PIETRO PERUGINO

Master of the Italian Renaissance

PIETRO PERUGINO

Master of the Italian Renaissance

Joseph Antenucci Becherer

PORTER FOUNDATION CURATOR FOR PERUGINO

WITH CONTRIBUTIONS BY

Katherine R. Smith Abbott

James R. Banker

Joseph Antenucci Becherer

Julia Conaway Bondanella and Peter Bondanella

Marilyn Bradshaw

Bruce Cole

Vittoria Garibaldi

Rosaria Mencarelli

RIZZOLI
NEW YORK

THE GRAND RAPIDS ART MUSEUM

Grand Rapids, Michigan

This catalogue has been published in conjunction with the exhibition *Perugino: Master of the Italian Renaissance*, organized by The Grand Rapids Art Museum, and held at the museum from November 16, 1997 to February 1, 1998.

The exhibition is presented under the grand patronage of The Jay & Betty Van Andel Foundation and is supported by The City of Grand Rapids, The City of Perugia, and Grand Rapids Sister Cities International. The catalogue is underwritten by The Richard and Helen DeVos Foundation.

First published in the United States of America
in 1997 by
    Rizzoli International Publications, Inc.
    300 Park Avenue South
    New York, New York 10010
    and
    The Grand Rapids Art Museum
    155 Division North
    Grand Rapids, Michigan 49503

Photography credits and captions for detail illustrations can be found on page 318.

Translations from the Italian of the statement by The Honorable Gianfranco Maddoli, and of the essays by Vittoria Garibaldi and Rosaria Mencarelli: Jody Shiffman
Map, page 20, by Yolanda Gonzalez
Designed by Susan E. Kelly with assistance by John Hubbard
Editorial assistance for Marquand Books by Norma Roberts
Produced by Marquand Books, Inc., Seattle

Typeset in Monotype Centaur

Printed and bound by C & C Offset Printing, Hong Kong

The Grand Rapids Art Museum
Perugino: Master of the Italian Renaissance

Project Directors
Judith Sobol, 1992–1995
Jane Connell, 1996–1997
Celeste Adams, 1997–1998

Project Guest Curator
Joseph Antenucci Becherer

Project Advisor
Bruce Cole

Project Editor
Jody Shiffman

Library of Congress Cataloging-in-Publication Data

Pietro Perugino : master of the Italian Renaissance /
    Joseph Antenucci Becherer, Porter Foundation
    curator for Perugino ; with contributions by
    Katherine R. Smith Abbott . . . [et al.].
       p.   cm.
    Published in conjunction with the exhibition
  and organized by the Grand Rapids Art Museum,
  held at the museum from Nov. 16, 1997 to Feb. 1,
  1998.
    Includes bibliographical references and index.
    ISBN 0-8478-2076-9 (hc : alk. paper). —
ISBN 0-942159-20-9 (soft : alk. paper)
    1. Perugino, ca. 1450–1523—Exhibitions.
2. Perugino, ca. 1450–1523—Criticism and interpretation. I. Becherer, Joseph Antenucci.
II. Abbott, Katherine R. Smith. III. Grand
Rapids Art Museum.
ND623.P4A4   1997
759.5—dc21   97-33981

Contents

THE EXHIBITION IS PRESENTED
UNDER THE GRAND PATRONAGE OF

The Jay & Betty Van Andel Foundation

Pietro Perugino: Master of the Italian Renaissance

THE CATALOGUE IS UNDERWRITTEN BY

The Richard and Helen DeVos Foundation

THE EXHIBITION IS SUPPORTED BY

The City of Grand Rapids
The City of Perugia
and
Grand Rapids Sister Cities International

*The Perugino Project is founded on the sister-city relationship between
Grand Rapids and Perugia, which is dedicated to cultural,
educational, and economic development.*

International Honorary Committee

The Honorable Peter Secchia
United States Ambassador to Italy,
    1989–93
and Mrs. Joan Secchia
Chairpersons

The Honorable Walter Veltroni
Vice President of the Council of
    Ministers and
Minister for Cultural Heritage and
    National Preserves

The Honorable Lamberto Dini
Minister of Foreign Affairs

The Honorable John M. Engler
Governor of Michigan
and Mrs. Michelle Engler

His Excellency Ferdinando Salleo
Ambassador of Italy to the
    United States
and Mrs. Anne Maria Salleo

The Honorable Michele Quaroni
Consul of Italy
and Mrs. Veronika Quaroni

The Honorable Gianfranco Maddoli
Mayor, City of Perugia

Dr. Mario Serio
Director General, Central Office for
    Archeological, Architectural,
    Artistic and Historic Assets,
    Ministry for Cultural Heritage
    and National Preserves

Mr. Giovanni Tarpani
Councilor for Culture, City of Perugia

Dr. Costantino Centroni
Superintendent of Arts, Umbria Region

Dr. Vittoria Garibaldi
Director, Galleria Nazionale dell'Umbria

The Honorable Reginald Bartholemew
United States Ambassador to Italy,
  1993–97
and Mrs. Rose-Anne Bartholomew

Dr. Lynne Cheney
Chairman, National Endowment for the
  Humanities, 1986–93

Dr. Bruce Cole
Distinguished Professor of Fine Art
Indiana University

Ms. Betty Ford
First Lady of the United States,
  1974–77

The Honorable John H. Logie
Mayor, City of Grand Rapids

Mr. Charles McCallum
President, Board of Trustees
The Grand Rapids Art Museum

Mr. Paul Polo
President, Order of Sons of Italy
  in America

Mr. Roger Randle
President, Sister Cities
  International

Mr. Frank D. Stella
Chairman, National Italian
  American Foundation

Mr. Casey Wondergem
Senior Public Affairs Counsel
Amway Corporation

Mr. Lew Chamberlin III
Mrs. Pamella DeVos
Perugino Project Development
Cochairs

Contributors and Sponsors

Grand Patron

Jay & Betty Van Andel Foundation

Patrons

Richard and Helen DeVos Foundation

Frey Foundation

Benefactors

CONEXPORT Umbria–Italy

Daniel G. and Pamella G. DeVos Foundation

The City of Grand Rapids

The Grand Rapids Foundation

Nestlé Perugina

Underwriters

Douglas and Maria DeVos Foundation

The Keeler Foundation

Porter Foundation

Sponsors

John and Marilyn Drake

Michigan Humanities Council

Charles and Stella Royce

Contributors

Peter C. and Pat Cook

Gainey Transportation Services, Inc.

Grand Rapids Community College

Mazda Great Lakes

Meijer, Inc.

Gretchen Minnhaar & Luis D. Tomatis, M.D.

National Italian American Foundation

Peter P. and Patricia Renucci

Peter and Joan Secchia

Universal Forest Products

Fellows

Edith J. Blodgett

Dick and Betsy DeVos Foundation

Grand Valley State University

Bob and Judy Hooker

George and Katy McAleenan

Sons and Daughters of Italy,
West Michigan Lodge

Marilyn Titche

Nan Van Andel

Steve and Cindy Van Andel

Warner Norcross & Judd L.L.P.

Peter M. Wege

Friends

ChoiceOne Insurance

Mart and Dottie Johnson

Deb and Hank Meijer

Lenders to the Exhibition

The Art Institute of Chicago

The Art Museum, Princeton University

The Cleveland Museum of Art

The Detroit Institute of Arts

Galleria Nazionale dell'Umbria, Perugia

The Metropolitan Museum of Art, New York

National Gallery of Art, Washington, D.C.

North Carolina Museum of Art, Raleigh

The Pierpont Morgan Library, New York

Sterling and Francine Clark Art Institute,
Williamstown, Massachusetts

Yale University Art Gallery

Foreword

The opportunity to bring together a group of important Renaissance paintings, many on panel, is rare indeed. Yet more extraordinary is the shared commitment among so many individuals in Italy and the United States who recognized the importance of this project at the outset and supported its development during the last six years. *Perugino: Master of the Italian Renaissance* is a concise exhibition of thirty-five works that clarifies issues of Perugino's style and his role upon the immense stage of Renaissance painting. So pervasive are the lessons of the Renaissance upon the next five hundred years of Western painting that we take for granted the distinction of these pivotal works in the history of art without reconfirming with our own eyes the particular characteristics and unique qualities that distinguish original works as we physically confront them. The Grand Rapids Art Museum takes special pride in organizing this exhibition and creating the opportunity for a professional and popular audience to encounter the works of the master Perugino in an intimate and reflective setting. The exhibition is a landmark international project for the museum and marks the beginning of a new era of institutional growth.

At the Galleria Nazionale dell'Umbria, Director Vittoria Garibaldi, in collaboration with Walter Veltroni, Lamberto Dini, and Mario Serio, has made this exhibition possible by the unprecedented loan of nine major works by Perugino, and the American lending museums have likewise generously supported this worthy project. The spirit and devotion of the staff members of the museum have been extraordinary. Jane Connell, who oversaw the project through its many stages of development, Linda Thompson, Roberta King, and Amy Heiney are all worthy of credit. Porter Foundation Guest Curator for Perugino and consulting curator at The Grand Rapids Art Museum, Joseph Becherer is the dynamic creative force that has driven the project and has been a loyal friend to all who have worked with him. Bruce Cole has rendered wise and quiet counsel.

Our gratitude to Ambassador Peter Secchia and Mrs. Joan Secchia, Mayor John Logie, Mayor Gianfranco Maddoli, and Charles and Stella Royce is abiding. Perugia Sister Cities cochairmen Carlo Vanin and Alma Valenti and, in Perugia, Daniela Borghesi have been constant friends to the project. In Grand Rapids, Casey Wondergem has been a champion of the exhibition, making it a reality for the museum and the city. Board President Charles McCallum has supported this exhibition with energy and purpose.

The Grand Rapids Art Museum thanks the many sponsors of this exhibition, first and foremost The Jay & Betty Van Andel Foundation, which provided a magnificent cornerstone gift and inspired other patrons and benefactors. This beautiful scholarly catalogue was made possible by The Richard and Helen DeVos Foundation. The Frey Foundation, The Daniel G. and Pamella G. DeVos Foundation, and The Grand Rapids Foundation are truly worthy of special recognition. We thank these and all our donors who place the mission of museums high in the order of social values by making this exhibition the focus of enlightened civic spirit.

Celeste Marie Adams
Director, The Grand Rapids Art Museum

Preface and Acknowledgments

Standing here in the Sistine Chapel, one encounters a sea of heads gazing upward at Michelangelo's Genesis scenes along the ceiling. However, a sizable number of visitors are inspecting the lower tier of frescoes, the chapel's premier decorations, by Perugino, Botticelli, and Ghirlandaio, among others. A few small groups stand immediately before Perugino's renowned *Delivery of the Keys to Saint Peter*, analyzing the masterful use of linear perspective, commenting on the classical nature of the architectural detail, and admiring the balletic figures which are at once mortal and divine. Knowingly or not, the membership of these groups has successfully summarized the very elements which made Perugino one of the most popular artists in Italy during the final decades of the fifteenth century and the opening years of the sixteenth.

This considered, the career of Pietro di Cristoforo Vannucci, or, familiarly, Pietro Perugino, justly deserves the attention and reevaluation offered by the present exhibition, *Perugino: Master of the Italian Renaissance*. As a prolific painter and prominent workshop master, Perugino's visual language speaks of an historical age with great clarity and beauty. This landmark exhibition and its accompanying catalogue mark the first international exhibition of the master in fifty years and serves as the inaugural presentation of his work in the United States. It provides a critical investigation of the master's oeuvre based on current scholarship, presents the historical context in which he endeavored, and details the realm of painting over which he reigned briefly, but subsequently lost to the next generation of artists like Michelangelo and his own student, Raphael.

Collectively, the catalogue essays, entries, and chronicle of Perugino's life address problematic areas such as the master's formative period, the function of drawings, and the broad dimensions of his relationship with his workshop and numerous followers. Critical new information is presented on a variety of topics including the recognition of Perugino's "late style," Vasari's biased biography of the artist, and issues of patronage and collecting.

For its years of planning and research, the exhibition itself is painfully brief. But the catalogue, the first major work on Perugino in English, allows for the longevity of the efforts of a team of nine scholars, two museums, and one unique sister-city relationship.

The foundation of *Perugino: Master of the Italian Renaissance* is the sister-city relationship between Grand Rapids and Perugia. Dedicated to cultural understanding, educational exchange, and economic development, it is a beautiful relationship driven by good will and fueled by the creativity of the respective citizenry. To this end, I must initiate my gratitude by acknowledging fellow members of the 1992 delegation from Grand Rapids to Perugia: Mayor John Logie, Carlo Vanin, Alma Valenti, and Chuck and Stella Royce. A special note of thanks is offered to Carlo Vanin, who functions as the indefatigable voice of Grand Rapids. The support of the entire Perugia Committee has been deeply appreciated. In Perugia, the ideals of a sister-city relationship have been nurtured by Mayor Gianfranco Maddoli, Giovanni Tarpani, Armando Alberati, Fabrizio Bracco, Patrizia Brutti, Renato Locchi, Lorella Mercanti, Bruno Braccalente, and Mario Valentini, among many others. A most deserved acknowledgment is extended to Daniela Borghesi for all her efforts and her constant, positive spirit.

It has been an honor to work with both the Galleria Nazionale dell'Umbria and The Grand Rapids Art Museum. Regarding the former, I am indebted to its director, Vittoria Garibaldi, and her wonderful staff. Rosaria Mencarelli, Brunella Loffredi, Piero Nottani, and Alessandra Raffa, in particular, have been most helpful and caring. Also, I am grateful to Costantino Centroni and to the office of the Soprintendenza for all the assistance it has provided. At The Grand Rapids Art Museum, I stand humble before its board and staff. My deepest gratitude is extended to Jane Connell, Linda Thompson, Kathleen Ferres, and Amy Heiney, who have been invaluable colleagues. Anne Armitage, Steve Ferris, Ann Van Tassel, Roberta King, and curatorial intern Kim Orcutt have also been of great support, and I appreciate their encouragement.

Sincere thanks are extended to Ambassador Peter Secchia and Mrs. Joan Secchia. Similarly, I wish to thank Casey Wondergem. Their belief in my efforts is something I will always hold dear. The assistance of the Italian Embassy in Washington, D.C., the Italian Cultural Institute in New York, and the United States Embassy in Rome is greatly appreciated.

This exhibition and catalogue result from the efforts of many who have been most helpful: Assia Landau, Michele and Veronika Quaroni, Samuel Sachs II, Cara Denison,

William Griswold, Keith Christiansen, Dorothy Kellett, Bill Eiland, Paul Richelson, David Alan Brown, Douglas Lewis, Eleonora Luciano, Victoria Rovine, Tom Russo, Earl A. Powell III, George Goldner, Larry Feinberg, Laurence Kanter, David Brooke, Steven Kern, Allen Rosenbaum, Betsy Rosasco, Cynthia Miller, Carol Ludwig, Daniela Maschi, Greg Lagano, Giuseppe Perrone, Barbara Bays, Fedora Bocca, Edgardo Abbozzo, Andrea Rondini and family, Mary Bruscia and family, Andrea Antonelli and family, and, of course, the unflappable Chuck Heiney. For this author, the immediate encouragement of Charles Chamberlain, Marianne Pierson, Carol Watson, Nick and Joan Antonakis, Marty and Sheree Alexander was crucial, just as the long-standing, long-distance "support groups" in Atlanta, Chicago, Columbus, and San Francisco are treasured.

It has been a distinct pleasure to work with each of my coauthors. I extend my deepest gratitude to each: Katherine Smith Abbott, James Banker, Julia Conaway Bondanella and Peter Bondanella, Marilyn Bradshaw, Bruce Cole, Vittoria Garibaldi, and Rosaria Mencarelli. To my mentors Bruce Cole and Marilyn Bradshaw, thank you for your support and direction at every turn! The support I have received from Grand Rapids Community College is of special note. Grant monies have been crucial to my research, and their understanding with regard to my time commitments outside the college has been priceless. So too, I am most appreciative of funding from the Porter Foundation, the Michigan Humanities Council, and the National Endowment for the Humanities.

Special acknowledgment is due to editor Jody Shiffman for her dedication to drawing together many voices and points of view into a cohesive whole, creating a catalogue of interest and benefit to scholarly and general readerships alike.

Finally, I must thank my family—an incredible and durable cast of characters. Their support, love, and prayers are unfailing; undoubtedly the glue in each of my endeavors. Words cannot express the debt I owe to my wife, Lisa, and our sons, Pino and Vito. You are angels of the highest order to me. My every effort is done with you at heart. *Grazie. Vi amo.*

Joseph Antenucci Becherer
Rome

Statements

THE HONORABLE REGINALD BARTHOLOMEW

AMBASSADOR OF THE UNITED STATES TO ITALY

This exhibition is a remarkable achievement that reveals a great deal about both the artistic vitality of fifteenth-century Perugia and the creative energy of Grand Rapids as we enter the twenty-first century. It also is a fine example of how private citizens and private institutions in two countries can do great things together as long as they have vision, drive, and a strong spirit of trust and cooperation. Private citizen exchanges are altering the face of international relations through programs like this one.

Not long ago, a major exhibition of the works of an important Italian Renaissance master like Pietro Perugino could only have been organized by one of the major museums in America's largest cities, or by the Italian government itself as an overseas cultural initiative. But we live in a new era, one in which education, economic growth, and advances in communication and transportation make possible yesterday's most impractical ideas. As the United States Ambassador to Italy, it is a pleasure to see the citizens of Grand Rapids and Perugia seize the opportunities presented by this new era.

Perugia and Grand Rapids are making the most of their sister-city relationship through this exchange. It is not easy for a city with Perugia's rich history to part with such a priceless part of its cultural heritage, even for a few months. But the director and staff of the Galleria Nazionale dell'Umbria recognized the value of the educational program The Grand Rapids Art Museum had planned. With Perugia's mayor and other municipal leaders, they made possible the key contribution that makes the exhibition whole.

I am sure this exhibition will lead to a greater understanding in the United States that the magnificent proofs of Italy's extraordinary contribution to Western culture are found not only in Rome, Florence, and Venice but also in important smaller cities like Perugia. Just as importantly, the exhibition is a perfect example of American creativity, public-spiritedness, and innovation in bringing an ambitious and valuable project to life. And it represents a fruitful collaboration between two cultural institutions—The Grand Rapids Art Museum and the Galleria Nazionale dell'Umbria—that come from different traditions, but also have a common mission of education in their regions.

This project should be just the beginning. It can be a gateway to greater understanding and to a rich sharing of cultural wisdom between the people of the Grand Rapids area and the people of the Umbrian region. I am proud of the small part the United States

Embassy in Rome has played in helping to make this exchange possible. In the end, however, it is the people of Grand Rapids and Perugia who must be congratulated for creating this opportunity to bring the Italian and American people closer together.

HIS EXCELLENCY FERDINANDO SALLEO
AMBASSADOR OF ITALY TO THE UNITED STATES

Perugino: Master of the Italian Renaissance is the first exhibition devoted to the Italian Renaissance master painter to be shown in the United States and constitutes a remarkable achievement in the cultural cooperation between the United States and Italy. It is also the first time that the works of this great artist travel from his birthplace and from all over the United States to come together in a major international collection of his work.

The exhibition will surely promote extensive research on the master's influence on central Italian style in the early sixteenth century, and we may envisage a renewed appreciation of Perugino as the leading personality in the spread of the early sixteenth-century Florentine canon to all central Italian workshops among the achievements of the Perugino Project. His soft, highly skilled and masterly organization of space, light, and color, as well as his development of perspective had a lasting influence not only on Raphael, one of his apprentices, but also on all the following generations.

The exhibition will feature thirty-five works. Nine of them are on loan from the Galleria Nazionale dell'Umbria, and twenty-six come from American museums. This joint venture has long had the support of Ambassador Peter Secchia. It offers us yet another chance to witness his long-standing effort to develop relations between our two countries at the highest cultural level, an effort initiated while serving as Ambassador of the United States to Italy in Rome.

The Perugino Project was also born of the sister-city relationship between Perugia and Grand Rapids. It is a signal that world relations and mutual understanding are carried on nowadays not only at the highest governmental level but in the encounters between local governments and in the close context among people as well. Italy can be considered the forerunner of this tradition in the development of the city-state system, which has surely contributed to the country's creativity throughout the centuries.

Perugia was, and still is, part of this system. Following the opening of its university, the city witnessed a period of extraordinary cultural vitality, becoming an important center in the intellectual life of the Italian Renaissance. Since then, Perugia has continued to produce a rich culture and is still renowned throughout the world for its prestigious universities, its art academy, its artistic collections, and, in a more modern perspective, its Umbria Jazz Festival.

I wish to congratulate the mayors of Grand Rapids and Perugia for their efforts, as well as the directors of The Grand Rapids Art Museum and the Galleria Nazionale dell'Umbria who have made possible this event in the realm of the arts, for which we all have cause to rejoice.

THE HONORABLE JOHN H. LOGIE
MAYOR OF GRAND RAPIDS

Dear Grand Rapids Neighbors and Art Lovers from around the World,

In 1992, I was privileged to lead a delegation from Grand Rapids to Perugia, Italy, to begin discussions which one year later led to the solemn signing, in Grand Rapids, of our sister-city agreement. During our visit to Perugia, we were dazzled and delighted to discover many of the original paintings by Pietro di Cristoforo Vannucci, better known as Perugino. These incredible works first inspired a significant fund-raising effort in our community to support this exhibition, and encouraged museums around the country to share masterpieces from their own collections.

For the first time in our country's history, we have an opportunity to experience first-hand the art of one of the greatest painters of the Italian Renaissance. On behalf of the citizens of Grand Rapids, I issue you a most hearty welcome. I know you are going to be as pleased as we are at this magnificent assemblage.

THE HONORABLE GIANFRANCO MADDOLI
MAYOR OF PERUGIA

I am certain that I speak for the entire population of the city when I say how proud Perugia is to know that one of its most illustrious sons has been chosen to act as our cultural ambassador to the New World.

For us, Perugino is not only the most famous and most important painter to emerge from the rich artistic environment of Perugia and Umbria in the Renaissance; he is much more. Perugino is one of its very symbols and yet at the same time he is a faithful interpreter of Perugia's civilization. His works reflect the sweet landscapes of the countryside and immortalize the faces of our ancestors and the images of our city while echoing the faith of an entire people. Our most beautiful churches, our monumental seats of temporal power and houses of the nobility have all been rendered more precious by the presence of his artistic creations. Moreover, Perugino knew how to illustrate popular feelings like piety, mysticism, and pride with incomparable mastery.

Within his art rests the identity of the community where he was born and lived. Our community, while proud of its traditions and concerned to maintain them intact, is no less directed toward the future: we are most interested in establishing new relations, constructing new friendships, instituting exchanges. The City of Perugia can present no better calling card to friends old and new than this exhibition devoted to Perugino and his works.

For these reasons we of Perugia feel ourselves to be part of your initiative and wish it all the best success. I am sure that once the citizens of Perugia and those of your great country have experienced the exhibition, its catalogue, and the accompanying festivities, they will better understand and love our fair city.

THE HONORABLE JOHN M. ENGLER
GOVERNOR OF MICHIGAN

In bringing the magnificent works of Pietro Perugino to Grand Rapids, the Perugino Project has joined together not only the museums in the sister cities of Perugia and Grand Rapids but it has also united the Italian Renaissance with the Grand Rapids community and the surrounding areas. As individuals come to see this great exhibition, they will be impressed by the number of Pietro Perugino's works that have been gathered for this show. Works that are rarely seen outside of private collections and Italian museums have made their way to Grand Rapids for this grand occasion. It is only through the growing relationship between Grand Rapids and her sister city Perugia that the citizens of Michigan and other states are able to enjoy this show. This relationship has allowed us to learn about history and individuals in other cultures as well as in our own, extending our world into Italy and beyond.

In celebrating the Perugino Project, The City of Grand Rapids will also bring to life the Italian Renaissance in Michigan. This exhibition of Pietro Perugino's works will bring a new understanding of Italian culture to our state in concert with complementary exhibitions and programs presented by the Gerald R. Ford Museum, the Van Andel Museum Center, the Frederik Meijer Gardens, the Grand Rapids Symphony Orchestra, and many others. As Michigan is already a state where the arts thrive, this extensive exhibition presents an excellent opportunity for all ages and cultures to learn something new.

I therefore extend my congratulations to The Grand Rapids Art Museum and its sister-city institutions for the fine exhibition they have organized. The individuals who have worked so hard to bring this collection of Pietro Perugino's works to Grand Rapids should be commended for their leadership and for the dedication they have shown to the Perugino Project.

HOC · PETRVS · DE · CHASTRO · PLEBIS · PINXIT

PIETRO PERUGINO

Master of the Italian Renaissance

VITTORIA GARIBALDI
GALLERIA NAZIONALE DELL'UMBRIA

Pietro Perugino of Perugia

from "Pietro, the painter of Città della Pieve" (M. Petri pictoris de Castro Plebis) *to "Pietro Perugino"* (Petrus Perusinus)

PIETRO VANNUCCI, Il Perugino, was considered by his contemporaries to be perhaps the greatest of the protagonists responsible for renewing Italian art at the height of the Renaissance. The level he achieved in his art and the historic import of his innovations were in fact so well understood in his own time that already by the end of the quattrocento he was unanimously regarded as "the best painter in Italy," as Agostino Chigi wrote to his father Mariano on November 7, 1500.[1] This judgment, as even Vasari notes, was the result of Perugino's new way of painting. This new style characterized the taste of an entire epoch. His crystalline art was diaphanous, made up of silences and the most insubstantial music, harmonies of color, studied yet endless perspectives. Its peasants and washerwomen were transformed by the magic of his brush into heroes, heroines, and divine figures full of delicate grace and sweet melancholy. His art, in short, aroused great emotions.

Hundreds of paintings more or less in Perugino's style were completed between the end of the fifteenth century and the beginning of the sixteenth century. His painting

> was so pleasing during his day that many artisans came from France, Spain, Germany and other countries to learn it. And many people traded in his works and sent them to various places before the appearance of the style of Michelangelo.[2]

His greatness was subsequently misunderstood and criticized following the failure of his Mantuan work commissioned by Isabella d'Este (see Chronicle, 1497, 1500, 1502–5), and that of the Santissima Annunziata Altarpiece (see Chronicle, 1506).[3]

It was not until the nineteenth and early twentieth centuries that scholars finally approached a better understanding of Perugino. Successive studies, however, have been marked by long intervals of stagnation or only marginal interest.[4] Even today, the grandeur of his classical language is often underestimated, so far is it from the tastes of a public brought up on contemporary art and the historic avant-garde movements. The recent renewal of interest in Perugino is to a great degree related to the resumption of research devoted to the young Raphael, rather than strictly to Perugino,[5] and is the result of specialized analyses.

The basic conditions which led to the formation of Perugino's artistic language must be sought in Florentine painting practices of the second half of the quattrocento. We know precious little about whether he received any artistic training in his hometown. Contrary to the poverty ascribed to him by Vasari (Perugino's first biographer and the sixteenth-century art historian responsible for many of our notions of Italian Renaissance art, though these are not always correct, as in this case; see Bondanella essay in this catalogue), Pietro Perugino was a member of one of the richest and most respected families in Castello della Pieve, better known as "Chastrum Plebis," a small fortified town in the Perugian countryside known today as Città della Pieve. According to Giovanni Santi, the father of Raphael, Pietro was born there in 1452.[6]

Almost no traces remain of local Umbrian paintings from the quattrocento, and it is probable that the young Pietro began his initial artistic training in nearby Perugia, a lively center of humanistic culture which also served as a meeting place for the exchange of figurative subjects and styles. Perugino may have acquired his profound knowledge of Piero della Francesca's spatial principles by direct observation of the altarpiece (fig. 58) that Piero was painting for the monks of Sant'Antonio in Perugia between 1455 and 1478, as well as by possibly accompanying the already famous master himself to Arezzo, Urbino, and San Sepolcro.[7] The very recent reconstruction of the life and career of Benedetto Bonfigli, the most representative painter in Perugia at the beginning of the Renaissance, also sheds new light on local artistic production at the moment of passage from "the painting of light" to the successive Perugian production.[8]

The first certain evidence we have for Perugino is from 1469, when he paid the wine tax in Castello della Pieve following his father's death. During the next year he is in Florence, completing his artistic training in the workshop of Andrea del Verrocchio, the goldsmith, sculptor and well-known painter. Here Perugino had occasion to meet and compare his work to that of such artists as Leonardo da Vinci, Botticelli, Ghirlandaio, and Lorenzo di Credi.

Florence played a particularly important role in these years. The city's artistic activity was dominated by expert master painters like Pollaiuolo and Verrocchio. These artists considered that the best way to fully master the fundamental concepts of anatomy and understand the structure of the human body was to draw from real life, removing the skin from cadavers. They then transferred the knowledge acquired through drawing to the medium of paint, devoting particular care to the rendering of movement and expression. The Florentine training he received did not displace the strong Umbrian component built into Perugino's cultural matrix. He creatively incorporated the new ideas suggested by his Florentine experience, interpreting them with sensitivity and elegance.

Perugino's artistic production clearly demonstrates the passage from the search for expression through the linearity of his drawing (characteristic of Perugino's early works) to a new way of painting. This new *maniera* (style) defined the artistic language which was to become prevalent in the cinquecento Rome of Popes Julius II and Leo X. In fact, it is Perugino who must be credited with creating this new classical style.

Another aspect worthy of evaluation is Perugino's role as designer of new artistic compositions in which human figures are inserted into vast realms of space. These arrangements were highly successful and exerted great influence, even though they were not always fully executed by the master himself. Often the master sketched out his idea in preparatory drawings that were then transferred to paint by his various followers and disciples. The same process took place in Raphael's workshop.

In 1472 Perugino was in Florence, as confirmed by his registration in the Company of Saint Luke. At this time he began his independent career as a painter, which took him to the major Italian cities of the time—Florence, Rome, Venice, and Perugia. Yet it is fruitless to attempt to single out works attributed to the period before 1473, for which we possess no certain data.[9] The first meaningful turning point in Perugino's career was the important commission granted him by the Franciscan Order in Perugia. Together the Franciscans and the city of Perugia were committed to promoting the cult of Saint Bernardino of Siena from both the religious and political viewpoints.[10] The role and degree of Perugino's involvement in conceiving and executing the so-called niche of Saint Bernardino (dated 1473), a group of panels for a niche in the oratory of the same name, has not yet been clarified.

The project's unitary nature is revealed through the passionate search for space as well as by the fantastic architecture present in the images, and visually attests to Perugino's having achieved a great mastery of composition.[11] The various scenes follow a previously constructed architectonic program laid out in drawings and etchings.[12] Their completion by six different artists, who thereby made names for themselves, does not call in question the integrity of the whole. This is a far cry from the decorative panels set up in other contemporary niches.[13]

It is possible to recognize Perugino's hand in the panel entitled *Saint Bernardino Healing the Ulcer of the Daughter of Giovanni Petrazio da Rieti* (fig. 1), and hence the work is universally attributed to him. The scene unfolds against the backdrop of an erudite rendition of the Arch of Titus, replete with Renaissance courtly motifs, while the center opens onto

Fig. 1. *Saint Bernardino Healing the Ulcer of the Daughter of Giovanni Petrazio da Rieti*, Galleria Nazionale dell'Umbria, Perugia

limitless space. The influence of Florentine painting is quite evident, especially in the group of figures at the left. The complex drapery of the male figure seen from behind recalls artistic practice prevalent in the period between Verrocchio and the young Ghirlandaio. The figure on the right seen from the front, perhaps an elegantly attired page, betrays the refined taste and predilection for graceful and light-hearted gestures which were to become hallmarks of Perugino's artistic work.

The magnificent open landscape seen through the arch is the first of many successive uses of this motif for the background. In part the fruit of Perugino's study of real landscape in the ever-green Umbrian countryside, it also reflects a knowledge, acquired in Florence or in Rome, of Flemish landscapes of the second half of the quattrocento. This cognizance of Flemish practice is implicit in Perugino's manner of rendering water and air, infused by the pearly drops of a light mist. The painter moves with absolute mastery within the architectonic layout. Figures, landscape, and a large part of the decorative array are constructed from pure color, undiluted by blacks or whites. The restrained, essential gestures diffuse a sense of peace and foreshadow Perugino's classical message.

To this phase of Perugino's activity belongs his *Adoration of the Magi* (fig. 2), generally dated 1476, painted for the Servite Order of Perugia. It is not difficult to explain the references to Florentine painting practice clearly discernible in this work as well, in light of the parallel results achieved by the great artists who shared the common training of Verrocchio's workshop. Yet insofar as it is possible to judge from the very different dimensions, the *Adoration* represents a step backward in comparison to the Saint Bernardino panel. The work seems to be that of a young painter rather than an accomplished master,

Fig. 2. *Adoration of the Magi*, Galleria Nazionale dell'Umbria, Perugia (see pl. 2)

based on the chronological expectations raised by too many "quotations."[14] Likewise, the presence of late Gothic motifs, the crowding of characters, the delineation of outlines, and the strong, heavy roundness of the figures all emphasize the artist's Umbrian matrix and a graphic ability which has not yet discovered its own sense of rhythm. Some elements do appear, however, that will become characteristic of Perugino's style, such as the figure of the young man wearing a turban and the refined young men with blond hair.

Very similar to the *Adoration of the Magi* is the processional banner of the *Pietà with Saints Jerome and Mary Magdalene* from the Franciscan convent in Farneto, now at the Galleria Nazionale dell'Umbria (cat. no. 9). In this case as well, the graphic composition still recalls that of Verrocchio, while the background landscape is quite close to that of Perugino's Saint Bernardino panel. Together these elements date the banner's production to the period prior to 1473, when Perugino had not yet redirected the strong Florentine component in his work toward sweeter and more sensual tones.[15]

On July 21, 1475, "M. Petri pictoris de Castro Plebis" (Pietro the painter of Città della Pieve) was in Perugia to decorate the Grand Salon in the Palazzo dei Priori ("in Sala Magna Superiori costruendarum e dipingendarum . . ."), but no trace of this decoration has survived. Given its collocation and the estimated payment of a thousand florins, the planned work must have been of no small importance.[16]

The fresco depicting Saints Romano and Roch (fig. 3) belongs to this same period. It contains a curious representation of the idealized town of Deruta in the lower section, and a *mandorla* (almond-shaped halo) with God the Father in the upper section. A fragmentary inscription dates it to 1477 or 1478. The fresco is particularly important for a

Fig. 3. *Saints Romano and Roch with the Eternal Benediction and View of Deruta,* Pinacoteca Comunale, Deruta

number of reasons, amongst which is its still legible original text. It reuses some elements from the *Adoration of the Magi,* such as the head of the magus King Balthazar for Saint Roch, and adopts the motif of the pavement with squares and diamonds from the Saint Bernardino panels.[17]

During this period when Perugino was predominantly working in Umbria, his fame was on the rise and commissions in the province followed one upon another. Some were of notable significance, such as the complex votive decoration of the chapel of Mary Magdalene in the Church of Santa Maria in Cerqueto. Still extant from the work is a section containing two fragments of Saint Roch and Saint Peter, as well as the entire figure of Saint Sebastian (fig. 4).[18] This representation of Saint Sebastian is the first splendid example of the saint whose constant presence in Perugino's repertory will almost make him the artist's symbol. The frail physical structure, which a knowing light sweetly illuminates, denotes perfect knowledge of anatomy. The smooth-faced youth, bound to a column and transfixed by arrows, expresses a vague sense of melancholy rather than pain. He seems moved only by a rhythmical cadence, although his feet are shown in perspective at the edge of the pavement. The references to Pollaiuolo and to Verrocchio are by now integrated into the artist's mature, personal language, which has transformed his earlier linearity into a soft lyrical rhythm. The very application of paint is directed toward creating a tonal painting fashioned only of color and luminous vibrations.

In the two decades that followed, the fame of Perugino was such as to induce him to keep two workshops actively functioning at the same time, one in Florence and the other in Perugia. In 1479 he was called to Rome to paint the Cappella della Concezione

Fig. 4. *Saint Sebastian*, Church of Santa Maria Assunta, Cerqueto

in Saint Peter's. The chapel was subsequently destroyed in 1609 to make room for the new Saint Peter's. Perugino's work must have pleased Pope Sixtus IV, who soon after commissioned him to decorate the Sistine Chapel together with a team of Florentine painters.[19]

The team, which included Botticelli, Ghirlandaio, and Cosimo Rosselli, reached Rome in the summer of 1481. Before long, Pintoricchio, Piero di Cosimo, and Luca Signorelli, their respective collaborators, arrived as well.[20] Although Perugino was one of the youngest artists within this group, he was the most esteemed, due to the innovative component of his style. Quite different from Botticelli's conception of pure drawing or Ghirlandaio's solid and robust structures, Perugino's style aimed at a new classicism.

The Sistine Chapel was to be decorated with a series of scenes from the Old and New Testaments illustrating the similarities between the lives of Moses and of Christ. Perugino played the most important role in this project, beginning his work in the area of the apse, where the pope and the cardinal's court performed their services.

Perugino proceeded to paint the *Baptism of Christ* (fig. 8) above which he wrote his own name (the only signed work in the entire chapel), the *Circumcision of Moses' Son,* and the very famous *Delivery of the Keys to Saint Peter* (fig. 32), which is laid out like a theatrical set and is unprecedented in its use of space. The latter work is subject to perfect intellectual control; no part of the work is casual. Classical references, already employed by Perugino in his Saint Bernardino panels, appear in *The Delivery of the Keys to Saint Peter* in the form of two triumphal arches, which copy the Arch of Constantine, and the small domed temple in the center of the work, constructed in the most modern style. The exceptional novelty of the composition made a great impression through its power and force.

Another extraordinary new element was Perugino's manner of rendering the human figure. The draperies, sometimes marked by sharp edges, other times falling in rhythmical folds, point to an artist in full possession of a vast repertoire painstakingly acquired. His sure and precise manner of drawing betrays his training with Verrocchio, reworked through the broader traditional Umbrian forms that owed much to the style of Piero della Francesca.

Placed in the foreground of a church courtyard whose pavement is decorated in the form of a perspectival grid, the figures are arranged in parallel lines and move naturally. The figures' heads, at times exceptional portraits composed with great ability, are silhouetted against the wide open background space. This treatment established an important precedent for Perugino's 1494 masterpiece *Portrait of Francesco delle Opere* (fig. 50).[21] When Perugino idealized figures, on the other hand, he painted images endowed with extreme elegance and refined sweetness. In the following years, thanks to the artist's increased mastery, the human figure was depicted in a classical manner.

Perugino continued to be drawn toward the Roman artistic environment for another ten years or so. Alternately residing in Florence and Perugia, he produced a number of masterpieces during this time. Since his assistants did not always follow him, he tended to hire them in the locale where he was working. This practice explains why his style sometimes assumed local characteristics while maintaining a substantial uniformity. Exemplifying the Roman period, with its susceptibility to Pintoricchio's decorative style, is the *Crucifixion with the Virgin, Saint John, Saint Jerome, and Saint Mary Magdalene* (also known as the Galitzin Triptych), dated to around 1485 (fig. 40). The fairy-tale landscape of the background also reveals Perugino's familiarity with the Portinari Triptych painted by the Flemish master Hugo van der Goes (see Chronicle, 1483).

Between 1482 and 1492 Perugino resided primarily in Florence, where he conceived his most modern innovations. He painted three panels, one of which was a *Pietà*,[22] for San Giusto alle Mura, the church of the Jesuates, during the first half of the 1480s. The perfect equilibrium of this *Pietà*, the definition of its forms, the rhythmical cadence of its figures, and the play of light which scans and molds the bodies inscribed against an architecture open toward limitless spaces, testifies to the greatness achieved by the Umbrian painter. During this same period he painted the *Last Supper* for the nuns of Foligno, where the architectonic motif is enlarged and developed just as it was in the *Vision of Saint Bernard* from 1489–90, today in Munich (fig. 82).[23] The light seems more diffuse and foreshadows future techniques for illumination. The landscape displays rolling hills, sweet rather than harsh, without traces of time or place.

The open architectonic backdrop of the Saint Bernardino panel is employed once again in the Albani Torlonia Polyptych of 1491 (fig. 42), but here it is inserted into the traditional altarpiece arrangement of two compositional planes and many sections. It is precisely the innovative backdrop that creates a unified space for the entire composition, wherein all elements have an equal role.

Perugino's fame in Florence surpassed that of all the contemporary, most fashionable Florentine artists. His workshop, the most active in the city, received the richest commissions. But Perugino's success was also due to the uncertainty of political and social conditions in Florence following the death of Lorenzo the Magnificent in 1492. This instability resulted in the subsequent preference for more devotional art as advocated by Savonarola (see Chronicle, 1490). Thus Perugino's serene, peaceful language, lacking violent emotions and extreme portrayals, satisfied the need in Florentine society (and in others as well) to find peace and inner concentration through art.

The successive phase of the artist's activity is documented in works like the panels painted for San Domenico in Fiesole (fig. 28; see Chronicle, 1493) and for Sant'Agostino in Cremona (see Chronicle, 1494). In August 1494, at the height of the splendor of Venice's great artists Carpaccio and the Bellinis, Pietro Perugino visited Venice. The master's later production reflects the strong influence of this trip. Elements such as the choice of subjects and the bearing of the figures, the compositional and spatial arrangements, the new selection of colors heightened by the addition of transparent coats of color, and the golden light all point to an ulterior qualitative improvement in works such as the *Lamentation over the Dead Christ* painted for the nuns of Santa Chiara of Florence (fig. 49; see Chronicle, 1495), the *Decemviri* Altarpiece for the chapel of the Palace of the Priors (fig. 64; see Chronicle, 1496), and also the *Crucifixion* for the Cistercians of Santa Maria Maddalena in Cestello (pl. 13; see Chronicle, 1496).

A fine illustration of this moment of grandeur is Perugino's 1499 polyptych for the Church of San Pietro in Perugia (see Chronicle, 1495, 1500). The polyptych constitutes one of the most emblematic examples of classicism achieved in the second half of the last decade of the fifteenth century. The central panel, of exceptional quality, employs for the first time the formula of two superimposed figure planes. The figures, full-formed and softly molded, suggest an ideal of perfection. The painting marks the high point of Perugino's career prior to painting the frescoes for the Collegio del Cambio (1496–1500), one of the most impressive programs of Italian Renaissance painting.[24]

Perugino's self-portrait, set among the frescoes he painted in this room, illustrates the master's ability to create effects using the fresco technique (fig. 33). These effects were no less refined than those he achieved in panel paintings. Depicting the self-portrait in a frame hanging by ribbons which seem real adds a genial touch. It appears to signal the painter's satisfaction with the fame he has earned. "PETRVS PERVSINVS EGREGIVS PICTOR," states the inscription below the image. Although Vasari recalls him with malevolent words

Fig. 5. *Fortitude, Temperance, and Six Ancient Heroes,*
Collegio del Cambio, Perugia

("Pietro was a man of very little religion, and no one could ever make him believe in the immortality of the soul . . ."),[25] his portrait depicts him with everyday features, rosy cheeks, and a full face—a man like any other man, but one who was capable of transforming himself into a great artist in front of a blank wall or panel.

In the two lunettes depicting the wise men and heroes of antiquity (fig. 5), it is surprising to see the level of classicism achieved in the delicacy of modeling and the use of a brilliant palette of strong colors: orange with green, yellow with blue, pink with green. This is expressed through an almost impressionistic technique employing the play of light. Here, light is color divided into an infinite number of vibrating fragments. These fragments are then recomposed in a unified final effect analogous to that achieved in later panel paintings. The landscape is simplified and the figures are arranged side by side in symmetrical fashion. There is a deliberate contrast between the foreground, where the figures rest their feet, and the luminous distant background. Atmospheric distance is created by employing simple thin layers of transparent color. The shadows on the land are sharp and both the young warriors and old wise men are elegantly posed. All in all, the style confirms the hand of a mature artist, a painter who has reached the peak of his expressive possibilities. These possibilities of expression anticipate many of the artistic developments to come during the course of the sixteenth century. The moment marked the great season of Italian painting.

Of the highest quality are the *Adoration of the Shepherds* (fig. 27) and the *Transfiguration,* also part of the Collegio del Cambio decorations. While the heads of the three apostles depicted in the *Transfiguration* are rendered in an exceptionally subtle manner, the human body now possesses a more defined structure. Some details suggest the collaboration of Raphael, such as the head of the apostle with the reddish complexion, the masses of color which have taken on plastic value, and the less atmospheric type of illumination.[26] If this is still Perugino, it is a different Perugino, devoting much care to how he renders forms and volumes. In the later *Adoration of the Magi* (pl. 18) that Perugino painted for Città della Pieve in 1504, this plasticity is totally absent and the application of paint is tenuous and soft.

At this moment when the artist was in such demand, reliance upon his workshop became almost a necessity. Requested by princes, rulers, and great lords, Perugino reserved his autograph paintings for the most special of occasions, exhibiting great moderation. This was typical of his personality, not only as a great artist, but as a careful protector and true entrepreneur of his image. He worked for the grandest and most refined patrons, such as Isabella d'Este, the Duchess of Mantua, who commissioned his famous painting *Combat between Love and Chastity* for her *studiolo* (study) in the Palazzo Ducale of Mantua (fig. 9; see Chronicle, 1497, 1500, 1502–5).

The *Combat between Love and Chastity* was a creation of great allegorical content, clearly inspired by the erudite humanist taste of the duchess. But it imposed upon Perugino a work of intimate content with which he was not at all comfortable, being accustomed to painting large altarpieces. Apart from the beautiful landscape, the composition is a bit confused. Isabella was unhappy with Perugino's product, finding it lacking in graphic ability with respect to other works in the same room painted by Mantegna. It was precisely at the height of his success that Perugino's style began to come under attack.

Shortly afterward, Perugino was commissioned to complete the altarpiece for the Church of the Santissima Annunziata in Florence, begun by Filippino Lippi prior to his death (see Chronicle, 1506). It was the last great work executed by Perugino in that city which had been one of the major centers of his activity and the place from whence his fame had spread. The altarpiece was savagely criticized. Vasari records that Perugino defended himself as follows:

> In this picture I have put figures which on other occasions were praised by all of you and which pleased you beyond measure. If now you don't like them and don't praise them, what can I do?[27]

In point of fact, since the early part of the 1500s, Perugino had adhered to a practice typical of mature artists. He had begun to reuse his own ideas, cartoons, and compositional arrangements. Their quality was assured by the painter's own expertise. But what had been accepted in the late 1400s was no longer the case in the first decade of the 1500s. Variety of invention, that is, creativity, had become fundamental in defining a first-rate artist (see Cole). Perugino, still thinking along fifteenth-century lines, had with the passing of the century become passé.

In the predella panels painted for the Annunziata Altarpiece, now in the Art Institute of Chicago and the Metropolitan Museum of Art (cat. no. 1a–e), the painter's technical ability was still excellent. Once again, the problem was that the composition, like that of the *Baptism of Christ*, to be considered below, was considered unoriginal. In early sixteenth-century Florence, where innovations appeared one after another at a breathtaking pace, Perugino's style was now rejected.[28]

From 1508 on, Perugino was no longer in demand in the larger artistic centers, including Florence. His frescoes on the vault of the Stanza dell'Incendio in the Vatican did not please Pope Julius II, who quickly settled his account with him (see Chronicle, 1508). His own disciples began looking for other sources of work and inspiration. Perugino's late production continued to be appreciated only by those patrons with traditional taste.

The restoration and studies recently carried out on the Sant'Agostino Polyptych (also known as the Sant'Agostino Altarpiece; see Chronicle, 1512) today allow us to rethink the negative judgment of Perugino's later oeuvre.[29] Two distinct phases of production have been discerned for the polyptych: the first between 1502 and 1512, and the second continuing until Perugino's death. The polyptych thus provides a reference point for reevaluating and dating all the artist's late works.

The complex two-sided altarpiece structure, conceived as true architecture and *not* as a rethinking of fifteenth-century tastes, was once constructed of twenty-eight or probably thirty paintings distributed within precious frames gilded on both surfaces. The woodwork, fashioned by Mattia da Reggio, was fitted together in various stages, beginning with the boxlike structure for the predella panels which was to serve as the support for all the other architectonic elements.

To the first phase belong the paintings facing the nave. The *Baptism of Christ* (fig. 45) includes Saints Augustine and Philip on the left, Saints Ercolano and James the Less on the right. Above is the angel of the Annunciation and the now-lost Virgin receiving the angel's message. The predella was executed by the workshop, using Perugino's drawings, probably in a great rush to meet the rigid deadline set by the friars.

All the paintings share a stylistic code which is quite evident. The lines, drawn in silverpoint, are very tenuous, delicate, precise. Often they are visible only through the use of infrared reflectography. The oil paint, notwithstanding its delicacy, furnishes body and density. The figures, details, flowers, jewels, and anatomical elements are all meticulously painted. Even the direction of the light and the consequent determination of shadows are consistent, coming from a single source on the left. This light source coincides with the natural illumination of the church during the afternoon.

The *Baptism of Christ* was executed in an outdated matrix which would have been technically correct for fifteenth-century practice. While not original, the composition is redeemed by its elegant forms. In particular the blond Christ displays an almost Apollo-like physiognomy. In addition, the delicate, suffused landscape is articulated by a splendidly gradual fading away of the forms, its depth suggested by a spectrum of very light colors.

Work on the components of the altarpiece facing the choir began in 1512, probably continuing throughout 1513, and then at more or less regular intervals until the death of the artist. In the center panel was the *Adoration of the Shepherds* (fig. 111), with *Saint Irene and Saint Sebastian* on the left and *Saint Jerome and Saint Mary Magdalene* (fig. 75) on the right. Two panels, *Young Saint with a Sword* and *Saint Bartholomew*, were set in the upper register.

To this period also belong the two panels for the top, which completed the altarpiece. An image of *God the Father* was placed facing the nave, while the *Pietà* faced the choir. The side panels, of which only the one to the left of the *Pietà* is extant, were in the form of tondi depicting the prophets David and Daniel.[30]

With the exception of the prophets, whose images were treated as decorative elements and painted using tempera, all of these panels may be characterized as drawings applied by brush. The drawings are very evident and their lines remain clear. The paint, ever so subtle and transparent, does not cover the drawings but allows their clearly-seen lines to delineate the figures. Even the rendering of landscape has changed; no longer are flowering lawns seen in the foreground. The naturalistic backgrounds have become simplified to allow figures to assume primary roles. The figures are exclusive and remain the central focus of the panels, as if Perugino had tried to eliminate anything that might distract from the impact of the images.

This was a particularly interesting period for the artist, who appeared to have been greatly inspired. Perugino had reached a level of quality comparable to that of his younger years. Forms assumed a new breadth attained through the exceptional employment of essentials and a rapid technique using filaments of color. The figures were grandiose, solemn, even monumental. Paint meshed with drawing in a manner never before witnessed— a new classicism which Perugino appears to have absorbed from Raphael.

In the final period of his life, which came to an end in February 1523 when he succumbed to the plague, Perugino was well on his way to renewing his style once again. The artist that emerged from this last period was more complex and versatile than had been previously imagined. Behind the protective aegis of official painter was hidden a character, a force, a spirituality and, last but not least, an unsuspected, creative imagination.

NOTES

1. ". . . è il meglio maestro d'Italia," in G. Cugnoni, "Agostino Chigi il Magnifico," *Archivio Romano di Storia Patria* 2 (1876): 481.

2. Giorgio Vasari, *The Lives of the Artists*, trans. Julia Conaway Bondanella and Peter Bondanella (Oxford: Oxford University Press, 1991), p. 267.

3. The references here are to the small painting of Love and Chastity for the Duchess of Mantua in 1505 and to the altarpiece begun by Filippino Lippi and completed by Perugino in 1507: see Pietro Scarpellini, *Perugino*, 2d ed. (Milan: Electa, 1991), pp. 52–53.

4. After the two volumes of Fiorenzo Canuti, *Il Perugino* (Siena: Editrice d'Arte "La Diana," 1931), the most complete work devoted to Perugino is the aforementioned study by Scarpellini.

5. Filippo Todini, "Una crocefissione del giovane Raffaello a Perugia," *Studi di Storia dell'Arte* 14 (1990): 113–45.

6. Giovanni Santi, *Cronaca rimata.*

7. For problems regarding the commission, the original structure, and the dating of the Sant'Antonio Polyptych, see *Piero della Francesco. Il polittico di Sant'Antonio*, ed. Vittoria Garibaldi (Perugia: Electa Editori Umbri, 1993).

8. The life and career of Benedetto Bonfigli are dealt with in the exhibition catalogue entitled *Un pittore e la sua città. Benedetto Bonfigli e Perugia*, exh. cat., ed. Vittoria Garibaldi (Milan: Electa, 1996).

9. A complete examination of the issue is offered by Scarpellini, pp. 18–28. Some new attributions are suggested in Filippo Todini, *La pittura umbra. Dal Duecento al primo Cinquecento*, 2 vols. (Milan: Longanesi, 1989).

10. Paola Mercurelli Salari, "I Francescani e l'oratorio di San Bernardino," in *Un pittore e la sua città. Benedetto Bonfigli e Perugia*, pp. 138–47.

11. Vittoria Garibaldi, "Bottega del 1473. Miracoli di San Bernardino da Siena," in the exhibition catalogue entitled *Rinascimento. Da Brunelleschi a Michelangelo. La rappresentazione della architettura*, ed. Henry Millon and Vittorio Magnago Lampugnani (Milan: Bompiani, 1994), pp. 448–52.

12. Regarding the complex situation of attributing architectonic backgrounds to a painter, architect, or architectural theorist, see the interesting suggestions of Laura Teza, "Bottega del 1473. Miracoli di San Bernardino da Siena," in *Galleria Nazionale dell'Umbria, Dipinti sculture ceramiche: studi e restauri*, ed. Caterina Bon Valsassina e Vittoria Garibaldi (Florence: Arnaud, 1994), pp. 216–20. Teza, from an idea of Bombe (Walter Bombe, *Geschichte der Peruginer Malerei bis zu Perugino und Pinturicchio* [Berlin: B. Cassirer, 1912], pp. 131–34), repropses the name of Francesco di Giorgio. See also the successive observations of Sylvia Ferino Pagden, "Bottega del 1473. Miracoli di San Bernardino da Siena," in *Rinascimento. Da Brunelleschi a Michelangelo. La rappresentazione della architettura*, pp. 447–48.

13. For contemporary niches by Benedetto Bonfigli, see Paola Mercurelli Salari, "Benedetto Bonfigli, Gonfalone di San Francesco al Prato," cat. no. 18; "Angeli che offrono rose," cat. no. 20; and "Angeli con cartigli e simboli della Passione," cat. no. 21, in *Un pittore e la sua città. Benedetto Bonfigli e Perugia*, pp. 150–51, 154–57.

14. The recent doubts regarding attribution on the part of critics and the proposed collaboration of painters such as Fiorenzo di Lorenzo or the young Signorelli are invalidated by the uniformity of the whole, which has emerged from the recent restoration of the work, as well as by the unmistakable manner of rendering the landscape in a clear and luminous manner. See Laurence B. Kanter, "Luca Signorelli, Piero della Francesca and Pietro Perugino," in *Studi di Storia dell'Arte* 1 (1977): 95–111.

15. Scarpellini, p. 26, finds compelling affinities between the group on the left of Perugino's *Adoration of the Magi* in Perugia and that of the *Adoration of the Magi* by Botticelli for the church of Santa Maria Novella in Florence, dated to 1475. Should this affinity not be dependent upon a common prototype, it would then make it very difficult to posit an earlier date for the *Adoration* in Perugia. Moreover, though advancing these two works by some years would on the one hand make it easier to understand important future commissions and fill in the lacuna before the execution of the Saint Bernardino panels, it would at the same time make it necessary to reconsider Vasari's suggestion that the date of Perugino's birth was 1445 or 1446. Until now, an intermediate date of 1448, halfway between the dates suggested by Vasari and by Giovanni Santi, has been accepted without documentary evidence in order to facilitate matters.

16. Canuti, 2: 120 and Scarpellini, p. 25 both give a mistaken indication of the day of payment (it was July 21 and *not* July 25), and do not give the exact estimated sum, i.e., one thousand florins, for the decoration of "certain figures." The five florins Perugino actually received must have been the payment for that day.

17. That the painting has not been repainted, except in the tiniest of areas, may be proven by the restoration in progress, which has, among other things, allowed us to see the decorative motif of the pave-

ment below a thin layer of dirt. The inscription correctly reads: DECRETO PVBLICO .)EFF)TA . ANNO . DNI. MCCCCLXXV[   ], allowing us to posit at least two IIs in the space after the date, thus making it 1478 or 1479.

18. The fresco, once signed PETRVS . PERVSINVS . P . / . A . MCCCCLVIII, comprises the first precious reference point for the activity of the painter: see Canuti, 1: 50–51 and 2: 10–12.

19. On the rear wall Perugino painted a false altarpiece with the *Assumption of the Virgin with Pope Sixtus IV* and on the sides were two paintings, the *Finding of Moses* and the *Nativity of Christ*, works which were destroyed to make room for the *Last Judgment* of Michelangelo. For the new compositional arrangements of the Assumption and the Nativity, see Scarpellini, p. 29, and the essay of R. Mencarelli in this catalogue.

20. On the Sistine Chapel, see also John Shearman, "La costruzione della cappella e la prima decorazione al tempo di Sisto IV," in *La Cappella Sistina: primi restauri: la scoperta del colore*, ed. Marcella Boroli (Novara: Istituto Geografico De Agostini, 1986), pp. 22–87; Rona Goffen, "Friar Sixtus IV and the Sistine Chapel," *Renaissance Quarterly* 39 (1986): 218–62; and Maurizio Calvesi, "La Cappella Sistina nel Quattrocento e i suoi pittori," in *Perugino e Pinturicchio in Vaticano*, ed. Stefani Macioce (Rome: Bagatto Libri, 1988), pp. 7–91.

21. Filippo Todini has suggested to me that the male portrait in the National Gallery of Art, Washington, D.C., formerly attributed to Lorenzo di Credi, should be assigned to Perugino, active in the Sistine Chapel, because it displays the same formal characteristics. The figure is defined with extreme subtlety, even from the psychological point of view, against a background with a rich and complex landscape. For the portraits of Perugino, see the essay of R. Mencarelli in this catalogue.

22. See Alessandro Cecchi, "La *Pietà* del Perugino per San Giusto degli Ingesuati," in *Restauri. La Pietà del Perugino e la Madonna delle Arpie di Andrea del Sarto*, Gli Uffizi. Studi e Ricerche, vol. 1 (Florence: Centro Di, 1984), pp. 29–35; and Alfio Del Serra, "Relazione tecnica sul restauro della *Pietà* di Pietro Perugino e della *Madonna delle Arpie* di Andra del Sarto," in *Restauri. La Pietà del Perugino e la Madonna delle Arpie di Andrea del Sarto*, pp. 36–38.

23. Riccardo Spinelli, "Vicende secentesche della *Visione di San Bernardo* del Perugino: una pala del Boschi e la copia del Ficherelli," in *Paragone* 35 (1985): 76–85.

24. For the Collegio del Cambio subsequent to its restoration, see Vittoria Garibaldi, "Un Perugino in Collegio," *Art Dossier* 101 (May 1995): 33–37; Sergio Fusetti and Paolo Virilli, "Secoli di interventi," *Art Dossier* 101 (May 1995): 101; V. Garibaldi, "Collegio del Cambio," in *Perugia. Segni di cultura* (Perugia: Quattroemme, 1994), pp. 89–94; and Elvio Lunghi, *Il Collegio del Cambio a Perugia* (Assisi: Minerva, 1996).

25. Vasari, p. 266.

26. Todini 1990, pp. 113–21.

27. Translation in Vasari, p. 265.

28. Christopher Lloyd, *Italian Paintings before 1600 in The Art Institute of Chicago* (Princeton: Princeton University Press, 1993), pp. 190–96.

29. Data and information have been acquired which allow us to better comprehend the most important work of Perugino's mature period. We can now establish some points regarding the original structure, the time period over which the individual parts were completed, and the amount of collaboration which took place in accomplishing the work: see Vittoria Garibaldi, "Il Polittico di Sant'Agostino, vicende storiche e critiche," in the journal of the *Associazione Comitato Italiano World Monuments Fund* (May 1996) [no pagination], and Vittoria Garibaldi, *Saggi in onore di A. Marabottini* (in press).

30. In 1512 the upper cornice had not yet been installed as two orders. The representation of *God the Father*, which always had been thought to have been facing the nave because it was traditionally placed above the *Baptism* (a hypothesis confirmed by the direction of the light), is stylistically removed from the first group of paintings and displays motifs similar to those depicted on the other side of the altarpiece facing the choir. The second, more valid reason is that during the restoration, traces of another *God the Father* were found underneath the circle containing the dove of the Holy Spirit in the panel of the *Baptism*. The earlier *God the Father* was evidently used previously, then covered and replaced by the Holy Spirit when the upper cornice was installed.

BRUCE COLE

INDIANA UNIVERSITY

What Was a Renaissance Artist?

IN MANY WAYS, Pietro Perugino's career exemplifies what it meant to be a Renaissance artist, and a most successful one at that. He came from a small town, began working in an artist's workshop in the nearby big city of Perugia, joined a Florentine shop with many soon-to-be well-known artists, and ended up managing two shops of his own while carrying out prestigious commissions all over Italy. But when we say "Renaissance artist," we must take care not to think of him in our twentieth-century sense. In fact, our concept of an artist is quite opposite from the idea held by Renaissance society. If we are to understand Perugino, we must place him in the context of his own time. To do this we will have to investigate how he and his Renaissance contemporaries learned to be artists, how they worked, what they thought about their art, and how society at large viewed them.

In order to understand the world of the Renaissance artist, it is necessary to say a word about what Renaissance art is and what it is not. If the phrase "Renaissance art" simply refers to that art produced in the Italian peninsula between 1250 and 1550, then the term has validity. However, if "Renaissance art" is used to label that same art as a generic entity distinguished by its commonalities rather than by its diversity, then the term is meaningless, for the differences between the local schools of Renaissance art are equal to or greater than their similarities.

Art, like society in the Renaissance, was intensely provincial. The Italian peninsula had, in fact, once been unified under Roman rule. With the decline of the empire, however, cities were depopulated and their inhabitants scattered throughout the countryside. The division and separation of the population were facilitated by Italy's mountainous topography (figs. 6, 11). Until the creation of a modern highway system in the last few decades, travel and all other forms of communication in the peninsula posed no small difficulties. Such conditions, combined with the lack of a central, unifying authority,

19

Fig. 6. Italy in the fifteenth century

encouraged the development of extreme localism during the Middle Ages. Notwithstanding the demographic shifts from the countryside back to the cities around the twelfth century, the culture of these burgeoning urban centers remained highly parochial. Particular dialects, special forms of government, individual currencies, and other major aspects of society had all evolved and were sustained into the Renaissance. Even today, despite the fact that Italy has existed as a unified country for over a century, localism is still a strong force influencing many aspects of contemporary culture and politics.

This localism was reflected in Renaissance art. Take, for instance, Florence and Siena, separated by not more than seventy-five miles. During the early Renaissance, these two cities, which were often at war with each other, independently developed their own schools of art. So different were they that it is still possible to trace the old borders between these two cities by analyzing the art in churches and town halls. On one side of the border the art is Florentine or Florentine-influenced; on the other side, there is Sienese or Sienese-influenced art. That is not to say that the Florentine and Sienese schools were totally separate entities, for they were not. Borrowing occurred among the members of both schools, and artists on each side were influenced by the advances of their colleagues. In the early fourteenth century, several Sienese artists were even given important Florentine commissions. Nevertheless, the fundamental components of style, iconography, and interpretation remained intensely local. It is precisely this localism which makes the term "Renaissance art" misleading when it is used to generically categorize the art of the period. When historians talk about "schools" or "centers" of Renaissance art—Florence, Siena, Perugia, Venice, Naples—they are in fact discussing the characteristics of this localism which allows them to identify and classify art by region and city.

It is surprising to learn that people during the Renaissance—and in this particular instance the period in question covers only the years 1250 through 1500—considered art to be a craft and thought artists such as Perugino were craftsmen, just like the butcher, baker, or candlestick maker. Each of these trades possessed roughly the same social and economic status, which was well below that of the merchant or banker, but slightly above the status of the manual laborer. Status in this period was fairly simple to comprehend: since the artist, like the laborer, worked with his hands, both were rather low on the social ladder. Artists therefore seldom achieved positions of power or status in Renaissance society. For instance, when Michelangelo, the younger contemporary and sometime-rival of Perugino, wanted to become an artist, his father Ludovico, a minor governmental official, tried to discourage him using beatings (among other things) because he felt such an occupation was beneath his son and his family. Michelangelo's sixteenth-century biographer Giorgio Vasari tells us,

In time the number of Ludovico's children grew, and since he was not well off and had little income, he placed his children in service with the Wool and Silk Guilds while Michelangelo, who was already grown, was placed with Master Francesco da Urbino in his grammar school, and because Michelangelo's genius attracted him to the pleasures of drawing, he spent all the time he could drawing in secret, for which he was scolded and sometimes beaten by his father and his elders, since they probably thought applying oneself to a craft they did not recognize was a base and unworthy undertaking for their ancient house.[1]

Conversely, becoming an artist could also constitute a step up the social ladder. An example of this was Giotto, who was said to be tending sheep when he was "discovered" by the great artist Cimabue. Giotto's father is likewise identified by Vasari as "a tiller of the soil and a humble person," yet he allows Giotto to become an artist (without beating him!) and eventually his choice is shown to be correct, as Giotto's wit and intelligence are praised alongside his artistic ability in literary works. Vasari likewise posits such a case for Perugino, who he claims was "raised in misery and privation" by a poor father in Castello della Pieve and was spurred on to success by the memory of this early poverty. This "fact" is probably not correct; rather it is probable that Vasari is coloring his tale to portray a non-Florentine artist as avid for wealth.[2]

Although the terms "art" and "artists" are used here, it would be incorrect to understand them in our modern sense of the words. In reality, there was no all-encompassing word for "artist" in the Renaissance. It was only late in the period that our concept of the artist as someone who, by his or her calling, stands apart from regular society was beginning to be formulated. Instead, those who produced works of art were known by the specific medium in which they worked: painter, sculptor, architect, and so forth. Nor was what they produced called "art." Today we tend to think of art as something more or less without a practical function, autonomous objects made to be collected and appreciated for their aesthetic, emotional, and philosophical characteristics, among other things. Art today is usually associated with decoration or with museums.

Museums did not exist in the Renaissance because art was never seen outside its functional context. Rather, art was tied to a specific location and meant to perform a certain, well-defined task. For example, an altarpiece was placed on an altar as both an aid and illustration to the rite of the Mass. Altarpieces were characterized by a specific, limited range of shapes, sizes, and subject matter developed over time for this exact purpose. As the Mass was said, images of the Pietà made visual the mystical presence of the body of Christ among the communicants. Images of the Madonna and Child with Saints, such as this example by Perugino for the high altar in the Duomo of Città della Pieve (fig. 7),

Fig. 7. View of the *Virgin and Child with Four Saints,*
Duomo, Città della Pieve

visualized the divine for believers. Other images were believed capable of performing miracles. Images were depicted on *cassoni* (storage chests), often in the form of legends from mythology and ancient history. These scenes not only decorated the chests, but also illustrated stories which were meant to morally and spiritually instruct and edify those who viewed them, especially children who saw them at eye level. So, while altarpieces and painted chests displayed paintings, they also performed specific functions.

In fact, this is true for almost all of Renaissance art, which can be easily classified according to type and function. In the Renaissance there was no hierarchy of categories: artists from the exalted to the humble were just as likely to decorate a chest or put geometric designs on a timbered ceiling as they were to paint an altarpiece or sculpt in marble. Perugino himself not only painted a number of "domestic" Madonna and Child images (see Abbott), but he also executed religious frescoes for churches, classical allegories for the Collegio del Cambio and the *studiolo* of Isabella d'Este, decorations for the Pope's investiture, and processional banners for confraternities. A good deal of artistic production involved things we would no longer consider to be in the realm of most contemporary artists, such as the painting of sculpture, furniture, or coats of arms.

Making art in the Renaissance was a craft, and artists were educated just like others who practiced trades during this period. When they were quite young, probably around ten to twelve years of age, boys were apprenticed to a master to learn their trade. These boys already possessed some rudimentary education, probably furnished by family members, as boys often pursued the family trade. While sons of merchants and bankers underwent formal schooling (the sort of grammar school which Michelangelo's father wished for his son), future artists' apprentices were taught to read and to do some simple mathematics at home, but not much more than that before being sent to learn the various art trades. A somewhat higher level of education than just reading and simple math became especially important to artists once patrons became more educated or had humanist scholars advising them on classical subjects and motifs to be painted—as the artists' compositions became more sophisticated, so they gained prestige and improved their status. Vasari describes the basic early education given an artist in his "Life of Luca della Robbia," stating that before Luca entered the shop of a goldsmith, he "was honestly brought up until he had learnt not only to read and write but also to cast accounts, in so far as it was likely to be needful, after the custom of most Florentines."

Boys like Luca della Robbia and Pietro Perugino would have studied with a master, an experienced artist who took complete charge of their education. As was common in all trades, the artist's workshop was a family business, often run out of the home. There was a real clan structure to many of these shops, with fathers, sons, nephews, and cousins working together over the generations. Shops were property to be inherited and their business carried on by younger relatives or pupils. Property was often passed down in wills as in, for example, the one made in 1625 by the Venetian painter Palma il Giovane in which he bequeaths

> everything pertaining to the profession of a painter—like finished paintings and rough sketches, drawings, reliefs—and all the implements of the profession. I leave them to my grandson Giacomo, the son of my daughter Crezia, who is to practice the profession of painting and to style himself "from the house of Palma" in memory of the famous Giacomo [Palma il Giovane]—and in memory of me.[3]

It is important to realize that boys like Palma's grandson and Perugino, among others, were accepted into the shop not because of their talent, which seems to have been of little importance, since Renaissance society did not believe in innate talent, but rather in the importance of training. Apprentices were taken on either because they were related to the master by blood or because they had been recommended by someone with connections to the shop. Often the apprentices, who frequently boarded with the master, were paid incrementally, with their wages increasing in proportion to the importance and difficulty of their tasks. Their stay in the shop seems to have been regulated by their progress rather than by guild law, although the guilds did sometimes try to control specific terms of apprenticeship. In his "Life of Michelangelo," Giorgio Vasari includes the text of a contract for Michelangelo's apprenticeship made between Michelangelo's father Ludovico and the painter Domenico Ghirlandaio. The terms of this contract were fairly typical:

1488. On this day, the first of April, I record that I, Lodovico di Lionardo di Buonarroti, place my son Michelangelo with Domenico and David di Tommaso di Currado for the next three years to come with these covenants and agreements: that the said Michelangelo must remain with the abovementioned for the stipulated period to learn to paint and to practice this trade, and to do whatever the abovementioned may order him to do, and during these three years, the aforesaid Domenico and David must give him twenty-four newly minted florins—six in the first year, eight the second, and ten the third, in all, a total of ninety-six lire.[4]

Occasionally, accomplished young artists were kept in the master's shop for a very long time. Taddeo Gaddi, a Florentine painter of the first half of the fourteenth century, remained in Giotto's shop for two decades, probably as principal helper. It is easy to understand how a master would be reluctant to part with a truly able student and how certain especially helpful apprentices became rather like junior partners who never left the shop during the master's lifetime.

Masters sometimes formed temporary partnerships for specific jobs or allowed their more mature apprentices to take on outside commissions. They even arranged for the sale of their apprentices' work. In his "Life of Botticelli" (Botticelli was a colleague who worked with Perugino on the great Sistine Chapel commission in the 1480s), Vasari includes an example of this in a little story he tells about the great painter's love of practical jokes:

Sandro [Botticelli] was a very pleasant person who played many practical jokes on his pupils and friends, and the story goes that one of his dependents named Biagio painted a tondo . . . and that after Sandro sold it for six gold florins to one of the citizens of Florence, he found Biagio and said to him: "I finally sold that picture of yours, but this evening it would be good to hang it up high so that it can be seen better, and then, tomorrow morning, you should go to the buyer's house and bring him here—this way, he can see it displayed in the right light and the right place; then he'll count out your money for you."[5]

Some apprentices, unable or unwilling to set up shops on their own, sought employment in already established shops where they remained for the rest of their careers. In some cases, an apprentice would be trained in one craft and then leave it for another—Botticelli, Ghirlandaio, Ghiberti, and Brunelleschi are all cases in point, having begun in goldsmiths' shops and then moved on to painting, sculpture, and architecture. A great deal of flexibility was inherent in the system of education and employment of Renaissance artists.

This system was predicated on the idea that almost any young boy could be sent to a workshop and *become* a good artist. In other words, Renaissance society believed that artists were made, and not born. Today we believe just the opposite. Present-day artists are trained only *after* they have demonstrated their talent to a committee at an art school or university. Unlike society in the Renaissance, we assume that talent is innate: one either has it or one does not. While training can improve an artist's work, it cannot create such an endowment.

This is not the venue to engage in a philosophical discussion of the nature of artistic talent, but it is clear that there was quite an abundance of it in the Renaissance. Whether this was the result of the availability of many naturally gifted youths or the outcome of the superior nature of their education is debatable. What we can say with certainty is that the Renaissance workshop was a remarkably effective educational institution. Boys entered a workshop with no experience and came out of it as artists with remarkable technical and formal skills, among the most advanced of any period of European art. The general level of art was astonishingly high and at its peak was unsurpassed by any other art-making civilization. One has only to think of the unceasing progression of exceptional Renaissance artists throughout the Italian peninsula, from Giotto to Perugino to Titian, to realize how much noteworthy art was being produced during the period.

How did all this come about? The answer lies in the way the workshop functioned. It was headed by a master, an artist who had himself been through the system. He obtained commissions, paid bills, and supervised all the shop's activities. Under him were apprentices who, as we have seen, came into the shop as adolescents. In addition, there were also part-time helpers, some of them artists, some of them unskilled workers, who were called in on an ad hoc basis when the shop had much work and needed more hands. We get a glimpse of just how many artists were associated with a busy workshop by looking at Vasari's list of Perugino's disciples. "Pietro made many masters in his own manner," Vasari tells us. Besides Raphael, the list includes Pintoricchio, Rocco Zoppo, Montevarchi, Gerino da Pistoia, and many others.

The apprentices learned their art, so to speak, from the ground up. Few documents about the course of artistic education in the Renaissance exist, but we are fortunate enough to possess a manuscript devoted to the subject. Written in the early fifteenth century by Cennino Cennini, a minor pupil of Agnolo Gaddi, *The Craftsman's Handbook* was intended for the instruction of fledgling artists. This manual includes recipes for artistic materials, hints on how to draw, principles of artistic education, and a wealth of other rare and curious facts, such as the proper altitude at which to find the best eggs for tempera painting and how to make a paint brush out of rat hair!

Beginning apprentices were taught the most basic of procedures. Their education was practical rather than theoretical, what today we would call "hands-on" training. They first learned all the material and mechanical aspects of their trade: how to make brushes, grind pigments, lay plaster for frescoes, prepare gesso, and the like. Years of such experience gave them an expertise in the handling of materials which is still visible in every well-preserved Renaissance painting. Craft—the ability to make things skillfully—was an important aspect in the selling and buying of Renaissance art. Patrons wanted things carefully made with the best material and craftsmanship. Our strict delineation between craft and art did not exist in the Renaissance, and contracts often specify in infinite detail exactly the materials to be used.

This concern with materials is well-illustrated in the contract agreed upon by Perugino and the Benedictine monks of San Pietro in Perugia. The contract is for an altarpiece to be placed on the high altar. Following a description of the witnesses present and the subjects to be painted, there is an interesting example of how the entity commissioning a work clearly stated the materials to be employed by the artist:

> The predella below is to be painted and adorned with stories according to the desire of the present Abbot. The columns, however, and the mouldings and all other ornaments of the panel should be embellished with fine gold and other fine colors, as will be most fitting, so that the panel will be beautifully and diligently painted, embellished and gilded from top to bottom as stated above and as it befits a good, experienced, honorable, and accomplished master.[6]

It is interesting to note that Perugino was expected to lay out the money for his paints, gold, etc., the costs of which were included in the total 500 gold ducats he was to be paid for the work within four years of the date he began painting.

Throughout their training, which could last for five or more years, the apprentices learned through imitation. Unlike today, where many art schools and the art world encourage students to be original and find their own idioms, Renaissance artists believed in the strict imitation of style and motif. Apprentices were to copy the work of the master until his style became their own. They were also encouraged to learn from the paintings and drawings of other masters. These works could furnish them with many types of compositions and motifs which would be of considerable benefit to them later on. This sort of copying was one of the major characteristics of Renaissance art and, in fact, of much Western art until this century.

Copying was of vital importance in the Renaissance workshop because the production of art in the period was collaborative. While the master would often create the designs for an individual painting or sculpture, the apprentices would carry them out on a work of any size, sometimes without the master's further participation. Consequently, they all had to be working in the same idiom in order to produce a seamless whole.

Art was not produced on an assembly line; it was made by many hands in a highly sophisticated, efficient manner. Take, for instance, the creation of a fresco. The shop plastered the walls. The master (and perhaps his best pupils) laid out the *sinopia* (preparatory design). Then the entire crew painted the frescoes, some doing landscape, another figures, and so forth. Fresco is a demanding and quite unforgiving medium which requires great speed and coordination, as the surface, once applied, dries very quickly. Such work could only have been successfully done with apprentices who were capable of closely imitating the master's style. Just how successful this imitation was (resulting in what might be called a "shop style") can be seen by examining almost any Renaissance fresco cycle. Most frescoes exhibit a seamless stylistic whole which appears to have been painted by a single individual rather than by an entire shop. Without this "shop style," a fresco cycle or an altarpiece would look like a crazy quilt of individual idioms.

Historians of art often use a twentieth-century paradigm of artistic originality to judge Renaissance works. This is misleading because, as we have just seen, the origin and development of style and interpretation were determined by the master and *not* by the fledgling artist. Moreover, unlike today, it was mainly a cooperative venture.

Most paintings and sculptures from the period before 1500 are unsigned, undated, and undocumented. Art historians have employed stylistic analysis to successfully, and even brilliantly, attribute and date these works, but they have frequently dealt with them as though they were products of the twentieth century. Given the collective nature of these paintings, it is inaccurate to think that, like modern works of art, they are the products of a single mind and a single set of hands.

Paradigms of modern artistic development are unfortunately no help in discussing Renaissance art. Most artists of the time learned a style from their masters, making few incremental modifications to that style as they matured. They did not exhibit the rapid and fundamental shifts of style which are so typical of the art of our time. It is therefore difficult or sometimes impossible to trace a linear development (or any other kind of development) in the works of many Renaissance artists. The norms of Renaissance art are seen in artists like Taddeo Gaddi and Neri di Bicci, whose style was unvarying, not in figures like Giotto or Donatello, who are notable exceptions. Piero della Francesca is a good case in point. Despite the efforts of several generations of art historians, the chronology of his paintings remains obscure simply because there is so little development in style between them.

All stylistic development in the Renaissance proceeded slowly and incrementally. The

Fig. 8. Perugino and assistants, *Baptism of Christ*, Sistine Chapel, Vatican

idioms of the individual artist, of the particular workshop, and of generations of artists succeeded each other in a steady progression. Such succession may be seen, for instance, in the dependence of the young Raphael on his master Perugino, immediately apparent in the classic comparison of their respective versions of the Marriage of the Virgin (pl. 17). Although there were several exceptions—Masaccio and Michelangelo, for example—most Renaissance artists were conservative and strongly dependent on tradition.

This dependence on the past also played a crucial role in how Renaissance artists conceived works of art. When a painter was given the commission for an Annunciation, he would not, as many modern artists do, reconfigure the subject. Instead, he would think about what paintings of the Annunciation he had seen and which of them could serve as models for the work he had in mind. Thus models, or parts of various models, were the inspiration for most Renaissance works of art. This use of prototypes was very much part of the mind-set of the Renaissance artist. Copying works themselves or copying drawings or prints of works of art also saved him time: efficiency was an important attribute of the successful artist. He did not, in other words, have to reinvent the wheel every time he received a new commission. And he was accustomed to copying from his earliest shop training.

Moreover, Renaissance artists frequently copied themselves. They often reused their own models or sketches to create replicas of works they had already sold. Perugino, for example, often reutilized his earlier work, as a comparison between his *Baptism of Christ* (c. 1481) from the Sistine Chapel (fig. 8) and the same subject from the Sant'Agostino Polyptych (1512) (fig. 45) reveals. A devotional or secular work was often copied and re-copied in the workshop. Vasari complains about this in his "Life of Perugino":

Pietro had worked so hard and always had such an abundance of paintings to complete that he quite often placed the same details in his pictures. He thus reduced the theory of his craft to such a fixed style that he executed all his figures with the same expression.[7]

The demand for copies of a particularly popular work, such as the portrait of a ruler or a miracle-working image, could continue for decades. Often these copies were delegated to apprentices, who would be expected to create faithful reproductions of the prototype.

"Prototype" is used here instead of "original," because the word "original"—which we so closely associate with important art today—is often not applicable to Renaissance art. An original is unique, while much of the art produced during the period was *meant* to be replicated. Sculpture in terra cotta, stucco, and bronze was often reproduced in many copies through the use of molds. Paintings, as we have just seen, were also copied many times to meet the demands of the numerous patrons who might have wanted the same or similar images. Today we think of paintings and sculpture as singular products. This was not the case in the Renaissance, where often there was no original, but merely a series of copies. Renaissance artists and their patrons saw nothing objectionable in this process, and did *not* equate artistic borrowing with plagiarism. Thus, as in the case of busy artists with large shops, such as Perugino, Ghirlandaio, or Giovanni Bellini, one can understand why there are so many works done not by the master but by his pupils.

Moreover, neither artist nor patron found any fault with the way works of art were commissioned, a process which would horrify today's artists (and probably most contemporary patrons as well) because it allowed the artist only limited, if any, free will. A contract was drawn up between artist and patron which often stipulated the size, material, and subject of the work to be done. A payment and delivery schedule were frequently included, with the amount of the final payment often being determined by a committee of fellow artists. But that was not all. Usually, in an altarpiece, for example, the identity of the saints, the colors of their robes, the attributes which they were to hold, and occasionally the facial expressions which they were to display were all stipulated. In 1455, the Florentine painter Neri di Bicci recorded the specifications of a contract for a fresco in his shopbook. This is a typical, although not overly specific, example of one of these contracts:

> Today I have agreed to paint for Abbot Benedetto of S. Pancrazio in Florence one arched bay of the cloister of this church in which I must make a figure of S. Giovanni Gualberto with ten saints and *Beati* of their order and below a kneeling abbot, these figures must be placed in a chapel which appears round; the sky must be blue and with stars and the arches should be carved and all well decorated.[8]

Fig. 9. *Combat between Love and Chastity*, Musée du Louvre, Paris (see pl. 20)

An even more particular set of contractual specifications was furnished for Pietro Perugino in 1503 by the famous Mantuan patron Isabella d'Este. Isabella was then decorating her *studiolo* with allegorical paintings and she was eager to include a work by Perugino (fig. 9). A detailed program for an allegory was composed by the humanist Paride de Ceresara and incorporated into the contract. What follows is only a small portion of the instructions given to Perugino:

> My poetic invention, which I wish to see you paint, is the battle of Love and Chastity—that is to say, Pallas and Diana fighting against Venus and Love. Pallas must appear to have almost vanquished Love. After breaking his golden arrow and silver bow, and flinging them at her feet, she holds the blindfold boy with one hand by the handkerchief which he wears over his eyes, and lifts her lance to strike him with the other. The issue of the conflict between Diana and Venus must appear more doubtful. Venus' crown, garland and veil will only have been slightly damaged, while Diana's raiment will have been singed by the torch of Venus, but neither of the goddesses will have received any wound.[9]

This contract was accompanied by a compositional sketch which the artist was to follow. Later Perugino asked for instructions about the height of the foreground figures.

Isabella then sent him a letter containing threads the exact length of these figures, adding however that "the other figures behind can be of any size that you like." To us, such contractual terms seem a surprising brake on an artist's originality, but they were accepted and even welcomed by Renaissance artists who did not share our idea that art is principally a creative process conceived and carried out by the artist alone.

It is reasonable to ask how any originality, in our sense of the word, could have existed in Renaissance art, in light of the artist's training, his conservative inclination to draw style and inspiration from the past, and the demands of his patrons. In fact, we know that there *was* much originality in the period. In most cases, however, it was not the striking, radical change which we have come to expect in our art. Today originality is hard to define because there are so few boundaries to cross and almost no mileposts to use as measurements. How does an artist know when he or she is really being original when so many are called original?

In the Renaissance, however, there were traditional styles, types, and interpretations which could be modified, albeit incrementally, to form new styles, types, and interpretations. Proof of this is easily found by looking at the changes between one generation of artists and the next. There was a major development in Renaissance art over the two and one-half centuries of the period's existence, but it was gradual and not the product of rapid, radical shifts.

Nevertheless, at the end of our period, around 1500, new attitudes were forming which began to foreshadow some of our modern ideas about art. In the sixteenth century, several artists (such as Michelangelo, Titian, and Perugino's most famous student, Raphael) were regarded by their contemporaries as more than simple craftsmen; they were viewed as divinely inspired creators standing apart from the common run of humanity. Vasari, our best guide here, tells us that in order to rid art of its many errors, the Almighty sent to earth Michelangelo,

> a spirit who, working alone, was able to demonstrate in every art and every profession the meaning of perfection in the art of design, how to give relief to the details in paintings by means of proper drawing, tracing, shading, and casting light, how to work with good judgement in sculpture, and how to make buildings comfortable and secure, healthy, cheerful, well proportioned, and richly adorned with various decorations in architecture. Moreover, He wanted to join to this spirit true moral philosophy and the gift of sweet poetry, so that the world would admire and prefer him for the wholly singular example of his life, his work, the holiness of his habits, and all his human undertakings, and so that we could call him something divine rather than mortal.[10]

Such statements were hardly conceivable much before Vasari wrote these words in the 1560s (see Bondanella). It was also Vasari who, with the support of Duke Cosimo de' Medici, established the Florentine Academy of Design in 1562 (see Chronicle, 1508). This was an institution meant to give artists the sort of academic, intellectual prestige already enjoyed by the more learned professions like literature and classical studies.

The work of artists became increasingly prized no longer solely for its functional qualities, but because it was now expressive of their particular minds and hands. The *process* of creating a painting or sculpture was becoming highly valued. Preparatory drawings, for example, once used simply as educational or compositional tools, were now being avidly collected. Before this time, drawings had been considered nearly worthless outside the studios of artists such as Perugino (see Mencarelli). In this new view, they were seen as revealing the stages of artistic creativity. Titian's student Palma il Vecchio, describing his master's preparatory oil sketches, tells us that

> the most sophisticated connoisseurs found such sketches entirely satisfactory in themselves, and they were greatly in demand since they showed the way to anyone who wished to find the best route into the Ocean of Painting.[11]

This description is important because it reveals a new attitude quite opposite that of the traditional appraisal of the nature of drawings. Drawings were no longer just considered a means to an end, but rather an end in and of themselves.

Famous artists such as Raphael and Titian were besieged by commissions from lay and secular powers who wanted any work that they might furnish, even mere sketches. The relation between patron and artist began to shift as these famous figures came to be treated as something other than subservient craftsmen. Of course, such treatment was not common, for most artists in the Italian peninsula were still viewed as craftsmen. Still, several great artists and their patrons were transforming ideas about art and artists. Raphael, Titian, and Michelangelo grew wealthy, were able to purchase grand houses, and lived in considerable luxury. Their abilities were extolled by humanists and their lives were considered worthy subjects for biography. In fact, much of what we know about Renaissance artists comes from Giorgio Vasari, an author to whom we have already referred several times. Vasari's *Lives*, first published in 1550, is a compendium of artists' biographies written to extol the progress of Florentine art from its beginnings in the fourteenth century with Giotto to its summit in Vasari's idol, Michelangelo. Such a book could not have been published before the sixteenth century because artists and their art would not have been considered fit for such extensive biographical treatment. In the Renaissance, in fact, Vasari and his many imitators initiated the study of the history of art through their books.

Thus, by the early years of the sixteenth century, ideas about art and artists had begun to change and to presage some of our own concepts about what art is, how it functions in society, and how and for whom it is made. The concept of the artist was being rethought as the painter, sculptor, and architect slowly metamorphosed from craftsman to genius. It was the Renaissance which gave birth to the Western artistic persona, beginning with Michelangelo and attaining romantic fruition in Jackson Pollock.

This transformation, however, did not fundamentally alter the training of artists. The workshop system, with its efficient and effective educational principles and its rational division of labor, remained intact for centuries to come. The training of Titian, Raphael, Caravaggio, Rubens, Van Dyck, and scores of other later artists diverged little from their fourteenth- and fifteenth-century ancestors.

Perugino, then, was a typical example of an early Renaissance artist. We know that he was trained in the workshops of more than one artist, although we cannot identify them all with certainty. Like his own master Verrocchio, who trained such future great artists as Botticelli and Leonardo da Vinci, Perugino taught Raphael of Urbino, whose fame ultimately eclipsed that of his teacher. Yet Perugino outdid most of his colleagues in needing two workshops, one in Florence and the other in Perugia, to accommodate the heavy load of work requested of him.

The locations of the two workshops are significant, for the political situation in these places remained in constant flux over the course of his life. In Florence, he lived through the transitions from the Medici rule to Savonarola's religious rule, to a short period of democracy, and then a return, through Papal intervention, to Medici control. In Perugia the government was likewise alternately controlled by powerful families, various popes, and by Cesare Borgia himself (see Banker). Having described the training he received, it is important to look at the history of Perugia, his adopted city, in order to understand Perugino and his development.

NOTES

1. Giorgio Vasari, *The Lives of the Artists*, trans. Julia Conaway Bondanella and Peter Bondanella (Oxford: Oxford University Press, 1991), p. 416.

2. Vasari's biographies are fictionalized to some degree so that he can praise Florentine artists, often at the expense of artists from other locales (such as the Umbrian Perugino). In one of his studies of the great compendium of artists' lives, Barolsky posits that Vasari himself did not object to poverty, as he felt it reflected the artist's devotion to his art rather than to luxury: Paul Barolsky, *Giotto's Father and the Family of Vasari's "Lives"* (University Park: The Pennsylvania State University Press, 1992).

3. Norbert Huse and Wolfgang Wolters, *The Art of Renaissance Venice: Architecture, Sculpture and Painting, 1460–1590* (Chicago: University of Chicago Press, 1990), p. 177.

4. Vasari, pp. 416–17.

5. Vasari, p. 228. The tale continues that, the next day when Biagio brings the buyer to see the tondo, Botticelli and another assistant had covered the angels' heads with red hoods to make them resemble the priors of the city of Florence. Biagio is too shocked to say anything, and the buyer has been let into the secret by Botticelli, so he praises the painting without noting the "change" in how the work had been described. Later, once the hoods were removed from the angels, Biagio is convinced by his colleagues that he was dizzy and never learns the truth.

6. Contract cited in *A Documentary History of Art*, selected and edited by Elizabeth Holt (Princeton: Princeton University Press, 1981), 1: 268 ff.

7. Vasari, p. 264.

8. This document is found in Anabel Thomas, *The Painter's Practice in Renaissance Tuscany* (Cambridge: Cambridge University Press, 1995), p. 107.

9. Julia Cartwright, *Isabella D'Este, Marchioness of Mantua, 1474–1539*, 2 vols. (New York: Dutton and Company, 1926), 1: 331.

10. Vasari, p. 414.

11. Marco Boschini, *La carta del navegar pitoresco*, ed. Anna Pallucchini, Fonti e documenti per la storia dell'arte veneta, no. 4 (Venice and Rome: Istituto per la collaborazione culturale, 1964), p. 711.

JAMES R. BANKER
NORTH CAROLINA STATE UNIVERSITY

The Social History of Perugia in the Time of Perugino

PEOPLE REFLECTING on the Renaissance in Italy usually conceive of the glories of the period through the achievements of the men and women of Venice, Florence, and Rome, with perhaps an acknowledgment of Siena's early contributions.[1] Fewer individuals are aware of the achievements of Perugia in this period. In the early Renaissance, Perugia and Siena were the most powerful city-states in the region between Florence and Naples. Perugia's culture evolved thanks to the city's substantial population, complex social and economic development, and political prowess. Those who have recognized Perugia's importance in the Renaissance have too often judged the city at the time of Perugino through the achievements and tragedies of the Baglioni, one of Perugia's most influential families. In viewing Perugia in this manner, today's historians have too easily dismissed the city's accomplishments and importance in the Renaissance.[2]

The failure of historians to appreciate Perugia's achievements is in part a consequence of the diversity of its citizens and their varied successes. For the period of the Renaissance, Venice can be viewed as the "Most Serene Republic" striving for command of the Mediterranean, Milan as populous but subject to the lordship of the Visconti and then the Sforza families, Rome as the home of the pope, and Florence as the center of art and of the experiments in republicanism. For Perugia there are no such simplistic generalizations; no overwhelming or dominant metaphor that would elevate the city's history to mythic or legendary proportions comes easily to mind.

The city of Perugia can be seen as a republic or as subject to the Baglioni family and/or the papacy, as a place of recurring violence or as a city in peaceful Umbria, as highly religious or violently opposed to the Christian Church. Perugia in the time of Perugino, therefore, evokes several contradictory and complementary images. Famous for its warriors and military commanders who were employed throughout Italy, Perugia was confounded by that very ferocity which it often directed at its own people and families. The city's population included wealthy families, artisans of great skill, and wide-ranging merchants, yet it was frequently devastated by recurrent attacks of bubonic plague and the fiercest warfare in Italy. Reports of great building projects and chronicles of high festivals appear alongside repetitive destruction of buildings in the city and decimation of rural villages and their harvests.

Several of the contrasts as well as the diversity in the culture were already recognized by contemporary Renaissance observers. They were best stated by the Perugian humanist Francesco Matarazzo, who wrote a description of the last years of the fifteenth century and the early years of the sixteenth century. His *Chronicles* are an excellent source for understanding Perugia. Describing the city in 1500, Matarazzo stated that

> every honest man was overborne by cut-throats who had the countenance of the gentlemen; and no citizen could call that which he had his own, nor could he dispose of his own property, and the gentlemen despoiled now one man, now another, taking from them their having and their goods. And they put up all offices for sale; and some they had abolished, taking to themselves the profits of them; and so grievously were the citizens plundered and oppressed that every man made moan all day long. . . . On the other hand the city was of good repute, because that there was in it such a crowd of men worshipful in every art and craft.[3]

This description possesses some degree of accuracy. Perugia at the time of Perugino can best be approached by acknowledging its diversity and rich culture as well as its violence. The most appropriate image of Perugia's history showcases the inhabitants' ability to create a human environment out of disparate materials through labor and cunning, despite the frequent changes of political regime and the destruction of human and material resources by warring internal factions. From the period of the Etruscans to the Renaissance, the people of Perugia had constructed a beautiful city upon an improbable and rugged site. By the time of Perugino, after man had occupied the site for more than two millennia, the inner city was still enclosed within mammoth walls built by the Etruscans, and many of the nobles' towers from the Middle Ages were still standing. The five *borghi* (districts) of the city emanated from the center along ridges and were enclosed within medieval walls (fig. 10). The people of Perugia valued the city's physical fabric and often commissioned artists to represent this image in paintings. As a result, Perugia is the Italian city whose likeness was most depicted in the fifteenth century.[4]

Perugia is located on the Tiber River. As the region's most populous city, it commanded much of Umbria during the Renaissance (fig. 11). The population trends of Perugia prior to and after the time of Perugino are clear in outline, even if one cannot attain

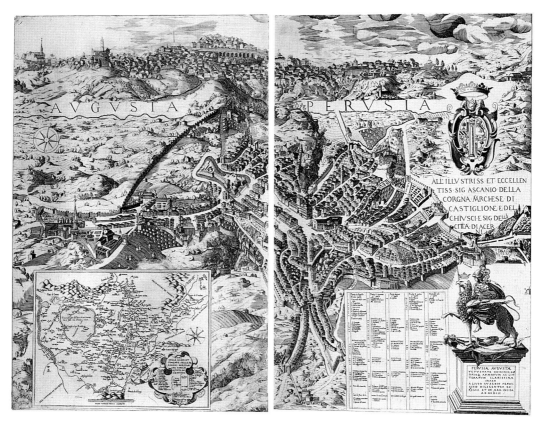

Fig. 10. Livio Eusebi, *Map of Perugia*, 1602 (modern impression), Gift of the City of
Perugia to the People of Grand Rapids

modern standards of accuracy. In common with other cities and towns of northern and
central Italy, Perugia's population expanded from about the year 1000 until 1300. In that
year the city's medieval walls enclosed approximately 28,000 individuals and its rural territory supported another 48,000.[5] Prior to the worst attack of bubonic plague in Italy, the
Black Death of 1348, these numbers had already begun to dwindle, but the 1348 attack and
subsequent outbreaks further reduced the population levels of both town and countryside. Even given the paucity of documents, one can estimate that Perugia suffered a loss
of from one-fourth to one-half of its population in 1348. Indeed, some areas within the
city walls were abandoned, as were numerous villages in the surrounding countryside. The
population continued to decline through the middle of the fifteenth century, with eight
attacks of bubonic plague occurring during the first half of that century, not to mention
several years of food scarcity and even famine. After mid-century, when the devastations
began to subside and changes in agricultural tenancy were implemented (shorter leases and
sharecropping with increased investment of capital), population levels in Perugia and
its countryside once more began to rise. That strategic changes had taken place is clearly
indicated by the population increase despite chronic episodes of plague in 1456, 1464,
1475–79, 1482, 1485, 1486, 1493–94, and 1499.[6] By 1500 Perugia housed approximately
27,500 persons within its walls, compared to approximately 28,000 in about 1300.[7]

Fig. 11. Egranzio Danti, *Map of Perugia and the Umbrian Countryside*, 1580–81, Musei Vaticani

In theory, the city belonged to the pope. But after the twelfth century, Perugia declared itself an autonomous republic, only occasionally acknowledging papal authority. The same political pattern was to occur in many of the cities and towns in the papal territory in Umbria and in the Marches as well. Renaissance Perugia thus inherited a tradition of political conflict. But the city was subject to social conflict as well. One of the principal sources of this conflict was the nobility. As the city's population grew in the twelfth and thirteenth centuries, many rural landowners with traditions of military valor and titles came to reside in the city. Most of these nobles retained their feudal values along with their country estates. Accustomed to command, the nobles resisted the efforts of the *popolo grasso* (the most wealthy merchants) to gain access to major political offices. The Perugian government reached the apex of its democratic development in the fourteenth century, when the *popolo grasso* united with the *popolo minuto* (artisans and shopkeepers) and at least nominally excluded the nobles from holding political office. Membership in one of the guilds of merchants, artisans, and shopkeepers became a requirement for political participation. Inasmuch as they were numerically greater and had more guilds, the *popolo minuto* then sought greater representation in office. Thus in the middle of the fourteenth century, political conflict centered around the two segments of the *popolo*. In the context of a papal attempt to grasp nearly total control of the city in 1371, the artisans and shopkeepers rebelled against the richer groups, but were quickly defeated. Thanks to this victory, the nobles were able to reestablish their social and political power in the city.

During the fifteenth century the nobility fused with the *popolo grasso*, forming an oligarchy. To achieve that unity, each group had to undergo subtle transformations, with many of the merchants obtaining titles of nobility from the city and others imitating noble behavior. At the same time, the nobles engaged in mercantile activities and clamored to join the city's two major guilds, those of the bankers and the merchants. A surprising number of noblemen even entered the socially inferior artisan guilds as makers or sellers of mattresses, leather goods, baskets, and purses, or as shopkeepers handling meat, oil, and cloth. The rapprochement of the two groups is most aptly seen in marriages between members of the merchant families and the older nobility.

The military captain Braccio Fortebraccio da Montone seized political power in Perugia in 1416. Until his death in 1424, he attempted to minimize the power of the city's political institutions. Braccio often ignored elections and the customary discussions in the city councils. His rule accelerated the aggregation of nobles and wealthy merchants, thus strengthening the ruling class of Perugia as he diminished the role of the guilds and their members in politics. The number of craftsmen decreased, and the oligarchy frequently participated in economic enterprises previously owned by the artisans of the *popolo minuto*. The oligarchy transferred profits from artisan production to rural investments, thereby impoverishing many of the artisans and shopkeepers.[8]

At the same time, an implicit alliance was forged between this newly formed oligarchy and papal officials, once again at the expense of the artisans and shopkeepers. In 1417, when the Christian Church in Europe had finally resolved the problem of two popes (one in Italy and the other in France), each claiming to be the "true" vicar of Christ, the papacy in Rome reasserted its ancient claims to possessions throughout central Italy. To this end, after the death of Braccio Fortebraccio, Pope Martin V proposed to restore papal authority in Perugia. In most instances and especially in 1371, artisans and shopkeepers had resisted papal attempts to assert authority in Perugia. During the fourteenth century the guilds had been the chief bulwark against papal as well as noble claims to dominate the city. The city had been ruled by ten priors drawn from the guilds, each prior serving a term of two months. Perugia submitted to papal authority in 1424 and the members of the new oligarchy were pleased with Martin V's settlement, which allowed them to maintain some of Perugia's ancient liberties, including a continuation of the magistracy of the priors. However, in the settlement, Perugians acknowledged the pope, represented by a cardinal legate, as their overlord. Though the legate was most often resident in Rome, he or his

Fig. 12. Coat of arms of the Baglioni family, Musei Vaticani

deputy exercised papal authority in Perugia, retaining the right to supervise the town's councils. This papal official often discussed problems with the town's leading citizens, thereby diminishing the importance of the priors and other councilors selected from the guilds. So after 1424, Perugia was jointly ruled by the city's traditional councils and by the papal legate and therefore is best called a dyarchy.[9]

The leading exponent of this cooperation with papal authority was Malatesta Baglioni. In return, he was made lord of the nearby town of Spello in 1425. The sixteenth-century chronicler of Perugia, Pompeo Pellini, believed that the eventual Baglioni predominance in Perugia derived from this grant of authority over Spello, which later was expanded to include Bastia and Cannaia. Under Malatesta Baglioni's son Braccio, the grant was confirmed for three generations by Pope Eugenius IV.[10]

The predominance of the Baglioni family (fig. 12) became clear in 1488 only after an extended period of contest within the oligarchical group for social and political leadership in Perugia. In this contest, the Baglioni were competing with the great houses of Oddi, Ranieri, Signorelli, Della Corgna, Baldeschi, Montesperelli, Montemelini, Montubiani Arcipreti (or Della Penna), Alfani, and Armanni (or Della Staffa).[11] Even during the half-century of Baglioni leadership from 1488 to 1540, these great houses as well as other families challenged the power of the Baglioni, often as exiles and in alliance with the papacy and other powers of central Italy. Despite the frequent conflicts between the great families of Perugia and the continued decline of the artisans in the second half of the fifteenth century, the population increased. The city's urban fabric underwent a transformation, as many of the oligarchical families united several medieval houses or towers into "palaces." These well-to-do families crowded into the older part of the central city surrounded by the Etruscan walls, while most of the average and poor families found themselves pushed into the districts near the medieval walls.

Though the Baglioni family leaders were not actually lords of Perugia in the period from 1488 to 1540, their many branches, when united into one clan, constituted the city's most important family. They exercised great authority, especially in foreign affairs and as employers of hundreds and at times thousands of soldiers. The Baglioni were composed of more than twenty households, and these numbers enhanced their political and military power, though as often as not conflicts between various Baglioni thwarted their attempts to gain political mastery over the city. The Perugia chroniclers and contemporary Italian historians, including Niccolò Machiavelli, were alternately enthralled and appalled by the military exploits of the Baglioni and by the viciousness of conflicts among the city's families. Who could not be excited by their military exploits and their physical prowess? By hiring them as their military commanders, the great princes and republics of Italy demonstrated the contemporary respect for the military skills of the Baglioni. So prominent were the Baglioni commanders that often one fought against another as each led the opposing armies of Florence, Siena, or Rome.

Portraits of the Baglioni by the contemporary chronicler Matarazzo, who worked closely with the family, attest to more than just military prowess. His discussion of Griffone Baglioni and his palace compels the reader to decry time's capacity to destroy the work of humans. For example, of Griffone he wrote that "for beauty he was a second Ganymede," with his wife "beautiful and winsome as he himself." They possessed a house "finer" than any other of the Baglioni:

> In it there was a room in which were portraits of all the Captains that ever ruled Perugia from the beginning till that day, and also of its famous intellectuals, each one painted in his likeness. The whole house was painted within and without from roof to foundation and it had two towers.[12]

In the middle of the sixteenth century, when Pope Paul III had gained control of Perugia and wished to remove every vestige of the Baglioni family, he chose to destroy this house, building a much-hated fortress on the site of this and other Baglioni houses. Despite Pope Paul's intentions, one can still see several of the Baglioni houses today, thereby gaining an idea of their size and structure, if not the original decoration and splendor. These houses survive because they served as the foundation of the fortress.

The Baglioni were known to be patrons of the arts. Perugino's altarpiece for the monastery of San Pietro was commissioned by the abbot, who was a Baglioni. The family also commissioned Pintoricchio and Perugino to paint in the churches of Spello, the town they ruled near Perugia. For work in their chapel in San Domenico in Perugia, the family commissioned Giannicola di Paolo in 1506-7.[13] In 1503 Matarazzo recalled earlier years of "splendor" under Baglioni leadership, before the cruel and justly short rule of Cesare Borgia (January–September 1503). His description of those Baglioni "good old days" reads as follows:

> You used to see resort in crowds men of position, men of wisdom, gentlemen, doctors, knights, citizens, and foreigners; and great abundance of soldiers and captains do honor to the magnificent House of the Baglioni. That family illumined with its brightness the whole of Tuscany, for any high gentleman that passed through our parts was honorably entertained by the magnificent House of the Baglioni: and they had in their pay a vast number of soldiers, and each one of them was very sumptuous in his expenses.[14]

The chronicler likewise called attention to Giovan Paolo Baglioni's possessing fifty of the fastest horses.

The Baglioni and the other great Perugian families supported *lo Studio* (the city's university), which was administered by the communal magistracy known as the *Savi dello Studio*. These nonprofessionals possessed considerable influence in choosing lecturers and determining which courses were to be taught. By the second half of the fifteenth century, professors of the university, together with the city's administrators, had begun to foster the revival of classical learning, an interest they shared with their contemporaries in Florence and other large cities. Around 1500, Matarazzo, the communal bureaucrat, humanist, and chronicler, employed his classical knowledge to suggest the subjects of Perugino's paintings for the walls of the Meeting Hall of the Bankers' and Money-changers' Guild (Collegio del Cambio) in the Palace of the Priors.[15]

The university also brought to Perugia men striving to master the new classical learning. A good example of such a scholar was a friend of the painters Piero della Francesca and Leonardo da Vinci. Fra Luca Pacioli da Borgo San Sepolcro lectured in the university from 1477 to 1480 on the new mathematics. While there, he wrote *Trattato di Arithematica et algebra*. Later, in 1494, Pacioli published his *Summa de Arithematica geometria proportioni et proportionalità*, regarded as the most important work on classical mathematics and geometry written in the fifteenth century. The Baglioni and other great families appreciated the humanists' knowledge and ability to compare them and their accomplishments to those of classical heroes, whereby they garnered prestige and respectability. The Baglioni were often praised in various humanistic genres, from poetry to medals.[16]

A good deal of Perugia's wealth derived from the employment of her nobles and common soldiers in the armies of other Italian cities. Matarazzo noted that Giovan Paolo's court and wealth "brought great tale of money, through his soldiers, into Perugia

Fig. 13. Interior of the *Mercanzia* meeting hall, Palazzo dei Priori, Perugia

every year."[17] But a greater amount of wealth derived from the city's artisans and merchants in league with agricultural workers. Though the most glorious days of the Perugian artisans were in the thirteenth and fourteenth centuries, the city registered more than forty guilds in the fifteenth century. Their meeting halls were erected in the very center of the city, in the area surrounding the Cathedral of San Lorenzo and the Grand Piazza, sometimes called the Piazza Comune.

The greatest of the guilds were the merchant guilds, of which the *Mercanzia* (merchants) and the *Cambio* (money-changers) were the most important. An essential contributor to the city's economic vitality from at least the twelfth century on, the *Mercanzia* achieved its position of supreme importance through profits from international trade. These merchants transported goods up the Tiber Valley to the area of Romagna and down the river to Lazio and Rome. Even more important was the Tuscan connection, in which Perugian merchants comprised the primary link between the port of Ancona and Tuscan cities, especially Florence. Merchant activity required the presence of money-changers, bankers who made it possible to exchange the various currencies circulating throughout central Italy. Merchants returning to Perugia with ducats and florins from Venice and Florence would exchange these gold coins for the silver coins based on the Perugian *lira* employed in small local transactions. Another possibility available to merchants was to buy a letter of credit, essentially a cashier's check, from a Perugian banker in Perugian silver *lire* that could then be exchanged in Florentine banks for florins or in Venetian banks for ducats. Often the letters of credit and exchanges of various types of money were means of hiding the loans with interest that bishops and popes of the church regarded as usurious and thus unchristian. Merchants, however, found these loans indispensable to their commerce.

Fig. 14. Sala dell'Udienza, Collegio del Cambio, Perugia

The *Mercanzia* and *Cambio* guilds maintained close relations, both spatially and politically, with the city's centers of power (fig. 13). Merchants and money-changers held more political offices in the fifteenth century than any other guildsmen. Both groups received communal permission to occupy rooms in the central political palace of the city, the Palazzo dei Priori (Palace of the Priors). As a means of enhancing their political and social authority, the *Cambio* granted the aforementioned commission to Perugino to paint their chamber with humanistic themes (fig. 14).

The guild of notaries had always held an important position in the political and social life of the city. The notaries formulated diverse types of economic and social transactions into legal and secure contracts. Many of these transactions today are considered simple exchanges of money and receipts. Payments for goods and services, rents and sales, pacifications between contentious factions, dowry exchanges, marriages, and a host of other agreements all required the intervention of a notary. Moreover, the city government required large numbers of notaries to document and embellish its recordkeeping. The guild of notaries gained social esteem as well because of the presence of the notarial curriculum in the university, and professors of this discipline comprised some of its most celebrated faculty. It is not surprising, then, that the political authorities of the city also conceded space (known today as the Hall of the Notaries) within their palace for the guild of notaries. The notaries built their own guildhall as well on the Grand Piazza, near the center of political power.

Fig. 15. Exterior of a surviving Renaissance workshop, Via Ritorta, Perugia

Important to the city's prosperity were the men of the *Lana* (wool) guild, who supervised the production and sale of wool. These merchants brought sheep fleece from the hills of Umbria and the Marches to Perugia and oversaw approximately thirty-five separate manufacturing processes. These processes required the employment of several hundred workers. Artisans carded and spun the fleece into yarn, made cloth on their looms, pounded the cloth to make it supple, dyed, cleaned the material several times, and wrapped the wool for sale in Perugia as well as throughout central Italy.

We have little idea today of the significance of the guild of leather finishers. The masters of leather employed a host of workers and brought great profits to the city. The guild of leather merchants and artisans enjoyed great political importance and occupied more offices in city government during the fifteenth century than any other guild except the *Mercanzia* and *Cambio,* though possessing less social prestige than the aforementioned guilds. The men of the leather guild bought hides throughout Umbria and neighboring regions and then employed others to cure the hides and make them into leather objects. Many of these leather goods were sold in Perugia and throughout central Italy. The artisans who produced saddles and other leather objects were often considered artists equal to painters, and had similar workshops in the city (fig. 15).[18]

As the discussion of wool and leather manufacturing illustrates, a good deal of the wealth of the city of Perugia derived from agricultural products of the countryside that were then finished in the city. As was largely true of all Italian Renaissance cities, Perugia was inseparable from its countryside, maintaining an especially close union of its rural and urban culture. The five populated ridges of the city that branched out from its center intersected cultivated land, parts of which were only a few hundred yards from the central piazza. Important events in the city's economic life during the Renaissance were Perugia's fairs, which brought agrarian products from the countryside into the main piazzas of the city.

Nearly equal in importance to the economic prosperity of Perugia was the religious fervor of Perugia's inhabitants. Christian worship in the town centered on the Cathedral of San Lorenzo, from which the bishop supervised forty-eight parish churches and their priests and organized much of the city's religious life. However, even more wealthy than these parish priests were the monks and nuns of the city's monasteries and convents. The latter were enlarged around 1500 due to the support of the oligarchy.[19] With more surviving daughters, the oligarchs chose to send many of them into convents as a means to avoid paying the large dowries required for the girls to find husbands. The city was also known for its confraternities of laymen and laywomen who came together to worship God and to provide charity for the city's less fortunate. The confraternities built their own small churches in almost every parish as centers for meetings and charity. While the members of the confraternities went to their parish priests for the sacraments, they also attended their own churches and hired their own priests for newer forms of lay devotion. These laymen performed religious rites that had previously been the exclusive preserve of the clergy. The confraternities constructed and administered hospitals, organized choirs that congregated nightly or weekly to sing praises to Mary and Christ, preached to each other, examined each other's behavior, required reform of character, and prayed for the well-being of the souls of deceased members.[20]

Many of the confraternities of Perugia and elsewhere in Italy had their origins in a peace movement of 1260 organized in Perugia by Fra Ranieri. This Franciscan called for the lay people of Perugia to hold processions and to flagellate themselves as a means of ending social conflict. Processions took place throughout central Italy that year, and subsequently confraternities of flagellants were organized. By 1500 these and other confraternities in Perugia had been integrated into a civic religion in which laymen often held processions on the traditional feast days of the liturgical calendar. During crisis periods, when plague raged or political crisis threatened the peace of the community, these laymen would lacerate their bodies in formal processions together with other confraternity members and clerics. Participants were arranged in an honorary formation to troop through the major streets of the city. During the plague of 1486, for example, the city organized three days of processions as a means "to placate the wrath of God," as Pellini reported.[21] The confraternities and ecclesiastical bodies were organized behind their *gonfaloni* (processional banners), which were often made and painted by the best artists of the day. For example, Perugino and his students fashioned several banners for confraternities and others for clerical corporations. He painted the *gonfalone* called the *Madonna della Giustizia* (cat. no. 12)

Fig. 16. Perugino and assistant (Giovanni di Francesco Ciambella, called Il Fantasia?), *Saint Francis and Four Members of the Flagellant Confraternity*, Galleria Nazionale dell'Umbria, Perugia

in 1501 for the confraternity known as Sant'Andrea (or Giustizia) that aided people condemned to death, and together with his assistant, Giovanni di Francesco Ciambella, painted a small banner for the Confraternity of San Francesco in 1499 (fig. 16).[22]

At the end of the Renaissance, forces greater than the Perugian people decided the city's fate, though we should not ignore the Perugian oligarchy's inability to unite in order to forestall a papal victory. Pope Paul III's insistence on taming the ferocity of Perugian independence came to be symbolized after 1540 by the fortress that was built on the foundations of several destroyed Baglioni palaces. The Fortezza Paolina (Pauline Fortress) was intended to protect papal officials from the Perugians, rather than to resist external invaders. Following the fortress' construction, Perugia came to be integrated into the modern Papal State. The city not only lost its political liberties, but also fell into social and economic torpor as it suffered losses in population. With the shift of major European commerce from the Mediterranean Sea to the Atlantic Ocean, Perugia's role as the link between Tuscany and Ancona decreased in significance, and the city earned still smaller profits. The halcyon days of the medieval commune and the Renaissance city of Perugino became faint memories that can only be recaptured by seeing again the city's past through its chroniclers' narrations and its painters' images.

NOTES

1. I wish to thank Christopher Black for reading a preliminary draft of this essay and offering criticisms and suggestions. Any remaining errors are my own.

2. In the last half-century, American and English scholars of the Renaissance have concentrated their attention on the history of Florence, Venice, and Rome and have largely ignored Perugia. There are two exceptions to this: Sarah R. Blanshei and Christopher Black have produced excellent studies of Perugia. For Blanshei, see "Perugia 1260–1340: Conflict and Change in a Medieval Urban Society," *Transactions of the American Philosophical Society* n.s. 66 (1976): 3–46 and "Population, Wealth and Patronage in Medieval and Renaissance Perugia," *Journal of Interdisciplinary History* 9 (1979): 597–619. For Black, see "The Baglioni as Tyrants of Perugia, 1488–1540," *English Historical Review* 85 (1970): 245–81; "Politica e amministrazione a Perugia tra Quattrocentro e Cinquecento," in *Storia e cultura in Umbria nell'età moderna (secoli XV–XVIII),* Atti del VII convegno di studi umbri, Gubbio, 1969 (Perugia: Facoltà di lettere e filosofia dell'Università degli Studi di Perugia, 1972), pp. 101–16; and "Commune and the Papacy in the Government of Perugia, 1488–1540," *Annali della fondazione italiana per la storia amministrativa* 4 (1967): 163–91. For a highly readable account of the history of Perugia based on the many chronicles of the city, see William Heywood, *A History of Perugia,* ed. R. Langton Douglas (London: Methuen, 1910). The interpretation of the leading Italian historian of Perugia, Alberto Grohmann, contributes to this dismissal of Perugia. Grohmann views the drastic decline of Perugia after 1540 as a result of the failures of the fifteenth century, despite the achievements of Perugia in the time of Perugino. The most important study of the history of Perugia is Grohmann's *Città e territorio tra medioevo ed età moderna,* 2 vols. (Perugia: Editrice Volumnia, 1981). A summary of his copious research is found in the more readable *Perugia,* 3d ed., in the series *Le città nella storia d'Italia* (Bari: Laterza, 1988).

3. Francesco Matarazzo, *Chronicles of the City of Perugia 1492–1503,* trans. Edward Strachan Morgan (1905; reprint, New York and Evanston, Ill.: Harper & Row, 1969), pp. 93–95. Though I shall use the name Matarazzo as the author of this chronicle, there has been a great debate as to whether he was the author; see Black 1970, p. 275, n. 2.

4. See the portrait of the city and fifteenth-century images in Grohmann 1981, 1: 27–35 and in Grohmann 1988, pp. 3–16.

5. Grohmann 1988, pp. 20–21.

6. Grohmann 1988, pp. 56–57.

7. Grohmann 1981, 1: 70–78 and Grohmann 1988, cf. pp. 56–57 with pp. 88–89. Grohmann appears reluctant to draw the conclusion that the population of Perugia by 1500 had nearly regained its earlier totals of about 1300, in part because he believes that the Perugian working classes in the city and countryside had become "proletariatized," and therefore, given their deprivation, were not engendering families. My estimate is derived from the number of occupied habitations in Perugia in 1493 determined by Grohmann multiplied by the number of assumed people in each habitation that he assumes elsewhere (5919 × 4.66). My approximation, derived from the number of taxed habitations (*focolari,* fireplaces), appears high given another of Grohmann's calculations that in 1529 the population was 12,000. His figure is based on the number of men fit for warfare. This low figure conflicts with Beloch's estimate that in 1551 the city of Perugia had 19,876 inhabitants. Grohmann's figures do imply a substantial drop in the countryside's population by 1493, though again, Beloch's figures for the Perugian countryside in 1551 are substantially higher: see K. J. Beloch, *Bevolkerungsgeschichte Italiens* (Berlin: De Gruyter, 1939), 2: 71–73. Perugia did suffer from devastating plagues in the 1520s, but Grohmann does not attribute population loss specifically to that plague.

8. Grohmann 1981, 1: 153–64, 278–79.

9. This discussion closely follows the research set out by Black 1970, pp. 250–53.

10. Pompeo Pellini, *Dell'historia di Perugia* (Venice: G. G. Hertz, 1664), 2: 296 and see Heywood, pp. 299–300.

11. Black 1970, p. 254.

12. Matarazzo, p. 96.

13. Blanshei 1976, pp. 616–17.

14. Matarazzo, pp. 240–41.

15. Grohmann 1988, p. 79.

16. Black 1970, pp. 276–77.

17. Matarazzo, p. 241; see also the discussion of Blanshei 1976, pp. 612–14.

18. The leather guild has been discussed as a means to illustrate the merchant-artisan guilds due to its intrinsic importance and also because it is one of the best researched; see Romano Pierotti, "Aspetti del mercato e della produzione a Perugia fra la fine del secolo XIV e la prima metà del XV: La bottega del cuoiame di Nicolo di Martino di Pietro," *Bollettino della deputazione di storia patria per l'Umbria* 72 (1975): 79–185 and 73 (1976): 1–131.

19. Grohmann 1981, 1: 381–82, 386–88, 404.

20. For this discussion of confraternities, see Giles G. Meersseman (with G. P. Pacini), *Ordo fraternitatis: Confraternite e pietà dei laici del medioevo*, 3 vols. in the series *Italia sacra*, vols. 24–26 (Rome: Herder editrice e libreria, 1977); Piero L. Meloni, "Per la storia delle confraternite disciplinate in Umbria nel secolo XIV," *Atti del convegno di studi umbri* (Perugia: Facoltà di lettere e di filosofia dell'Università degli Studi di Perugia, 1971), 2: 533–87 and James Banker, *Death in the Community: Memorialization and Confraternities in an Italian Commune in the Late Middle Ages* (Athens, Ga., and London: University of Georgia Press, 1988).

21. Pellini, 2: 831–32.

22. For the first banner, see F. Santi, *Gonfaloni umbri del Rinascimento* (Perugia: Editrice Volumnia, 1976), p. 34, tav. XXIII, and for the second banner, F. Santi, *Galleria Nazionale dell'Umbria a Perugia* (Rome: Istituto poligrafico dello Stato, 1955), pp. 102–3.

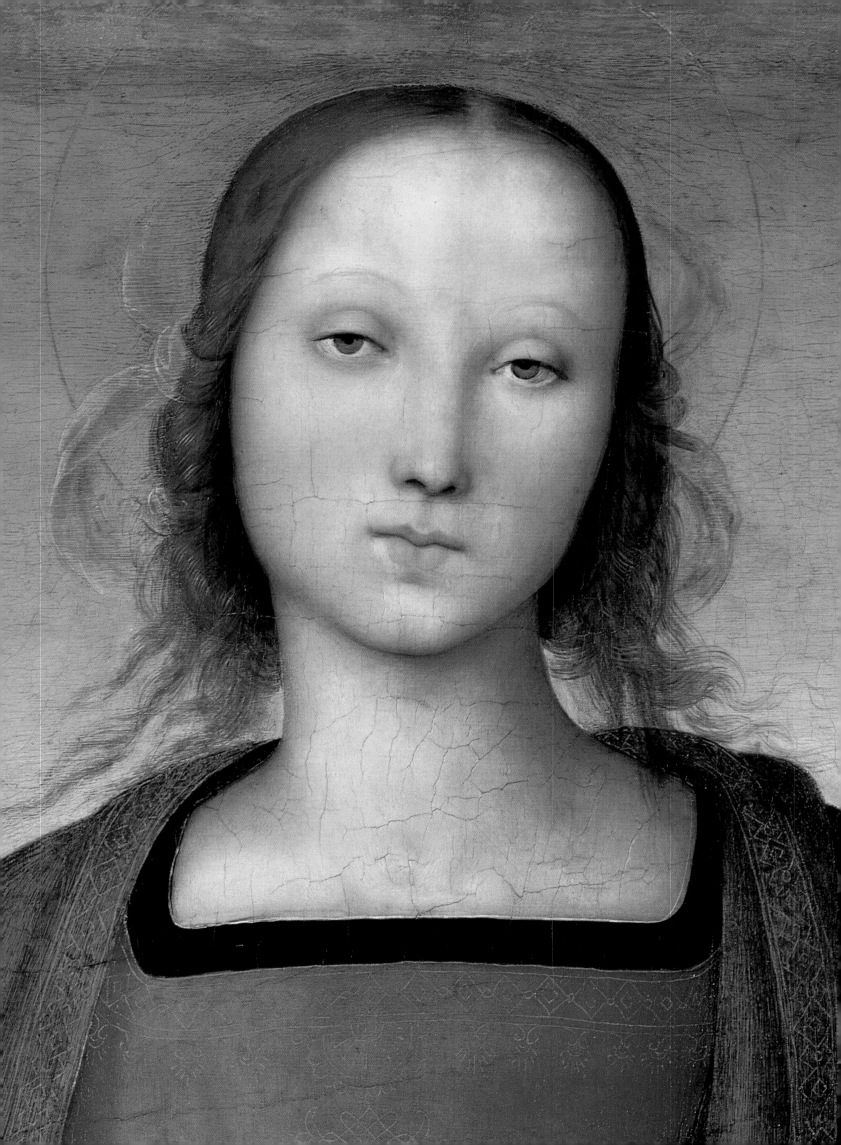

KATHERINE R. SMITH ABBOTT
MIDDLEBURY COLLEGE

Defining a Type: Perugino's Depictions of the Virgin Mary

PERUGINO'S *Madonna and Child*, dated to 1500 and now in the Ford Collection of the Detroit Institute of Arts (cat. no. 5), provides an ideal example of the stylistic and iconographic elements that sealed the artist's popularity as a painter of Marian imagery. Moderate in scale (31¾ × 25½ in. [80.7 × 64.8 cm]), the painting nonetheless maintains an immediacy and an accessibility vital to its success as a focus for personal prayer and devotion. The Virgin is placed in a three-quarter relationship to the picture plane, yet her face and torso are nearly frontal, facing the viewer in a direct and open manner. Christ is seated on the Virgin's right knee, her right hand supporting his back, her left hand gently gesturing toward and steadying him. Given this compositional arrangement, as well as the Virgin's monumentality and the suppression of background detail, Perugino's intent seems clear: he consciously crafted images of the Virgin familiar in their reflection of contemporary ideals of female beauty and decorum, and at the same time generalized enough in type to satisfy a broad audience, both devout *and* discriminating. As we know from visual imagery as well as from contemporary documents, by the late fifteenth century the Virgin had become more than an abstract symbol. She was still revered as the Mother of God, her virtue continually regarded as superhuman and inimitable. Yet she was increasingly and emphatically depicted as a human mother—a flesh-and-blood reflection of the role so familiar to women of the Renaissance.

Artists such as Fra Filippo Lippi working in Florence, Giovanni Bellini in Venice, and Perugino in Perugia sought to craft an image of the Virgin that was at once idealized and familiar. A complex dichotomy was thereby established in paintings such as the Detroit *Madonna and Child*, for even as fifteenth-century viewers found in the image of Mary a new kind of accessibility, they were simultaneously reminded of the gulf which separated this impossible ideal from their own flawed lives. Because Perugino's audience was

53

Fig. 17. Tiberio d'Assisi, *Madonna and Child Enthroned with Saint Francis and Saint Louis of Toulouse,* Church of the Madonna della Luce, Perugia

exceedingly familiar with a vocabulary of visual form quite remote from our own, they would have responded favorably to an image of the Virgin as beautiful, yet earthbound; richly dressed, yet direct in her glance, open in her appeal to the viewer. While Perugino did not invent this new visual type, he perfected it through constant repetition, proffering to his Umbrian audience an increasingly familiar form on which to project their own culturally ingrained expectations and personal aspirations.

Perugino's depictions of the Virgin Mary are steeped in time-honored imagery and religious customs evident even today. Roadside shrines and tabernacles, painted on walls rising from cobblestoned streets, still mark the intersections of wandering alleys and grace the façades of fourteenth-century buildings throughout Italy. They are placed there for the daily devotions of Christian passersby (fig. 17). Some of these images are quite faded, suggesting that they were painted either long ago or in an inexpensive and short-lived pigment. Others are fresh or retouched and bear testimony, through the bouquets of flowers which surround them, to their ongoing importance in the lives of present-day citizens. Many are simply, even crudely, painted, and occasionally sculptural details create the sense that the image is intended to project into and become part of the viewer's space and experience. With very few exceptions, each of these images depicts the Virgin Mary and is dedicated to her.

While few outdoor shrines visible today can be dated with confidence to the Renaissance, they reflect a tradition for communal as well as private devotional imagery with roots in the Middle Ages. Giorgio Vasari writes, for instance, of the fourteenth-century

Sienese painter, Pietro Lorenzetti: ". . . in Florence, next, opposite to the left-handed door of the church of Santo Spirito, on the corner where today there is a butcher, he painted a shrine which . . . deserves the highest praise from every discerning craftsman."[1] Like the fresco in figure 17 painted by Tiberio d'Assisi, Lorenzetti's shrine was notable both for its skill of execution and for its prominent placement, where it could be viewed, studied, and worshiped by a variety of contemporary individuals.

Fifteenth- and early sixteenth-century inhabitants of Umbrian or Tuscan towns of any size could expect to see representations of the Virgin Mary, Christ, and local name saints on a daily basis and in contexts which might seem strange to twentieth-century sensibilities. Certainly local churches, baptisteries, and monastic chapterhouses contained the lion's share of religious imagery. Civic commissions, however, competed equally for the talents of prominent artists who would be paid to paint large-scale devotional images of the enthroned Virgin, the miracles of a particularly revered local saint, or Christ in Triumph. Both grand and humble in scale and in the talent they reflect, these images underscore a central truth of Renaissance visual, social, and civic experience: rigid boundaries between the sacred and the secular simply did not exist. Holy personages were readily invoked for assistance in corporate as well as in private affairs, and as the fourteenth century gave way to the fifteenth, their painted images became increasingly familiar in appearance, dress, and demeanor.

Renaissance popular imagery was, therefore, religious in subject and functional in nature. Even as a monumental altarpiece dedicated to the Virgin might grace the altar of the Cathedral in Perugia, serving as a focus for healing prayers in times of plague or for military might in times of war, so too could a tempera rendering by Perugino entitled *Madonna and Child with Saints Costanzo and Ercolano* of around 1515 find a home in the kitchen of the Palace of the Priors (cat. no. 13).[2] Echoing the compositional format and iconography of the kind of roadside shrine seen in figure 17, Perugino's painting exemplifies the way in which smaller-scale and rather intimately conceived devotional images were placed in the context of large-scale civic structures.

Enthusiasm for just this kind of image—accessible in style, format, and in the rendering of saintly physiognomies—is documented by the sheer number of closely related works attributed to Perugino. In the absence of written testimony by Perugino's patrons, we may look to the establishment of a specific Madonna and Child type as a means of ascertaining the popularity of his trademark treatment of this favored imagery. The root of the popularity of the Madonna as produced by Perugino may be established by reading these images in their original socio-historical context. Beyond reacting to the influence of his artistic forerunners and contemporaries, Perugino fashioned his image of the Virgin Mary as a mirror of contemporary ideals of female beauty, decorum, and restraint.

Fig. 18. Filippo Lippi, *Madonna and Child*, Galleria degli Uffizi, Florence

He was not unique in doing so, as may be easily discerned by observing an image such as Filippo Lippi's *Madonna and Child* from 1465, now in the Uffizi (fig. 18). His extraordinary consistency and excellent reception in these efforts is addressed in what follows.

Marian devotional imagery, found in both public and private paintings in the quattrocento, is rooted in the cult of the Virgin as it evolved from the twelfth and thirteenth centuries onward throughout Europe.[3] Documented on a monumental scale in the Gothic churches of France and Italy, the cult also led to the discovery and invention of relics throughout the Latin West and ultimately to the creation of vast numbers of painted and sculpted representations of the Virgin. The Virgin was seen as Annunciate, as mother of the infant Christ, as mourner at the Crucifixion, and as triumphant companion at the Last Judgment. In nearly all of these roles, Mary acted as intercessor, performing the most sacred and sought-after of functions for contemporary viewers: proffering hope of salvation and aiding in the working of miracles. In a diary entry of June 12, 1482, the Florentine Luca Landucci testifies to the specific power of the Virgin in contemporaries' lives:

At this time there was much talk of the worship of an image of Our Lady at Bibbona, or rather in a tabernacle about a bowshot from Bibbona. It is, namely, a Virgin seated and holding the dead Christ in her arms, after He has been taken down from the Cross; which is called by some a *Pietà*. This worship began on the 5th April, when it was transfigured: that is, it changed from blue to red, and from red to black and divers colours. And this is said to have happened many times between then and now, and a number of sick persons have been cured, and a number of miracles been performed, and quarrels reconciled; so that all the world is running there. Nothing else is talked of at this moment; I have spoken to many who tell me that they themselves have seen it transfigured, so that one must perforce believe it.[4]

Landucci's observations are tremendously revealing—not only does he communicate the sense of popular enthusiasm that attended the transformation of the tabernacle at Bibbona, he also registers the way in which multiple voices of testimony were tantamount to material proof.

Despite one's devotion to a local or name saint, an individual's most powerful ally was always the Virgin herself. She was perceived as spiritual superior, but also as fellow flesh-and-blood human by the Renaissance viewer: this dual nature empowered the Virgin to ensure the miraculous even as she appeared before the observer as a familiar, accessible, and empathetic listener. From the fifth century, Mary's role as *Theotokos* (God-bearer) was established to underscore that Christ was divine, albeit human. As mother of Christ, Mary was remote, a vehicle for the mysterious and awesome workings of God. But in the hands of the late fifteenth-century painter, she became the idealized reflection of contemporary woman and contemporary motherhood: a model of beauty, reserve, and compassion for women, and for men, the reinforcement of a fervently sought ideal. The wild success of Perugino's images of the Virgin can be attributed, in part, to the ways in which they incorporate these ideals while retaining certain time-honored iconographic elements. Exemplifying a kind of conservative modernity for the moment in which they were produced, these devotional paintings would ultimately redefine the Virgin Mary "type," advancing this ideal to the next generation of painters such as Raphael.

Michael Baxandall has pointed to the "general, unparticularized, interchangeable types," in Perugino's religious paintings as a means of explaining the popularity of these images. He states that "they [the figural types developed by Perugino] provided a base— firmly concrete and very evocative in its patterns of people—on which the pious beholder could impose his personal detail, more particular but less structured than what the painter offered."[5] These observations are especially germane to a discussion of Perugino's devotional images of the Madonna and Child, particularly those which functioned in a private, domestic setting. In Perugino's depiction of the Madonna and Child with Saints and Angels, dated about 1490 and now in the Louvre, the Virgin sits on a low throne, cradling the infant Christ in her right arm and steadying him with her left (fig. 19). She is flanked on either side by female saints who may be identified as Saint Catherine of Alexandria and Mary Magdalene.[6] Standing on a low parapet above and behind the saints are two angels who clasp their hands and cast their eyes downward in

an attitude of prayer. Tightly constructed, the scene is set in the corner of a courtyard or on a porch overlooking a Renaissance estate or garden. This compositional arrangement is striking, for the strong rectilinear arrangement of the setting is at odds with the circular format of the work itself.

Perugino's Louvre painting is a tondo, a round panel which was most likely intended to decorate the interior of a private residence. Tondi were extremely popular in central Italy, especially in Florence, during the last quarter of the fifteenth century, and painters typically illustrated subjects such as the Nativity, the Epiphany, or the Adoration of the Child in these paintings.[7] Participating in a broad scheme of painted and sculpted domestic adornment, tondi echoed the shape and many of the messages of proudly displayed *deschi da parto*—brightly painted and inscribed trays which were heaped with fruit and candies and either brought to new mothers as congratulatory gifts after the birth of a child or given to new brides upon the occasion of their marriage.[8] The content of tondi such as Perugino's Louvre panel mirrored the smaller-scale tabernacles dedicated to the Virgin Mary which could be found in the bedrooms, receiving rooms, and other living chambers of Renaissance palazzi.

In style and figural approach, Perugino crafted a work that could harmonize with the relative opulence of the room in which it was placed, while eschewing any sense of specificity that might conflict with a viewer's own sense of the appearance of the saints, the Virgin, and Christ. Margaret Miles has referred to religious paintings as the "media images of medieval people, informing their self-images and ideas of relationship, God, and world in strong and immediate ways."[9] To the extent that the figures in medieval and

Renaissance devotional images served as "informants" or models, they needed to be standard enough, iconographically, to allow for immediate recognition on the part of the viewer, and generic enough in type to allow for the superimposition of an individual's own sense of the Virgin, Christ, and other holy personages. Functioning within the matrix of domestic ornament, images such as Perugino's Louvre *Madonna* were both decorative and didactic. A kind of generalized appeal which invited the owner/viewer to participate to a limited extent in the holy activity depicted was essential to the success of these images.

The 1454 handbook known as the *Zardino de Oration* (The Garden of Prayer), illustrates the perceived relationship between viewer and image in the fifteenth century. Subsequently printed in Venice, the *Zardino* was widely read and cited. The handbook urged young women to imagine their friends and acquaintances as stand-ins for religious figures:

> And then too you must shape in your mind some people, people well-known to you, to represent for you the people involved in the Passion—the person of Jesus Himself, of the Virgin, Saint Peter, Saint John the Evangelist, Saint Mary Magdalene, Anne, Caiaphas, Pilate, Judas and the others, every one of whom you will fashion in your mind.[10]

By mid-century, then, the pious viewer was prompted not just to reflect on the achievements and sacrifices of Christ, the Virgin, and the saints, but to actively "shape," to participate in creating the appearance of these sacred individuals, so that they became specific, personal, and meaningful in the viewer's own terms.

Turning from the mental image constructed in private moments of devotion and reverie to the "reality" of a painted representation, the viewer was thus compelled to make adjustments, to accommodate the painted image while maintaining the powerful and familiar interior presence recently conjured forth. The viewer enjoyed a definite advantage before an image such as the Louvre *Madonna.* However specific the figures of the Madonna and saints may be in presentation, attributes, and demeanor, they are exceedingly general in physiognomy, expression, body type, and dress. They are the "base" to which Baxandall refers, and they exemplify the opportunity given to a viewer to superimpose more specific ideals or more familiar attributes in order to further increase the specificity and accessibility of the holy personages. While Perugino undoubtedly intended to attract his viewer's interest through the rich, warm hues of the cascading drapery, and to hold his viewer rapt in contemplation of the impossibly idealized beauty of the female saints and the Virgin, he was committed to keeping this beauty generic, even bland, while emphasizing symmetry and balance. In the Louvre tondo, as in most of Perugino's devotional panels, a sense of inevitability permeates the compositional arrangement, as though the figures simply could not be made to fit harmoniously in any other configuration. By embracing a stolid and predictable compositional symmetry, the artist crafts a sense of immobility, permanence, and universality.

The familiarity which characterizes the appearance of Perugino's figures is also reflected in the function of Perugino's Louvre tondo. Jeryldene Wood notes that "tondi are part of a genre frequently related to the celebration of marriage, and the Biblical allusions in Perugino's picture suggest his painting may have been a nuptial commission. . . ."[11] Among the most significant of these allusions is the closed garden environment in which the Madonna and Child are seated. With its roots in the Song of Songs, wherein Mary is extolled as the bride of Christ, the enclosed garden came to symbolize the virginity and thus the holiness of Mary.[12] Saint Catherine is also seen in other paintings of the period as a type for the Virgin Mary, for, according to tradition, the Alexandrian saint was joined to Christ in a mystical marriage ceremony.[13]

This emphasis on marriage, and particularly on virginity, underscores the probable function of Perugino's painting as a matrimonial commission, for chastity had long been understood as fundamental to a strong and dependable marriage. Chastity, according to Margaret King,

> assured future husbands of the purity of their line, the legitimacy of their heirs, and the reputation of their family. Thus, the guarding of chastity was the primary business of the daughters of the Renaissance. Their honor consisted in the maintenance of their chastity; their fathers' honor consisted in their supervision of the chastity of their daughters and wives.[14]

As contemporary documents make exceedingly clear, a woman's marriageability had nothing to do with her as an individual, her interest in a particular husband, or her own aspirations, and everything to do with her status as a chaste, noble, and preferably wealthy woman. The Venetian Francesco Barbaro, for example, in a treatise entitled *On Marriage*, counseled: "Virtue, therefore, should be considered first, because its power, its dignity is such that, if all other advantages are lacking, yet the marriage is desirable; and if they are present, they render it joyous."[15] Leon Battista Alberti's *The Book of the Family* (1433–39) is a dialogue wherein the ideals and values of good marriage are discussed at length. Through the words of his dying father Lorenzo, Alberti lists in detail the traits a young man should seek out in a wife:

> It is said that in taking a wife, you must look for beauty, relatives, and wealth. I think beauty in a woman may be judged not only in her charms and in the gentleness of her face but even more in her person, which should be shaped and adapted for carrying and giving birth to a great number of beautiful children.

And among the beauties of a woman, above all, are her good manners; for while an unkempt, wasteful, greasy, and drunken woman may have a beautiful body, who would call her a beautiful wife? And the most important manners worthy of praise in a woman are modesty and purity.[16]

Carefully placed images of the Virgin Mary were among the most effective of the myriad strategies for consistently impressing the value of her own chastity upon a young woman. The Virgin occupied a unique, even strange position among all other women in the approbation and reverence which she received. Being human, she seemed to represent a reasonable role model for contemporary women, yet no flesh-and-blood woman could hope to effectively emulate her. She was a mother, but her purity, underscored by the symbolic shorthand of Perugino's enclosed garden, placed her in a special, super-human category. In addition, as Miles points out, "the Virgin represented a fantasy of a totally good mother. She was a mother who could be counted on to nurse not only her son but, through him, all Christians."[17] Appearing with female saints who also embodied the virtues of repentance, chastity, the ideal bond between mother and child, and an undying commitment to the faith, the Louvre *Madonna* would have symbolized the most essential and highly prized qualities for a new bride. Seen in the context of other religious and mythological paintings intended to reinforce these ideals, the Louvre tondo might well have served to elicit both devotion and admonishment.[18]

Fig. 20. *Madonna and Child,* Samuel H. Kress Collection, © Board of Trustees, National Gallery of Art, Washington, D.C.

A series of small-scale devotional panels depicting the Virgin and Child, with or without attendant saints and angels, follows the Louvre panel chronologically as well as schematically. This group of conceptually related works includes the *Madonna and Child* in the National Gallery of Art, Washington, D.C. (fig. 20), the *Madonna and Child with Saint John the Baptist* in the Staedelsches Kunstinstitut, Frankfurt (fig. 21), the *Madonna and Child between Saints Rose (?) and Catherine of Alexandria,* in the Kunsthistorisches Museum, Vienna (fig. 22), the *Madonna and Child* in the Detroit Institute of Arts (cat. no. 5) and the *Madonna and Child with Saints Costanzo and Ercolano,* now in the Galleria Nazionale dell'Umbria (cat. no. 13). While the paintings in this group are dated between 1493 and 1515, most were produced at the height of Perugino's popularity as a mature painter, around 1493–1500. They suggest that the artist had become particularly well-known and admired for devotional panels of this type. Conscious of this reputation, he took advantage of his success by repeating motifs and delivering a popular, albeit predictable, ideal.

In each of the five paintings, the Virgin appears in a form borrowed, then abbreviated from the Louvre Virgin type. In the Frankfurt, Vienna, Detroit, and Perugia panels, she looks out into the viewer's space with a soft, pensive, rather somber expression, while in the Washington painting, her eyes are cast down at her son. Despite this slight variation, each representation of the Virgin follows tradition by placing the child within her arm and having one of her hands gesturing toward him. The gesture can also be read as a hand resting on and supporting the child, a type known as the *Hodegetria*.[19] Rejecting the hieratic formality of the Byzantine-inspired prototypes he must have known, Perugino

Fig. 21. *Madonna and Child with Saint John the Baptist,* Staedelsches Kunstinstitut, Frankfurt

Fig. 22. *Madonna and Child between Saints Rose (?) and Catherine of Alexandria,* Kunsthistorisches Museum, Vienna

retains the placement of the Virgin's hands in gentler form as though she is pointing to Christ and acknowledging the infant as future leader and redeemer.

The typology of the Virgin Mary, so distant from our own visual vocabulary, was part of the lexicon which Perugino's patrons brought to the viewing and reading of his works. What seems subtle, even imperceptible to our eyes would have been overt to viewers in the last decade of the quattrocento. Even as he renders the Virgin in these paintings as soft, gentle, and familiar, Perugino includes time-honored iconographic elements in order to communicate that we are to understand the Virgin as intercessor, guide, and source of knowledge.

In considering this group of devotional panels, one quickly perceives that Perugino consciously repeated not only the facial and figural types of the Virgin and Child as he moved from one commission to the next, but even retained details such as finger placement, hair arrangement, and the neckline of the Virgin's bodice. This repetitive approach characterizes Perugino's working method throughout much of his career, but is particularly striking in elements such as the position and expression of the Christ Child. His appearance is nearly identical in all but the Vienna panel, where he is simply transposed from the left to the right side of the composition, implying that Perugino must have reversed his working cartoon when creating the underdrawing for the work. Writing in 1979, John Pope-Hennessy noted that "the immense success of Perugino's style was due to two main factors, its other-worldliness and its predictability."[20] He credits the vast space in which Perugino's compositions are set for this sense of "otherworldliness," while arguing that

> the predictability of Perugino was a product of the way in which he and his studio worked, and this in turn was dictated by his extraordinary popularity. Once a cartoon (for the figures in his paintings, not the landscape) had been invented and had proved successful, it was repeated and recombined, often in paintings that are in large part autograph.[21]

While this kind of working procedure was by no means uncommon in fifteenth-century workshops, the overwhelming regularity of its implementation suggested by this group of Perugino devotional panels bespeaks a level of public enthusiasm matched only by the artist's willingness to respond repeatedly in a familiar format.

By establishing a workshop environment in which copying occupied a position of centrality (see Cole, Mencarelli), Perugino bequeathed to his assistants an approach wherein the repetition of forms, compositional devices, and poses was encouraged. Within this context, Perugino's own commercial success evinced the fact that the popularity of an artist's conceptions was reflected in the sheer demand placed on him for like compositions. More difficult to document, though of tantamount importance for an understanding of Perugino's approach, is the degree to which the repetition of a specific *female* ideal in the artist's oeuvre was propelled through the positive reinforcement of patron commissions. In an article on Perugino's workshop practices, Sylvia Ferino notes that in the absence of firm documentation, "all that we can discover about the means by which those working for Perugino learned to handle his style has to be deduced . . . from the works themselves. . . ."[22] The same is true for our knowledge of the ways in which contemporary discussions on female beauty and decorum shaped the artistic vision of the Virgin Mary. Extant paintings serve as our documents, urging us to understand Perugino's interpretations as inextricably connected to the fifteenth-century perception of the Virgin as both accessible and remote.

Although both impossible and inevitable as a role model for contemporary women and mothers, the Virgin took on a heightened immediacy in paint. Through this mimetic medium, she appeared to her audience as a palpable presence, seemingly as sympathetic to the travails of daily life as she was distant from them. Few late quattrocento artists were unaware of the power of paint, and few remained unaffected by the evolving tendency to depict the Virgin in contemporary dress, her hair, veil, and even jewels reflecting current taste. Few, however, equaled Perugino in recognizing the potential impact and sustainable popularity of a codified, idealized representation of the Virgin. Deftly balanced between the generic and the particular, Perugino's images of the Virgin reinforced deeply rooted cultural ideals, while inviting the intensely personal response of individual viewers.

NOTES

1. Giorgio Vasari, *Le vite de' più eccellenti pittori scultori ed architettori,* ed. Gaetano Milanesi, 9 vols. (Florence, 1906), 1: 473, cited in Eliot Rowlands, "Sienese painted reliquaries of the Trecento: their format and meaning," *Konsthistorisk tidskrift* 48, no. 3 (1979): 122–38.

2. For the provenance of this panel, see *Pittura in Umbria tra il 1480 e il 1540: premesse e sviluppi nei tempi di Perugino e Raffaello* (Milan: Electa, 1983), p. 77, and *L'opera completa del Perugino,* ed. Carlo Castellaneta and Ettore Camesasca (Milan: Rizzoli, 1969), p. 108.

3. For thorough treatments of specific aspects of the cult of the Virgin throughout Europe, see Marina Warner, *Alone of All Her Sex: The Myth and the Cult of the Virgin Mary* (New York: Knopf, 1976) and Michael P. Carroll, *The Cult of the Virgin Mary: Psychological Origins* (Princeton: Princeton University Press, 1986).

4. Luca Landucci, *A Florentine Diary from 1450 to 1516,* trans. Alice de Rosen Jarvis (1927; reprint, New York: Arno Press, 1969), p. 35.

5. Michael Baxandall, *Painting and Experience in Fifteenth Century Italy* (Oxford: Oxford University Press, 1972), p. 46.

6. Jeryldene Marie Wood, "The Early Paintings of Perugino" (Ph.D. diss., University of Virginia, 1985), p. 185. Wood notes that the saints have in the past been identified as Catherine of Alexandria and Rose of Viterbo. While accepting the identification of Saint Catherine, whose hand-held book alludes to her learnedness, Wood sees the companion saint as Mary Magdalene, "who traditionally was paired with St. Catherine to embody the concepts of Penitence and Wisdom."

7. Ibid., p. 179.

8. As gifts to new brides, the trays were likely to have served as "talismans of fertility": see Bruce Cole, *Italian Art 1250–1550: The Relation of Renaissance Art to Life and Society* (New York: Harper & Row, 1987), pp. 49–53.

9. Margaret R. Miles, "The Virgin's One Bare Breast: Nudity, Gender, and Religious Meaning in Tuscan Early Renaissance Culture," in *The Expanding Discourse: Feminism and Art History*, ed. Norma Broude and Mary D. Garrard (New York: Harper & Row, 1992), p. 32.

10. Baxandall, p. 46.

11. Wood, p. 182.

12. "A garden locked is my sister, my bride, a garden locked, a fountain sealed" (Song of Solomon 4:12).

13. This mystical marriage occurred during a vision. Catherine's most common attribute is a broken wheel (not evident in the Louvre painting). It refers to the spiked wheel which the Emperor Maxentius invented to torture the fourth-century Christian, but which was broken by a thunderbolt from heaven. Catherine is sometimes depicted holding a book inscribed *Ego me Christo sponsam tradidi* (I have offered myself as a bride to Christ); cf. James Hall, *Dictionary of Subjects and Symbols in Art* (New York: Harper & Row, 1983), p. 58.

14. Margaret King, *Women of the Renaissance* (Chicago and London: University of Chicago Press, 1991), p. 29.

15. Francesco Barbaro, *De re uxoria liber*, cited in King, p. 32.

16. Leon Battista Alberti, *The Book of the Family* (1433–39), translated and excerpted in *The Renaissance Reader*, ed. Julia Conaway Bondanella and Mark Musa (New York: New American Library, 1987), p. 170.

17. Miles, p. 35.

18. Lilian Zirpolo's article, "Botticelli's *Primavera*, A Lesson for the Bride," *Woman's Art Journal* 12, no. 3 (fall 1991/winter 1992): 24–28, details the way in which the mythological paintings completed for the nuptial chamber for Lorenzo di Pierfrancesco de' Medici and Semiramide d'Appiani served to supply the bride "with lessons on chastity, submission, and procreation" (p. 24). According to a reconstruction of the nuptial chamber and an adjoining room, Botticelli's *Primavera, Camilla and the Centaur*, and an anonymous *Madonna and Child* were all found in the bedroom itself.

19. The term *Hodegetria* derives from a famous icon of the Virgin and Child, said to have been a portrait painted by Saint Luke. According to tradition, this painting was acquired by Eudocia, wife of the Byzantine Emperor Theodosius II, during a pilgrimage to the Holy Land in the early fifth century. The icon was subsequently sent to Constantinople and was placed in a church known as the Hodegon, built specifically to house it. The compositional format of the icon—the Virgin seated, the infant Christ cradled by her left arm—became one of the most popular of the medieval period, and was copied repeatedly. For more on this type, see James Hall, *A History of Ideas and Images in Italian Art* (New York: Harper & Row, 1983), pp. 90–91.

20. John Pope-Hennessy, "The Ford Italian Paintings," *Bulletin of the Detroit Institute of Arts* 57, no. 1 (1979): 20–21.

21. Ibid., p. 22.

22. Sylvia Ferino, "A Master-painter and his Pupils: Pietro Perugino and his Umbrian Workshop," *The Oxford Art Journal* 3 (1979): 11.

ROSARIA MENCARELLI

GALLERIA NAZIONALE DELL'UMBRIA

The Role of Drawings and Compositional Arrangements in Perugino's Work

DURING THE EARLY PHASES of artistic production in the Italian Renaissance, drawings and sketches were not considered a significant reflection of the artist's ability to compose his works. At that time, an artist would sketch out his design on a cartoon to be transferred to a surface, such as a wall for a fresco, and nothing more was thought about the fact that the drawing was thereby lost in the process. The drawing might even be sketched directly on the wall (see Cole). As the Renaissance progressed, it became clear how significantly the practice of drawing brought about developments in the way figures were represented and how details were added to a work. Compositions could be planned by uniting various sketches in a larger overall arrangement and alternating them to form adaptations based on a common theme. Students could learn to emulate their master's drawing style, thus ensuring a continuity of style before adding their own particular manner to that of their masters. Due to the importance of drawing for Perugino in particular, this essay will examine the categories of sketches the artist employed, and how he put these categories together to form a repertoire of compositional arrangements that made him one of the most sought-after artists of the Renaissance.

Perugino created a new style which greatly contributed to his artistic fortune. This new style gave form to religious as well as human and divine ideals and was defined by Giorgio Vasari (see Bondanella) as "charming and full of color . . . and this manner endured in Italy, being copied until the style of Michelangelo came into fashion."[1] As a result of the papal commission to supervise as well as participate in the project to paint the walls of the newly built Sistine Chapel in the early 1480s, Perugino became one of Europe's most qualified and desirable painters: "He was held in so much esteem in so few years that not only Florence and Italy, but France, Spain, and the many other countries where they were sent, were full of his works."[2]

But no sooner had Vasari richly sung Perugino's praises than he informed us of his true sentiments with regard to the artist who, having come from the provinces, had known how to monopolize the wider art market: "Pietro had worked so hard and received so much work, that he painted the same things over and over again."[3] While Vasari's intent was to emphasize the painter's artistic stagnation, his comment provides us with a useful vantage point. Through it, we are better able to understand Perugino's need to organize his workshops and manage his assistants over the course of his long working life so as to get the most out of the artistic production sanctioned in his name.

Perugino opened his first workshop in Florence, perhaps during the early 1470s. It was in this workshop that several artists were trained—the Florentines Rocco Zoppo, Gerino da Pistoia, il Bacchiacca, as well as the young Raphael of Urbino. These men were known both as Perugino's assistants and as independent artists in their own right. The workshop's practices would not have differed much from the structures of artistic production known in other fifteenth-century shops.[4] In 1501, Perugino opened another permanent workshop, this one in Perugia, where he trained the greater part of the painters who were to spread his artistic style while adding their own personal contributions.[5]

The practice of drawing as part of the workshop experience proved to be one of the most significant elements in popularizing the Peruginesque style. Drawing had become essential to the formation of the Renaissance artist (see Cole); entire generations of artists concentrated their efforts on copying their teacher's drawings as a form of training prior to producing independent works. Thus we can confidently say that behind every painting existed a rich series of preparatory drawings which were related either to the entire work or to its details, as well as life-size cartoons used to transfer the composition from paper to the surface to be painted, be it panel, canvas, or fresco.[6] And indeed this was how Perugino worked. The Galleria Nazionale dell'Umbria possesses a few drawings that can be associated with surviving works, as well as some drawings executed for works that are no longer extant. As final cartoons ready for transfer have rarely been preserved, their original forms can nevertheless be reconstructed by examining the preparatory drawings visible below the layers of color of surviving works. Such drawings can be detected through infrared reflectography (fig. 23), or by the naked eye when the pigments applied over them age and become transparent, allowing the underdrawing to be revealed.

In general, the drawings attributed today to Perugino can be classified in three groups. First there are sketches for compositions in which the most important features of the completed work can be recognized. Then there are studies of single figures. The final category consists of studies of heads, some of which are true-to-life portraits, but more often they are idealized creations. Perugino apparently did not execute studies of drapery, a subject frequently drawn by contemporary artists such as Verrocchio, Filippo Lippi, or

Fig. 23. *God the Father* (from the Sant'Agostino Polyptych), detail of infrared reflectography

Leonardo, nor did he make studies of architecture or copies of ancient works.[7] It is important to understand that these groups are not mutually exclusive: a sketch for a composition may consist of a single figure for example, or a group of drawings may create a composition, and so forth.

Representative of the first group is an interesting landscape drawing conserved in the Metropolitan Museum of Art (cat. no. 14). The work has been attributed to Perugino by George Goldner.[8] The image is a brush drawing on prepared paper, done in brown ink with white heightening. On one side is a pen sketch in brown ink of a landscape seen from a wide view. The composition was then given final touches and more details on the other side,[9] where the minutely executed drawing of a thick wood sloping down to the banks of a river or lake can be seen. The proposed attribution to Perugino is a convincing possibility, given the freedom of expression and swift immediate line with which the work was drawn. Goldner has suggested the drawing was a study for the landscape portrayed in the background of Perugino's *Vision of Saint Bernard*, now in the Alte Pinakothek, Munich (fig. 82; see Chronicle, 1489).[10]

The larger first category of sketches, which illustrates the principal idea of the composition, includes works from the next group of drawings, that is, individual figures which were subsequently inserted into larger pictorial contexts. The drawings *Old Man Leaning on a Staff*,[11] *Standing Nude*, and two *Madonna and Child* studies[12] all belong to this category. These drawings are a rare testimony of the graphic activity of the young Perugino and can be dated to the end of the 1480s. The sure swift line, in some cases delineating only what is most essential—as for example the old man's beard—demonstrate a freedom of invention that will be lost in later drawings, and reveals the painter's technical ability as well as his potential creativity.

Fig. 24. *Blessed James of the Marches,* Gabinetto Disegni e Stampe degli Uffizi, Florence

While we have no sure point of reference for the *Old Man,* the figure in *Standing Nude* is surprisingly similar to that of Saint Roch in the fresco executed for the Church of Santa Maria Assunta in Cerqueto, near Perugia, between 1477 and 1478 (see Chronicle, 1478). This youthful study holds a particularly important place in the repertoire of figurative arrangements conceived by Perugino. Perugino's compositions always favor a youthful figure in a pose characterized by strong *contrapposto,* one hand on the subject's hip and the other resting on the thigh. This was to become one of the artist's most popular inventions. Likewise, the arrangement of the Madonna seated with the Christ Child in the third drawing resembles many of the groups of women present in Perugino's fresco *Circumcision of Moses' Son,* in the Sistine Chapel (see Chronicle, 1480), as well as the Madonna depicted in the *Adoration of the Magi*[13] predella from the polyptych of San Pietro in Perugia (fig. 104), whose parts are now scattered among a variety of museums in France (see Chronicle, 1495).[14]

Blessed James of the Marches (fig. 24)[15] is an illustration of the second category of individual figures, where the entire composition consists of a single figure. This drawing of the Blessed James corresponds exactly to the *gonfalone* (processional banner) painted by Perugino for the Confraternity of Saint Jerome of Perugia and now in the Galleria Nazionale dell'Umbria in Perugia (cat. no. 7). Notwithstanding the drawing's poor state of conservation, it is possible to discern the subtlety of execution as well as the formal construction of the figure, which recalls the classical ideal of the early Cinquecento. Perugino wholeheartedly adheres to this ideal in his works after this date.

Fig. 25. *Study for the Head and Foot of the Madonna,*
The Royal Collection, Windsor Castle

The larger (first) category of sketches for compositions includes both groupings and unique subjects. Sketches could be put together to form an overall composition before laying out the final cartoon. Among the most articulated of Perugino's extant composition drawings are the *Study for the Adoration of the Magi* in the British Museum, London (fig. 90),[16] the *Adoration of the Shepherds* in a private English collection,[17] and the *Studies for Birth of the Virgin.*[18] The third work comprises a lively and summary rough draft of the scene depicted on the predella of the altarpiece in Fano (see Chronicle, 1497). Such drawings later served as models to be reused with slight variations in other works. Drawings of subjects unique in Perugino's repertoire, and not considered models for reuse, also exist. These are well-thought-out and well-drawn preliminary sketches for specific paintings, such as the famous drawing *Apollo and Marsyas* (also known as *Apollo and Daphne*) in the Galleria dell'Accademia in Venice,[19] clearly related to a small painting now in the Louvre.[20]

Having briefly examined the overlapping categories of studies for compositions and figures, the third group can now be considered. Studies of heads, drawn from real life as well as idealized, are particularly important for Perugino's pictorial formulations. Few drawings of this type have been preserved, although Perugino's works are not short on portraits, a genre quite in vogue during the second half of the quattrocento.[21] The sureness of line, the intensity of expression, the solid construction of the portraits—such as the *Portrait of a Man* in the National Gallery of Art in Washington, D.C.,[22] dated perhaps to the period of his employment in the Sistine Chapel, or the *Portrait of Francesco delle Opere*[23] from 1494 (fig. 50)—confirm the intense effort Perugino devoted to drawing. These results may perhaps be compared to those achieved in the *Head of a Youth* drawing.[24]

Perugino's ideal of compositional and emotional equilibrium finds its most eloquent expression in the sweet harmonious facial type most often employed for the Virgin. One such example is the drawing in the Royal Collection, Windsor Castle (fig. 25).[25] This image is clearly related to the head of the Virgin in the altarpiece *Virgin Mary and Child with Saints John the Baptist and Sebastian*,[26] painted by Perugino for the Martini Chapel in the Church of San Domenico in Fiesole (fig. 28; see Chronicle, 1493). The scholar Caterina Caneva has called this drawing a perfect example of "golden equilibrium achieved by the artist, employing the sweetest outlines, a composition harmonically balanced in its every part."[27] This image of the Virgin's head fully embodies Perugino's pictorial ideal and immediately becomes reproducible, as attested by its presence in successive works: *Virgin and Child with Saints Peter, John the Evangelist, Paul, and John the Baptist* in the Kunsthistorisches Museum, Vienna (see Chronicle, 1493);[28] a panel with the analogous subject in Sant'Agostino in Cremona, signed and dated to 1493;[29] the later *Madonna of the Confraternity of the Consolazione* (where the drawing has been reversed) in the Galleria Nazionale dell'Umbria in Perugia (fig. 76; see Chronicle, 1498);[30] and the *Madonna in Glory and Saints* in the Pinacoteca Nazionale in Bologna.[31] Another work which can be added to this group is the processional banner, *Madonna della Giustizia*, in the Galleria Nazionale dell'Umbria in Perugia (cat. no. 12). The employment of this facial type in the *Madonna della Giustizia* is a clear indication that the model was still popular around 1501, when the banner was probably painted.

Having discussed the categories of preparatory drawings which can be associated with Perugino's works, there is also the next type of drawing employed by the Renaissance artist: the cartoon. No examples of cartoons for frescoes, even more fragile due to their particular purpose and use, are extant. Only a few examples of any cartoons have survived. One of the oldest is the *Beheading of a Saint*, now in the Uffizi.[32] The drawing cannot be related to any specific work, but the composition was a favorite with Perugino's followers. An adaptation of the subject can be recognized in a scene depicting the beheading of Saint Catherine in the church of Santa Illumunata at Montefalco, executed by the workshop of Antonio Melanzio.

Some cartoons, however, can be related to extant works. For example, the cartoon *Head of Saint Joseph of Arimathaea* has been linked to the *Lamentation over the Dead Christ* in the Galleria Palatina of Florence (fig. 49; see Chronicle, 1495).[33] It is possible that the cartoon of Saint Augustine preserved in the Kupferstichkabinett of Berlin (fig. 52) may have been prepared for the panel painting *Saint Augustine with Members of the Confraternity of Perugia*, in the Carnegie Museum of Art, Pittsburgh (fig. 51),[34] just as the drawing in the Ashmolean Museum of Oxford (fig. 46) may have been for the predella panel *Christ and the Woman of Samaria*, in the Art Institute of Chicago (cat. no. 1c; see Chronicle, 1502).[35]

Fig. 26. *Assumption of the Virgin with Saints*, Galleria dell'Accademia, Florence

Perugino's workshop developed and perfected certain compositional arrangements which met with particular approval from the public. These designs enjoyed favor not only due to their basic idea, which was more or less new, but because they gave substance to a whole range of works in which various elements—such as tradition, devotion, taste, and even fashion—could be intimately associated. The creation of these new compositional arrangements was closely connected to the practice of drawing. It is precisely from the drawings that we can comprehend the variety of compositions conceived by Perugino and better grasp the genesis and use that the artist made of some of his compositional schemes. For this reason the most commonly used arrangements will be examined here.

The oldest recognizable compositional arrangement is found among the Sistine Chapel frescoes. We know that in addition to the frescoes on the side walls, which are still preserved today, Perugino was commissioned to paint the *Assumption of the Virgin* on the altar wall. Although the work was subsequently destroyed to make room for Michelangelo's *Last Judgment*, its composition is known to us thanks to a drawing by one of Pintoricchio's students.[36] The arrangement, repeated numerous times, was even adopted by Perugino for the Ascension of Christ. In the *Assumption of the Virgin* we see the first use of the formulaic division of a scene into two parallel planes, almost without communication between them. The Madonna, or Christ in glory among angels and cherubs, is placed in the upper part,

Fig. 27. *Adoration of the Shepherds,* Collegio del Cambio, Perugia

while in the lower part apostles or saints are arranged in lines or groups and portrayed as dictated by the iconographic program. This compositional plan recurs in the Fano Altarpiece (around 1489; Chronicle, 1497);[37] in the Vallombrosa *Assumption of the Virgin with Saints* now in the Galleria dell'Accademia in Florence (fig. 26; see Chronicle, 1500);[38] in the *Madonna in Glory and Saints* (where the arrangement is slightly modified in order to adapt to the subject) dated 1500–1501 in the Pinacoteca Nazionale in Bologna;[39] in the 1507 panel for the Church of the Santissima Annunziata in Florence;[40] in the painting in the Duomo of Naples, executed between 1507 and 1508;[41] and in the 1513 altarpiece of the Church of Santa Maria a Corciano.[42]

This arrangement was equally popular in its adapted form for the Ascension of Christ. It is present in the painting of this subject from 1496–1500, now in Lyons (originally in the Church of San Pietro in Perugia;[43] see Chronicle, 1495), and in the altarpiece for the Duomo of San Sepolcro,[44] painted during the first decade of the sixteenth century (see Chronicle, 1509), to name but two examples. It is also not unusual in other paintings to find the painter employing only the upper-plane motif consisting of the *mandorla* with polychrome bands surrounded by cherubs which, in smaller form, circumscribe the figure of Christ in the act of blessing or God the Father.

The theme of the Nativity may have also found its compositional prototype in Perugino's youthful endeavors. Vasari recalls that Perugino painted two Nativities around 1480, one in San Giusto alle Mura in Florence (razed during the war in 1529–30; see Chronicle,

Fig. 28. *Virgin Mary and Child with Saints John the Baptist and Sebastian*, Galleria degli Uffizi, Florence (see pl. 8)

1486), and the other in the Sistine Chapel, it too destroyed along with his *Assumption of the Virgin* to make room for Michelangelo's *Last Judgment* fresco.[45] Traces of these early motifs may be seen in the *Kneeling Musical Angel* in the Biblioteca Reale in Turin[46] and in the *Head of a Young Man Bent Forward* in the Uffizi, which Sylvia Ferino Pagden believes was a study for one of the kneeling shepherds.[47] At the top of a long list of paintings with this subject is the Albani Torlonia Polyptych, in the Villa Albani collection in Rome, signed and dated 1491 (fig. 42).[48] This work offers us a model with three receding planes for the Nativity (also known as the Adoration), which will be repeated again and again by Perugino and his workshop.

The most significant variant in the model is the background in which the scene takes place. The vast architectural and perspectival constructions of the Albani Torlonia Polyptych tend to become more simple over time, and result in the canonical compositional arrangement of figures in the foreground, a cottage behind them, and a simple, unadorned landscape in the background. The most notable example is the *Adoration of the Shepherds* in the Collegio del Cambio in Perugia[49] (fig. 27; see Chronicle, 1500), in which the composition centers on the symmetrical frontality of the figures "on stage." Perugino's new vision means that the representation of depth has decreased in importance. The sense of volume and size of the human figure is no longer based on the figure's placement within a scene constructed according to the laws of perspective, for it is the figure in and of itself that generates its own volume. This arrangement for the Nativity recurs without substantial variation in the lunette of San Francesco di Monteripido in Perugia, painted around 1502 and now in the Galleria Nazionale dell'Umbria,[50] as well as in the 1503 work in the Church of San Francesco in Montefalco.[51] Perugino continued to utilize this arrangement even in later life, as for example in the central panel of the Sant'Agostino Polyptych, now in the Galleria Nazionale dell'Umbria (fig. 111; see Chronicle, 1512).[52]

Sketches for compositional arrangements provided patrons with a means to influence the outcome of the work they were commissioning. Among the designs available for Perugino's patrons to choose from, according to their own particular desires and tastes, the Madonna and Child with Saints occupied a position of great importance (see Abbott). Returning to the square altarpiece format depicting the *sacra conversazione* (sacred conversation), conceived in Florence during the first half of the quattrocento,[53] Perugino proposed a design whose impact was enormous. In his panel *Virgin Mary and Child with Saints John the Baptist and Sebastian,* for the Church of San Domenico in Fiesole[54] (fig. 28; see Chronicle, 1493), the Madonna is seated on a throne placed upon a pedestal under a slightly foreshortened portico, with two or more figures placed around her under a covered colonnade. At least two other works by Perugino directly descend from this Florentine prototype: the 1493 panel in the Kunsthistorisches Museum in Vienna,[55] and the panel in the Church of Sant'Agostino in Cremona.[56] It is clear in these cases that the figures of the Madonna were derived from the same cartoon, which was also employed, with few variations, for the Senigallia panel, painted around 1489 for the Church of Santa Maria delle Grazie (see Chronicle, 1497), and for the Fano panel for the Church of Santa Maria Nova,[57] executed in the same time period.

It is interesting to note the important change that took place in the representation of the Madonna during this phase of Perugino's artistic production. In works prior to the 1493 altarpiece of Fiesole, the Madonna was depicted as a young woman bedecked with refined clothing and precious jewels. After this work, she is transformed into a more mature woman dressed in simple robes with an air of austerity on her face. This iconographic change occurs significantly between the end of the last decade of the fifteenth century and the first decade of the sixteenth, when works were being produced in a Florence whose cultural climate had been strongly affected by the words of Girolamo Savonarola (see Chronicle, 1490). Scholars thus see a direct reflection of the changes taking place in Florence's cultural, religious, and social life in the iconography and the spirit of works by Perugino, as well as by other artists working in and around that city.[58] Perugino continued to employ this arrangement in the stereotyped compositions of around 1494, formerly in the Baltimore Museum of Art,[59] and in the 1521 fresco in Santa Maria Maggiore in Spello,[60] an exact copy of the previous example, except for the number of saints.

Finally, there is the compositional arrangement associated with Saint Sebastian, a subject Perugino had handled many times since his first depiction of the saint in his early fresco at Cerqueto (fig. 4; see Chronicle, 1478). Beyond changes in style and pictorial rendering, the model is consistent in representing the saint as an Apollo-like youth draped in only a cloth around his hips, languidly leaning against the column of his martyrdom. Duplicated in compositions where the saint appears as either the sole subject or alongside other saints in more crowded paintings, the arrangement provides an ideal prototype for commissions of private devotion, allowing the painter to best express the intimate nature of the subject. Apart from the *Saint Sebastian* in the Nationalmuseum of Stockholm,[61] shown with his arms tied above him, the most recurrent pattern is that depicted in the painting in the Louvre dated to around 1490 (fig. 53).[62] The same arrangement had already been employed by Perugino a few years earlier in the altarpiece of Fiesole (related to a drawing in the Cleveland Museum of Art [cat. no. 4]) and in the work dated to around 1500 currently in the Museo de Arte di São Paolo in Brazil.[63]

It has often been stated by scholars that Perugino's final twenty years of production, up to his death in 1523, were distinguished solely by a monotonous repetition of previously conceived subjects and compositional arrangements.[64] From a certain point of view, the works described here might even confirm this thesis. However, it must be stressed that in the eyes of Perugino and his contemporaries, the "quality" of a work was not determined so much by the artist's inventiveness as it was by his technical ability. In this sense, the judgment expressed by Agostino Chigi is illuminating. Writing to his father Mariano in Siena, Agostino states: "I tell you that, wishing to paint *with his own hand,* He is the best Master in all Italy."[65] This opinion was expressed in 1500, when Perugino had already re-used numerous compositional arrangements worked out in the past. Evidently the frequent duplication of a subject was *not* considered a lack of compositional originality. It is also worth reiterating that artists painted according to the very explicit requests of their patrons, who at times described the subject to be painted in minute detail in their contracts (see Cole). Perugino thus maintained an inventory of drawings and cartoons which could be employed with minimum modification on any number of occasions. He was copying himself precisely because he was being *asked* to do so.

It is also important to emphasize the fundamental role played by Perugino's workshop. We must acknowledge that he was a great businessman, blessed with an excellent ability for organization. Not only did Perugino journey all over Italy painting the various commissions he had received, but at the same time he managed to maintain workshops in both Florence and Perugia, supervising the work being carried on there as well as executing some of it himself. So while it is certain that he personally executed the drawings that were to be transferred to paint, the painting of some parts of works were entrusted at times to the students in his workshop. When a work was of great difficulty and prestige, then Perugino painted the entire work himself. Many paintings that Perugino signed, thereby claiming full paternity, included work by his assistants as well. The frescoes completed in 1500 for the Collegio del Cambio in Perugia provide a good example of this: although the master depicted his self-portrait in the room (fig. 33) as a sort of seal of guarantee and of immortality, we know that his students made notable contributions to the work.[66]

Within the confines of the workshop, students not only collaborated in the execution of paintings, but actively practiced drawing. This explains why a great number of drawings once considered to have been by Perugino have now been reattributed to his students. Quite often the students were not only making their own drawings, but were copying the master's drawings that were at their disposal. The so-called Sketchbook of Raphael now in the Galleria dell'Accademia, Venice, is an illuminating case in point. The critical fortune of this collection of drawings has been widely discussed. Today the collection is believed to have been the work of an artist either contemporary with or slightly younger than Raphael, who conceived it as a choice of significant drawings copied from the inventories of other artists, among them Perugino and Raphael.[67]

An example of this reuse of Peruginesque inventions is the drawing on sheet 57 in the Sketchbook. This sheet includes a copy of the famous *Little Idol*[68] drawing in the Uffizi and a study of a kneeling leg which resembles the one in the painting of *Saint Jerome* (cat. no. 11) in the Galleria Nazionale dell'Umbria in Perugia. Another example is sheet 33, which on the recto and verso depicts Saint Sebastian bound to a tree, copied from the preparatory studies made for the painting of the same subject by Perugino in the Nationalmuseum of Stockholm.[69] Drawing 17 has a crouching lion on the recto that resembles the Peruginesque invention in the paintings *Saint Jerome and Mary Magdalene*,[70] in the Galleria Nazionale dell'Umbria in Perugia, the above-mentioned *Saint Jerome*, and the analogous subject in the Kunsthistorisches Museum in Vienna,[71] executed with a great deal of help from collaborators.

It is the author's belief that this reuse of designs and cartoons may also help us to understand how the art of Perugino could have been called original and innovative in its time and why it met with such great success among his contemporaries. Perugino's art marks the passage from expression through drawing above all, characteristic of the first phase of the Renaissance, to the manifestation of classicism, which was to become the new language of the cinquecento. This new language was one that Raphael, Perugino's most gifted student, would know how to master before the death of his own master.[72]

NOTES

1. ". . . vaga et ornata di colori . . . e durò tal cosa per Italia a imitarsi fin che venne la maniera di Michele Agnolo Buonarroti," in Giorgio Vasari, *Le Vite de' più eccellenti architetti, pittori, et scultori italiani, da Cimabue, insino a' tempi nostri*, ed. Luciano Bellosi and Aldo Rossi, 2 vols. (Turin: Einaudi, 1991), 1: 537.

2. "Venne in pochi anni in tanto credito, che de l'opre sue s'empiè non solo Fiorenza et Italia, ma la Francia, la Spagna e molti altri paesi, dove furono mandate," in Vasari, 1: 530.

3. "Avea Pietro tanto lavorato e tanto gli abondava sempre de lavorare, che e' metteva in opera le medesime cose," in Vasari, 1: 534.

4. An interesting exhibition on just this form of entrepreneurial enterprise in fifteenth-century Florence was organized in 1992 by Mina Gregori, Antonio Paolucci, and Cristina Acidini Luchiant. The exhibition examined the artistic industry of Florence during this period in all its aspects, including the artist's training, organization of work, collaborative relationships between teacher and students, dissemination and repetition of models, specialization in various artistic genres, and ways and means of adapting to changes in the culture. It is a shame that the Florentine workshop opened by Perugino, perhaps in the early 1470s, was not among the many workshops investigated by the exhibition. The exhibition catalogue is entitled *Maestri e botteghe. Pittura a Firenze alla fine del Quattrocento* (Florence: Silvana editoriale, 1992).

5. Nevertheless, there is still no academic contribution that considers the "Perugino phenomenon" as a whole, above all for its effects on his contemporaries and on painters who were working in the first decades of the sixteenth century. The large study by Filippo Todini, *La pittura umbra. Dal Duecento al primo Cinquecento*, 2 vols. (Milan: Longanesi, 1989), remains essential.

6. This custom is also described in Jill Dunkerton, Susan Foister, D. Gordon, and Nicholas Penny, *Giotto to Dürer. Early Renaissance Paintings in The National Gallery* (London: National Gallery Publ. Ltd., 1991), pp. 164–74. For a broad and in-depth discussion, consult Gigetta Dalli Regoli, "Il disegno nella bottega," in *Maestri e botteghe. Pittura a Firenze alla fine del Quattrocento*, pp. 61–69. The concepts expressed by Dalli Regoli can be considered relevant to Perugino and his workshop.

7. A vast collection of such drawings can be seen in the exhibition catalogue entitled *Il Disegno fiorentino del tempo di Lorenzo il Magnifico*, ed. Annamaria Petrioli Tofani (Florence: Silvana editoriale, 1992).

8. George Goldner, "New Drawings by Perugino and Pontormo," in *Burlington Magazine* 136 (1994): 365–67. The drawing was acquired by the Metropolitan Museum of Art at the December 15, 1992 auction at Christie's, London.

9. 20.4 × 28 cm.

10. Inv. W.A.F. 764. For the image, see Pietro Scarpellini, *Perugino*, 2d ed. (Milan: Electa, 1991), figs. 73, 75.

11. Gabinetto Disegni e Stampe degli Uffizi, inv. 10908 F, 21.1 × 11.4 cm. Pen on yellowed white paper mounted on a new backing. See Sylvia Ferino Pagden, *Disegni umbri del Rinascimento da Perugino a Raffaello* (Florence: Olschki, 1982), pp. 27–28, fig. 5.

12. Gabinetto Disegni e Stampe degli Uffizi, inv. 205 F, 25.7 × 9.8 cm. Metalpoint on paper prepared yellow. Inv. 56 E, 21.8 × 17.3 cm. Pen on yellowed white paper (recto and verso). See Ferino Pagden 1982, pp. 28–29, figs. 6, 7.

13. Rouen, Musée des Beaux Arts (inv. D 803–34); Scarpellini, fig. 130.

14. Scarpellini, pp. 93–94, figs. 124–133.

15. Inv. 5887 Horne; 36.2 × 25 cm. Pen, stylus, on yellowed white paper.

16. Sylvia Ferino Pagden, "Perugino's Use of Drawing: Convention and Invention," in *Drawings Defined*, ed. Walter Strauss and Tracie Felker (New York: Abaris Books, 1987), p. 80, fig. 3.

17. Francis Russell, "A late drawing by Perugino," in *Master Drawing* 15 (1972): 257–58, pl. 10.

18. Sheet 366E in the Gabinetto Disegni e Stampe degli Uffizi. See Alessandro Marabottini, "Raffaello fino all'ottobre del 1504," in *Raffaello giovane e Città del Castello*, exh. cat. (Rome: Edizioni Oberon, 1983), pp. 45–46.

19. Sylvia Ferino Pagden, *Disegni umbri, Gallerie dell'Accademia di Venezia* (Milan: Electa, 1984), n. 54.

20. Musée du Louvre, inv. R.F. 370, 39 × 29 cm. See Todini, fig. 1163. It is evident that the work was inspired by the ancient classical style, especially the figure of Apollo, which calls to mind the *Meleager* of Scopas, known in the Renaissance only through copies.

21. See the recent monograph on this subject edited by Gloria Fossi, *Il ritratto: gli artisti, i modelli, la memoria* (Florence: Giunti, 1996).

22. Inv. 636; cf. Todini, fig. 1154.

23. Florence, Uffizi, inv. 1700. See Scarpellini, fig. 101.

24. Gabinetto Disegni e Stampe degli Uffizi, inv. 416 E, 10.5 × 10.3 cm. Pen with brown wash, white lead, traces of black pencil, darkened white watermarked paper. See *Gabinetto disegni e stampe degli Uffizi. Inventario I. Disegni esposti*, ed. Annamaria Petrioli Tofani (Florence: Olschki, 1986), p. 187.

25. The drawing, inv. 12744, is done in silverpoint and white lead, on paper prepared pink; 234 × 224 mm.

26. Florence, Uffizi, inv. 1453. See Ilaria Della Monica, "Pietro Vannucci detto il Perugino. Madonna col Bambino in trono fra i santi Giovanni Battista e Sebastiano," in *L'Officina della Maniera: varietà e fierezza nell'arte fiorentina del Cinquecento fra le due repubbliche, 1494–1530* (Venice: Marsilio editore, 1996), p. 80.

27. Caterina Caneva, "Pietro Perugino. Testa della Vergine," in *Il Disegno fiorentino del tempo di Lorenzo il Magnifico*, pp. 115–16.

28. Inv. 615; see Scarpellini, fig. 85.

29. Ibid., fig. 91.

30. Inv. 270; ibid., figs. 143–44.

31. Inv. 579; see Carla Bernardini, "Pietro Vannucci detto il Perugino. Madonna col Bambino in gloria e i Santi Michele Arcangelo, Caterina d'Alessandria, Apollinare e Giovanni Evangelista," in *La Pinacoteca Nazionale di Bologna*, ed. Andrea Emiliani (Bologna: Nuova Alfa editoriale, 1987), p. 72, fig. 104.

32. Gabinetto Disegni e Stampe degli Uffizi, inv. 1116 E, 19.2 × 16.9 cm, pen and brown wash, white lead, strongly yellowed white paper. The drawing has been pricked along the outlines of the figures. See Ferino Pagden 1982, pp. 36–37, fig. 15.

33. Inv. 164, see Scarpellini, fig. 96.

34. Ibid., figs. 203–4.

35. Christopher Lloyd, *Italian Paintings before 1600 in The Art Institute of Chicago* (Princeton: Princeton University Press, 1993), p. 195, fig. 2.

36. Ibid., p. 151, fig. 40.

37. Ibid., p. 201, fig. 123.

38. Inv. 8366; ibid., p. 242, fig. 198.

39. Inv. 579; see Bernardini, p. 72, fig. 104.

40. Scarpellini, p. 266, fig. 240.

41. Ibid., p. 278, fig. 262.

42. Ibid., p. 281, fig. 268.

43. Ibid., p. 202, fig. 124.

44. Ibid., p. 271, fig. 249.

45. Giorgio Vasari, *Le Vite de' più eccellenti pittori scultori ed architettori*, ed. G. Milanesi, 9 vols. (Florence: G. C. Sansoni, 1878–85), 3: 575, 579.

46. Scarpellini, p. 29.

47. Gabinetto Disegni e Stampe degli Uffizi, inv. 1313 F; see Ferino Pagden 1982, pp. 33–34.

48. Todini, fig. 1160.

49. Vittoria Garibaldi, "Un Perugino in Collegio," in *Art Dossier* 101 (1995): 33–37.

50. Inv. 358, see Paola Mercurelli Salari, "Pietro Vannucci detto il Perugino. Adorazione dei Pastori," in *Galleria Nazionale dell'Umbria. Dipinti, sculture e ceramiche: studi e restauri*, ed. Caterina Bon Valsassina and Vittoria Garibaldi (Florence: Arnaud, 1994), pp. 247–48.

51. Scarpellini, p. 253, fig. 216.

52. Inv. 268; ibid., p. 283, fig. 274; see also the essay by V. Garibaldi in this catalogue.

53. Peter Humfrey, "Il dipinto d'altare nel Quattrocento," in *La pittura in Italia. Il Quattrocento*, ed. Federico Zeri (Milan: Electa, 1987), pp. 541–42.

54. Florence, Uffizi, inv. 1435; see I. Della Monica, p. 80.

55. Inv. 615; see Scarpellini, p. 179, fig. 85.

56. Ibid., p. 183, fig. 91.

57. Ibid., p. 198, figs. 114, 115.

58. Alessandro Cecchi, "La prima Repubblica. 1492–1512," in *L'Officina della Maniera*, pp. 72–73; and Della Monica, p. 80.

59. Inv. 38.229; see Scarpellini, p. 261, fig. 229.

60. Todini, fig. 1181.

61. Inv. 2703; see Scarpellini, p. 173, fig. 75.

62. Inv. R.F. 957; ibid., p. 181, fig. 87.

63. Inv. 13; ibid., p. 240, fig. 193.

64. Among these is Federico Zeri, "Il Maestro dell'Annunciazione Gardner," in *Bollettino d'Arte* 38 (1953): 238–39. For another opinion resulting from recent restorations conducted in the Galleria Nazionale dell'Umbria, see the essay by Vittoria Garibaldi in this catalogue as well as her article "Il polittico di Sant'Agostino, vicende storiche e critiche," in *Associazione Comitato Italiano World Monuments Fund* (May 1996).

65. The judgment is cited in G. Cugnoni, "Agostino Chigi il Magnifico," in *Archivio della Società Romana di Storia Patria* 2 (1879): 481.

66. The panorama of jobs in the workshop is effectively laid out by Sylvia Ferino, "A Master-Painter and his Pupils: Pietro Perugino and his Umbrian Workshop," in *The Oxford Art Journal* 3 (1979): 9–14. In the essay "Modelli fortunati e produzione di serie," in *Maestri e botteghe*, pp. 145–56, Venturini asserts that Perugino's workshop followed Quattrocento workshop practice, briefly mentioning Perugino on p. 152.

67. Ferino Pagden 1984, pp. 13–31.

68. Gabinetto Disegni e Stampe degli Uffizi, inv. 531 E.

69. Inv. 2703; see Scarpellini, figs. 76, 77.

70. The panel is part of the Sant'Agostino Polyptych. The Polyptych is partially preserved in the Galleria Nazionale dell'Umbria: see Garibaldi 1996.

71. Inv. 617; see Scarpellini, fig. 205.

72. On this subject, see also Sylvia Ferino Pagden, "I disegni del Perugino," in *Perugino, Lippi e la Bottega di San Marco alla Certosa di Pavia, 1495–1511*, exh. cat. (Florence: Cantini Edizioni d'Arte, 1986), p. 48.

JULIA CONAWAY BONDANELLA AND PETER BONDANELLA
INDIANA UNIVERSITY

Giorgio Vasari, Pietro Perugino, and the History of Renaissance Art

WITH HIS *Lives of the Artists,* Giorgio Vasari (1511–1574; fig. 29), the inventor of art history, established a hierarchy of artists that has continued to influence artistic taste and preference down to the present. Two editions of this work appeared in the Renaissance, the first in 1550 and the second, expanded and enlarged, in 1568.[1] For this work, Vasari enunciates both honorific and didactic purposes: first, to honor his fellow artists, and, second, to inform his readers of his own opinion.[2] Among the first scholars to conceive of a cultural renaissance, he uses the term *rinascita* to refer to the reawakening of the arts along with aesthetic standards derived from those of classical antiquity. His appraisal of the career and works of Pietro di Cristoforo Vannucci, known as Perugino[3] (c. 1450–1523; fig. 30) reflects his theory of progress in the arts, his aesthetic criteria based on those of the ancients, his bias about the craft of painting, and his ideas on the technical and psychological formation of artists.

Although Vasari organizes his *Lives* in a generally chronological fashion, the structure and significance of the final edition clearly derive as much from his evolutionary theory of artistic revival as from simple chronology. Through a detailed exploration of the works of Italian artists from the thirteenth to the mid-sixteenth centuries, he conceived of artistic progress as a slow organic process of growth and development.[4] The first stage was set into motion by the stylistic discoveries of Cimabue and Giotto.[5] The second stage was marked by the more sophisticated techniques of design, perspective, and coloring that Vasari identified in the works of Masaccio, Brunelleschi, and Donatello. Vasari believed the third stage reflected a state of perfection in the arts and was dominated by the special genius of Perugino's greatest student, Raphael, and that of Michelangelo. In the *Lives,* Vasari delineates the art historian's task, through his own example, as one of drawing qualitative distinctions among artists on the basis of stylistic traits and aesthetic qualities

Fig. 29. Giorgio Vasari, *Saint Luke Painting the Virgin (Saint Luke: A Self-Portrait of Vasari)*, Church of Santissima Annunziata, Florence

Fig. 30. Woodcut portrait of Perugino from the 1568 edition of Vasari's *Lives of the Artists*

after long and careful study of their works.[6] He claims to imitate writers of history who have earned a reputation for good judgment by

> investigating with every care and even greater curiosity the methods, manners, and means that these valiant men have employed in the management of their artistic enterprises; and [who] have taken pains to explore their errors as well as their successes and remedies and the prudent decisions they sometimes made in handling their affairs, and, in short, all those ways in which wisely or foolishly, with prudence, compassion, or magnanimity, such men have behaved.[7]

His aim has been

> not only to tell what such men did, but . . . to pick out the better works from the good ones, and the best works from the better ones, noting with some care the methods, colors, styles, traits, and inventions of both painters and sculptors.[8]

In illustrating and arguing his thesis, Vasari refers mainly to Florentine and Tuscan artists,[9] but includes artists like Perugino from other regions, especially if they had ties to the Florentine school or in some other way embodied the artistic principles he evokes in his *Lives.* Vasari's Tuscan nationalism was frequently expressed through an unnecessarily severe critique of non-Florentine artists, such as the Umbrian Perugino or even the great Venetian master Titian, both of whom receive what we perceive as unfounded harsh evaluations because of their supposedly defective talents as masters of design. Vasari prized *disegno* (design) above almost every other talent in painting and believed that this design was a specifically Florentine skill. His value judgments of non-Florentines such as Perugino, therefore, have been criticized by subsequent generations of art historians, especially in the twentieth century, who have seen more clearly than Vasari the rich diversity of style and talent in Renaissance Italy. Today we recognize that if Raphael was a genius, he learned much of his craft from his master Perugino.

In writing his artistic biographies, Vasari regularly uses a specific series of terms and concepts to express his evaluative distinctions, which he claims to be "the special vocabulary and terms characteristic of artists . . . their own words in their own language."[10] He often describes works or techniques that please him as *bello* (beautiful); this term refers to the overall finish of a work of art, reflecting the degree to which the artist has mastered a variety of skills in depicting things naturally: *quanto il vivo* (as if alive). These skills would include the artist's knowledge of perspective and anatomy, his use of color and light, and, above all, his mastery of *disegno* (design, drawing, or draftsmanship), which refers both to the skill of drawing and the ability to design a work of art in a manner both natural and beautiful. In Vasari's view, *disegno* is the foundation of all good art, a higher level skill essential to achieving art's fundamental goal of imitating nature.[11] Vasari praises most highly an energetic and vigorous artistic style based on good technique and sound invention, rejecting any kind of pedantic or academic style, or any work which seems laborious or strange. Rather the effect of the whole should be inspired and graceful. In his *Lives*, *grazia* (grace) develops into an aesthetic standard differing from beauty and proportion, and evident only to the sound critical judgment.[12] When Vasari speaks of *grazia*, he refers to the quality of a painting which carries it beyond simple craftsmanship or beauty; it may refer to a certain softness or sweetness of style as well as to the ease and naturalness with which the work depicts its subject.

Within this theoretical and aesthetic context, Vasari explores Perugino's contributions to the craft of painting, and while his verdict is not always positive, it fairly depicts Perugia's great master as an important precursor to the artists, who, in Vasari's opinion, strove to achieve a high level of perfection in his third stage of artistic development. Vasari emphasizes, for example, the major commissions Perugino executed in the Sistine Chapel in Rome and in the Collegio del Cambio in his native Perugia as proof of his artistic greatness. And, of course, the fact that Vasari identifies Raphael as Perugino's pupil underlines Perugino's role as an influence on the third or heroic age of Italian painting.

In the "Life of Perugino," we find not only aesthetic judgments but psychological insights, for Vasari always attempts to discover environmental factors that may have influenced the development of the artists whose lives he relates. Hence, he examines the circumstances of Perugino's birth and early apprenticeship, his training in Florence, his discipline and hard work, the effects of poverty on his art, and his greatest achievements. We learn not only about his contributions to the craft of painting, especially his ability to use color, but also about his weaknesses in *disegno*, his difficulty in dealing with his sometimes less-than-gracious competitors, and his wage-earner's attitude toward painting. A comparison of the 1550 edition of the *Lives* with the expanded and revised edition of 1568 reveals that Vasari's initial judgment of Perugino's achievements was, in the main, confirmed by his increasing knowledge of Perugino and his contemporaries as well as the artists of the third period. In the 1568 edition, he expands considerably his commentary on the Perugian's work, especially upon some of his most successful paintings, but he retains essentially the same opinions about Perugino's achievement.[13]

The actual placement of Perugino's "Life" in the context of Vasari's great history reveals much about the way in which Vasari reworked the 1550 edition. In the first edition of the *Lives* (1550), the "Life of Perugino" holds a crucial position in Vasari's project of delineating the progress of the arts through his analysis of individual artists' styles.[14] Vasari's judgments of Perugino's paintings are sometimes more positive in the first edition, where Perugino's "Life" concludes the second part of the work. In the revised edition of 1568, however, Vasari's praise for Perugino's style is somewhat more muted, even though he expands his analysis of the Perugian's artistic production. This change in emphasis stems from Vasari's growing understanding of the crucial role of technique—especially what he calls *disegno*—in all great art.[15] Perugino's "Life" has now been displaced by three other biographies, two of which contain multiple lives. These include a number of painters from different regions, such as Vittore Carpaccio (1465–c. 1525), whose own biography is brief and is inserted into a discussion of the lives of various other Venetian and Lombard painters; Jacopo (1476–1526) and Francesco Torni (1492–1562), whose works have not been recovered and about whom little is known; and Luca Signorelli (1441–1523).[16] Whereas Carpaccio is praised for his skill, his use of perspective and color, and the variety of his figures, Signorelli, unlike Perugino, is praised specifically for his ability in *disegno*. In an effort to underscore Signorelli's links to the artists of the third period, Vasari recounts that Michelangelo both praised and imitated his work. At the end of Signorelli's "Life," Vasari points to Signorelli's skills of invention and design as the factors which made him the true precursor to the artists of the third stage:

> Thus, with the end of this man's life, which came in 1521,[17] we bring to an end
> the second part of these lives, concluding with Luca as the man who, by means
> of the fundamentals of design, especially those of his nudes, and by means of

his graceful invention and the composition of his scenes, opened the way to the ultimate perfection of art for the majority of the artisans whom we shall discuss from here on, and who, in following, were able to give it the finishing touches.[18]

It is clear that Vasari had specific aesthetic and theoretical reasons for placing the lives of Carpaccio and Signorelli after that of Perugino in the 1568 edition of the *Lives of the Artists*.

Nonetheless, Vasari devotes considerably more space to Perugino's "Life" than to those of either Carpaccio or Signorelli. The space Vasari devotes to Perugino, even when displacing his life from the concluding chapter of the second book in the 1568 edition, underscores Perugino's role as a major transitional figure. Both editions of the *Lives* call attention to Perugino's initial promise and growing reputation, with Vasari's account of how the young artist first worked with an unknown painter from Perugia, who "was not very skilled in this trade but who held in great veneration this profession and the men who excelled in it."[19] Perugino eventually came to Florence, where he studied with the likes of Andrea del Verrocchio and received early acclaim for his studiousness, his diligence, and the respect he showed for his craft.

The fact that Perugino was praised by the Florentines is significant. Often Vasari recounts the positive opinions of other artists about their colleagues, and, in his view, the opinion of Tuscan artists is uniquely important, since he believed Florence to be the environment most likely to produce great art and good judges. After recounting how Perugino took his first teacher's advice to study in Florence, where "more than anywhere else, men came to be perfect in all the arts, and especially in the art of painting," he states—without any modifications in the second edition—that Perugino "had considerable success, since in his day works in his style were held in the greatest esteem."[20] In this way, Vasari qualifies his praise for Perugino's style, by suggesting that he had "considerable," if not exceptional success, and that while this style was outstanding in its day, it soon became dated, as Perugino failed to modernize his approach to his craft, especially with regard to *disegno*.

In the 1568 edition, Vasari sometimes reevaluates certain works by the Perugian painter, delineating their artistic qualities more sharply, particularly in light of his increasing understanding of the technical skills necessary to rise to new levels of achievement in the arts. Vasari cites one early painting which contained the kind of anatomical design much admired by the Florentines, a painting of Saint Jerome on a wall in the Badia at Camaldoli.[21] In the 1550 edition, he simply had referred to the great admiration of the Florentines for the painting,[22] but he elaborates in the 1568 edition, specifying that the painting was admired for the way in which Perugino depicted the saint "as a lean and wizened figure with his eyes fixed upon the cross and so emaciated that he looks like a skeleton."[23] Expanding on his earlier statement about this painting, Vasari explains why the figure was so admired. In Vasari's view, *disegno* (good design) is an essential element of excellence in painting, and Perugino's attention to human anatomy is evident in his depiction of the angular body of the emaciated saint.

Although Vasari finds much to admire in the Perugian painter's work, his assessment of Perugino's contribution is generally more restrained in the final edition of the *Lives*, where he simply eliminates certain statements of unqualified praise, however brief, made in the 1550 edition. For example, when he first describes the impact of a panel of the dead Christ (1495) painted for the nuns of Santa Chiara in Florence (fig. 49) in his 1550 edition of the *Lives*, he discusses the painter's fresh technique:

> Pietro worked for the nuns of Santa Chiara on a panel of a dead Christ painted in such a delightful and novel way with the most lively colors that he confirmed the opinion of the artisans that he was an excellent and marvelous painter, but among the people he was much more famous and admired, for when they saw the originality of his almost modern style, they exalted him with endless praise.[24]

This highly favorable assessment of the painting calls particular attention to the admiration of the artisans for Perugino's inventive use of color, but it contains a caveat. Vasari pointedly observes that the "people" were far more impressed than Perugino's colleagues, the Florentine artists who would naturally set the ultimate standards of artistic excellence. In the 1568 edition, Vasari modifies his account of the Florentine artisans' response to this work by weakening the entire anecdote about the reception of this painting:[25]

> Pietro worked for the nuns of Santa Chiara on a panel of the dead Christ with such delightful and novel colouring that he made all the artisans believe he had the ability to become marvelous and pre-eminent.[26]

In revising his original anecdote, Vasari now declares that these Florentine artists recognized no more than Perugino's *potential* for excellence, having eliminated both the reference to his fame and the characterization of his style as original and similar to the style of the third and greatest phase of painting ("the originality of his almost modern style").[27]

When describing the response to the landscape in this same panel of the dead Christ, Vasari likewise attenuates the more direct praise of the 1550 edition, which relates that the landscape was "considered very great."[28] In 1568, Vasari places his judgment of Perugino's landscape within the context of the changing techniques of landscape painting: "He painted a landscape that was then considered extremely beautiful, since the true method of painting them had not yet been seen as it has been since that time."[29] Once again, he suggests that Perugino has not achieved technical or artistic superiority by adding a comment in the 1568 edition about the deterioration of a crucifixion painted by the artist around 1478.[30] In the 1550 edition, Vasari notes the *diligenza* (care) with which the painting was completed,[31] but in 1568, he mentions only that its poor condition is the result of poor technique: "Pietro could not have known this, since it was only in his own day that they had begun to paint well in oil."[32] Likewise, in speaking of a panel painting of Christ in the garden with the sleeping apostles, originally painted for the church of San Giusto alle Mura, he eliminates a reference in praise of Perugino's "fresh and lovely style."[33]

Vasari's careful assessment of Perugino's contributions to the art of painting finds its psychological basis in a brief analysis of the artist's childhood. Like other contemporary biographies and autobiographies of artists, Vasari's work provides much information, often anecdotal, about his artists' early lives. Such stories about origins reflect the tradition in Western heroic narrative of proving the hero's worth by creating a lineage which can be traced to divine or superhuman origins.[34] In the Renaissance, the importance of family life and its effects upon individual talent were outlined long before Vasari in works such as Leon Battista Alberti's *The Book of the Family* (1433–39).[35] As Paul Barolsky has demonstrated in *Giotto's Father and the Family of Vasari's "Lives,"* Vasari displays the same interest in individual artists' origins as found in stories written about Cellini, Bandinelli, and Michelangelo.[36] Like other early histories, Vasari's *Lives* contain fictional character sketches, especially unusual events in the artists' childhoods or anecdotes representing their special genius. As he examines the artists' achievements, he rarely fails to elaborate on their origins, so important are they to the formation of the artists' characters and their artistic predilections. Thus, he links what he believes to be Perugino's limitations as an artist to his childhood experiences. The salient event of Perugino's childhood as recounted by Vasari, whether fact or fiction, offers clues to the Perugian artist's inability to rise above himself and his contemporaries. The sources of his "defects" can be found, as one might expect in a Renaissance narrative, in his early upbringing, specifically in his treatment by his father and the advice of his first teacher. In this light, the details of Perugino's early life and family foreshadow his reticence to take risks in order to push his art toward new stylistic and conceptual horizons.

Significantly, both versions of Perugino's "Life" relate what Vasari believed to be the harsh poverty of his early years and how it affected his art. The 1550 edition is slightly more optimistic about the effects of poverty on success. Vasari calls poverty a stimulus to the creation of great art, able to elevate potential genius: "it is a powerful way of making them become perfect at the highest levels of excellence."[37] The 1568 edition proclaims:

How beneficial poverty may sometimes be to those with talent, and how it may serve as a powerful goad to make them perfect or excellent in whatever occupation they might choose, can be seen very clearly in the actions of Pietro Perugino.[38]

Nonetheless, Vasari's analysis of the consequences of poverty on Perugino's art, common to both editions of the *Lives*, ultimately diminishes its ability to stimulate artistic invention, and gives greater emphasis to its negative effects. In both versions, Vasari depicts Perugino as a disciplined, dedicated artisan and an honest man, who initially sacrificed everything for his craft. According to Vasari, Perugino worked so hard that "he made night into day."[39] Although hard work is one of the essential ways of achieving greatness in the arts,[40] Vasari suggests that Perugino worked constantly to alleviate the fear of falling back into the poverty he had known as a child, when his father sent him away from home, not merely to paint but to earn his own keep: "Raised in misery and privation, he was given by his father as an errand-boy to a painter from Perugia. . . ."[41]

Perugino's first master encouraged him to take up the profession of painting by teaching him esteem for the craft, but he always emphasized the rewards for which the best painters could hope:

He never did anything with Pietro but talk about how profitable and honorable painting was to anyone who did it well. And by telling of the rewards already earned by ancient and modern painters, he encouraged Pietro to study it.[42]

In this way, Vasari casts some doubt on Perugino's motivations to excel in the art of painting, with the implication that Perugino took his master's advice too much to heart. Thus, in Perugino's case, poverty and the teaching of his first master left the artist dedicated to his craft, but far too concerned with monetary success. In this analysis of Perugino's childhood and early apprenticeship, Vasari finds many ways to imply that the artist's aims were perhaps less lofty than those of painters who, never having experienced such dire want, could be less concerned with profit, or who, through better fortune, were placed with better masters. For instance, the young Luca Signorelli, the dependent and student of Piero della Francesca, "tried very hard to imitate his master and even to surpass him."[43]

It is the goal of continuously trying to surpass one's teachers, one's contemporaries, and oneself that Perugino never attains, according to Vasari. In what is a thinly veiled criticism common to both the 1550 and 1568 editions, Vasari writes that whereas Perugino's poverty had empowered him to strive for excellence in painting, it had not necessarily inculcated in him the desire to rise to the top of his profession and to surpass his teachers, like Signorelli. Instead it inspired the more modest and much less praiseworthy or honorable desire to earn his keep through his craft:

> But need spurred him on since he desired to rise from such a miserable and lowly position—if not perhaps to the summit and supreme height of excellence, then at least to a point where he would have enough to live on.[44]

Vasari bolsters this less-than-flattering portrait of the prolific Umbrian painter with the statement that "he took no notice of cold, hunger, discomfort, inconvenience, toil, or shame, if he could only live one day in ease and repose."[45] Furthermore, he also attributes to Perugino the prosaic and materialistic proverb "that after bad weather, good weather must follow, and that during the good weather houses must be built for shelter in times of need."[46]

In Vasari's view, this supposed desperation to make money had a negative impact on Perugino's capacity for improving his art. When he came back to Florence later in his career, he faced a more hostile audience after a younger generation of artists had abandoned his way of painting in favor of the new style of Michelangelo. As recounted in both the 1550 and 1568 editions, his return to Florence had unhappy results because he had allowed his work to stagnate. Vasari observes that in search of economic independence, Perugino produced so many paintings that his work never improved, but merely repeated itself:

> Pietro had worked so hard and always had such an abundance of paintings to complete that he quite often placed the same details in his pictures. He thus reduced the theory of his craft to such a fixed style that he executed all his figures with the same expression.[47]

Preoccupied by money, Vasari believed that Perugino had failed to reflect seriously upon his craft, to search for new solutions, and to remain inventive and vigorous in his approach to art. He ceased to strive for perfection, the only worthy goal of great art, once he had achieved financial security. It is Vasari's judgment in both editions that he

> placed all his hopes in the gifts of Fortune, and he would have struck any evil bargain for money. He earned great wealth, and in Florence he built and bought houses, while in Perugia and Castello della Pieve, he acquired a great deal of real estate. He took as his wife a very beautiful young woman and had a number of children by her, and he took great delight in the fact that she wore, both inside and outside the home, charming head-dresses which, it is said, Pietro himself often arranged for her.[48]

Fig. 31. Filippino Lippi and Perugino, *Deposition of Christ from the Cross* (from the Annunziata Altarpiece), Galleria dell'Accademia, Florence (see pl. 21)

Vasari's observations, essentially identical in both the 1550 and 1568 editions, are devastatingly clear: Perugino's reputation was based on the promise of his early work, and he merited severe criticism in his later career:

> And seeing that the greatness of his own reputation, which he had acquired entirely because of his very promising beginnings, was being overshadowed, he constantly tried to use sarcastic remarks to insult those who were working [in this manner].[49]

Seeing his own reputation diminished because of the stylistic innovations of Michelangelo and incapable of accepting this humiliation, Perugino insulted those who followed the younger painter's example. Vasari indicates that Perugino earned Michelangelo's criticism of his works as "clumsy," one of the most negative judgments that could be pronounced about an artist's work.[50] In Vasari's account, all the young artisans attack the *Deposition of Christ from the Cross* (fig. 31),[51] which Perugino completed around 1507 for the main altar of the Servite friars in Florence:

> It is said that when this work was uncovered, it was very harshly attacked by all the young artisans, most especially because Pietro had re-used figures which he had placed in his works on other occasions, and even his own friends, question-

ing him, said that he had not taken sufficient pains and had neglected the good method of working, either out of avarice or out of a desire to save time.[52]

The attack on the work focuses upon the lack of good techniques and fresh invention. Perugino's uncomprehending response to criticism, even from friends, further demonstrates his inability to change with the times.[53]

While critical of his later career, Vasari never discredits Perugino's contributions to painting or demeans his character or honesty. However, he makes clear in both editions of the *Lives* that the Perugian painter was at fault for concentrating more on accumulating wealth than on exploring new methods and seeking improvements in his own style. In both editions, Vasari praises Perugino's works, even some of the late ones, but in the 1568 edition he tends to leave unmodified only those remarks which already contain a cautious appraisal of the Perugian's work. He often deletes uncategorical praise, or he adds some qualifying remark to provide a context. For example, Vasari declares that none of Perugino's pupils, with the exception of Raphael, equaled the master's "diligence or the grace with which he used colors in his own personal style." Vasari continues by noting that many artisans from outside Italy came to learn from him and that his works were sold widely. But he qualifies both statements with the observation that the style was pleasing and popular only in its time, and that Perugino's work sold well only before "the appearance of the style of Michelangelo."[54] Yet few masters in all of Vasari's *Lives* ever produced a genius of a pupil such as Raphael.

When Vasari offers unqualified praise for a particular painting, it usually meets the test of the aesthetic standards of judgment formulated by him in the 1568 edition, with particular emphasis on technique, especially design, coloring, stylistic grace, and invention. Vasari praises Perugino's use of perspective, light, and colors in both fresco and oil, along with his fresco technique and his ability to create lifelike figures of charm and elegance. During Perugino's early days in Florence (after 1472), as his reputation was growing, he painted a *Nativity with the Magi* for a cloister in the convent of the Jesuates which was later destroyed. Vasari claims that this painting showed "exquisite detail, which Pietro completed perfectly with charm and great elegance."[55] Vasari calls attention to a number of portraits in this *Nativity*, including one of Verrocchio and one of the prior of this convent painted as an architectural decoration, saying the latter was "so lifelike and painted in such a fine style that it was judged by the most skillful artisans to be the best thing Pietro ever did."[56] For another cloister in this same convent, he did a scene of Boniface VIII approving the habit for the order; in describing this scene, Vasari praises Perugino's use of perspective, another of the techniques central (according to Vasari) to the exceptional quality of art in the third period. Perugino, says Vasari, "made this technique a specialty of his."[57]

Fig. 32. *The Delivery of the Keys to Saint Peter*, Sistine Chapel, Vatican (see pl. 3)

Still another *Nativity of Christ* and some half-figures were executed "in such a beautiful style that it was considered to rank among the best fresco paintings Pietro ever did on a wall."[58] Of particular importance among these early paintings was a *Dead Christ with Saint John and the Madonna* done above the side door on the exterior of San Pietro Maggiore, which resisted the elements for many years:

> He did this in such a way that even though exposed to rain and wind, it has been preserved with the same freshness as if Pietro had just now completed it. Pietro's mind certainly knew how to use colors, both in fresco and in oil, and as a result all skilled artisans are indebted to him, since through him they have gained knowledge of the use of light, which can be seen in all his works.[59]

Perugino's fame was so great as a result of these works that he obtained many commissions throughout Italy, including one from Pope Sixtus IV to work in the Sistine Chapel along with other great painters of the time (fig. 32).[60] Among the many works he did upon his return to Perugia, none receive the lavish praise of the works of his first period in Florence. Of the paintings in the Collegio del Cambio (fig. 33), Vasari states:

> This work, which was extremely beautiful and praised more lavishly than any other Pietro had completed in Perugia, is today held in esteem by the citizens of that town in memory of this praiseworthy artisan from their native city.[61]

Fig. 33. *Self-Portrait*, Collegio del Cambio, Perugia

Vasari especially notes that poverty and the urge to earn money never made Perugino dishonest, adding a long anecdote in the 1568 edition to testify to the Perugian's moral character. During a long discussion of Perugino's work in the Jesuates' church and convent, Vasari recounts an episode about the desire of the prior to use ultramarine blues lavishly in these paintings. The prior insisted on being present whenever Perugino painted with ultramarine, a very expensive material. By dipping his brush in the water with some frequency, Perugino managed to use a great deal of the ultramarine, eliciting a complaint from the prior about the amount of paint the plaster was absorbing. When the prior was absent, Perugino took the ultramarine from the basin in which he dipped his brush and saved it. Finally, to make amends, Pietro returned a great quantity of ultramarine to the prior with the remark: "'Father, this is yours: now learn to trust honest men who never deceive those who trust them but who know how very well, if they wish, to deceive suspicious men such as yourself.'"[62]

The fact that Vasari's most serious criticism of Perugino remains the same in both editions demonstrates that his opinion of the Perugian painter's contributions to art had not changed in a significant fashion for over two decades, even though Vasari had visited Perugia in 1566, at which time he encountered a significant number of new paintings to examine and consider. What he saw apparently reconfirmed his judgment that although

Fig. 34. Perugino and Raphael, *Trinity with Six Benedictine Saints Above and Six Other Saints Below*, Church of San Severo, Perugia (see pl. 24)

Perugino made substantial contributions to the art of painting, he had never consistently stretched his imagination, nor had he kept up with the younger generation in their studies of anatomy and design. Vasari finds much to be admired in the Perugian's work—his use of color, light, and perspective along with his ability to create lifelike figures in a graceful style—but his admiration is always qualified by the standards of excellence set by the new generation of artists, including Perugino's own pupil Raphael (fig. 34), who "surpassed his master by far,"[63] and such Florentine luminaries as Leonardo and Michelangelo.

In his revisions of Perugino's "Life," Vasari carefully shapes his judgments to fit his theory of artistic progress. His changing opinion of Perugino, based primarily upon Vasari's analysis of the artist's obsession with poverty, need not hinder a contemporary appreciation of Perugino's works. We know today that Perugino actually came from a middle-class background. He enjoyed a brilliant career and managed one of the largest and most successful of Renaissance shops, producing an amazing number and range of great works. He was very likely *not* dominated by a tireless search for wealth any more than other artists of the day and was certainly less engaged in the kind of obsequious courtiership to obtain commissions typical of Vasari's career as an artist and architect.

Vasari's portrait of Perugino's life and career is thus flawed by a number of personal prejudices, such as his goal of inserting every Italian artist into his highly influential three-stage picture of progress in the arts of his time. Many other important figures, especially those from outside Florence (Siena, Venice, southern Italy) suffered equally severe criticism when compared with what to Vasari was the incomparable talent of his idol Michelangelo.

Vasari's focus on a poverty-stricken craftsman struggling for survival has neither stood the test of time nor the scrutiny of subsequent art historians. Yet Vasari's praise of Perugino's many talents stands as the first, if not the most accurate, assessment of his greatness as one of Renaissance Italy's influential figures.

NOTES

1. All references to the Italian will be to recent editions of Vasari's two versions of the *Lives:* vol. 1 of Giorgio Vasari, *Le vite de' più eccellenti architetti, pittori, et scultori italiani, da Cimabue insino a' tempi nostri*, 2 vols. (Turin: Einaudi, 1986), which is based on the 1550 text, known in the critical literature on Vasari as the Torrentino edition; and vol. 3 of Giorgio Vasari, *Le vite de' più eccellenti pittori, scultori e architettori*, 9 vols. (Novara: Istituto Geografico de Agostini, 1967), which comes from the final edition of 1568, known in the literature as the Giuntina edition. All references to these two volumes will state the original year of publication and the page number. Occasional references to other volumes of the 1568 edition will be noted by referring to the volume number. All references in English are from Giorgio Vasari, *The Lives of the Artists*, trans. Julia Conaway Bondanella and Peter Bondanella (Oxford: Oxford University Press, 1991) and will be cited in the notes by the English title *The Lives* and the page number.

2. Vasari discusses his work as a tribute to his fellow artists in the "General Preface" to the work (*Proemio*, 1550, pp. 16–17; 1568, 1: 43–44). He discusses his didactic purpose in the "Preface to Part Two of the *Lives*," *The Lives*, p. 48 (1550, pp. 207–8; 1568, 2: 80).

3. Few scholarly books on Perugino have been published. Among the most useful are Lionello Venturi, *Il Perugino: Gli affreschi del Collegio del Cambio*, ed. Giovanni Carandente (Turin: Edizioni Radio Italiana, 1955) and *L'opera completa del Perugino*, ed. Carlo Castellaneta and Ettore Camesasca (Milan: Rizzoli, 1966).

4. In the "Preface to the *Lives*" (*The Lives*, pp. 5–6), Vasari establishes this organic metaphor to assist the reader in understanding his theory of the progress of art: "the nature of this art resembles that of the others, which, like human bodies, are born, grow up, become old, and die." (1550, p. 101; 1568, 1: 190).

5. Vasari typically uses the term *maniera* to refer to style; this term appears frequently throughout the *Lives.*

6. The *Lives* reflects Vasari's emphasis on the crucial role of visual acuity and intelligence in the art historian's task.

7. *The Lives*, p. 47 (1550, p. 207; 1568, 2: 79).

8. *The Lives*, p. 48 (1550, p. 207; 1568, 2: 80).

9. Although the contemporary Italian word *artista* (artist) is absent from the *Lives*, we use the terms artisans, artists, or craftsmen to refer to the artists whose lives Vasari describes. Vasari normally employs the words *artigiano* (artisan) or *artefice* (artificer, from the Latin *artifex*, often used in theological writings for God the Creator), along with the *pittori, scultori, e architettori* of his title.

10. "General Preface," authors' translation (*Proemio* 1550, pp. 16–17; 1568, 1: 44). An examination of his terminology reveals much that derives from classical treatises on art, modern discussions of art beginning with Petrarch, books of courtesy, and even poetry: see Patricia Lee Rubin, *Giorgio Vasari: Art and History* (New Haven: Yale University Press, 1995), pp. 231–85, for discussion of Vasari's rhetoric.

11. The significance of design is discussed at some length in the "Life of Battista Franco" in part three.

12. As an aesthetic standard, *grazia* may be related to Baldessar Castiglione's concept of *sprezzatura* (a certain ease in performing social functions and a naturalness of bearing). In his *Book of the Courtier* (1528), Castiglione developed a new concept of civilized behavior in his portrait of the courtier, a cultured individual, often involved in politics and diplomacy on behalf of a ruler, with a broad education and the qualities of grace, dignity, and perfect manners. *Sprezzatura* is his ability to do the right thing in any

social situation with great ease and without apparent effort.

13. A comparison of the two editions of the *Lives* reveals that Vasari made significant changes in the lives at the beginning and end of the first two parts of the work to reflect what he had learned during his travels in 1566, when he visited a number of Italian cities. His changes also reinforce his interpretation of the progress of the arts in Italy during the Renaissance.

14. In the "Preface to the *Lives*" (*The Lives*, pp. 3–4), Vasari establishes nature as the origin of the arts (1550, pp. 93–4; 1568, 1: 171). The goal of artistic style is always to represent nature in the most beautiful and lifelike manner possible. Early artists more frequently created works deficient in naturalness and beauty, which Vasari describes as *rozzo* and *goffo* (rough, or crude and awkward).

15. Modifications of the first six lives in part two tend to focus on the matters of technique that Vasari came to see as being central to artistic success in the 1568 edition.

16. It is interesting to note, however, that Signorelli is a Tuscan rather than an Umbrian painter, although he had studied with Piero della Francesca, as it is likely Perugino had. Vasari sees Signorelli as part of the Florentine tradition of innovation in style. Signorelli is particularly praised by Vasari for his ability "to execute nude figures," which only with difficulty and great skill could "be made to seem alive" (*The Lives*, p. 268; 1568, 3: 365). Signorelli's life is not included in the 1550 edition. Rubin, p. 228, argues that Vasari places Signorelli's "Life" at the end of part two to underscore his idea of historical development in the arts, not only because of his abilities in invention and drawing but also because of his ties to Michelangelo and Vasari himself.

17. Actually in 1523.

18. *The Lives*, p. 273 (1568; 3: 373–74).

19. Ibid., p. 257 (1550, p. 529; 1568, 3: 306).

20. Ibid., p. 258 (1550, p. 530; 1568, 3: 307).

21. This painting may be the fresco now in the F. Mason Perkins Collection at Assisi. It is considered an early painting.

22. 1550, p. 530.

23. *The Lives*, p. 258 (1568, 3: 307–8).

24. 1550, p. 530 (authors' translation).

25. Such modifications suggest that Vasari's accounts are often fictionalized to support his thesis.

26. *The Lives*, p. 258 (1568, 3: 308).

27. Throughout his *Lives*, Vasari makes clear that Florence is the real birthplace of artistic genius; it is the judgment of the artisans of Florence that can establish or ruin an artist's reputation. In Perugino's "Life," Vasari explains that Pietro went to the Tuscan city to study because everyone he asked praised Florentine art. He adds that in Florence the environment produces free spirits and high critical standards along with the desire to work hard to earn glory. It is for this reason that the reactions of the Florentines to Perugino's work are of crucial importance.

28. 1550, p. 530 (authors' translation).

29. *The Lives*, p. 258 (1568, 3: 308).

30. There is some debate about whether this painting dates from the early career of Perugino, or from around 1500 (see 1568, 3: 311, n. 3). Some critics also claim that Signorelli may have been involved in painting some of the figures.

31. 1550, p. 531.

32. *The Lives*, p. 259 (1568, 3: 312).

33. 1550, p. 531 (authors' translation). This assessment disappears from the last edition (see *The Lives*, p. 259; 1568, 3: 311). The work in question is *Agony in the Garden (Orazione nell'orto)*, now in the Galleria degli Uffizi, Florence.

34. These stories range from classical epics and Matthew's Gospel to the medieval *chansons de geste* and Dante's famous utterance in his *Divine Comedy*: "I am no Aeneas or Paul" (Dante Alighieri, *The Inferno of Dante*, trans. Robert Pinsky [New York: Noonday, 1996], 2: 26).

35. The Italian title of Alberti's treatise is *Della Famiglia*. Written in the vernacular, like Vasari's *Lives*, this book expresses the ideals of the middle-class merchants and businessmen who helped create the Renaissance. Alberti discusses the fact that some families may exhibit more *virtù* than others, and that through the careful management, good practices, honest customs, humanity, openness, and civility of their "solicitous and diligent fathers," family members may "reach the heights of supreme happiness

and not be forced in time to succumb to inequitable and unforeseen Fortune"; cited from *The Italian Renaissance Reader,* ed. Julia Conaway Bondanella and Mark Musa (New York: Penguin, 1987), p. 167.

36. Paul Barolsky, *Giotto's Father and the Family of Vasari's "Lives"* (University Park: The Pennsylvania State University Press, 1992), p. xvii.

37. Vasari states that poverty "sia potente cagione di fargli venire perfetti ne' sommi gradi delle eccellenzie" in the 1550 edition (p. 528).

38. *The Lives,* p. 256. The 1568 edition reads: "Di quanto benefizio sia agli ingegni alcuna volta la povertà e quanto ella sia potente cagione de fargli venir perfetti et eccellenti in qual si voglia facultà, assai chiaramente si può vedere nelle azzioni di Pietro Perugino" (3: 304).

39. *The Lives,* p. 256 (1550, p. 528; 1568, 3: 305). This comment is found in both editions.

40. In the "Preface to Part Two of the *Lives*" (*The Lives,* p. 48), Vasari writes that it "is certainly true that although greatness in the arts is achieved by some artists through hard work, by others through study, by others through imitation, and by still others through a knowledge of all the sciences which assist these arts, there are some artists who succeed through most or all of the abovementioned qualities." (1550, p. 208; 1568, 2: 80).

41. *The Lives,* p. 257 (1550, p. 529, 1568, 3: 306). The facts about Perugino's childhood remain the same in both editions.

42. Ibid. This comment is found in both editions.

43. Ibid., p. 268 (only in 1568, 3: 365).

44. Ibid., p. 256 (1550, p. 528; 1568, 3: 305–6). This comment, along with the next five quotations, is found in both editions.

45. Ibid.

46. Ibid. (1550, pp. 528–29; 1568, 3: 305–6).

47. Ibid., p. 264 (1550, p. 534; 1568, 3: 319).

48. Ibid., p. 266 (1550, p. 535; 1568, 3: 322).

49. Ibid., p. 264 (1550, p. 534; 1568, 3: 319).

50. Ibid. Vasari often uses the word *goffo* or "clumsy" to describe the works produced before Cimabue and Giotto in the "Greek" manner: "that is, not in the fine, ancient style of Greece, but rather in that awkward, modern style of their times" (*The Lives,*

p. 8; this statement appears in 1568, 1: 198, but not in the 1550 edition). Vasari tells us that Perugino brought an embarrassingly unsuccessful suit for slander against Michelangelo before the Tribunal of the Eight in Florence.

51. Begun by Filippino Lippi in 1503, the painting was recommissioned to Perugino after Lippi's death in 1504. Perugino worked on it between 1505 and 1507 (and perhaps afterwards).

52. *The Lives,* p. 265 (1550, p. 535; 1568, 3: 320–21).

53. Ibid.: "In this picture, I have put figures which on other occasions were praised by all of you and which pleased you beyond measure. If now you don't like them and don't praise them, what can I do."

54. Ibid., p. 267 (1550, p. 537; 1568, 3: 327–28). Although the comparison with Michelangelo is present in the 1550 edition, Vasari expands the last paragraph in Perugino's "Life" to clarify his specific role in the progress of the arts.

55. *The Lives,* p. 260 (1550, p. 531; 1568, 3: 312).

56. Ibid. The phrasing in the 1550 edition is slightly different, stating that this work was considered to be Pietro's most consistently excellent painting ("era stimata la più continuata in eccellenza"), but the effect is essentially the same.

57. Ibid.

58. Ibid.

59. Ibid., p. 261 (1550, p. 532; 1568, 3: 314).

60. Perugino's major contribution to the Sistine Chapel is *The Delivery of the Keys to Saint Peter;* his *Assumption* was destroyed when Michelangelo painted *The Last Judgment* in 1536. A drawing of Perugino's *Assumption* remains.

61. *The Lives,* p. 264 (1568, 3: 318). This passage is not in the 1550 edition.

62. Ibid., p. 261 (1568, 3: 313). This passage is not in the 1550 edition.

63. Ibid., p. 267 (1568, 3: 323). Much of the long passage devoted to Perugino's pupils was added in the 1568 edition, including the comment about Raphael.

JOSEPH ANTENUCCI BECHERER

THE GRANDS RAPIDS ART MUSEUM AND GRAND RAPIDS COMMUNITY COLLEGE

Perugino in America: Masterpieces, Myths, and Mistaken Identities

THIS ESSAY BEGINS with an introduction to its final pages, which consist of a composite list of works in American collections, those by Perugino and those attributed to the master's school and immediate followers, known and unknown.[1] This list is the fruition of a seven-year, nationwide survey as well as a great many pilgrimage tours aimed at a more complete understanding of Perugino, Renaissance painting in Umbria, and American collecting. It is the first attempt to recognize this significant body of the artist's work in American public and private collections. Ultimately, such a study of Perugino in America both illuminates the complexities inherent to a prolific and influential master and reflects the larger history of collecting in this country from the late nineteenth century through the present.

Casual readers and scholars alike may be surprised to discover that there are more of Perugino's paintings, as well as works attributed to his school and unknown followers, in American museums than almost any other Italian master of the fifteenth century.[2] Indeed, the total number of Perugino's surviving panel paintings and frescoes in Europe and America is nearly overwhelming until one considers the popularity the master enjoyed throughout his career and the participation of large numbers of assistants in his active workshop.[3] Vasari accurately comments on both factors when he records that Perugino's work was traded and collected widely because his style "was so pleasing to his own day that many artisans came from France, Spain, Germany, and other countries to learn it."[4]

While Perugino's popularity and the activity of his workshop and followers offers the fundamental rationale for the number of surviving works, it can also serve as the cornerstone for the many attribution problems encountered by collectors and wrestled with by scholars. For example, the Currier Gallery of Art's *Madonna and Child* (fig. 35) is among the many works once given to the master, but now reattributed. It is a subject and composition Perugino addressed numerous times throughout his career, beginning in the 1490s.

Fig. 35. School of Perugino, *Madonna and Child,* The Currier Gallery of Art, Manchester, N.H.; Currier Funds, 1952.2

Fig. 36. Follower of Pietro Perugino (Sinibaldo Ibi?), *Baptism of Christ,* Yale University Art Gallery, University purchase from James Jackson Jarves

In fact, with precious few changes, save the exclusion of a landscape background, the figural composition mirrors in reverse the *Madonna and Child* from the collection of Mr. and Mrs. Edsel Ford in the Detroit Institute of Arts (cat. no. 5). The author of the Currier panel was undoubtedly aware of the Detroit image and even may have had access to its cartoon. However, the weak modeling throughout, the rough brushstrokes, and the linearity of Mary's head and hands fall short of the angelic quality and sweetness with which Perugino's work was celebrated in contemporary accounts.[5]

The first two works attributed to Perugino in the listing entered American collections in the 1870s. The Yale University Art Gallery's *Baptism of Christ* (fig. 36) was purchased by the university in 1871 from the James Jackson Jarves collection after having been exhibited in New York as Perugino's work in 1860 and in 1863. Jarves (1818–88), one of the period's most influential writers on art and aesthetics, lived in Italy for an extensive period and encouraged the collecting of Renaissance masters, likening the growing economic strength of industrial America to that of fifteenth-century Italy.[6] His personal collection, among the most renowned of the nineteenth century, contained more than one hundred twenty paintings, which surveyed the development of the Italian Renaissance from Byzantine icons through works then attributed to Cimabue, Giotto, Angelico, Masaccio, Botticelli, Leonardo, Ghirlandaio, Perugino, Pintoricchio, and Raphael.[7] The appearance of the collection on American soil was extolled as the "first attempt to make the new world a sharer in the great art-heritage of Europe's old civilization" and was expected to "perform a similar civilizing office for the rising world on the other side of the Atlantic."[8] The significance of this transatlantic move is most fully appreciated when one understands that few works by European old masters, let alone extensive collections of them, existed in America at this time.

According to museum records, Jarves claims to have acquired the *Baptism of Christ* from the Badia, the Benedictine abbey in Florence.[9] This subject was popular throughout the Renaissance epoch and was painted several times by Perugino, beginning with his celebrated fresco of 1481–83 in the Sistine Chapel. Later versions by Perugino are the panels in the Duomo of Perugino's native Città della Pieve; the Kunsthistorisches Museum, Vienna; the centerpiece of the monumental Sant'Agostino Polyptych in the Galleria Nazionale dell'Umbria (fig. 45); and the now-damaged fresco in the Church of the Nunziatella in Foligno.[10] Although size and media differ, each of these later works concentrates on the figures of Christ and Saint John the Baptist, whose pose and position in the central foreground ultimately derive from the Sistine fresco. The Yale panel, though thoroughly repainted and in a ruinous state, is reminiscent of the Vienna version in its tight, vertical format, treatment of the landscape, and inclusion of kneeling attendant angels. The inclusion of the wreathed figure of God the Eternal Father and the flanking angels above the baptism are found only in the Sistine fresco.[11]

In comparing the Yale *Baptism of Christ* to the Vienna version, or to any of the aforementioned autograph works, one begins to question its attribution to Perugino. At a glance, the overall composition and the hilly Umbrian landscape reveal a debt to the master, but a number of awkward elements support the current attribution to a follower of Perugino. The sky is uncharacteristically crowded, the kneeling angels are clumsily rendered, and even the main figures of Christ and the Baptist lack the organic and balletic ease one associates with Perugino. Each of these elements is an independent passage executed without fully understanding the harmony necessary to the unified vision typical of the master and his most skillful students. As early as 1916, this panel was posited to be "School of Perugino" and has occasionally and erroneously been attributed to Sinibaldo Ibi of Gubbio. Charles Seymour was most succinct in describing the work as "an eclectic and rather provincial reflection of Perugino and his ablest followers."[12]

The fluid "science" of connoisseurship was in its infancy during the late nineteenth and early twentieth centuries. The Yale *Baptism of Christ* exemplifies the type of work that was attributed to a well-known master like Perugino because of the recognizable quotes made from documented, or at least venerated, works of the artist. When one considers the popularity Perugino enjoyed at the height of his career and the number of able, and even fine painters that emerged from his workshop, it is amazing that the list of works at one time attributed to the master, and now assigned to students or followers, is not lengthier.

The second of the two earliest Perugino works to enter an American collection is undoubtedly the more intriguing and closely related to the master's work.[13] *Anonymous Bearded Saint* (fig. 37), a small roundel measuring only 8⅛ inches in diameter, is held in a gilded, mid-nineteenth-century frame. The saint is shown in three-quarter length in the

Fig. 37. Perugino (?), *Anonymous Bearded Saint*, Olana State Historic Site, New York State Office of Parks, Recreation, and Historic Preservation

center of the image. Following the movement of his right hand, the body twists slightly to the left from the hips, but the head and glance look decidedly to his right. The figure stands out against a dark, solid wall.

The *Anonymous Bearded Saint* is included in the extensive collections of the renowned American landscape painter Frederic Edwin Church (1826–1900) at his exotic, oriental-style house-museum at Olana, in Hudson, New York. As a historic site operated by the New York State Office of Parks, Recreation, and Historic Preservation, Olana maintains a sizable collection of old master paintings acquired by Church during the last third of the nineteenth century. There is a photograph taken between 1892 and 1900 that shows the dining room, which doubled as a gallery, and provides a postmodern audience with a wonderful record of Victorian personal tastes in collecting and display. The panel attributed to Perugino is found among continental Baroque landscapes, other religious images, and portrait paintings hung salon style, while a variety of tapestries and rugs cover floors and furniture.[14]

As with so many American artists of the late nineteenth and early twentieth centuries, Church traveled to Europe to study and collect works that formed the Western tradition. The roundel is recorded for the first time shortly after 1880 in Church's handwritten list of his old masters. Here it is attributed to Perugino. It is not known when or how Church acquired the painting, but its absence from earlier inventories of those paintings he purchased in Rome suggests the work may have been purchased in New York City between c. 1870 and 1885.[15] More than likely, Church took stock in a dealer's inscription and a red wax seal found on the reverse of the panel. The inscription "Petrvs pervsinvs pinxit,

A.D. 1521" (Pietro Perugino, painter, 1521) in black ink is written directly on the panel; in the seal a blurred coat of arms is flanked by heraldic lions, surrounded by laurel and the largely illegible text, "Gio Paslin[   ] Ass[   ]s."

The *Anonymous Bearded Saint* is almost entirely unknown to scholars. The few existing opinions on record indicate that the work is accepted as sixteenth century and that some relationship to Perugino is acknowledged. In 1991, Everett Fahy suggested the author may be Gerino da Pistoia and that the roundel was certainly taken from an altarpiece predella, *cassone*, or some larger work of art. The following year the work was examined by Laurence Kanter, who felt the Perugino attribution might be correct. Without doubt, Fahy's observation that the *Anonymous Bearded Saint* is taken from a larger work like an altarpiece is accurate, for the unfortunate practice of dismantling large Renaissance painting ensembles and reframing individual elements as independent works of art was all too common in the nineteenth century. Accepting the Perugino attribution, however, requires further attention.

The size of this work and the compositional format of a single figure set against a dark background is strikingly similar to those of the roundels, the *Mourning Virgin* and *Mourning Saint John the Evangelist* from the North Carolina Museum of Art (cat. no. 21a, b). These three works are also related in that, according to Camesasca, each of the North Carolina panels also had a dealer inscription "Petrvs Pervsinvs pinxit" on its reverse while in the Dudley Collection, London.[16] As discussed in their catalogue commentary, the *Mourning Virgin* and *Mourning Saint John the Evangelist* are thought to have once flanked a central roundel of the *Dead Christ* in the Pinacoteca Civica, Montefortino (fig. 98). These four works are alike in the thinly applied paint and sketchy brushstrokes typical of the final works by Perugino, such as the *Pietà with Angels and Saints John the Evangelist and Mary Magdalene* in Spello, dated 1521. This late style of Perugino is decidedly loose in comparison to those hallmark, early works of firm definition for which the master is so well-known. As with many of Perugino's final works, the involvement of studio assistants is probable, and therefore the attribution of the North Carolina panels to Perugino and studio or to the studio of Perugino meets with little resistance among scholars.

It stands to reason that at one time these roundels may have formed the predella of an altarpiece with Christ at the center, Mary at the viewer's left, and John at the viewer's right and that these were followed by the Olana panel. The pose of the bearded saint would connect him to Christ with his glance and perhaps to another figure on his right indicated by the gesture of the right hand. Impending conservation, including further pigment analysis, is essential to support this hypothesis.[17] The aforementioned information considered, it is reasonable to suggest that Frederic Edwin Church did indeed purchase the first Perugino for an American collection.

Fig. 38. *Madonna and Two Saints Adoring the Child*, The Pierpont Morgan Library, New York

Returning to our list, the majority of works were acquired for American collections beginning in the 1890s and peaking with the monumental acquisitions of the 1930s. By all accounts, this period of zealous collecting mirrored the national trend in which captains of industry, self-anointed American aristocracy, and moneyed families in general raided Europe of its available old master paintings and sculptures. Some collectors were well-informed, attentive to scholarly advice, and critical, rather than romantic with regard to both visual analysis and provenance. Others, too eager to fill their salons with the glint of gilded frames and aged canvases, fell prey to the many nefarious dealers whose vocational descendants still slither through the corridors of the international art world. The breadth and energy of collecting in late nineteenth- and early twentieth-century America is perhaps best summarized by biographer Lewis Corey, who writes, "the aristocracy of money transformed its mansions into art galleries, plundering Europe of its paintings and sculptures, its furniture and tapestries, occasionally transporting castles stone by stone and resurrecting them on the American scene."[18] In retrospect, the acquisition of historical objects from the treasuries of Europe confirmed America's position as the heir to a pedigreed Western history. Today many of the works that once filled these private art galleries hang in museums, and several of the remaining mansions and castles have been opened to the public.

J. P. Morgan (1837–1913) was doubly generous among America's ennobled, contributing major works to public collections like the Metropolitan Museum of Art and the Wadsworth Atheneum, and, through his only son and heir, opening his palatial New York residence, now known as The Pierpont Morgan Library, to the public in 1924. Biographers tell us that Morgan began collecting in the 1870s and 1880s, but only with the death of his father in 1890 did his accumulation of art, rare books, and manuscripts burgeon.[19] Like most of his fellow collectors, Morgan focused his interests on masterpieces of an established European tradition, intentionally ignoring the phenomenon of contemporary art in the wake of Impressionism. As David Alan Brown accurately comments, "The search for more authentic art led in two directions: avant-garde artists and cultural visionaries who tried to subvert the classical tradition, while conservative collectors (like Morgan) sought to reinforce it by going back to the roots of the past."[20] Perugino's *Madonna and Two Saints Adoring the Child* (fig. 38) embodies the masterpiece of historical pedigree and aesthetic quality that Morgan eagerly sought.

The subject of the panel is a variation of Madonna and Child devotional images and the centerpiece of traditional Nativity scenes. Mary and the saints are reverently distanced from the Christ Child, who acknowledges their devotion with a loving gaze. This composition stems from the central panel of the Albani Torlonia Polyptych of 1491 (fig. 42), but is most closely related to a series of works executed around 1500. Specifically, the Morgan panel is allied with the *Virgin and Child with Saints* in the National Gallery, London, and the *Madonna del Sacco* in the Palazzo Pitti, Florence, except for the addition of the saints who flank the Virgin. When the work was purchased by Morgan in 1911 from the Sitwell collection in England, it bore the title *The Three Marys;* today the figure on the left is accurately described as a young man and may represent Saint John the Evangelist, and the figure on the right has recently been identified as Saint Sophronia.[21]

Madonna and Two Saints Adoring the Child is a visual summary of Perugino's style at the height of his popularity. With oval faces of graceful countenance and hands poised in prayer appearing from within bulky and seemingly woolen robes, the adult figures are characteristically Peruginesque. These saints are prominent figural types which, like the Christ Child, appear frequently, with varying modification, throughout the master's oeuvre and that of his students and followers. Perugino's forms are developed of an unfailingly rich palette—one of the most significant yet least discussed elements of his paintings. The color transitions of this masterfully uncomplicated landscape are nothing less than sublime. It is color that binds the mood of solemn adoration. Although of a later date, the frame's Latin inscription: "Fairer in beauty are you than the sons of men; grace is poured out upon thy lips; thus God has blessed you forever," seems to summarize the sentiments of timeless devotion and eternal tranquility that Perugino intended and that Morgan would have appreciated as he looked upon the work hanging in his beloved West Room (fig. 39).[22]

As a private study, the West Room was the epicenter of Morgan's world. Herbert Satterlee, Morgan's son-in-law and first biographer, later recalled, "No one could really

Fig. 39. View of the interior of the West Room,
The Pierpont Morgan Library, New York

know Mr. Morgan unless he had seen him in the West Room. This was because the room expressed his conception of beauty and color in varied and wonderful forms."[23] From the antique wooden ceiling purchased in Florence to the flocked burgundy walls hung with fifteenth- and sixteenth-century paintings to the great carved fireplace and numerous bronze and maiolica objects, it seems the seat of a Renaissance patrician. The aesthetic is a singular, historical statement and contrasts greatly with the ensemble previously encountered in the dining room of Church's Olana. Perugino's *Madonna and Two Saints Adoring the Child* remains one of the dominant works in the West Room, balanced to the left of the fireplace by a *Madonna and Child* by Francesco Francia, a contemporary of Perugino. Unquestionably, Perugino's *Madonna* is among the finest by the master in America and assures Morgan's place among the most important collectors of his era.

Perhaps the most significant work by Perugino to enter an American collection is the National Gallery of Art's altarpiece, *Crucifixion with the Virgin, Saint John, Saint Jerome, and Saint Mary Magdalene* (fig. 40; see Chronicle, 1483). The painting probably dates to 1482–83, shortly following the execution of the frescoes in the Sistine Chapel.[24] It was purchased between 1930 and 1931 by none other than Andrew Mellon (1855–1937)—then the world's leading art collector—from the Hermitage Gallery in Leningrad through Knoedler and Company. This work was acquired along with Botticelli's *Adoration of the Magi*, Raphael's *Alba Madonna*, Titian's *Venus with a Mirror*, and Van Eyck's *Annunciation* with the intention that they would serve as the cornerstones of a national art collection in Washington, D.C.

By all accounts, the *Crucifixion* is remarkable in terms of intrinsic value, provenance, and circumstances of acquisition. In time-honored fashion, the center panel depicts the

Fig. 40. *Crucifixion with the Virgin, Saint John, Saint Jerome, and Saint Mary Magdalene,* Andrew W. Mellon Collection, © Board of Trustees, National Gallery of Art, Washington, D.C. (see pl. 4)

crucified Christ between his mother Mary and his beloved apostle John. The intimacy of these three figures reflects upon the text of John 19: 26–28 wherein Christ entrusts the care of his mother to John.[25] On the side panel to the right of Christ is Mary Magdalene, who is also recorded as being present at the Crucifixion; on the side panel to the left of Christ is the aged and penitential Saint Jerome (A.D. 342–420), one of the four Latin (Western) Fathers of the Church. The altarpiece epitomizes the carefully articulated composition and development of landscape space for which Perugino was to become so well-known. Human and landscape forms on both sides of the cross are nearly symmetrical, just as the golden earth tones of the foreground and early middle ground pass through an interlude of green to find balance with the blues of the distance and the skies. Additionally, the viewer is offered evidence of several important components for Perugino's early style: the great attention to detail reveals the influence of Netherlandish painting; the significant space given over to the landscape testifies to pioneering efforts to incorporate believable and inviting terrain; and the nearly identical forms of John and Mary Magdalene suggest the common practice of repeating, with slight variations, standard figural types within a singular work of art. In the end, the *Crucifixion* repositioned the apex of late quattrocento painting and served as the basis for later versions in fresco, on panel, and in illuminated manuscripts by the master and a plethora of followers and imitators.[26]

The National Gallery's *Crucifixion* was commissioned by Bartolomeo Bartoli, a prominent Dominican theologian of the Renaissance who briefly became confessor to the Borgia pope, Alexander VI (1492–1503). In G. V. Coppi's *Annali, memorie ed huomoni illustri di San Gimignano* of 1685, the altarpiece is recorded as one of the many gifts Bartoli presented to the church of San Domenico in his native San Gimignano. Coppi erroneously listed the young Raphael as the author of the work—an attribution maintained until the late nineteenth century, when increased scrutiny revealed it to be a landmark in Perugino's career.[27] The *Crucifixion* remained in San Domenico for more than three hundred years. It subsequently turned up in two Italian collections (Moggi and Buzzi), and from there was acquired in 1800 by the Russian Ambassador to Rome, Prince Alexander Galitzin. The work was inherited by Galitzin's son, Prince Theodore, who in 1862 sent it to the family museum in Moscow, where it remained until its purchase by Czar Alexander III in 1886 for the Hermitage.[28] The altarpiece was installed in the Hermitage for nearly fifty years until the Soviet leadership's need for hard cash resulted in its being sold once more.

In the brief period between 1929 and 1931, Mellon was responsible for one of the greatest coups in the history of collecting. He acquired twenty-one important old master works from the Hermitage for less than seven million dollars.[29] In addition to the Perugino *Crucifixion* and the aforementioned works by Botticelli, Raphael, Titian, and Van Eyck, this most august company was to include four works by Rembrandt, four works by Van Dyck, two works by Hals, one by Chardin, one by Veronese, and another by Raphael. The entire group was given to the nation in 1937, ten years after Mellon's earliest known discussion of building what was to become the National Gallery of Art.[30] How fortuitous that the Soviets' needs should overlap with Mellon's interest in acquiring important works for the delight and cultural nourishment of the American people!

Today neither the National Gallery of Art nor the prominence of Italian Renaissance paintings in America would be complete without a discussion of Samuel H. Kress (1863–1955). An immensely successful retail merchant, Kress began buying works of art in the 1920s, but his great purchases were made in the years between the death of Andrew Mellon in 1937 and his own death in 1955.[31] Ironically, these two decades were the final years for the large-scale purchase of old masters by American collectors. The Kress Foundation owned more than 1,300 paintings, but the lion's share of 377 were given to the National Gallery of Art.[32] The remaining panels were distributed across America to more than sixty metropolitan and university museums in an effort to reach and inform a broad and diverse audience. Kress purchased most of his Perugino and Perugino-related panels from his primary agent and advisor, Count Contini Bonacossi, in Florence during the late 1930s and early 1940s. Indeed, eleven of the total works in the list that accompanies this essay are gifts of his foundation.

Fig. 41a. *Saint John the Baptist*, The Metropolitan Museum of Art, Gift of the Jack and Belle Linsky Foundation, 1981

Fig. 41b. *Saint Lucy*, The Metropolitan Museum of Art, Gift of the Jack and Belle Linsky Foundation, 1981

Two of the final works by Perugino to enter an American collection are *Saint John the Baptist* (fig. 41a) and *Saint Lucy* (fig. 41b). They were purchased in 1961 by Mr. and Mrs. Jack Linsky from Rosenberg and Stiebel of New York after having spent nearly a century in the collection of the Dukes of Saxe-Meiningen. In 1981, the Linsky Foundation donated the pair of paintings to the Metropolitan Museum of Art. These are the latest works by Perugino to enter an American public collection and are among the most important acquisitions of Italian Renaissance painting in recent years. Without doubt, they are connected with one of the more complex and most controversial commissions of the master's career.

Originally these large panels were part of a monumental altarpiece which stood in the tribune of Florence's magnificent Servite church, the Santissima Annunziata.[33] Contracts for the framework of the altarpiece date to 1500; in 1503, Perugino's contemporary, Filippino Lippi, was given the commission to paint a large central panel depicting the *Deposition of Christ from the Cross* (fig. 31). The *Deposition* was to face the nave of the church, while a second large panel was to face the choir, and six smaller panels of saints were to be placed in pairs in the front, back, and rear of the church. In 1504, however, Filippino died, having only begun the *Deposition*, and the commission was passed on to Perugino the following year. Although documented payments continue through 1512, Perugino probably finished *Saint John the Baptist* and *Saint Lucy* with the other Annunziata panels by 1507. The altarpiece remained intact in the church until it was removed in 1654. Today only one of the eight aforementioned works remains in the Annunziata, albeit in a side chapel. The remaining seven panels are dispersed among the collections of the Galleria dell'Accademia, Florence; the Galleria Nazionale di Arte Antica, Rome; the Lindenau Museum, Altenburg; the Metropolitan Museum of Art, New York; and a private collection.[34]

As with each of the six panels depicting saints, *Saint John the Baptist* and *Saint Lucy* are shown full length, standing within niches. Conceived of as pairs, the works in question originally flanked the *Deposition* and faced the church's nave. With the exception of differences in the position of the heads, the respective forms of the Baptist and Lucy were created to mirror one another. From the positioning of slender arms and hands to the diagonal flow of the drapery from the torso, the figures would have served as a visual parenthesis around the larger, more dramatic central panel. Most startling is the strength of Perugino's warmly subdued palette. A rich, burgundy-brown pervades. Detail is minimal, and consequently the viewer is delighted by the broad passages of color and the opportunity to travel through the respective tonal variances. Considering Perugino's handling of color and the fact that the saints were created as mirror images, one can earnestly support Keith Christiansen's statement that "No other fifteenth-century artist conceived his work in such a remarkably abstract way."[35]

At the time of their completion and installation, however, the panels were not appreciated: Perugino's Annunziata Altarpiece met with immediate criticism. Of primary concern was the fact that the figures lacked originality—they had been reused from earlier compositions. In truth, many of the figures arise from a stock vocabulary the master had originated decades before. This, in combination with the degree of repetition employed in what was one of the most prominent works of its day, offers insight into the attacks Perugino endured. According to Vasari, Perugino's response to his critics was swift:

> In this picture, I have put figures which on other occasions were praised by all
> of you and which pleased you beyond measure. If now you don't like them and
> don't praise them what can I do?[36]

The practice of reusing figural types was traditional for most fifteenth-century Renaissance masters like Perugino. However, in these opening years of the sixteenth century, the aesthetic standards in Florence were being challenged by a new generation of progressive artists, like Michelangelo and momentarily Perugino's own student Raphael, who were to call into question the products and practices of established generations of painters and sculptors.

Having discussed *Saint John the Baptist* and *Saint Lucy* as the latest works by Perugino to enter an American collection, it is natural to ask if the list accompanying this essay is finite. Unfortunately, too many factors prevent a clear-cut response. It must be noted that very few documented works by Perugino remain in private collections, but there are those occasional and appreciated surprises. Should a work become available, any desire for acquisition is immediately met with a troubling, two-fold concern: the inflated international art market and the dwindling acquisition funds available to most institutions. However, there is both market and acquisition potential with regard to those works by the school of Perugino and his known and unknown followers; herein lies the need for more research.

Many of the works listed below have not yet been thoroughly examined in order to identify their independent significance or the contribution they may offer to a greater understanding of Perugino and Umbrian painting. General audiences and scholars alike are the intended beneficiaries of this work, with the hope of eliciting continued study. A collective companion, it has been compiled to assist in appreciating important masterpieces, unraveling a few myths, and realizing the historical circumstances of some mistaken identities as represented under the rubric of Perugino in America.

PERUGINO IN AMERICA: THE PAINTINGS

Pietro Perugino (c. 1450–1523)

1. *Adoration of the Christ Child*, 1500/1505, tempera on panel, transferred to canvas, 10⁵⁄₁₆ × 18¼ in. (26.2 × 46.4 cm), The Art Institute of Chicago, Illinois (1933.1025).
NOTES: Unanimously accepted as Perugino; purchased by Martin A. Ryerson from Durand-Ruel, Paris and New York, 1893.

2. *Baptism of Christ*, 1500/1505, tempera on panel, transferred to canvas, 10¾ × 18¼ in. (27.3 × 46.3 cm), The Art Institute of Chicago, Illinois (1933.1023).
NOTES: See information for no. 1 above.

3. *Christ and the Woman of Samaria*, 1500/1505, tempera on panel, transferred to canvas, 10¾ × 18¼ in. (27.3 × 46.3 cm), The Art Institute of Chicago, Illinois (1933.1024).
NOTES: See information for no. 1 above.

4. *Noli me Tangere*, 1500/1505, tempera on panel, transferred to canvas, 10¾ × 18¼ in. (27.3 × 46.3 cm), The Art Institute of Chicago, Illinois (1933.1026).
NOTES: See information for no. 1 above.

5. *Saint Bartholomew*, post-1515–20, tempera on panel, 35¼ × 28¼ in. (89.5 × 71.7 cm), Birmingham Museum of Art, Alabama (1961.103).
NOTES: Unanimously accepted as a part of the dismantled Sant'Agostino Polyptych; Kress acquisition, 1938, from Alessandro Contini Bonacossi, Florence.

6. *Saint Augustine with Members of the Confraternity of Perugia*, c. 1500, oil on panel, 37 × 25⁵⁄₁₆ in. (94 × 64.3 cm), The Carnegie Museum of Art, Pittsburgh, Pennsylvania (61.42.1).
NOTES: Unanimously accepted as Perugino; purchased by Mr. and Mrs. Erikson through Wildenstein, New York; sold to Mrs. A. M. Scaife in 1961 and donated to the Carnegie Museum of Art.

7. *Sepulcrum Christi*, 1498, oil with tempera on panel transferred to fabric on panel, 36⁷⁄₁₆ × 28¼ in. (92.6 × 71.8 cm), Sterling and Francine Clark Art Institute, Williamstown, Massachusetts (947).

NOTES: Unanimously accepted as Perugino; purchased by Robert Sterling Clark from P. & D. Colnaghi & Obach, London, in 1914.

8. *Madonna and Child*, c. 1500, tempera on panel, 31¾ × 25½ in. (80.7 × 64.8 cm), The Detroit Institute of Arts, Michigan (77.3).

NOTES: Unanimously accepted as Perugino; purchased by Mr. and Mrs. Edsel Ford from Duveen Brothers, Paris, 1932.

9. *Saint Lucy*, c. 1500–1505, oil (?) on wood, 63 × 26⅜ in. (160 × 67 cm), The Metropolitan Museum of Art, New York (1981.293.2).

NOTES: Unanimously accepted as Perugino from the dismantled Santissima Annunziata Altarpiece; purchased by Mr. and Mrs. Jack Linsky in 1961 through Rosenberg and Stiebel, New York.

10. *Saint John the Baptist*, c. 1500–1505, oil on wood, 63 × 26⅜ in. (160 × 67 cm), The Metropolitan Museum of Art, New York (1981.293.1).

NOTES: See information for no. 9 above.

11. *Resurrection*, 1500/1505, tempera on wood panel, 10½ × 18 in. (26.7 × 45.7 cm), The Metropolitan Museum of Art, New York (1911.65).

NOTES: Unanimously accepted as Perugino in association with the four-part series from The Art Institute of Chicago; purchased with the Frederick C. Hewitt Fund from R. Langton Douglas, London, 1911.

12. *Madonna and Child*, after 1500, oil on wood panel, 27⅝ × 20 in. (70.2 × 50.8 cm), National Gallery of Art, Washington, D.C. (1939.1.215, formerly 326).

NOTES: Unanimously accepted as Perugino; Kress acquisition, 1936.

13. *Crucifixion with the Virgin, Saint John, Saint Jerome, and Saint Mary Magdalene*, c. 1485, oil on panel, transferred to canvas, center panel: 39⅞ × 22¼ in. (101.3 × 56.5 cm); side panels: 37½ × 12 in. (95.2 × 30.5 cm), National Gallery of Art, Washington, D.C. (1937.1.27 a, b, c).

NOTES: Although today the work is unanimously accepted as Perugino, it was considered a Raphael from 1695 until 1896; purchased by Andrew Mellon, 1930–31, from the Hermitage Museum and donated to the National Gallery of Art, 1937.

14. *Mourning Virgin*, c. 1520, tempera and oil on panel, 8¹⁄₁₆ in. (20.5 cm) diam., North Carolina Museum of Art, Raleigh (GL.60.17.33).

NOTES: Kress acquisition, 1938, as Perugino from Alessandro Contini Bonacossi, Florence; attributed to Perugino by Fiocco, Longhi, Perkins, Suida, Venturi, and Scarpellini; Shapley discusses the work as studio of Perugino.

15. *Mourning Saint John the Evangelist*, c. 1520, tempera and oil on panel, 8⅜ in. (21.3 cm) diam., North Carolina Museum of Art, Raleigh (GL.60.17.34).

NOTES: See information for no. 14 above.

16. *Madonna and Two Saints Adoring the Child,* c. 1500, tempera on panel, 34¼ × 28⅜ in. (87 × 72.1 cm), The Pierpont Morgan Library, New York.

NOTES: Unanimously accepted as Perugino; purchased in 1911 by J. P. Morgan from the Sitwell collection, Chesterfield, England.

17. *Madonna and Child,* c. 1520, oil on panel, 24¾ × 19³⁄₁₆ in. (62.9 × 48.7 cm), The Walters Art Gallery, Baltimore, Maryland (37.475).

NOTES: Acquired by Henry Walters in 1909; unanimously accepted as Perugino, except for 1903 sale at American Art Association, New York, where it is listed as school of Perugino.

School/Studio/Circle of Perugino

1. *Madonna and Child With Saints and Angels,* oil on panel, 39 × 35½ in. (99 × 90.2 cm), The Corcoran Gallery of Art, Washington, D.C. (26.153).

NOTES: Purchased by William Clark from Sir George Donaldson, London, 1907, and donated, 1926, as Perugino; attribution to Perugino maintained through 1946, when workshop participation was first noted; current attribution dates to 1977.

2. *Madonna and Child,* c. 1495, tempera on panel, 24 × 29½ in. (60.9 × 74.9 cm), The Currier Gallery of Art, Manchester, New Hampshire (1952.2).

NOTES: Early attribution to Perugino by Berenson; Bombe and Zeri accept work as school of Perugino.

3. *Saint Nicholas of Tolentino Saving a Boy from Drowning,* c. 1500, tempera on panel, 10½ × 20½ in. (26.7 × 52.1 cm), The Detroit Institute of Arts, Michigan (27.10).

NOTES: Purchased by Ralph A. Booth, 1927 from the Alphonse Kann collection, Paris; published as the work of Eusebio da San Giorgio prior to the sale and by Berenson and Gnoli; Valentiner attributed the work to early Raphael; current attribution dates to 1982.

4. *Saint Nicholas of Tolentino Restoring Two Partridges to Life,* c. 1500, tempera and panel, 10¼ × 20½ in. (26 × 52.1 cm), The Detroit Institute of Arts, Detroit, Michigan (25.146).

NOTES: Purchased by the museum from Alessandro Contini Bonacossi, Florence and Rome, 1925, probably as Raphael.

5. *Madonna and Child with Saints,* c. 1493, tempera on panel, 31¾ × 23¹¹⁄₁₆ in. (80.6 × 60.2 cm), The Hyde Collection, Glen Falls, New York (1971.32).

NOTES: Acquired from Jacob M. Heimann as Perugino in 1940; attribution of school of Perugino first suggested by Valentiner.

6. *Anonymous Bearded Saint* (possibly Saint Peter), oil and tempera (?) on panel, 8⅛ in. (20.6 cm) diam., Olana State Historic Site, Hudson, New York (OL.1980.1912).

NOTES: Attribution to Perugino dates to c. 1880, when recorded by Frederic Edwin Church; overpaint and varnishes prevent conclusive attribution to Perugino.

7. *Saint Sebastian,* c. 1500, oil on panel transferred to canvas on pressed wood panel, 30³⁄₁₆ × 21¹⁄₁₆ in. (76.7 × 53.4 cm), Gift of the Samuel Kress Foundation to the New

Jersey State Museum; transferred to The Art Museum, Princeton University, New Jersey (1995–330).

NOTES: Known through the nineteenth and early twentieth centuries as an early Raphael; attributed to Raphael as late as 1954, but also attributed to Giannicola Manni, Eusebio da San Giorgio, Sinibaldo Ibi, and Master of the Greenville Tondo; Kress acquisition, 1948, from Alessandro Contini Bonacossi, Florence.

8. *Nativity,* c. 1505–10, egg tempera on panel, 16 × 12⅛ in. (40.6 × 30.8 cm), Yale University Art Gallery, New Haven, Connecticut (1943.265).

NOTES: Attribution to school of Perugino dates to van Marle, 1933; acquired by Maitland F. Griggs in Paris, 1927.

Unknown Followers of Perugino

1. *Madonna and Child Enthroned with Four Saints,* oil on panel transferred to canvas, 80¾ × 80½ in. (205.1 × 204.5 cm), formerly Baltimore Museum of Art, Maryland (38.229).

NOTES: Deaccessioned, sold Christie's, New York, October 1991; purchased (1909) and bequeathed (1938) as Perugino; relationship to Perugino supported by van Marle, Berenson, Oberhuber, Scarpellini.

2. *Portrait of a Man,* tempera and oil on panel, 22⅞ × 17⅜ in. (58 × 44 cm), The Brooklyn Museum, New York (34.497).

NOTES: First attributed to Perugino by Berenson in 1909 while in Friedsam collection, but doubts by Bombe and, most recently, Scarpellini persist; current attribution to follower of Perugino initiated by Todini in 1989.

3. *Two Angels* (surrounding fourteenth-century *Madonna and Child with Male Donor*), fresco transferred to canvas, entire work: 54¾ × 37¼ in. (139.1 × 94.6 cm), Fogg Art Museum, Harvard University, Cambridge, Massachusetts (1923.46.1).

NOTES: Acquired by Edward W. Forbes in 1923 from the dealer Brizzi in Assisi and donated to the Fogg Art Museum; current attribution first suggested by Edward Fahy; formerly attributed to Lo Spagna and Melanzio by Longhi.

4. *Decorative Frieze with Putti and Grotesquerie,* fresco transferred to canvas, 17 × 33½ × 9½ in. (43.2 × 85.1 × 24.1 cm), Hearst Castle, San Simeon, California (529-9-88).

NOTES: Purchased by Randolph Hearst from Leone Ricci, New York, in 1920.

5. *Nativity,* c. 1505–10, tempera and oil on panel, 30½ × 30¼ in. (77.5 × 76.8 cm), The Minneapolis Museum of Art, Minnesota (22.25).

NOTES: Early erroneous attribution to Perugino based on inscription found in architecture (HOC/PETRVS//DE/PERVSIA//PINXIT MCCCCXXCII), now known to have been painted in at a later date.

6. *Saint Jerome in the Wilderness,* tempera on panel, 24⅝ × 16½ in. (62.5 × 41.9 cm), National Gallery of Art, Washington, D.C. (1939.1.280).

NOTES: Kress acquisition, 1937, from Alessandro Contini Bonacossi, Florence; Perugino attribution unchallenged until published as school of Perugino in 1968 posthumous edition of Berenson; current attribution formally accepted in 1984.

7. *Saint Jerome in the Wilderness*, oil on panel, 11 × 9 in. (27.9 × 22.9 cm), San Diego Museum of Art, California (1944.020).

NOTES: Donated by the New York dealer Jacob M. Heimann; generally accepted as follower of Perugino, although attribution to Lo Spagna has been presented and refuted.

8. *Scene from the Life of Saint Nicholas of Tolentino*, oil on panel, 12 × 40³⁄₁₆ in. (30.5 × 102.1 cm), Sedgwick Collection, University of California at Santa Barbara (60.9).

NOTES: Early attributions to Perugino and Granacci; current attribution to a Pisan follower of Pintoricchio initiated by Fahy in 1976.

9. *Madonna and Child with Saint John*, tempera on panel, 30⁵⁄₁₆ in. (77 cm), diam., The Frances Lehman Loeb Art Center, Vassar College, Poughkeepsie, New York (17.1.17).

NOTES: Purchased from the William Graham collection as school of Perugino by the Carrington collection in 1886; later purchased by Osvald Siren for Charles M. Pratt, who donated it to Vassar in 1917 as Giannicola di Paolo (Manni); attributed to an Umbrian follower of Perugino by Zeri in 1964 and to a Florentine follower of Perugino by Fahy in 1984.

10. *Crucifixion*, oil on parchment, 10⅞ × 7¼ in. (27.6 × 18.4 cm), The Walters Art Gallery, Baltimore, Maryland (37.1174).

NOTES: Acquired 1902 by Henry Walters from the Massarenti collection, Rome, as Perugino; accepted as Perugino throughout the early twentieth century.

11. *Baptism of Christ*, c. 1510, tempera on panel, 21½ × 16½ in. (54.6 × 41.9 cm), Yale University Art Gallery, New Haven, Connecticut (1871.93).

NOTES: Published in 1860 and 1863 as Perugino; purchased as Perugino in 1870; attributed to Sinibaldo Ibi by Offner in 1927; current attribution from Seymour, 1970.

Giannicola di Paolo, active 1484–1544

1. *Annunciation*, c. 1510–15, tempera on panel, 15⅞ × 14⅛ in. (40.3 × 35.9 cm), National Gallery of Art, Washington, D.C. (266).

NOTES: Early attributions assign the work to Raphael; attributed to Perugino by Zeri, Camesasca, and Shapley; attributed Giannicola di Paolo by Berenson, Brown, and Scarpellini; Kress acquisition, 1935, from Alessandro Contini Bonacossi, Florence.

2. *Crucifixion*, c. 1505, 12¾ × 10⅜ in. (32.4 × 26.4 cm), The Philbrook Museum of Art, Tulsa, Oklahoma (1945.26.1).

NOTES: Attribution predates 1945 accession; donated by Robert Lehman through Harold Woodbury Parsons.

3. *Crucifixion with Holy Women*, c. 1520, tempera on wood, 23⅛ × 16 in. (58.7 × 40.6 cm), Portland Art Museum, Oregon (61.37).

NOTES: Kress acquisition, 1938, from Alessandro Contini Bonacossi, Florence; listed as Giannicola di Paolo since first exhibited in 1941.

4. *Angel Annunciate*, 10¾ × 12½ in. (27.3 × 31.8 cm), formerly The Snite Museum of Art, University of Notre Dame, Indiana.

NOTES: Deaccessioned 1974 through Chicago Art Galleries as "Anonymous Italian, late 15th century"; purchased at the end of World War II by E. W. Curley, Chicago, with attribution to "Flemish School with the influence of Botticelli"; Fredericksen and Zeri reattribute it to Giannicola in 1972.

5. *Adoration of the Magi*, c. 1500, oil on panel, 16½ × 16³⁄₁₆ in. (41.9 × 41.1 cm, tondo), The Walters Art Gallery, Baltimore, Maryland (37.440).

NOTES: Acquired 1902 by Henry Walters from the Massarenti collection, Rome as Pintoricchio; attributed to Giannicola di Paolo by Zeri, 1976; published as Fiorenzo di Lorenzo, 1922, 1929; published as Tuscan-Florentine School, 1909.

Lo Spagna (Giovanni di Pietro), active Perugia by 1504–d. Spoleto 1528

1. *Saint Catherine of Siena*, 1510–15, tempera and oil on panel, 42½ × 19¾ in. (108 × 50.2 cm), The Art Institute of Chicago, Illinois (1937.1008).

NOTES: Unanimously accepted as Lo Spagna since first published in 1906; an old inscription "originale di [   ] Perugino" on the back of the panel attributes the work to Perugino.

2. *Christ on the Mount of Olives*, oil on panel, 19 × 17 in. (48.3 × 43.2 cm), Clowes Fund Collection, Indianapolis Museum of Art, Indiana (IMA–CL10059).

NOTES: Perugino attribution accepted until 1988, when follower of Perugino was put forward by Ian Frasier; attribution to Lo Spagna first suggested by Becherer in 1994.

3. *Madonna and Child with a Monk Saint and Saint Catherine of Siena*, oil (?) on panel, 19⅝ × 14⅞ in. (49.8 × 37.9 cm), John G. Johnson Collection, The Philadelphia Museum of Art, Pennsylvania (145).

NOTES: Purchased by Johnson in 1909 from Ehrlich Gallery, New York, at the suggestion of Bernard Berenson.

4. *Madonna and Child*, fresco transferred to canvas, 52¾ × 24⅜ in. (134 × 62 cm), formerly The Art Museum, Princeton University, New Jersey.

NOTES: Deaccessioned 1989, sold Sotheby's, New York, July 1989.

5. *Pietà*, c. 1510, tempera on panel, 14¾ × 18½ in. (37.5 × 47 cm), St. Phillip in the Hills, Tucson, Arizona (Kress 1186).

NOTES: Kress acquisition, 1939, from Alessandro Contini Bonacossi, Florence; unanimously accepted as Lo Spagna.

Antonio da Viterbo (also known as Pastura), active 1489–1513

1. *Madonna and Child*, c. 1490, tempera on panel, 17¼ × 13¹⁵⁄₁₆ in. (43.8 × 35.4 cm), Fogg Art Museum, Cambridge, Massachusetts (1900.6).

NOTES: Most nineteenth-century literature related to this work refers to it as a Raphael; purchased Rome, 1899, and donated 1900.

2. *Pietà*, c. 1505, tempera on panel, 11⅝ × 17 in. (29.5 × 43.2 cm), High Museum of Art, Atlanta, Georgia (58.50).

NOTES: Kress acquisition, 1935, as Perugino from Alessandro Contini Bonacossi, Florence; exhibited as Perugino until 1964; Viterbo first suggested by Berenson and Zeri; current attribution dates to 1968.

3. *Madonna and Child with Saints Jerome and John*, oil (?) on panel, 78.7 × 53.5 in. (199.9 × 135.9 cm), John G. Johnson Collection, Philadelphia Museum of Art, Pennsylvania (43).

NOTES: A part of Johnson's collection by 1904; provenance is unknown.

4. *Madonna and Child with Saint John and Angel*, Phoenix Museum of Art, Arizona (1961.103).

NOTES: Further information unavailable.

5. *Madonna and Child*, tempera (?) on panel, 20 × 14½ in. (50.8 × 36.8 cm), Ringling Museum of Art, Sarasota, Florida (SN30).

NOTES: Purchased with the erroneous attribution to Bellini at Christie's in 1928; currently attributed to the studio of Antonio da Viterbo.

6. *Madonna and Child with Two Angels*, c. 1500, tempera on panel, 31⅛ × 16⅜ in. (79 × 41.6 cm), Worcester Art Museum, Massachusetts (1914.44).

NOTES: Purchased from Levesque et Cie., Paris, in 1914 with the current attribution and date proposed in 1914 by Gnoli and accepted by Berenson.

Gerino da Pistoia

1. *Crucifixion*, c. 1500, oil on panel, 22¹⁵⁄₁₆ × 15¹⁄₁₆ in. (58.3 × 38.3 cm), The Walters Art Gallery, Baltimore, Maryland (37.454).

NOTES: Current attribution dates to 1908 and is generally accepted; only Weinberger tentatively attributed the work to Perugino; purchased at the Galerie Georges Petit, Paris, from the Cheramy sale.

Master of the Greenville Tondo

1. *Madonna and Child with Angels*, oil on panel, 40¾ in. (103.5 cm) diam., Bob Jones University Art Museum, Greenville, South Carolina (59.12).

NOTES: Most literature through 1958 assigns this work to Perugino, except for an attribution as early Raphael by Fiocco and Salmi; current attribution to the Master of the Greenville Tondo was first put forward by Zeri in 1959 and is generally accepted.

2. *Adoration of the Christ Child by Mary and Joseph*, oil on panel, 39 × 30½ in. (99.1 × 77.5 cm) [oval], Museum of Fine Arts, St. Petersburg, Florida (76.3).

NOTES: Purchased by Dr. and Mrs. Vance D. Bishop for the museum in 1976 from Sotheby-Parke-Bernet, New York, with current attribution.

Anonymous, Fifteenth-Century Umbrian

1. *Saint Sebastian*, fresco transferred to canvas, 58½ × 26 in. (148.6 × 66 cm), formerly Museum of Fine Arts, Boston, Massachusetts, now private collection.

NOTES: Deaccessioned, sold William Doyle Galleries, October 1986 (lot 61); in 1947, G. H. Edgell favored an attribution to Melanzio, supported by Cesare Festi, 1972.

2. *Crucifixion*, panel, 35 × 21 in. (88.9 × 53.3 cm), The Detroit Institute of Arts, Michigan (09.11).

NOTES: Attributed to Perugino through 1910; sold in estate of Earl of Buckingham at Stowe House, 1846; acquired as Perugino by the Scripps family, who donated it to the museum in 1909.

3. *Madonna and Child with Two Saints*, formerly Los Angeles County Museum of Art, California (53.73).

NOTES: Deaccessioned, sold Sotheby's, Los Angeles, November 1977 as attributed to Raphael.

4. *Portrait of a Man*, formerly Nelson-Atkins Museum of Art, Kansas City, Missouri (49.50).

NOTES: Deaccessioned, sold Christie's, New York, as circle of Luca Signorelli, May 1991; X-ray studies suggest the work is nineteenth century.

5. *Adoration of the Shepherds*, tempera on panel, 11 × 19½ in. (27.9 × 49.5 cm), formerly New York Historical Society, New York (1867.25a).

NOTES: Published as both school of Perugino and copy after Perugino, sold December 2, 1971, as after Raphael at Parke-Bernet Galleries; listed as fifteenth-century Umbrian by Fredericksen and Zeri, 1972.

6. *Resurrection*, tempera on panel, 11 × 19½ in. (27.9 × 49.5 cm), formerly New York Historical Society, New York (1867.25b).

NOTES: See information for no. 5 above.

Anonymous, Sixteenth-Century Umbrian

1. *Madonna and Child with Saints Jerome and Francis*, tempera on panel, 24⅝ × 16¾ in. (52.54 × 42.5 cm), The Metropolitan Museum of Art, New York (32.100.74).

NOTES: Attributed to Antonio da Viterbo by Berenson, van Marle, and Zeri; current attribution dates to 1990; purchased in 1916 by Michael Friedsam from Kleinberger Galleries.

2. *Madonna and Child with Infant Saint John the Baptist*, tempera on panel, 21¾ × 17¼ in. (55.2 × 43.8 cm), The Philbrook Museum of Art, Tulsa, Oklahoma (61.9.21).

NOTES: Kress acquisition, 1939, from Alessandro Contini Bonacossi, Florence; attributed to a follower of Perugino by Longhi and Perkins while Suida and Venturi noted it as close to Pintoricchio.

3. *Anonymous Nun Saint*, fresco fragment, 13⅜ × 12½ in. (34 × 31.8 cm), formerly San Diego Museum of Art, California.

NOTES: Deaccessioned 1989, sold Christie's, New York, under the title of *Saint Claire*, as Umbrian School, June 1990; early attributions to Perugino.

4. *Holy Family with the Baptist,* c. 1500–1505, oil on panel, 23⁹⁄₁₆ in. (59.8 cm) diam., The Walters Art Gallery, Baltimore, Maryland (37.506).

NOTES: Acquired 1910–15 by Henry Walters from Bernard Berenson who attributed the work to an unknown Florentine between Piero di Cosimo, Raffaellino di Garbo, and Francesco di Garbo; other early attributions to Giovanni Battista Utili are now refuted.

5. *Portrait of Perugino,* c. 1500, oil on panel, 20⅝ × 16 in. (52.4 × 40.6 cm), The Walters Art Gallery, Baltimore, Maryland (37.1060).

NOTES: Acquired 1902 by Henry Walters from the Massarenti collection, Rome.

6. *Saint Francis of Assisi,* c. 1510–15, oil on panel, painted surface: 27 × 16⅞ in. (66.6 × 42.9 cm), The Walters Art Gallery, Baltimore, Maryland (37.640).

NOTES: Acquired 1902 by Henry Walters from the Massarenti collection, Rome, as Eusebio da San Giorgio; Berenson and van Marle attributed the work to Antoniazzo Romano.

NOTES

1. Each work is entered according to its current attribution, followed by information regarding date, medium, size, museum collection, museum accession number, and, when applicable, notes significant to the attribution or to the history of the work. This list includes those works by Perugino's pupils wherein a great many attribution problems existed at the time of acquisition, and, in some instances, have persisted. The works of the master's most celebrated pupil, Raphael Santi, are not included, since voluminous scholarship on their relationship exists. For the most complete source on Raphael's work in American collections, see David Alan Brown's *Raphael and America* (Washington, D.C.: National Gallery of Art, 1983).

2. According to Fredericksen and Zeri's venerable *Census of Pre-Nineteenth-Century Italian Paintings in North American Collections* (Cambridge, Mass.: Harvard University Press, 1972), only a few other masters, like Botticelli and Giovanni Bellini and their respective schools and anonymous followers, appear in larger numbers in American collections.

3. The phenomenon of Perugino's popularity is most concisely articulated in André Chastel's *Studios and Styles of the Italian Renaissance,* trans. Jonathan Griffin (New York: Odyssey, 1966).

4. Giorgio Vasari, *The Lives of the Artists,* trans. Julia Conaway Bondanella and Peter Bondanella (Oxford: Oxford University Press, 1991), p. 267.

5. One important contemporary account is a letter from an agent of the Duke of Milan around 1490, wherein Perugino is described as an exceptional master and his works as having an angelic air and being very sweet; this letter and its significance are discussed in Michael Baxandall's *Painting and Experience in Fifteenth Century Italy* (Oxford: Oxford University Press, 1972), pp. 25–27.

6. Regarding this point, see James Jarves' "A Lesson for Merchant Princes," in *Italian Rambles* (New York: G. P. Putnam and Sons, 1883), pp. 361–80.

7. Although a great many of these attributions have been challenged and changed, the most complete document on the Jarves collection as it was known to nineteenth-century audiences is Russell Sturgis' *Manual of the Jarves Collection of Early Italian Pictures* (New Haven: Yale College, 1868). The only rival of the Jarves collection in America was that of Thomas Jefferson Bryan (1802–1870), donated in large part to the New York Historical Society.

8. Letter of M. T. Trollepe in the *London Atheneum* of February 12, 1859, as cited in Sturgis, pp. 101–2.

9. The summary document discussing this work and others purchased from Jarves is the catalogue by Charles Seymour Jr., *Early Italian Paintings in the Yale University Art Gallery* (New Haven: Yale University Press, 1970).

10. Additionally, it is found as a predella panel for the San Pietro Polyptych, now in the Musée des Beaux Arts, Rouen, and for the Santissima Annunziata Altarpiece, now in the Art Institute of Chicago (cat. no. 1b).

11. God the Father is also shown, but as an independent image above the *Baptism of Christ* in both the Sant'Agostino Polyptych and the Nunziatella fresco.

12. Seymour, p. 233.

13. I wish to thank Laurence Kanter, Curator, Robert Lehman Collection, The Metropolitan Museum of Art, New York, for introducing me to this work.

14. The panel attributed to Perugino is probably the square blurred at the far right end, second from the top in this image. A later photo, taken around 1905, records a similar view, where the *Anonymous Bearded Saint* is more clearly seen in the same position as the c. 1892–1900 image.

15. Museum records and correspondence of February 22, 1994 and August 1, 1994.

16. *L'opera completa di Perugino,* ed. Carlo Castellaneta and Ettore Camesasca (Milan: Rizzoli, 1966), p. 122.

17. All works at Olana are required to be restored only to their 1891–1900 state in keeping with the condition in which Church would have displayed them, and not to their original state.

18. Lewis Corey, *The House of Morgan: A Social Biography of the Masters of Money* (New York: AMS Press, 1969), p. 236.

19. See *In August Company: The Collections of the Pierpont Morgan Library* (New York: Harry N. Abrams, 1993),

and Francis Henry Taylor, *Pierpont Morgan: Collector and Patron, 1837–1913* (New York: Pierpont Morgan Library, 1970).

20. Brown, p. 31.

21. *In August Company*, p. 45.

22. Psalms 45:3: "Speciosus forma prae filiis hominum; diffusa est gratia in labiis tuis; proptera benedixit te Deus in aeternum" (cited from *The New American Bible*, Saint Joseph Edition).

23. *In August Company*, p. 22.

24. Although the altarpiece is often dated to around 1485, Jeryldene Wood's case for 1482–83 is most sound. See J. Wood, "The Early Paintings of Perugino" (Ph.D. diss., University of Virginia, 1985), p. 243.

25. "When Jesus saw his mother and the disciple whom he loved (John), he said to his mother, 'Woman, behold your son.' And from that hour, the disciple took her into his home" (John 19:26–28, cited from *The New American Bible*, Saint Joseph Edition).

26. Perugino's most notable versions of the Crucifixion are the monumental fresco in the chapterhouse of Santa Maria Maddalena dei Pazzi in Cestello near Florence, the Albani Torlonia Polyptych (lunette) in Rome, the San Girolamo delle Poverine Altarpiece in the Uffizi, Florence, and the manuscript illumination in the *Foglio di Messale*, attributed to the master, in the Vatican Library, Rome.

27. For notice of the initial challenge to Coppi's attribution to Raphael, see F. Harck's "Notizen über italienische Bilder in Petersburger Sammlungen," *Repertorium für Kunstwissenschaft* 19 (1896): 413–14.

28. Pietro Scarpellini, *Perugino*, 1st ed. (Milan: Electa, 1984), p. 80.

29. According to David Koskoff's biography *The Mellons: The Chronicle of America's Richest Family* (New York: Croswell, 1978), p. 331, the total cost of the Hermitage acquisitions through their primary agent Knoedler and Company, was $6,654,000, and three works (two Leonardos and a Giorgione) were passed up as "overpriced."

30. For a complete discussion of Mellon's founding role in the National Gallery of Art, see John Walker's essay, "The Founding Benefactors," in *The National Gallery of Art, Washington, D.C.* (New York: Abrams, 1984), pp. 24–48.

31. Ibid., p. 37.

32. For a complete discussion of the Kress paintings specific to the topic of this essay, see Fern Rusk Shapley's *Paintings from the Samuel H. Kress Foundation: Italian Schools XV–XVI Century* (London: Phaidon, 1968).

33. For the most recent and complete history of the altarpiece, see Jonathan Nelson, "The High Altarpiece of SS. Annunziata in Florence: History, Form and Function," *Burlington Magazine* 139 (1997): 84–94.

34. Predella panels from the Art Institute of Chicago and the Metropolitan Museum of Art (cat. no. 1a–e) are also considered to have been part of the Annunziata Altarpiece. For a more complete discussion of this commission and all its panels, consult Scarpellini, pp. 113–14.

35. Keith Christiansen, *Metropolitan Museum of Art: Notable Acquisitions* (New York: Metropolitan Museum of Art, 1982), pp. 38–39.

36. Vasari, p. 265.

Catalogue of the Exhibition

JOSEPH ANTENUCCI BECHERER

1

Pietro Perugino

FIVE SCENES FROM
THE LIFE OF CHRIST

1a ADORATION OF THE
CHRIST CHILD

c. 1500/1505
Tempera on panel, transferred to canvas, 10⁵⁄₁₆ × 18¼ in. (26.2 × 46.4 cm)
The Art Institute of Chicago, Mr. and Mrs. Martin A. Ryerson Collection (1933.1025)

1b BAPTISM OF CHRIST

c. 1500/1505
Tempera on panel, transferred to canvas, 10¾ × 18¼ in. (27.3 × 46.3 cm)
The Art Institute of Chicago, Mr. and Mrs. Martin A. Ryerson Collection (1933.1023)

1c CHRIST AND THE WOMAN OF SAMARIA

c. 1500/1505
Tempera on panel, transferred to canvas, 10¾ × 18¼ in. (27.3 × 46.3 cm)
The Art Institute of Chicago, Mr. and Mrs. Martin A. Ryerson Collection (1933.1024)

1d RESURRECTION

c. 1500/1505
Tempera on wood panel, 10½ × 18 in. (26.7 × 45.7 cm)
The Metropolitan Museum of Art, Frederick C. Hewitt Fund, 1911 (11.65)

The Art Institute of Chicago
PROVENANCE (a–c, e): 1852–57(?), Alexander Barker, London; 1868, William Ward (d. 1885),
First Earl of Dudley, London; 1892, sold Christie's, London (June 25), nos. 76, 77, 79, 80, to
Durand-Ruel, Paris and New York, on behalf of Martin A. Ryerson; 1893, sold Durand-Ruel,
Paris and New York, on behalf of Martin A. Ryerson (d. 1932); 1893–1933, intermittently on loan
to The Art Institute of Chicago; 1933, bequeathed to The Art Institute of Chicago.

The Metropolitan Museum of Art
PROVENANCE (d): 1852–57(?), Alexander Barker, London; 1868, William Ward, (d. 1885), First
Earl of Dudley, London; 1892, sold Christie's, London (June 25), no. 78; 1892, Thomas Agnew
and Sons, London; 1892–1911, Frederick Anthony White, London; 1911, R. Langton Douglas,
London; 1911, The Metropolitan Museum of Art purchase, Frederick C. Hewitt Fund.

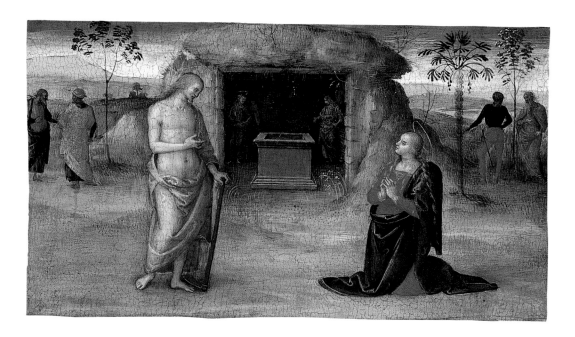

1e NOLI ME TANGERE
(Touch Me Not)

c. 1500/1505
Tempera on panel, transferred to canvas, 10¾ × 18¼ in. (27.3 × 46.3 cm)
The Art Institute of Chicago, Mr. and Mrs. Martin A. Ryerson Collection (1933. 1026)

THROUGHOUT THE RENAISSANCE, religious and secular histories and legends were successfully communicated through the visual arts. In painting, such storytelling, known as narrative, found expression in large fresco cycles and panel paintings of varying scale. Predella panels, such as this fine series from the Art Institute of Chicago and the Metropolitan Museum of Art, were originally situated at the base or pedestal of a large altarpiece. Whereas the surmounting main scene or central panel of an altarpiece is typically a grand, singular vision intended to be seen from a great distance, predella panels are intimate and intended to be read in chronological order from left to right.

These works, reunited for the first time in more than a century, recount five stories from the life of Christ as recorded in the New Testament: the Adoration of the Christ Child, Baptism of Christ, Christ and the Woman of Samaria, Resurrection, and Noli me Tangere.

The series appropriately begins with the *Adoration of the Christ Child* as recorded in the Gospel of Luke (2: 1–20). In the central foreground is the Holy Family: a reclining infant Christ is flanked by his parents, Mary and Joseph. Like many Renaissance depictions of this subject, the swaddling clothes and manger described by Luke are omitted. Instead, a nude child rests atop a simple cloth spread on the ground as a means of remembering the human nature of Christ in a scene where all gestures are reactions to his divinity. The child gazes affectionately upward at his mother, who kneels before him with her hands gently

Fig. 43. Attributed to Perugino, *Adoration of the Shepherds*, Accademia Carrara di Belle Arti, Bergamo

Fig. 42. *Nativity* (central panel, Albani Torlonia Polyptych), Museo di Villa Albani, Rome

brought together in prayer. Joseph appears behind the child on bended right knee, his hands drawn back in awe. Directly behind these figures is a simple, timber-frame stable housing an ox and an ass, which testify to Christ's humble birth. To the right and left of this structure are the shepherds visiting from the surrounding countryside, as recorded in the gospel. In the pair at the right, the standing shepherd receives the announcement of the child's birth from a tiny angel hovering in the sky, while the other figure focuses forward in adoration as do the two figures at the left. As in each of the panels of this series, Perugino arranges all forms in a perfectly balanced and uncluttered composition in order to speak clearly and directly to the viewer.

Perugino's format for the *Adoration of the Christ Child* was initiated with the central panel of the Albani Torlonia Polyptych (fig. 42) of 1491 and subsequently reinterpreted several times both on panel and in fresco. The most prominent version is part of the renowned fresco cycle of the Collegio del Cambio in Perugia, Italy, dated to 1500 (fig. 27). Although the Chicago example is measurably smaller, it suggests the volume and depth encountered in the much larger Cambio version. Three other surviving predella panels depict the Adoration of the Christ Child by the shepherds. Of these, the Chicago panel is most closely related to that found in the Accademia Carrara in Bergamo (fig. 43).[1]

The next panel depicts one of the most popular themes in the history of Christian art, the Baptism of Christ. All four of the Gospels record that Christ came before John at the Jordan River to be baptized—a historical act of purification. As a prophet who forecast the coming of the Messiah, John was at first reluctant to baptize Christ, whom he recognized as the fulfillment of his prophecy. In keeping with Renaissance tradition,

Fig. 44. Andrea del Verrocchio, *Baptism of Christ*, Galleria degli Uffizi, Florence

Fig. 45. *Baptism of Christ* (central panel, Sant'Agostino Polyptych), Galleria Nazionale dell'Umbria, Perugia (see pl. 23)

Perugino describes the very moment when the cloaked John raises a small vessel with water above the head of Christ, who, disrobed, stands humbly and ponders the significance of the event. The positioning of these graceful figures in the shallow waters of the river in the immediate central foreground underscores the significance of their biological and theological relationship to one another.[2] One standing and one kneeling angel border the main figures to the left and right sides, thereby maintaining the very sense of balance and symmetry initiated with the shepherds in the *Adoration of the Christ Child*. Although these angels do not appear in the biblical descriptions of this event, they are commonly included by artists. The only traditional element lacking here is the descending dove of the Holy Spirit, which typically appears above the head of Christ in scenes of his Baptism.

Perugino first addressed the Baptism of Christ with his celebrated fresco of 1481–83 in the Sistine Chapel (fig. 8). Although this work is rendered active by its numerous groups of figures, it is easy to identify the central characters of John and Christ which established the visual precedent for the Chicago panel. For Perugino, these and all other versions of the subject recall a notable altarpiece of 1470–72 (fig. 44) by his Florentine master, Andrea del Verrocchio. Each of the eight known examples of the Baptism of Christ by Perugino reflects his debt to Verrocchio's composition and figure types.[3] Of these, the Chicago panel most closely mirrors (although on a diminutive scale) the poses and gestures found in the large central panel of the monumental Sant'Agostino Polyptych, now preserved in the Galleria Nazionale, Perugia (fig. 45).

Christ and the Woman of Samaria is the third painting in the series and the least familiar to most audiences. Only the Gospel of John (4: 1–30) records the meeting of Christ and the woman at the ancient well of Jacob outside the town of Sychar in Samaria. Christ requests a drink of water from the woman, a known prostitute. This event symbolizes Christ's willingness to cross several traditional social boundaries by reaching out to a Samaritan, with whom the Jews held a long-standing hatred, and to a strange woman who was a member of an ill-reputed profession as well. When she questions his decision to request a drink of her, Christ responds in a metaphor alluding to salvation: "Everyone who drinks this water will be thirsty again; but whoever drinks the water I shall give will become in him a spring of water welling up to eternal life."[4] Perugino strategically separates the main figures on either side of the perspectively correct well, thereby eliminating any indication of a close relationship as encountered in the earlier scene with Christ and John the Baptist. The Woman of Samaria is elegantly dressed and coiffed in the manner typical of Renaissance courtesans. The figures found in the middle ground and distance do not interact or connect with those figures in the foreground, reflecting Perugino's attempt to articulate the happenstance nature of this encounter.

The story of Christ and the Woman of Samaria is not a staple of Renaissance art, and the panel presented is the sole example by Perugino. This considered, it is interesting to note that the only known drawing related to the Chicago/New York series was created in preparation for *Christ and the Woman of Samaria.* The black chalk drawing (fig. 46) in the Ashmolean Museum, Oxford, has incised outlines and auxiliary perspective lines plotted out by pinpointing; in addition, the reverse of the drawing has been blackened, indicating that the drawing was used for transferring the design, probably onto the cartoon.[5] The uniqueness of the subject may have required Perugino to create a preliminary work, whereas the other panels of the series can be clearly linked to existing works by the master, for which multiple drawings may have been readily available. Finally, and perhaps most

Fig. 46. *Christ and the Woman of Samaria,* Ashmolean Museum, Oxford

Fig. 47. Perugino and assistants, *Resurrection*, Musée des Beaux Arts, Rouen

accurately, the precise, geometric quality of the well may have merited such a clearly articulated preparatory drawing.

Following this is the panel depicting the Resurrection. According to Christian tradition, Christ rose from the dead on the third day after his death by crucifixion. This event serves as the very foundation of Christianity and was consequently among the most popular images requested of Renaissance artists. Each of the Gospels records the entombment and the discovery of the empty tomb two days later, but not the actual moment of resurrection, at which there were no witnesses. Perugino's version is standard in that it attempts to visualize the triumphant moment of victory over death. The *Resurrection* has Christ positioned above a marble sarcophagus at the center with a set of Roman guards on either side, thereby maintaining the carefully balanced compositions encountered in each of the other predella panels. Visually, this image is the least complicated of the series in that it contains the fewest figures, presents the least active foreground, and, as a result, fully reveals the simple grandeur of the landscape.

Like most central Italian artists of the late fifteenth century, Perugino was undoubtedly familiar with Piero della Francesca's *Resurrection* fresco of the early 1450s. Here, against a landscape backdrop, the risen Christ steps triumphantly from the sarcophagus above the heads of the sleeping guards. The essence of Piero's work is retained by Perugino, although the latter artist proves more successful at integrating figures into the landscape. The New York *Resurrection* is closely linked to a nearly contemporary predella panel from the San Pietro Polyptych attributed to Perugino and assistants, now in the Musée des Beaux Arts, Rouen (fig. 47). The compositions mirror one another except that the New York panel has fewer figures and landscape details. The forms of Christ and the opened sarcophagus upon which he stands are nearly identical but reversed, suggesting the possibility of a common cartoon.

The series concludes with the *Noli me Tangere (Touch Me Not)*. According to John 20: 14–20, Mary Magdalene was the first to discover the empty tomb of Christ, finding two angels where the body had been laid to rest only days earlier. This panel follows the text, illustrating that although she was the first person to encounter Christ after the Resurrection, she was told not to touch him, for he had not yet ascended to God the Father. A penitent prostitute, Mary Magdalene is one of the only women within Christ's immediate circle of followers and, most significantly, one of the few figures present at the time of his Crucifixion. This considered, it is understandable why she appears so frequently in Christian painting and sculpture and why the Noli me Tangere subject was so familiar to Renaissance audiences. Perugino's image provides all the elements described by John. In the *Noli me Tangere*, Perugino has added anecdotal figures in the middle ground and poignantly separated the main figures as he had done in *Christ and the Woman of Samaria*.

Although the figure of Mary Magdalene appears frequently in the work of Perugino, and the Noli me Tangere subject was commonly addressed in the Renaissance, this is its only depiction by Perugino. However, it should be noted that this panel is symbolically related to the third panel of the Chicago/New York series. Both Mary Magdalene and the Woman of Samaria were prostitutes. The appearance of two such subjects in a series would probably be misread if emphasis were placed on their vocation (or former vocation) and respective relationships with Christ. Instead, it is the theological connection between the aforementioned messages of promised eternal life and fulfilled resurrection represented by the scenes that is intended.

An examination of the Chicago/New York predella series as a whole reveals several important characteristics of the master's style. Primary is the concern for composition. Originally positioned at the heart of the series, *Christ and the Woman of Samaria* is arguably the most carefully organized panel. The geometric quality of the well reveals Perugino's concern for linear perspective and provides the perfect vehicle around which organic, if not balletic, figures are positioned. In this work, as in each panel, the main characters of the story are emphasized in the central foreground, and from here the viewer is led through the middle ground by those secondary figures which have been carefully, often symmetrically, positioned. As the viewer moves into the distant spaces of the background, the landscape becomes as important as the main characters encountered in the foreground. The horizon line remains constant from scene to scene, enabling the viewer to move through the series with ease. Finally, these panels collectively reveal Perugino's use of repetition for the sake of both economy and cohesion. For example, the same figure of Christ is presented in the Baptism, at the well, and before Mary Magdalene with only slight variation, and probably arose from a single design.[6] Renaissance masters like Perugino clearly recognized that this simple practice was time-efficient and supportive of compositional unity.

Each of the panels in this series has been created using a bright, almost pastel-palette. Topaz blues of sky and water gracefully extend along the dusty lime-greens of grassy valleys and hills. Carefully observed flesh tones are quiet near the high key pinks and peach-oranges encountered in several of the costumes. Of particular merit is the use of such an orange amid steel blue in the garment of the Woman of Samaria; this striking and unusual combination merges the very colors seen in the two separate articles of clothing worn by Christ in the same image. Perugino's loose brushwork encourages the liveliness of color. Paint has been applied in a sketchy manner with short strokes. Considering that the very size of predella scenes requires close examination, it is obvious that the artist wished to engage the viewer through both color and brushwork. Finally, it should be noted that every panel has a painted border intended to simulate an actual frame. A thin ochre band is found on each of the respective sides with the upper and left edges lined in black and the bottom and right edges lined in white. The effect of this border would have added to the illusion of depth originally encountered when these works were an integral part of the framework of a large Renaissance altarpiece.

Scholars have considered this series in association with two of Perugino's important altarpiece commissions in the first decade of the sixteenth century: the masterwork for the high altar of the Church of the Santissima Annunziata in Florence, which was completed in 1507, and the Chigi Altarpiece for the Church of Sant'Agostino in Siena, which was completed in 1506. The former has been traditionally discussed and widely accepted even though no mention of a predella has been found in the numerous surviving original documents.[7] The latter proposal is more recent and has renewed interest in deciphering the original context of the panels.[8] Although no consensus exists today regarding a specific context, scholars have long agreed that the panels come from a single altarpiece. The unfortunate history of an overwhelming number of Renaissance altarpieces, including several by Perugino, is that they were taken apart in later centuries: individual elements were reframed and sold as independent works of art. The Chicago/New York series were in England by the middle of the nineteenth century and remained together until 1892, when the *Resurrection* was sold separately. Christopher Lloyd was most astute in his observation that "Perugino may have regarded the compositions used in these predellas as smaller versions of large-scale works."[9] Consequently, the compositional strength of each panel enables it to stand as an independent work of art and may have contributed to the dismantling of the series more than a century ago.

NOTES

1. In addition to the Chicago and Bergamo examples, there is a version from the Signorelli Altarpiece in the Galleria Nazionale dell'Umbria, Perugia (cat. no. 10b), and a version that is part of the high altarpiece in the Church of Santa Maria, Corciano.

2. According to tradition, John and Christ were biological relatives through their mothers. In terms of their theological relationship, John is seen as the last of the great prophets and the final expression of the old law; Christ, however, is viewed as the realization of this prophecy and the beginning of the new law.

3. In addition to the aforementioned works, versions of the Baptism of Christ can also be found in the Musée des Beaux Arts, Rouen; the Kunsthistorisches Museum, Vienna; the Church of the Nunziatella, Foligno; the Duomo, Città della Pieve; and two examples in the Galleria Nazionale dell'Umbria, Perugia (fig. 45 and cat. no. 10c).

4. John 4: 13 (*The New American Bible*, Saint Joseph Edition, New York, 1986).

5. Lloyd, p. 195.

6. This is also true of the figures of Mary, the mother of Christ, in the *Adoration of the Christ Child* and Mary Magdalene in the *Noli me Tangere*.

7. The connection of the Chicago/New York series to the Annunziata Altarpiece was first proposed by Zeri in 1964 and Laclotte in 1965. The most recent and complete investigation of the surviving documents surrounding the commission and execution of this monumental project is Nelson's cited article.

8. Keith Christiansen first proposed the relationship to the Chigi Altarpiece in 1983.

9. Lloyd, p. 196.

LITERATURE*

W. Burger, *Trésors d'art exposés à Manchester en 1857*, (Paris, 1857); J. A. Crowe and G. B. Cavalcaselle, *A History of Painting in Italy* (1866); B. Berenson, *Central Italian Painters of the Renaissance* (1909); Bryson Burroughs, "A Painting by Perugino," *Bulletin of the Metropolitan Museum of Art* 6 (1911): 130–31; Bryson Burroughs, *The Metropolitan Museum of Art: Catalogue of Paintings* (New York: Metropolitan Museum of Art, 1914); U. Gnoli, *Pietro Perugino* (1923); U. Gnoli, *Pittori e miniatori* (1923); Arthur McComb, "Francesco Ubertini (Bacchiacca)," *Art Bulletin* 8 (1926): 250; Daniel Catton Rich, "The Paintings of Martin A. Ryerson," *Art Institute of Chicago Bulletin* 27 (1933): 12; Harry Wehle, *The Metropolitan Museum of Art: A Catalogue of Italian, Spanish and Byzantine Paintings* (New York: Metropolitan Museum of Art, 1940); *Tutta la pittura del Perugino* (1959); F. Zeri, "Appunti sul Lindenau-Museum di Altenburg," *Bolletino d'arte* 49 (1964): 51; *L'opera completa del Perugino* (1969); B. Fredericksen and F. Zeri, *Census of Pre-Nineteenth-Century Paintings* (1972); Denys Sutton, "A Lawyer from Philadelphia," *Apollo* 109 (1979): 387–93; F. Zeri and E. E. Gardner, *Metropolitan Museum of Art: Italian Paintings* (1980); Keith Christiansen, "Early Renaissance Narrative Painting in Italy," *Metropolitan Museum of Art Bulletin* 41, no. 2 (1983): 31–32; P. Scarpellini, *Perugino*, 1st ed. (1984); S. Ferino Pagden, *Die Kirchen von Siena* (1985); F. Todini, *La pittura umbra* (1989); C. Lloyd, *Italian Paintings before 1600* (1993); J. Nelson, "The High Altar-piece of SS. Annunziata" (1997).

---

*Works are cited in the Literature section in chronological order. Full bibliographical information for the short titles employed here may be found in the Bibliography for Literature Cited in Catalogue Commentary following the Catalogue.

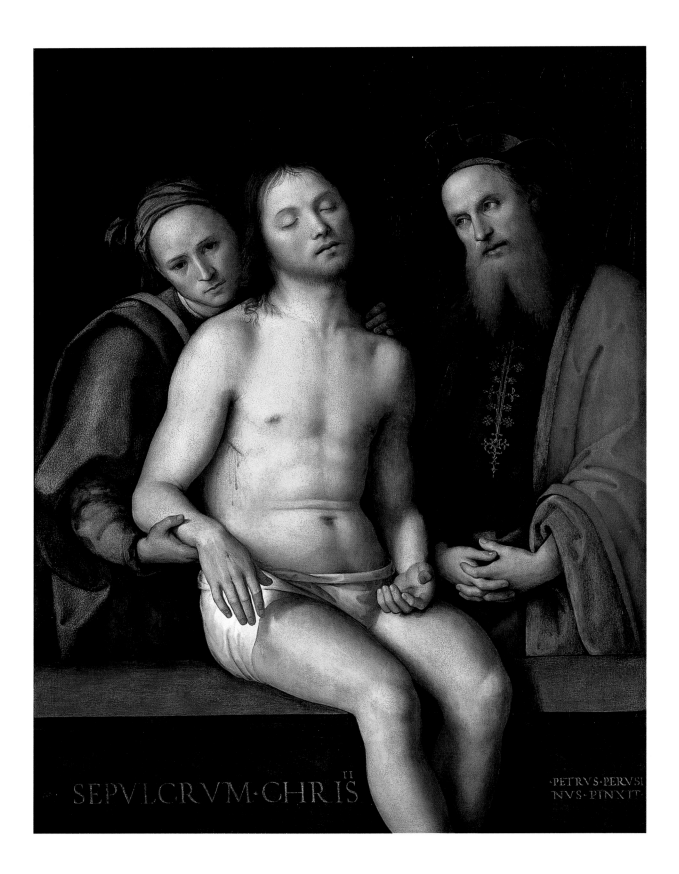

SEPVLCRVM·CHRIS͡ TI

·PETRVS·PERVSI
NVS·PINXIT·

2

SEPULCRUM CHRISTI

1498
Pietro Perugino
Oil possibly with tempera on panel, transferred to fabric on panel,
36⁷⁄₁₆ × 28¼ in. (92.6 × 71.8 cm)
Signed: SEPVLCRVM·CHRIS*TI* (at bottom left); PETRVS·PERVSI/NVS·PINXIT (at bottom right)
Sterling and Francine Clark Art Institute, Williamstown, Massachusetts (947)

PROVENANCE: 1850, (as of) Henry Labouchere, Quantock Lodge, Bridgewater, Somerset,
England; 1914(?), collection of Mrs. Edward Stanley, Quantock Lodge, Bridgewater, Somerset,
England; to P. & D. Colnaghi & Obach, London; 1914, collection of Robert Sterling Clark;
1955, bequeathed to the Sterling and Francine Clark Art Institute.

Sepulcrum Christi is a unique work in Perugino's career for its subject matter and style. The painting depicts the devotional theme of the Pietà—a sorrowful scene in which the recently expired Christ is mourned by a single figure or small group and is simultaneously presented to the viewer with the intention of soliciting a similar emotional response. Traditional representations place the deceased Christ with his mother Mary, and may involve Mary Magdalene and John the Evangelist, but this moving example includes only Joseph of Arimathaea and Nicodemus. Although the Gospels discuss the involvement of these men in the events between the death of Christ and his entombment, and Renaissance artists frequently depict them within the context of a larger group of mourners, as in the lunette of the Fano Altarpiece (fig. 48), it is unusual to encounter them alone with Christ. This is the only such version by Perugino.

    The three figures are firmly positioned at the edge of the picture plane. Space is shallow. The dark, murky background lends emphasis to the human drama taking place here. The dead Christ has been placed on the rim of a sepulcher, or tomb, and is supported from behind by the turbaned Nicodemus, who supplied myrrh and aloes to anoint the corpse.[1] Joseph stands near, gazing solemnly upon the figure that would soon fill his own tomb.[2] Through the placement of the lifeless body and the outward gaze of Nicodemus, the intimacy of the moment that these men share with Christ has been poignantly extended

Fig. 48. *Dead Christ* (*Cristo Morto*) (lunette above the *Virgin Mary and Child Enthroned*), Church of Santa Maria Nova, Fano

to include the viewer. The prominence of the physical body of Christ alludes to the Christian ritual of Communion and the Eucharist, and, by extension, the tomb calls to mind an altar table. The limp hand that Nicodemus lifts forward allows for the inspection of the wound incurred through crucifixion and is an intentional reminder of Christ's Passion. Ultimately, the carefully defined anatomy and sensual form of this central figure is intended to juxtapose death and promised resurrection, ideas of mortality and divinity. The mood of the work encourages individual devotion. This, in combination with its size, suggests the painting may have been commissioned for a private, domestic context.

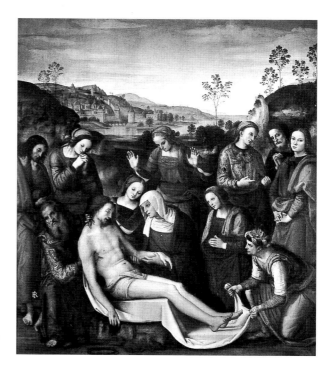

Fig. 49. *Lamentation over the Dead Christ*, Galleria Palatina, Palazzo Pitti, Florence (see pl. 11)

Fig. 50. *Portrait of Francesco delle Opere,* Galleria
degli Uffizi, Florence (see pl. 10)

Sepulcrum Christi has long been associated with one of Perugino's most celebrated
works, the enormous altarpiece, *Lamentation over the Dead Christ,* signed and dated 1495, and
now conserved in the Galleria Palatina, Florence (fig. 49).[3] In general terms, the scenes are
thematically related, even though the drama earlier painting is played out by a sizable
group of mourners. Specifically, the works contain similar figures of Christ, Joseph, and
Nicodemus. The body type and countenance of Christ are definitely based on the same
model. In the *Lamentation,* the bearded, contemplative Joseph is easily recognized as the
figure supporting the torso of Christ, and the figure in the second row, third from the
right, is clearly linked to Nicodemus in the Clark painting.[4] This practice of recreating
characters from a common model was customary for Perugino and all Renaissance masters. However, it should be noted that the attention to detail encountered in the facial features of those individuals common to both paintings parallels Perugino's talents as
portraitist, as evidenced in the nearly contemporary *Portrait of Francesco delle Opere* of 1494
(fig. 50).[5]

   Any examination of the Clark painting would be incomplete without a discussion
of color. The success of the unfailingly rich, if not velvet, palette begins with the blackened background and extends forward in numerous passages of shadow. The red of
Joseph's garment is intensified by its blue trim, just as the lavender sleeve enhances the

green of Nicodemus' cloak. Such color frames the golden flesh tones of Christ's body. Among Italian painters of this period, few displayed such sensitivity to color as did the Venetians. Perugino himself is recorded in Venice in 1494 and 1495 (see Chronicle 1494, 1495); undoubtedly, his experiences there amidst the works of the Bellini family inform the palette of the *Sepulcrum Christi*, the *Lamentation*, and other paintings of this period.

NOTES

1. "Nicodemus, the one who had first come to him at night, also came bringing a mixture of myrrh and aloes weighing about one hundred pounds" (John 19: 39, cited from *The New American Bible*, Saint Joseph Edition).

2. "When it was evening , there came a rich man from Arimathaea named Joseph, who was himself a disciple of Jesus. He went to Pilate and asked for the body of Jesus; then Pilate ordered it to be handed over. Taking the body, Joseph wrapped it [in] linen and laid it in his new tomb that he had hewn in the rock" (Matthew 27: 57–59, cited from *The New American Bible*, Saint Joseph Edition).

3. The relationship of the *Sepulcrum Christi* to the *Lamentation* was pointed out as early as 1857 by G. F. Waagen in his *Treasures of Great Britain*, when the former work was in Somerset, England. The *Lamentation*, 84 5/16 × 76 13/16 in., was originally created for the nuns of Santa Chiara in Florence.

4. Some scholars recognize the figure at the feet of Christ in the *Lamentation* as Nicodemus.

5. Although the portrait, 20½ × 17 5/16 in., was briefly attributed to Raphael, it was correctly ascribed to Perugino in 1815; since 1833, it has been in the Galleria degli Uffizi, Florence.

LITERATURE

Gustav Friedrich Waagen, *Treasures of Great Britain* (London, 1854–57); J. A. Crowe and G. B. Cavalcaselle, *A History of Painting in Italy* (1866); B. Berenson, *Central Italian Painters of the Renaissance* (1909); U. Gnoli, *Pietro Perugino* (1923); Alfred Frankfurter, "Now the Old Masters at Williamstown," *Art News* 56, no. 8 (1957): 52; Helen Comstock, "The Connoisseur in America: Old Masters in the Clark Collection," *Connoisseur* 134, no. 566 (1957): 278; Carlo L. Ragghianti, "La Collezione Clark," *Sele Arte* 34 (1958): 36; *Tutta la pittura del Perugino* (1959); *Sterling and Francine Clark Art Institute, Italian Paintings and Drawings* (Williamstown: The Sterling and Francine Clark Art Institute, 1961); B. Fredericksen and F. Zeri, *Census of Pre-Nineteenth-Century Italian Paintings* (1972); *List of Paintings in the Sterling and Francine Clark Art Institute* (Williamstown: The Sterling and Francine Clark Art Institute, 1972); Francis Russell, "Two Italian Madonnas," *Burlington Magazine* 120, no. 900 (1978): 152; Samson Lane Faison Jr., *The Art Museums of New England: Massachusetts* (Boston: D. R. Godine, 1982, revised edition of S. L. Faison Jr., *Guide to the Art Museums of New England*, New York: Harcourt Brace, 1958); P. Scarpellini, *Perugino*, 1st ed. (1984); D. A. Brown, *Andrea Solario* (Milan: Electa, 1987).

3

KNEELING FIGURE AND TWO HEADS

n.d.
Pietro Perugino
Metalpoint drawing on prepared paper, 8⅝ × 5⅜ in. (21.9 × 13.7 cm)
Sterling and Francine Clark Art Institute, Williamstown, Massachusetts (1458)

PROVENANCE: n.d., collection of Count Giovanni Carlo Conestabile; n.d., collection of
J. P. Heseltine (with L. 1507 on reverse); 1917, acquired by R. S. Clark from Colnaghi, London;
1955, bequeathed to the Sterling and Francine Clark Art Institute.

RENAISSANCE MASTERS EXECUTED and employed a wide variety of drawings. Figure studies, compositional sketches, and full-scale preparatory works, or cartoons, were a vital means to an end in the creation of both panel paintings and frescoes. For prolific masters like Perugino, drawings were central to the success of an active workshop and a single drawing could be easily and efficiently utilized in the creation of several paintings. This well-preserved sheet from the Sterling and Francine Clark Art Institute is a preliminary study that may have been instrumental in the creation of several devotional images painted by Perugino from 1496 through 1500.[1]

A full-length kneeling figure is the primary focus of the drawing. Emphasis has been placed on an accurate rendering of the subject's cumbersome garment in relation to the position of the body. Although the head of this figure is loosely addressed, a more detailed study of the face and its features appears directly above. Toward the top right of the sheet is a sensitive examination of another, unrelated head shown in near profile.

The kneeling figure and the head above it are closely associated with a stock character that appears in paintings Perugino executed for confraternities, or companies, such as the *Saint Augustine with Members of the Confraternity of Perugia*, c. 1500 (fig. 51) and the *Madonna of the Confraternity of the Consolazione*, 1496–98 (fig. 76). These confraternities were fraternal organizations sanctioned by the church. As lay brothers, members dedicated themselves to anonymous acts of charity and goodwill. The traditional hooded costumes they wore were ecclesiastical in air and intended to cloak the identity of the individual.[2] In both paintings, confraternity members similar to the one found in the Clark drawing are shown gathered around a large, central figure—the group's patron saint.

Fig. 51. *Saint Augustine with Members of the Confraternity of Perugia,*
Carnegie Museum of Art, Pittsburgh, Acquired through
the generosity of Mrs. Alan M. Scaife

The figure in the drawing offers a most obvious comparison to the forward-most figure at the right of the saint in each painting.[3] Specifically, the upward gaze and tilt of the head encountered is most closely allied with that of the confraternity member in the Saint Augustine panel. Perugino could easily have utilized this cursory sketch of a kneeling form as the basis for a cartoon, which in turn would result in a painted image. A cartoon for the seated Saint Augustine (fig. 52) is preserved in the Kupferstichkabinett, Berlin. It shares the concern for accuracy in the fit of the garment to the figure and echoes the sure, yet delicate draftsmanship encountered in the Clark drawing.

Fig. 52. *Preparatory drawing for Saint Augustine,*
Kupferstichkabinett, Staatliche Museen
zu Berlin—Preussischer Kulturbesitz

NOTES

1. In addition to the *Madonna of the Confraternity of the Consolazione* and the *Saint Augustine with Members of the Confraternity of Perugia* discussed, Perugino and his workshop also executed a *Saint Francis and Four Members of the Flagellant Confraternity* (Galleria Nazionale dell'Umbria, Perugia) in 1499 (fig. 16).

2. F. Santi, *Gonfaloni umbri del Rinascimento* (1976).

3. If the figure in the drawing were reversed, it would be comparable to the figure to the left of the saint in each painting. Such a drawing, with the figure reversed, is found in the Metropolitan Museum of Art (1972.118.263). For a more complete discussion of such practices, see B. Cole's essay in this catalogue.

LITERATURE

O. Fischel, "Die Zeichnungen der Umber" (1917); Sterling and Francine Clark Art Institute, *Italian Paintings and Drawings* (Williamstown: The Sterling and Francine Clark Art Institute, 1961); Gordon Bailey Washburn, "Two Notable Pictures for Pittsburgh," *Carnegie Magazine* (1962): 41–44; H. Bull Teilman, *Catalogue of the Painting Collection* (Pittsburgh: Carnegie Institute Museum of Art, 1973).

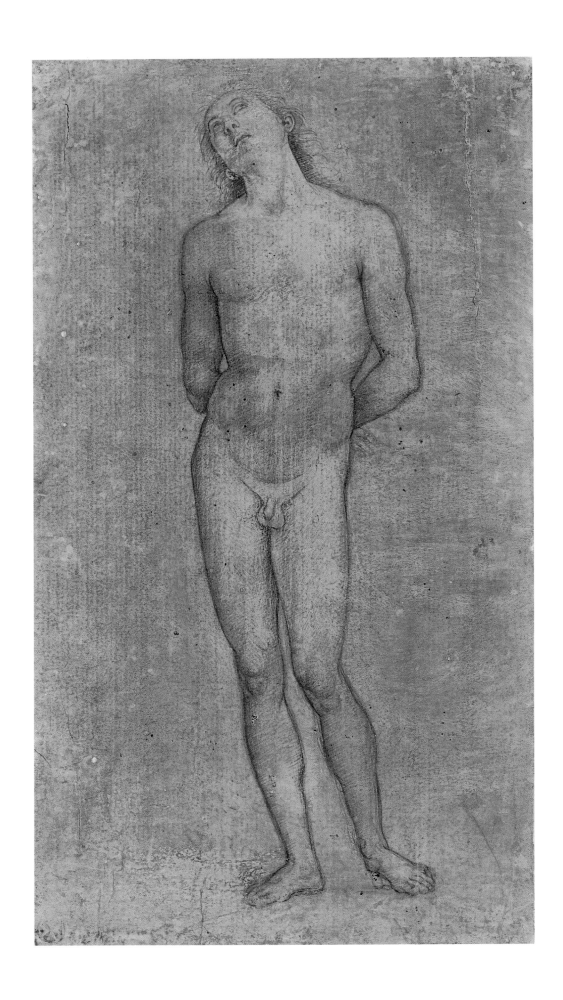

4

SAINT SEBASTIAN

c. 1493
Pietro Perugino
Metalpoint on prepared paper, 10¹/₁₆ × 5¾ in. (25.6 × 14.6 cm)
The Cleveland Museum of Art, Dudley P. Allen Fund (1958.411)

PROVENANCE: c. 1820, collection of Count Moriz von Fries, Vienna; n.d., collection of the
Prince of Liechtenstein; 1958, purchased by the Cleveland Museum of Art from
Herbert N. Bier, London.

SAINT SEBASTIAN, the subject of this striking drawing from the Cleveland Museum
of Art, is one of the most recognizable figures in the history of Christian art and a prominent personality in Renaissance imagery. Ironically, little is known of this late-third-
century martyr and saint from ancient Rome. Tradition holds that Sebastian was an officer
of the Praetorian guard during the reign of Emperor Diocletian (A.D. 284–305) and a secret convert to Christianity. When his faith was revealed, he was condemned to death. First
he was stripped of his armor, then bound and placed before an executioner's squad of
archers. His legend maintains that miraculously none of the arrows pierced his organs, and
although gravely wounded and left for dead, he was nursed to health only to return before the emperor physically restored and spiritually strengthened. Sebastian was again condemned, clubbed to death and his body cast into the sewers of Rome. In the following
centuries, the legend of his deliverance and restoration was emphasized and he was viewed
by the faithful as a protector against illness, especially the plague.[1]

Renaissance masters were often called upon to portray Saint Sebastian, a symbol of
hope and deliverance, as a part of a pious group or as a singular devotional image. Perugino represented the saint in at least eleven paintings throughout the course of his career,
beginning as early as 1478.[2] The Cleveland drawing has been traditionally linked to two
works the artist executed at the height of his career, *Virgin Mary and Child with Saints John the
Baptist and Sebastian* (fig. 28), signed and dated 1493, in the Galleria degli Uffizi, and the
nearly contemporary *Saint Sebastian* (fig. 53) in the Musée du Louvre.[3] Specifically, these
painted versions of the saint mirror the soft athletic body, graceful *contrapposto* pose, and
upward-looking, otherworldly gaze presented in the drawing. Close inspection of the

Fig. 53. *Saint Sebastian*, Musée du Louvre, Paris (see pl. 9)

Fig. 54. Master of the Gubbio Cross, *Cross with Two Sides*, verso: *Flagellation with Two Angels and a Bishop*, Galleria Nazionale dell'Umbria, Perugia

drawing reveals that the outline contour of the figure has been emphasized. Such emphasis suggests that it may have been a popular model traced and copied often within the context of Perugino's active workshop.

Artists of the Renaissance welcomed the opportunity to portray Saint Sebastian, for the subject served as a vehicle to express their quasi-scientific knowledge of human anatomy. The figure encountered in the Cleveland drawing undoubtedly results from Perugino's study of the male nude. It is surely indebted to the tradition of anatomical truth initiated by Masaccio in the 1420s and clearly revealed in the paintings and prints executed by Antonio del Pollaiuolo in the 1460s and 1470s.[4] This considered, it is interesting to note that Perugino's nude also maintains the lyrical movement and softness of musculature encountered in late thirteenth- and early fourteenth-century imagery like that of the painted crucifix given to the Master of the Gubbio Cross. An image of the Flagellation (fig. 54) appears on one side of this work. Here, one encounters the gentle S-curve of the torso and delicate positioning of the feet which typify many of Perugino's representations of Saint Sebastian.

NOTES

1. For further discussion of the saint and his attributes, see James Hall, *Dictionary of Subjects and Symbols in Art* (New York: Harper & Row, 1974), pp. 276–77.

2. The earliest example (fig. 4) is the *Saint Sebastian* fresco, Church of Santa Maria Assunta, Cerqueto, which has been dated as early as 1473 by some, while others maintain the 1478 date from a modern inscription painted beneath the work. Other examples include: *Saint Sebastian,* panel, National Museum, Stockholm; *Saint Sebastian* (head and torso only), panel, The Hermitage Museum, St. Petersburg; *Saint Sebastian,* canvas, Museo de Arte, São Paolo; *Madonna and Child with Saints Nicholas of Tolentino, Bernardino of Siena, Jerome, and Sebastian* (executed with Eusebio da San Giorgio), panel, Galleria Nazionale dell'Umbria, Perugia (fig. 108); *Martyrdom of Saint Sebastian* from the *Ghastlier Manuscript,* British Museum, London; *Martyrdom of Saint Sebastian,* fresco, Church of San Sebastiano, Panicale (pl. 19); *Saint Irene and Saint Sebastian* (from the Sant'Agostino Polpytych), panel, Musée des Beaux Arts, Grenoble; and *Martyrdom of Saint Sebastian,* panel, Galleria Nazionale dell'Umbria, Perugia (fig. 94).

3. The Uffizi panel is signed on a scroll attached to Mary's throne, "PETRVS. PERVSINVS. PINXIT. MCCCCLXXXX.III." It was commissioned for the Salviati family chapel in the Church of San Domenico, Fiesole. The Louvre panel has been dated to 1493–97.

4. A pivotal work toward the accurate representation of the human nude is Masaccio's *Expulsion,* c. 1425, in the Brancacci Chapel, Church of Santa Maria del Carmine, Florence. Closer to Perugino are the anatomical investigations as expressed in Antonio del Pollaiuolo's engraving, *Battle of the Ten Nudes,* 1465, and the *Martyrdom of Sebastian,* 1475, National Gallery, London.

LITERATURE

A Year in Review, Bulletin of The Cleveland Museum of Art 46 (1959); Louise E. Richards, "Three Early Italian Drawings," *Bulletin of The Cleveland Museum of Art* 49, no. 7 (1962): 171–73; *L'opera completa del Perugino* (1969); *Handbook of The Cleveland Museum of Art* (Cleveland: Cleveland Museum of Art, 1978); "Pérugin et l'école ombrienne," *Revue du Louvre* 29 (1979): 479; P. Scarpellini, *Perugino,* 1st ed. (1984); Daniela Parenti, "Maestro della Croce di Gubbio," catalogue entry in *Dipinti, sculture e ceramiche* (1994); *Drawings in Midwestern Collections,* vol. 1, *Early Works,* ed. Burton Dunbar and Edward Olszewski (Columbia and London: University of Missouri Press, 1996).

5

MADONNA AND CHILD

c. 1500
Pietro Perugino
Tempera on panel, 31¾ × 25½ in. (80.7 × 64.8 cm)
The Detroit Institute of Arts, Bequest of Eleanor Clay Ford (77.3)

PROVENANCE: 1784, collection of Francesco Baglioni, Perugia; 1828, Giovanni Metzger
(dealer), Florence; 1831, collection of Ludwig I, King of Bavaria, Bavaria; 1850, on deposit at the
Alte Pinakothek, Munich; 1925, Drey collection (dealer), Munich, sold by exchange to Duveen
Brothers, London/New York; 1927, collection of John D. Rockefeller Jr., New York; 1930,
Duveen Brothers, New York; 1932, collection of Mr. and Mrs. Edsel B. Ford, Detroit; 1977,
bequeathed by Eleanor Clay Ford (Mrs. Edsel Ford) to The Detroit Institute of Arts.

IT HAS BEEN SUGGESTED that Perugino's immense popularity in the final decades
of the fifteenth century and the opening years of the sixteenth century was based on the
otherworldliness and predictability of his style.[1] This notion is certainly confirmed when
one considers the serene *Madonna and Child*, c. 1500, from the Detroit Institute of Arts and
the master's related Marian imagery of the period (see Abbott). At first the figures seem
as familiar as any young mother and child encountered in a portrait, yet they are intended
as sacred ideals in human form, majestic and removed. Perugino was certainly fortunate
in that, as a prolific painter and skillful workshop master, his visions were perfectly
matched with the Renaissance's long-established and seemingly insatiable demand for
images of Mary and the infant Christ. A recent survey of Perugino's career reveals that
such imagery is the central theme of more than thirty surviving works.[2]

The Detroit panel fits securely within a prominent group of related paintings executed between 1493 and 1504—a period that parallels the very height of the master's pop-
uarity.[3] Shown frontally, the seated maiden and cherubic son appear with slight variations
in private devotional works, large altarpieces, and even frescoes. The moderate size of this
painting, in combination with its connection to the Baglioni household, suggests that it
was probably intended for private devotion in a domestic context. Four closely related versions of the Detroit panel are known, testifying to both the appeal of this type of image
and the significance of its function for Renaissance audiences.[4] In each, the very position

Fig. 55. Marino di Elemosina, *Madonna and Child, Angels, and Saints Paul and Peter Celestino*, Galleria Nazionale dell'Umbria, Perugia

and gestures of Mary and the Christ Child are maintained or simply reversed, supporting the notion that the paintings resulted from a common preparatory drawing, or cartoon. Although such practices may seem foreign compared to our modern ideas about originality and art, Renaissance masters like Perugino commonly reemployed successful cartoons in order to sustain the esteem of their reputation, fulfill the desires of patrons, and facilitate the productivity of an active workshop (see Cole).

An examination of the Detroit *Madonna and Child* provides the opportunity to consider several fundamental elements which brought its creator such widespread acclaim. Perugino and his contemporaries sought to construct visions of divine, otherworldly personalities that were familiarly human yet ideally angelic. There can be little doubt that such visions are the heirs of the masters and monuments first available to him in Perugia. Certainly Perugino's earliest exposure to the courtly beauty of early Renaissance painting, as

Fig. 56. Gentile da Fabriano, *Madonna and Child Enthroned with Angels*, Galleria Nazionale dell'Umbria, Perugia

exemplified in the work of Marino di Elemosina (fig. 55) and Gentile da Fabriano (fig. 56), was significant.[5] However, the impact of more current representations of Mary and the Christ Child, as expressed by Fra Angelico in the San Domenico Altarpiece (fig. 57) and Piero della Francesca in the Sant'Antonio Altarpiece (fig. 58), was profound.[6] In fact, Perugino's concept of the Madonna and Child relies on the sweet serenity of the former, yet maintains the sober, if not solemn, distance of the latter. Color in this work is triumphantly rich. Mary wears a ruby tunic encased in a lapis cloak. Flesh tones are warm, nearly golden, against an ethereal palette of blues employed for earth, sky, and costume. Embroidery is imitated by pencil-thin gilding beneath the Virgin's neckline and along the cloak's trim. The star on her left shoulder is not a personal ornament but a reference to her title, *Stella Maris,* "Star of the Sea," and refers to the protection she offers sailors and travelers.

Fig. 57. Fra Angelico, *Madonna and Child Enthroned with Angels* (central panel, San Domenico Altarpiece), Galleria Nazionale dell'Umbria, Perugia

Fig. 58. Piero della Francesca, *Madonna and Child Enthroned* (detail, Sant'Antonio Altarpiece), Galleria Nazionale dell'Umbria, Perugia

Perugino's contemporary *Madonna and Child* in the National Gallery of Art, Washington, D.C. (fig. 20), is clearly related to the Detroit panel. Although Mary's pose differs, her form is based on the same model. All the other elements which make up the presented visual and the suggested spiritual effects are preserved.

NOTES

1. Pope-Hennessy, p. 20.

2. See Scarpellini.

3. This time frame is established by the completion dates of two prominent paintings signed by Perugino: the *Virgin Mary and Child with Saints John the Baptist and Sebastian* of 1493, Galleria degli Uffizi, Florence (fig. 28), and the *Adoration of the Magi* of 1504, in the Oratory of the Bianchi, Città della Pieve (pl. 18).

4. *Madonna and Child between Saint Rose and Saint Catherine, and Two Angels*, Musée du Louvre, Paris (fig. 19); *Madonna and Child with Saint John the Baptist*, Staedelsches Kunstinstitut, Frankfurt (fig. 21); *Madonna and Child between Saints Rose (?) and Catherine of Alexandria*, Kunsthistorisches Museum, Vienna (fig. 22); and *Madonna and Child with Two Saints*, Palazzo Pitti, Florence. As noted, each version includes intercessory saints flanking the Madonna and Child. The Detroit panel is the only Marian image at this period of Perugino's career to singularly address Mary and the infant Christ.

5. This artist is also known as Marino da Perugia.

6. Fra Angelico's altarpiece, c. 1447, was painted for the Guidalotti Chapel in the Church of San Domenico, Perugia. Piero's monumental work was originally found in the Church of Sant'Antonio at the Porta Sant'Angelo, Perugia. The c. 1460–70 dating follows the research of Keith Christiansen, "Alcune osservazioni critiche sulla pala di Perugia e sulla sua collocazione nella carriera di Piero della Francesca," in *Piero della Francesca. Il polittico di Sant'Antonio*, ed. V. Garibaldi (Perugia: Electa Editori Umbri, 1993). Both works are preserved in the Galleria Nazionale dell'Umbria, Perugia.

LITERATURE

J. A. Crowe and G. B. Cavalcaselle, *A History of Painting in Italy* (1866); Ivan Lermolieff (G. Morelli), *Kunstkritische Studien uber italienische Malerei—Die Galerien zu München und Dresden* (Leipzig, 1891); B. Berenson, *Central Italian Painters of the Renaissance* (1909); W. Bombe, *Perugino* (1914); F. Canuti, *Il Perugino* (1931); L. Venturi, "A Pietro Perugino" (1932); *Tutta la pittura del Perugino* (1959); F. Zeri, "Appunti sul Lindenau-Museum di Altenburg," *Bolletino d'arte* 49 (1964): 51; F. R. Shapley, *Paintings from the Samuel H. Kress Collection* (1968); *L'opera completa del Perugino* (1969); B. Fredericksen and F. Zeri, *Census of Pre-Nineteenth-Century Paintings* (1972); Frederick J. Cummings, "Annual Report 1976–1977," *Bulletin of the Detroit Institute of Arts* 56, no. 1 (1977): 9; John Pope-Hennessy, "The Ford Italian Paintings," *Bulletin of the Detroit Institute of Arts* 57, no. 1 (1979): 15–23; F. Zeri and E. E. Gardner, *Metropolitan Museum of Art: Italian Paintings* (1980); D. A. Brown, *Raphael and America* (1983); Keith Christiansen, "Early Renaissance Narrative Painting in Italy," *Metropolitan Museum of Art Bulletin* 41, no. 2 (1983): 31–32; P. Scarpellini, *Perugino*, 1st ed. (1984); S. Ferino Pagden, *Die Kirchen von Siena* (1985); F. Todini, *La pittura umbra* (1989); C. Lloyd, *Italian Paintings before 1600* (1993); J. Nelson, "The High Altar-piece of SS. Annunziata" (1997).

6

SCENES FROM THE LIFE OF
SAINT NICHOLAS OF TOLENTINO

SAINT NICHOLAS OF TOLENTINO (c. 1246–1305) was an Augustinian hermit whose life was devoted to preaching and good works. He is associated with numerous miracles and, like Saints Sebastian and Roch, was frequently invoked for protection and deliverance from dire illness and plague. His canonization in 1446, combined with the popularity of the Augustinian order, made Nicholas a favorite subject in Renaissance painting. In each of these panels from the Detroit Institute of Arts, Nicholas is shown in the traditional black habit of the order, performing the very type of wondrous acts that endeared him to the faithful in Italy and Spain from the fifteenth through the seventeenth centuries. The delicate size, rectangular format, and narrative content of both works strongly suggest that they were originally part of the predella of a large altarpiece.

In the first panel, *Saint Nicholas of Tolentino Rescuing a Boy from Drowning*, the saint is shown rescuing a youth from a narrow stream. The event is witnessed by a nun in Augustinian habit kneeling at the left and two men in contemporary dress at the right. Behind the nun are two anecdotal figures apparently deep in conversation and a mule standing before a simple stone farmhouse. The remainder of the middle ground and distance is devoted to receding hillsides and valleys, undoubtedly inspired by the tranquil terrain of the Umbrian countryside. Although the sky is a light, soft, atmospheric blue, the dominant tone of the immediate landscape is a rather sober palette of olive green and brown. Rather surprising, yet tantalizing to the eye, is the vibrant pink used to describe portions of the costume of the drowning boy, the witnesses to the right, and one of the two figures standing in the arched doorway of the farmhouse. The entire scene is bordered by a dark gray-green band painted with thin stripes of black and white to enhance the illusion of a frame.

6a SAINT NICHOLAS OF TOLENTINO RESCUING A BOY FROM DROWNING

c. 1500
Circle of Perugino
Tempera on panel, 10½ × 20½ in. (26.7 × 52.1 cm)
The Detroit Institute of Arts, Gift of Ralph Harman Booth (27.10)

PROVENANCE: until 1923, Alphonse Kahn collection, Paris; 1927, American Art Association;
1927, sold (as Raphael) to Ralph H. Booth and donated to the museum.

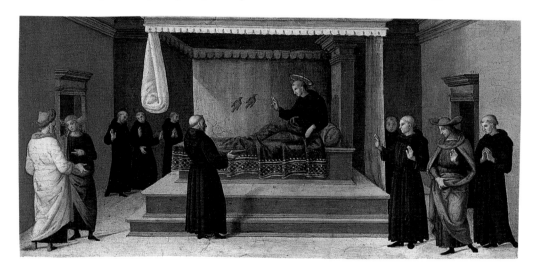

6b SAINT NICHOLAS OF TOLENTINO RESTORING TWO PARTRIDGES TO LIFE

c. 1500
Circle of Perugino
Tempera on panel, 10¼ × 20½ in. (26 × 52.1 cm)
The Detroit Institute of Arts, Founders Society Purchase,
Elizabeth Champe Fund (25.146)

PROVENANCE: until 1925, Alessandro Contini Bonacossi, Florence and Rome;
1925, museum purchase (as Raphael).

Fig. 59. Raphael, *Saint Jerome Punishing the Heretic Sabinian*, North Carolina Museum of Art, Raleigh, Purchased with funds from Mrs. Nancy Susan Reynolds, the Sarah Graham Kenan Foundation, Julius H. Weitzner, and the State of North Carolina

Fig. 60. Follower of Perugino, *Nativity*, Minneapolis Institute of Arts, Gift of John R. Van Derlip in memory of Ethel Morrison Van Derlip

The second panel, *Saint Nicholas of Tolentino Restoring Two Partridges to Life*, re-creates one of the most popular legends associated with the saint. According to tradition, Nicholas, shown here on the bed in the middle of the room, had become gravely ill and was offered roasted partridges in order to regain his strength. His love of animals prevented him from eating the birds; consequently, he restored their lives by making the sign of the cross over them. This panel depicts the very moment of resurrection as the birds take flight amidst an astounded audience of both Augustinian monks in their simple black robes and three colorfully attired, secular figures. This miracle is staged in a typical Renaissance bedroom with a large, stepped bed in the center. The dusty rose walls and terra-cotta floor underscore the grand simplicity of the event. This panel has the same border employed in *Saint Nicholas of Tolentino Rescuing a Boy from Drowning*.

A third predella panel, *Saint Nicholas of Tolentino Saving Two Hanged Men*, in a private collection, has been discussed in association with the two Detroit panels.[1] Beyond the similar subject matter, the relationship is supported by the nearly identical size and comparable style displayed by all three works. The addition of this third scene would complete the predella of a sizable altarpiece.[2] The history of these three panels parallels that of so many Renaissance predelle: the series was first removed from the altarpiece base, and then the panels were separated, reframed, and sold as independent works of art. It is through good fortune that two of the panels were reunited in Detroit in 1927.

The artistic paternity of *Saint Nicholas of Tolentino Rescuing a Boy from Drowning* and *Saint Nicholas of Tolentino Restoring Two Partridges to Life* has been disputed. Attributions to Perugino and to his well-known students, from Eusebio da San Giorgio to, most intriguingly, Raphael, have been considered. The concern for the landscape in the first panel and the pose of many of the figures in both works derive from Perugino. However, these figures lack the fluidity and sculptural presence encountered in predella scenes by Perugino such as the *Marriage of the Virgin* from the 1497 altarpiece in Santa Maria Nova, Fano. Some scholars have pursued an attribution to the young Raphael, but an examination of his early predella panel, *Saint Jerome Punishing the Heretic Sabinian* (fig. 59), restates the very arguments present in an attribution to Perugino.[3] In any thorough examination of Perugino's works, one must acknowledge numerous quality paintings executed by his students and followers. In fact, the charm and aesthetic merit of the Detroit panels, like that of the *Nativity* in the Minneapolis Institute of Arts (fig. 60), place them among the most respectable images securely given to an anonymous follower of Perugino.

NOTES

1. This work was formerly part of the Schiff collection, Rome. It was first illustrated in connection with the two Detroit panels by Berenson in the 1968 edition of his work from 1909 (p. 123, illus. no. 1158), with the attribution of Eusebio da San Giorgio. The current location of this work is unknown.

2. In an unpublished catalogue entry written in 1982 for the Detroit Institute of Arts, Burton Fredericksen (pp. 2, 4–5) suggests that the predella may have been complete with the three panels thus considered. He discounts the inclusion of a fourth panel depicting another miracle of Saint Nicholas in the Sedgwick Collection, University of California at Santa Barbara.

3. This attribution was promoted by Valentiner, while Venturi linked the Detroit panels to Raphael's *Coronation of Saint Nicholas of Tolentino* Altarpiece painted in 1500–1501.

LITERATURE

B. Berenson, *Central Italian Painters of the Renaissance* (1909); U. Gnoli, *Pittori e miniatori* (1923); Wilhelm Reinhold Valentiner, "Two Predella Pictures," *Bulletin of the Detroit Institute of Arts* 7 (1925): 29–30; "Zwei Predellen zu Raffaels frühestem Altarwerk," in *Festschrift für Max J. Friedländer zum 60. Geburtstage* (Leipzig: Verlag von E. A. Seemann, 1927), 244–58; Detroit Institute of Arts, *Catalogue of Paintings in the Permanent Collection of the Detroit Institute of Arts of the City of Detroit* (Detroit: Detroit Institute of Arts, 1930); R. van Marle, *The Development of the Italian Schools of Painting* (1937); A. Venturi, "Quattro parti di predella raffaellesca," *L'Arte* 43 (1940): 134–39; Wilhelm Reinhold Valentiner, "Note on the two Raphael Predella Panels," *Bulletin of the Detroit Institute of Arts* 20 (1941): 70–72; Detroit Institute of Arts, *Catalogue of Paintings* (Detroit: Detroit Institute of Arts, 1944); Carlo Volpe, "Notizia e discussione zu Raffaello giovane," *Arte antica e moderna* 17 (1962): 80; Detroit Institute of Arts, *Paintings Checklist* (Detroit: Detroit Institute of Arts, 1965); Luitpold Dussler, *Raphael: A Critical Catalogue of His Pictures, Wall-paintings and Tapestries*, trans. Sebastian Cruft (London: Phaidon, 1971); B. Fredericksen and F. Zeri, *Census of Pre-Nineteenth-Century Paintings* (1972); S. Beguin, "Un nouveau Raphael: un ange du retable de Saint Nicolas de Tolentino," *Revue du Louvre* 32 (1982): 113; B. Fredericksen, unpublished catalogue entries for the Detroit Institute of Arts, 1982; D. A. Brown, *Raphael and America* (1983); F. Todini, *La pittura umbra* (1989).

7

BEATO GIACOMO DELLA MARCA
(Blessed James of the Marches)

c. 1512
Pietro Perugino
Tempera on canvas, 63³⁄₁₆ × 34½ in. (160.5 × 87.5 cm)
Galleria Nazionale dell'Umbria, Perugia (no. 241)

PROVENANCE: by 1532, Company of Saint Jerome, Perugia; late eighteenth century, church of
San Francesco al Prato, Perugia; 1810, transferred to the Accademia di Belle Arti, now in the
Galleria Nazionale dell'Umbria.

ALTHOUGH RELATIVELY UNKNOWN TODAY, Saint James of the Marches (1394–
1476) was a revered and, at times, controversial figure in the church of the fifteenth century. He was born into poverty at Montebrandone (Marches of Ancona), traveled to
Assisi to join the Franciscan Order, studied with the immensely popular preacher, Bernardino of Siena, and later read law at Perugia. James led a penitential lifestyle, hardly eating
and sleeping. As an influential preacher in his own right, he traveled throughout Italy into
Hungary and Bosnia. Itinerant preaching became an essential part of his life. James is
known to have refused ecclesiastical promotions which would have interfered with his zeal
for evangelizing; according to legend, he is said to have preached at least once every day
for forty consecutive years. During his life, James was immersed in the controversies between the various branches of the Franciscan Order and was denounced for his views regarding the precious nature of the blood of Christ. In later years, he became embroiled in
the controversies between the Dominicans and the Franciscans. Unlike his mentor Bernardino, who was canonized, or sainted, soon after his death, James was not canonized until
1726. At the time Perugino painted this image, James was beatified, a posthumous decla-
ration of heavenly stature and a precursor to canonization, hence the title, *Blessed James of
the Marches.*

This painting was commissioned as a *gonfalone* (processional banner) for the Company of Saint Jerome in Perugia.[1] The commission was well-suited to the confraternity, for Jerome, like James, was a popular penitential saint. In his *Blessed James of the
Marches,* Perugino presents the saint at the very edge of the picture plane. He is dressed
in the simple brown robes characteristic of the Franciscans and is posed in the classical

Fig. 61. *Saint Anthony of Padua*, Church of Santa Croce, Florence

Fig. 62. *Saint Anthony of Padua and a Patron*, Pinacoteca Comunale, Bettona

contrapposto position. The lowered left hand holds a book while the right hand raises up a small reliquary upon which is inscribed "SANGUINE CRISTE" (Blood of Christ), a reference to James' beliefs regarding the precious nature of the blood of Christ.[2] A few paces behind the figure is a low wall separating the saint from the barren landscape in the distance. The pose of the figure and general compositional format of this work are reiterated in several other paintings by Perugino. A panel, *Saint Anthony of Padua*, in the Church of Santa Croce, Florence (fig. 61), and a banner representing the same subject in the Pinacoteca Comunale, Bettona (fig. 62), differ little from the *Blessed James* except for the depiction of the heads (fig. 63) and the attributes held in the right hands. It is logical to consider that the paintings result from a single preparatory drawing, or cartoon. In fact, a drawing in the Uffizi (fig. 24) is probably the sketch for that very cartoon.[3] The prominence of the figure in each painting versus the simplicity of the background encourages devotional focus and would have been highly effective as the banners were moved within the context of ceremonial processions.

Fig. 63. *Blessed James of the Marches* (detail, cat. no. 7)

NOTES

1. Inventory lists from 1532 for the Company of Saint Jerome discuss the work, but an earlier list of 1517 does not mention it, leading some scholars to date the work immediately following 1517.

2. The reliquary is typical of those produced in Perugia during the Renaissance and has been compared to the Reliquary of Santa Spina conserved in the convent of San Francesco al Prato; see F. Santi, *Galleria Nazionale dell'Umbria a Perugia* (1955), pp. 111–12.

3. For further discussion of this drawing, please see the essay by R. Mencarelli in this catalogue. The drawing has been variously attributed to Perugino, his workshop, and his followers.

LITERATURE

J. A. Crowe and G. B. Cavalcaselle, *A History of Painting in Italy* (1866); M. Guardabassi, *Indice-guida* (1872); B. Berenson, *Central Italian Painters of the Renaissance* (1909); A. Venturi, *Storia dell'arte italiana* (1913); W. Bombe, *Perugino* (1914); U. Gnoli, *Pietro Perugino* (1923); Jean Alazard, *Pérugin* (Paris: Henri Laurens, 1927); F. Canuti, *Il Perugino* (1931); R. van Marle, *The Development of the Italian Schools of Painting* (1937); F. Santi, *Galleria Nazionale dell'Umbria a Perugia* (1955); *Tutta la pittura del Perugino* (1959); F. Santi, *IV Mostra di opere restaurante* (1963); *L'opera completa del Perugino* (1969); *Pittura in Umbria tra il 1480–1540* (1983); P. Scarpellini, *Perugino*, 1st ed. (1984); F. Santi, *Dipinti* (1985); F. Todini, *La pittura umbra* (1989).

8

CRISTO MORTO
(Dead Christ)

1495
Pietro Perugino
Oil on panel, 21⅞ × 22½ in. (55.5 × 57 cm)
Galleria Nazionale dell'Umbria, Perugia (no. 248)

PROVENANCE: through 1797, Chapel of the *Decemviri*, Palazzo dei Priori, Perugia; 1863,
transferred to the Pinacoteca Vannucci, now the Galleria Nazionale dell'Umbria.

IN 1483 PERUGINO RECEIVED an important commission from the *Decemviri*, the
ten communal magistrates of the city of Perugia, to paint a grand altarpiece for their private chapel in that city's town hall, the Palazzo dei Priori (Palace of the Priors). Although
this commission was withdrawn the same year, it was reinstated in 1495 and the work was
completed in the following year.[1] This moving image originally formed the *cimasa*, or finial,
above the sizable main panel, which depicts Mary and the Christ Child enthroned among
the patron saints of Perugia: Ercolano (Herculanus), Costanzo (Constantius), Lawrence,
and Louis of Toulouse (fig. 64). The entire altarpiece remained in the chapel until 1797,
when a Napoleonic legion removed the main panel from the Palazzo dei Priori and
brought it to France. The *Dead Christ* remained in Perugia, but the main panel was eventually brought to Rome. The relationship of the *cimasa* to the main panel can be better understood by examining a contemporary work by Pintoricchio, the Santa Maria dei Fossi
Altarpiece (fig. 65). Both works strategically juxtapose the playful innocence of the Christ
Child in the main panel with the mournful image in the *cimasa.*

The subject of the Dead Christ, also known as Christ at the Sepulcher, was a popular one throughout the history of Renaissance painting. Whether a single devotional
image or part of a larger work, such images afforded the viewer an opportunity to examine the wounded, lifeless body of Christ and to grieve, for these are icons of mortality.
It is interesting to note that this subject was first addressed by Perugino in one of his earliest known works, a diminutive panel now in the Louvre, datable to the early 1470s
(fig. 66).[2] In the *Dead Christ* from the *Decemviri* Altarpiece, the artist has upheld the conventional downward tilt of the head, curve of the torso, taut muscularity, and position of

Fig. 64. *Virgin and Child Enthroned with Saints* (*Decemviri* Altarpiece), Musei Vaticani (see pl. 12)

Fig. 65. Bernardino di Betto, called Pintoricchio, Santa Maria dei Fossi Altarpiece, Galleria Nazionale dell'Umbria, Perugia

Fig. 66. *Christ at the Tomb*, Musée du Louvre, Paris

the hands which appear in the Louvre panel. However, the references to the Passion and Crucifixion of Christ have been eliminated in favor of the void produced by the solid black backdrop. This single gesture reinforces the immediate presence of the figure and increases the potential to create emotional impact.

If the description of the corpse in the *Dead Christ* is compared with a slightly later version, such as that in the 1498 *Sepulcrum Christi* (cat. no. 2), differences in the anatomical description of Christ become immediately apparent. The former is gaunt and fragile, almost brittle, while the latter is sensual and relaxed, as if slumbering. In the *Dead Christ*, Perugino seems to be working closer to models provided by established Umbrian painters such as Bartolomeo Caporali (fig. 67) and Fiorenzo di Lorenzo, rather than in terms of the idealized beauty which typifies his style throughout the last twelve to fifteen years of the quattrocento and opening years of the cinquecento, as reflected in both the main panel of the *Decemviri* Altarpiece and the *Sepulcrum Christi*.[3] Perhaps the *Dead Christ* predates the main panel originally located beneath it. Alternatively, and perhaps more accurately, Perugino fully considered its intended context and realized that from below, the image of the *cimasa* should make an immediate impact. Hence, stylistic affinities with imagery of the 1470s were an appropriate means to that end.

Fig. 67. Bartolomeo Caporali and Sante di Apollonio del Celandro, *Dead Christ between the Virgin and Saint John the Evangelist* (predella, Triptych of the Confraternity of the Giustizia), Galleria Nazionale dell'Umbria, Perugia

NOTES

1. For further discussion of this commission of the *Decemviri* Altarpiece and its history, see Scarpellini, pp. 89–90 and Chronicle 1483, 1496.

2. This panel is traditionally dated to the early 1470s for its stylistic affinities with the eight panels of the *Miracles of the Life of Saint Bernardino of Siena*, dated 1473.

3. *Dead Christ between the Virgin and Saint John the Evangelist* has been dated as early as 1460–70 by Gnoli and as late as 1476 by Berenson.

LITERATURE

C. Crispolti, *Perugia Augusta* (1648); G. F. Morelli, *Brevi notizie* (1683); Lione Pascoli, *Vite de' pittori, scultori, architteti perugini* (Roma, 1732); B. Orsini, *Vita, elogia e memoria* (1804); A. Mezzanotte, *Della vita* (1836); Adamo Rossi, *Il Palazzo del Popolo in Perugia* (Perugia, 1864); J. A. Crowe and G. B. Cavalcaselle, *A History of Painting in Italy* (1866); A. Lupatelli, *Catalago* (1885); B. Berenson, *Central Italian Painters of the Renaissance* (1909); A. Venturi, *Storia dell'arte italiana* (1913); W. Bombe, *Perugino* (1914); F. Canuti, *Il Perugino* (1931); L. Venturi, "A Pietro Perugino" (1932); R. van Marle, *The Development of the Italian Schools of Painting* (1937); C. Gamba, *Pittura umbra del Rinascimento* (1949); F. Santi, *Galleria Nazionale dell'Umbria a Perugia* (1955); *Tutta la pittura del Perugino* (1959); F. Santi, *IV Mostra di opere restaurate* (1963); *L'opera completa del Perugino* (1969); Giorgio Vasari, *Le Vite de' più eccellenti pittori, scultori e architettori*, ed. Paola Barocchi, 7 vols. (Florence: Studio per Edizioni Scelte, 1971); *Pittura in Umbria tra il 1480–1540* (1983); P. Scarpellini, *Perugino*, 1st ed. (1984); F. Santi, *Dipinti* (1985); F. Todini, *La pittura umbra* (1989).

9

PIETÀ TRA SAN GIROLAMO E LA MADDALENA
(Pietà with Saints Jerome and Mary Magdalene)

c. 1470
Pietro Perugino
Tempera on canvas, 51½ × 65 in. (130 × 165 cm)
Galleria Nazionale dell'Umbria, Perugia (no. 220)

PROVENANCE: until 1863, Franciscan convent of Farneto (outside Perugia); 1863,
transferred to the Pinacoteca Vannucci, now the Galleria Nazionale dell'Umbria.

THE PIETÀ, or lamentation over the dead Christ, is among the most poignant subjects in the history of Christian art. In this moving example from the Galleria Nazionale dell'Umbria, the fragile and ashen-colored corpse of Christ is held by his mother Mary. Mother and son are flanked by the renowned penitent saints Mary Magdalene at right, and Jerome at left, kneeling in respect and adoration. Close at hand are the traditional symbols of these figures—the perfume chalice of the former and the lion associated with the latter. The rocky hillsides behind each saint not only extend the balance of the composition but may allude to the retreat into hermitage that, according to tradition, both saints accepted during the course of their lives. Scenes of the pietà do not illustrate a distinct recorded event: while Mary Magdalene was a contemporary and early follower of Christ, Jerome lived centuries later (c. A.D. 341–420). Their joint appearance visualizes the mystical timelessness of the event, which ultimately invites the faithful of every epoch.

Pietà with Saints Jerome and Mary Magdalene is one of the few known early works by Perugino. Unfortunately, precious little is known of his early career. Discussions of his training in Perugia and Florence and his work prior to the historic commission to paint frescoes in the newly built Sistine Chapel in 1480 are particularly complex.[1] It is generally accepted that while in Perugia, the young Perugino became familiar with that city's leading masters, such as Fiorenzo di Lorenzo (active 1460–1522) and Bartolomeo Caporali (c. 1420–1503/5), and while in Florence, he worked in the bustling workshop of Andrea

Fig. 68. Leonardo da Vinci, *Annunciation*, Galleria degli Uffizi, Florence

del Verrocchio (1435–1488) among other emerging prodigies like Leonardo da Vinci and Sandro Botticelli. This considered, an examination of the *Pietà* suggests several of the fundamental currents that characterize Perugino's formative period.

Without doubt, *Pietà with Saints Jerome and Mary Magdalene* reveals Perugino's debt to Florentine painting. The carefully balanced composition, articulation of the landscape, pursuit of anatomical truth, and attention to the detailed cascades of draperies are among the elements that the young Perugino, Leonardo, and Botticelli all would have gleaned from Verrocchio. Such comparative elements can also be comfortably analyzed in one of Leonardo's first independent works, the *Annunciation* (fig. 68). In addition, one cannot help but consider that the inception of Perugino's Mary Magdalene and Leonardo's Virgin and Angel arise from a similar pursuit of ideal beauty. Alternatively, Perugino's depiction of Saint Jerome refers to a traditional Umbrian concept of aged male saints realized throughout the careers of Fiorenzo di Lorenzo and Bartolomeo Caporali. A notable *Adoration of the Shepherds* (fig. 69), which has been attributed to both artists, features a balding Joseph that illustrates this concept.[2] Although this painting is nearly contemporary with the *Pietà*, its crowded composition, awkward landscape and attenuated figures illustrate Perugino's growing favor for Florentine, rather than Umbrian, painting.

Finally, it must be noted that *Pietà with Saints Jerome and Mary Magdalene* functioned as a *gonfalone*, or processional banner. The *gonfalone* was a popular type of Renaissance artwork.[3] This is the earliest of several surviving examples known to have been painted by Perugino. The Pietà is not a rare subject for a *gonfalone*, and other examples are known (fig. 70). The emotive power of the theme must have been equally felt by the faithful as the banner moved by during a procession or stood in place in a chapel, church, or confraternity.

Fig. 69. Bartolomeo Caporali, *Adoration of the Shepherds*, Galleria Nazionale dell'Umbria, Perugia

Fig. 70. Giovanni Boccati, *Gonfalone with the Pietà*, Galleria Nazionale dell'Umbria, Perugia

NOTES

1. The most concise resource on Perugino's early career is Jeryldene Wood's 1985 doctoral dissertation from the University of Virginia, "The Early Paintings of Perugino."

2. This panel has been traditionally attributed to Fiorenzo di Lorenzo, early 1470s. However, recent research supports Caporali as the artist. Payment documents to the latter have been discovered which may date the work to 1475–76. For further discussion, see Scarpellini's catalogue entry in *Dipinti, sculture e ceramiche* (1994), pp. 235–38.

3. For further information, consult F. Santi's *Gonfaloni umbri del Rinascimento* (1976).

LITERATURE

J. A. Crowe and G. B. Cavalcaselle, *A History of Painting in Italy* (1866); M. Guardabassi, *Indice-guida* (1872); A. Lupatelli, *Catalago* (1885); Jean Carlyle Graham, *The Problem of Fiorenzo di Lorenzo* (Perugia-Roma, 1903); Siegfried Weber, *Fiorenzo di Lorenzo* (Strasbourg, 1904); B. Berenson, *Central Italian Painters of the Renaissance* (1909); A. Venturi, *Storia dell'arte italiana* (1913); W. Bombe, *Perugino* (1914); F. Canuti, *Il Perugino* (1931); L. Venturi, "A Pietro Perugino" (1932); R. van Marle, *The Development of the Italian Schools of Painting* (1937); C. Gamba, *Pittura umbra del Rinascimento* (1949); F. Santi, *Galleria Nazionale dell'Umbria a Perugia* (1955); *Tutta la pittura del Perugino* (1959); F. Santi, *IV Mostra di opere restaurante* (1963); *L'opera completa del Perugino* (1969); F. Santi, *Gonfaloni umbri del Rinascimento* (1976); *Pittura in Umbria tra il 1480–1540* (1983); P. Scarpellini, *Perugino*, 1st ed. (1984); F. Santi, *Dipinti* (1985); F. Todini, *La pittura umbra* (1989); *Dipinti, sculture e ceramiche* (1994).

10

Pietro Perugino

THREE SCENES FROM
THE LIFE OF CHRIST

10a L'ANNUNCIAZIONE
(Annunciation)

1507
Oil on panel, 6⅝ × 14¾ in. (16.8 × 37.2 cm)
Galleria Nazionale dell'Umbria, Perugia (no. 267)

174   JOSEPH ANTENUCCI BECHERER

10b IL PRESEPIO
(Adoration of the Christ Child)

1507
Oil on panel, 6⅜ × 14⅝ in. (16.2 × 37 cm)
Galleria Nazionale dell'Umbria, Perugia (no. 268)

10c IL BATTESIMO
(Baptism of Christ)

1507
Tempera and oil on panel, 6¾ × 14⅜ in. (17.1 × 36.6 cm)
Galleria Nazionale dell'Umbria, Perugia (no. 269)

PROVENANCE: 1517 (?), Church of Santa Maria dei Servi, Perugia; c. 1540, transferred to the
Graziani Chapel, Santa Maria Nuova; by 1784, placed in the sacristy of Santa Maria Nuova,
Perugia; 1863, transferred to the Pinacoteca Vannucci, now the Galleria Nazionale dell'Umbria.

PREDELLA PANELS are a standard feature of Renaissance altarpieces. The works were originally placed at approximately eye level in the base of the altarpiece's framework, where they afforded the viewer a direct line of visual communication. These three diminutive panels from the Galleria Nazionale dell'Umbria are the latest of several surviving predella series by Perugino. The Annunciation, Adoration of the Christ Child, and Baptism of Christ are the subjects depicted. Among the artist's known panels, these are approximately half the size of Perugino's standard predelle. For the most part, each subject is represented in a manner that would have been quite familiar to viewers of the period, but the size of the panels invites close inspection, fostering the immediacy of interaction one would traditionally experience with illustrations in a book or manuscript.

The Annunciation is the first scene of the series. According to the Gospel of Luke, the angel Gabriel came before Mary with the news that she would conceive and bear a son to be called Jesus.[1] In the panel, Gabriel appears in the foreground on bended knee offering a lily (symbolic of purity) to Mary. Overwhelmed by the messenger and the message, Mary raises her hands in incredulity. She turns slightly as if wishing to escape, but the impact of the message arrests her motion. Although scenes of the Annunciation are typically staged in a domestic interior, Perugino presents the drama on an open terrace before a low-rising wall which leads to the undulating hills of the distant landscape. The idea of an enclosed space may loosely refer to Mary's purity or even her Immaculate Conception.[2] Perugino's decision to include four additional angels in the *Annunciation* is a unique compositional device.

The following scene is that of the Adoration of the Christ Child. Mary and Joseph appear on either side of the Child, who is placed in the immediate foreground. Three shepherds holding their staffs kneel in the middle ground, which includes the customary representation of the ox and the ass.[3] Finally, two angels appear in the distance at the edge of a vale. The moment of adoration transpires in the open landscape. As in the *Annunciation*, all references to traditional architectural spaces have been eliminated in favor of expansive stretches of airy terrain. The infant Christ is not only the central focus of adoration, but the compositional point of balance for the singular panel and, in summary, the entire predella series.

The Baptism of Christ is the final scene of the series. The waters of the Jordan River flow to the very edge of the picture plane. Here one encounters John and Christ at the moment of baptism. On the shore to the right, two figures await baptism; at the left are two angels whose presence at the event is standard and whose physical appearance unquestionably relates them to the standing angels of the *Annunciation*. At first glance, the figures found in the *Baptism of Christ* appear as a constant frieze against bands of green and blue, but close

Fig. 71. *Transfiguration* (from the Signorelli Altarpiece),
Galleria Nazionale dell'Umbria, Perugia

inspection reveals the rhythmic current of subtle movement flowing from left to right. As with each of the panels, tranquillity in support of contemplation is intended.

Most scholars believe these three panels once served as the predella of the Signorelli Altarpiece. The surviving central panel, also conserved in the Galleria Nazionale dell'Umbria, depicts the mystical event of the Transfiguration (fig. 71). Perugino received the commission for the altarpiece from Adreana Signorelli in 1517. Although the work was originally placed in the Signorelli family chapel in the Church of Santa Maria dei Servi, it was transferred to a new family chapel in Santa Maria Nuova in 1542 upon the demolition of the first church. In keeping with the previous discussion of the predella panels, the *Transfiguration* maintains a similar positioning of figures in the immediate foreground and upholds the measurable quantity of open land and sky.

It should be noted that some scholars believe the *Annunciation, Adoration of the Christ Child,* and *Baptism of Christ* formed the predella of the Schiavone Altarpiece of 1507.[4] Commissioned for the private chapel of Giovanni di Matteo Schiavone, also in the Church of

Fig. 72. *The Virgin and Child with Saints Jerome and Francis*,
The National Gallery, London

Santa Maria dei Servi, the central panel depicts the Virgin and Child with Saints Jerome
and Francis (fig. 72), also known as the *Madonna di Loreto*. The work is now in the National
Gallery, London. Contracts for the Schiavone Altarpiece do stipulate the inclusion of a
predella, but scholars who do not support the relationship between the London painting
and the panels in the Galleria Nazionale have rallied around a discussion of stylistic quality and upheld the physical connection between the *Transfiguration* and the predella panels
that was made in the nineteenth century.[5] Ultimately, the aesthetic quality of each panel
commands individual attention.

The Galleria Nazionale series is deceivingly similar to another notable predella series, now divided between the Art Institute of Chicago and the Metropolitan Museum of
Art, New York (cat. no. 1a–e). Although two of the subjects, the Adoration of the Christ
Child and the Baptism of Christ, are shared, and the nearly pastel palette and some color
combinations are comparable, the brushwork is markedly different. Paint has been applied
in a series of thin veils and with energetic, if not staccato, strokes. With the latter, it appears as if traditional Renaissance painting and drawing techniques converge. For Perugino, such characteristics are hallmarks of his late style and consequently may render
necessary reconsideration of a date as early as 1507. A rare drawing related to the Adoration panel has been published in support of both the unique late style of the master and
a date beyond 1507.[6] Measurably small, each scene draws the viewer inward yet, when re-
leased, the viewer undoubtedly recalls the presence of something quite grand.

NOTES

1. Luke 1: 26–31 (*The New American Bible*, Saint Joseph Edition, New York, 1986).

2. Throughout the Renaissance an enclosed garden space traditionally referred to Mary's purity, but the walled- or fenced-in space without the garden is more correctly identified with the concept of the Immaculate Conception (Anne's miraculous conception of Mary).

3. The ox and the ass ultimately refer to Isaiah 1:3: "An ox knows it owner, and an ass its master's manger; but Israel does not know, my people has not understood" (*The New American Bible*, Saint Joseph Edition, New York, 1986).

4. Scarpellini, pp. 117–18.

5. For the most current discussion of the predella panels in association with both altarpieces, see Scarpellini's catalogue entry in *Dipinti, sculture e ceramiche* (1994), pp. 245–46.

6. See Russell, pp. 257–59.

LITERATURE

B. Orsini, *Vita, elogia e memoria* (1804); S. Siepi, *Descrizione topologica-istorica* (1822); A. Mezzanotte, *Della vita* (1836); J. A. Crowe and G. B. Cavalcaselle, *A History of Painting in Italy* (1866); M. Guardabassi, *Indice-guida* (1872); A. Lupatelli, *Catalogo* (1885); A. Venturi, *Storia dell'arte italiana* (1913); W. Bombe, *Perugino* (1914); U. Gnoli, *Pietro Perugino* (1923); F. Canuti, *Il Perugino* (1931); R. van Marle, *The Development of the Italian Schools of Painting* (1937); M. A. Mochy Onory Vicarelli, "Il gusto e l'arte di Pietro Perugino," *Bolletino della Deputazione di Storia Patria per l'Umbria* 42 (1945): 5–178; F. Santi, *Galleria Nazionale dell'Umbria a Perugia* (1955); *Tutta la pittura del Perugino* (1959); F. Santi, *IV Mostra di opere restaurante; L'opera completa del Perugino* (1969); Francis Russell, "A Late Drawing by Perugino," *Master Drawings* 15, no. 3 (1977): 257–59; *Pittura in Umbria tra il 1480–1540* (1983); P. Scarpellini, *Perugino*, 1st ed. (1984); F. Santi, *Dipinti* (1985); F. Todini, *La pittura umbra* (1989); *Dipinti, sculture e ceramiche* (1994).

11

SAN GIROLAMO
(Saint Jerome)

c. 1512–15
Pietro Perugino
Oil on canvas, 51⅝ × 42⅜ in. (131 × 107.5 cm)
Galleria Nazionale dell'Umbria, Perugia (no. 242)

PROVENANCE: by 1822, sacristy of Sant'Ercolano, Perugia; 1836, Sodality of San Martino,
Perugia; 1863, transferred to the Pinacoteca Vannucci, now the Galleria Nazionale dell'Umbria.

SAINT JEROME (c. A.D. 341–420) is one of the four Latin Doctors of the Church (with Saints Ambrose, Augustine of Hippo, and Gregory) and a prominent figure in Western art from the Middle Ages onward. He is known to have been well-educated in both Greek and Latin traditions and to have traveled extensively prior to his decision to become a monk. Upon arriving in Palestine on a pilgrimage, Jerome became a hermit in the desert for several years and dedicated his attention to learning Hebrew and studying Scripture. He was later ordained a priest, but never said Mass. In Constantinople, Rome, and finally in Bethlehem, he devoted himself to scholarly writings and translations of Christian texts. His crowning achievement was without doubt the enormous task of translating the Hebrew Bible and the Greek New Testament into Latin. This painting from the Galleria Nazionale dell'Umbria is a conventional depiction of Jerome, shown gray-haired and bearded, accompanied by his typical attributes of the lion and the cardinal's hat. Artists routinely depict the saint as a scholar at work in his study or a bare-chested penitent in the desert. The latter arises from a description in one of Jerome's letters in which he describes beating his breast in order to expel vivid sexual hallucinations. To emphasize the physicality of penance, artists introduced the stone in his hand and the trickle of blood down his chest.

Like most Renaissance masters, Perugino was called upon numerous times to represent Jerome.[1] The earliest known representation of the saint attributed to the artist is a fresco, now transferred to canvas, dated prior to 1480 (fig. 73).[2] Whether or not the authorship of this work is ever definitively established, it testifies to a thematic and compositional format which ultimately gives rise to the *Saint Jerome* of c. 1512–15 exhibited here:

Fig. 73. *Saint Jerome*, Galleria Nazionale dell'Umbria, Perugia

Fig. 74. Attributed to Perugino, *Saint Jerome*, Musée des Beaux Arts, Caen

the aged saint is shown kneeling in the foreground, his hat and companion lion near, a rock clenched in his right hand. Yet the upward, otherworldly gaze of the c. 1512–15 figure differs greatly from the standard compositional format: it represents an attempt to visualize spiritual longing and gain at the expense of the physical pain which has displaced sexual desire. The landscape in the *Saint Jerome* is surprisingly open and topographically uncomplicated. In comparison to a panel ascribed to Perugino (fig. 74), the landscape seems serenely desolate.[3] This low-lying and far-reaching terrain is in direct opposition to the immediacy of the figure. Such awkwardness is atypical for Perugino, but becomes clear when one considers that the *Saint Jerome* was intended to function as a *gonfalone*, for the figure of the saint would have been clearly discernible, like an emblem, during transport. Stylistically, the *Saint Jerome* is closely related to the second phase of paintings Perugino executed for the enormous Sant'Agostino Polyptych between 1512/13 and his death in 1523. A side panel of the polyptych, depicting Saint Jerome and Saint Mary Magdalene (fig. 75), presents a similar conception of Jerome and reveals the light palette, thin application of paint, and sketchy brushwork integral to Perugino's late period.

Fig. 75. *Saint Jerome and Saint Mary Magdalene* (from the Sant'Agostino Polyptych), Galleria Nazionale dell'Umbria, Perugia

NOTES

1. *Pietà with Saints Jerome and Mary Magdalene,* Galleria Nazionale dell'Umbria (cat. no. 9); *The Penitent Jerome,* Galleria Nazionale dell'Umbria; *Crucifixion with the Virgin, Saint John, Saint Jerome and Saint Mary Magdalene,* National Gallery of Art, Washington, D.C. (fig. 40); *Madonna and Child with Saints Nicholas of Tolentino, Bernardino of Siena, Jerome, and Sebastian,* Galleria Nazionale dell'Umbria (with Eusebio da San Giorgio; fig. 108); *Saint Jerome in the Desert,* Kunsthistorisches Museum, Vienna (attributed to Perugino); *Crucifixion,* Pinacoteca Comunale, Bettona; Sant'Agostino Polyptych side panel with Mary Magdalene (fig. 75); and *Saint Jerome,* Musée des Beaux Arts, Caen (attributed to Perugino; fig. 74). In addition, numerous images of the saint were executed by Perugino's students and followers.

2. Although this work has been ascribed to Fiorenzo di Lorenzo, scholars beginning with Berenson have also attributed the work to the young Perugino for its close stylistic relationship to the saint as seen in the *Pietà with Saints Jerome and Mary Magdalene* (cat. no. 9).

3. This panel has been attributed to Perugino by Knapp, Berenson, Bombe, Canuti, and Camesasca; however, some doubts persist. It has been dated as early as 1498 and as late as 1516.

LITERATURE

B. Orsini, *Vita, elogia e memoria* (1804); S. Siepi, *Descrizione topologica-istorica* (1822); A. Mezzanotte, *Della vita* (1836); J. A. Crowe and G. B. Cavalcaselle, *A History of Painting in Italy* (1866); B. Berenson, *Central Italian Painters of the Renaissance* (1909); A. Venturi, *Storia dell'arte italiana* (1913); F. Canuti, *Il Perugino* (1931); R. van Marle, *The Development of the Italian Schools of Painting* (1937); Achille Bertini Calosso, *Quattro secoli di pittura in Umbria* (Perugia: Galleria Nazionale dell'Umbria, 1945); F. Santi, *Galleria Nazionale dell'Umbria a Perugia* (1955); *Tutta la pittura del Perugino* (1959); F. Santi, *IV Mostra di opere restaurante* (1963); *L'opera completa del Perugino* (1969); *Pittura in Umbria tra il 1480–1540* (1983); P. Scarpellini, *Perugino,* 1st ed. (1984); F. Santi, *Dipinti* (1985); F. Todini, *La pittura umbra* (1989).

12

MADONNA DELLA GIUSTIZIA

1501

Pietro Perugino

Tempera and oil on canvas, 85⅞ × 55³⁄₁₆ in. (218 × 140 cm)

Galleria Nazionale dell'Umbria, Perugia (no. 278)

PROVENANCE: 1501, commissioned by the Confraternity of Sant'Andrea, Perugia; 1534, transferred to the Oratory of San Bernardino, Perugia; 1683, conserved in the new Oratory of Sant'Andrea, Perugia; c. 1863; transferred to the Pinacoteca della Confraternita; 1879, entered the Accademia di Belle Arti, now the Galleria Nazionale dell'Umbria.

ON FEBRUARY 11, 1501, the *Decemviri*, Perugia's ten communal magistrates, granted a subsidy to the Confraternity of Sant'Andrea della Giustizia for a new *gonfalone*. With their assistance, the confraternity, whose membership was devoted in part to aiding those condemned to death, was able to commission this painting from Perugino. The *Madonna della Giustizia*, also referred to as the *Madonna and Child in Glory with Saints and Angels*, was in the care of the confraternity until 1534, when it merged with Perugia's renowned Confraternity of San Bernardino. At this time, the work was transferred to the Oratory of San Bernardino. Here it also came to function as an altarpiece.[1] The subject is highly symbolic, both as *gonfalone* and as altarpiece, and uniquely suited to reflect the religiosity and history of Perugia in the early sixteenth century.

Mary and the Christ Child are depicted enthroned in glory among the clouds. The benevolent maiden and toddler are clearly related to the larger body of Perugino's Marian imagery (see Abbott) produced at the very height of his mature period, for example, the *Madonna of the Confraternity of the Consolazione* (fig. 76). Two praying angels are hovering on each side. Conceived as mirror images, their role is attendant adoration, thereby successfully establishing the banner's formal tone of devotion. Five seraphim, bodiless angels ensconced in three sets of wings, surround the celestial vision and sanction its mystical nature. In the immediate foreground are the kneeling Saint Francis of Assisi (c. 1182–1226) on the left, and Saint Bernardino of Siena (1380–1444), a most prominent Franciscan follower, on the right. The visage and demeanor of Francis derives from Perugino's standard repertory of youthful male saints and heroes, but the gaunt face and slight features of Bernardino arise from a standard depiction of the saint employed by Umbrian and Tuscan

Fig. 76. *Madonna of the Confraternity of the Consolazione*, Galleria Nazionale dell'Umbria, Perugia (see pl. 14)

Fig. 77. Benedetto Bonfigli, *Gonfalone of Saint Bernardino*, Galleria Nazionale dell'Umbria, Perugia

artists.[2] Among the most favored saints of the period, they serve as intercessory figures for the representative citizenry of Perugia shown gathered at their knees. The simple gesture of Francis summarizes the very intervention desired by these lilliputian figures. Of special note are the hooded confraternity members of Sant'Andrea who appear in the back row of figures: their apparel ensured anonymity and thereby deterred individuals from receiving praise for the meritorious acts of the group. Finally, the viewer is provided with the skyline of Perugia as it was known to Perugino and his contemporaries. The inclusion of such detail is important historical documentation and visualizes the protection offered by the Virgin and Child to the entire community.

The *Madonna della Giustizia* merits consideration in relation to several important monuments of Umbrian painting. Primary is the celebrated *Gonfalone of Saint Bernardino* from 1465 (fig. 77), executed by Perugia's preeminent fifteenth-century master, Benedetto Bonfigli (c. 1418/20–1496). The hierarchy of relations is evident as the saint appeals to the sumptuously enthroned Christ on behalf of the people of Perugia below. This work provided Perugino with an established tradition for a *gonfalone* that poignantly described the apparel, customs, and faith of the people of Perugia.[3] In turn, throughout the sixteenth century, Perugino's *Madonna della Giustizia* undoubtedly served as a point of departure for numerous artists and their respective processional banners, altarpieces, and general devotional imagery. A notable comparison can be made to a work by Berto di Giovanni (documented 1488–1526), his *gonfalone* of 1526 in San Lorenzo, Perugia's cathedral (fig. 78). Throughout the Renaissance, the prevalence of the processional banner in Perugia, and more broadly in Umbria, was fostered by the immense popularity of confraternities (see Banker).[4]

Fig. 78. Berto di Giovanni, *Gonfalone of Christ with Saint Joseph, the Virgin, and Saint Costanzo,* at base: *The City and the People of Perugia,* Duomo, Perugia

As early as 1509, the *Madonna della Giustizia* was altered from the original form painted by Perugino. At this time, a crown of silver and gold was added to the head of the Virgin. Subsequent repainting and a disastrous restoration attempt in 1789 were carried out.[5] The current presentation of the work follows recent evaluation and painstaking restoration in order to realize as clearly as possible the original intentions of the artist.

NOTES

1. For the most concise discussion of the commission and history of this work, see Scarpellini, p. 105.

2. In Perugia, the definitive image for Saint Bernardino is the relief sculpture of Agostino di Duccio on the façade of the Oratory of San Bernardino, 1457–61.

3. Perugino would have been quite familiar with this particular example of Bonfigli's work, for he was among several artists to execute small decorative panels originally lining the cabinet, or cupboard, where this *gonfalone* was maintained. For further discussion, see V. Garibaldi's essay in this catalogue.

4. For further reading on the subject, see F. Santi's *Gonfaloni umbri del Rinascimento.*

5. F. Santi, *Dipinti,* pp. 104–5.

LITERATURE

C. Crispolti, *Perugia Augusta* (1648); G. F. Morelli, *Brevi notizie* (1683); A. Mezzanotte, *Della vita* (1836); Raffaello Marchesi, *Principali Monumenti D'Arte in Perugia* (Perugia, 1857); J. A. Crowe and G. B. Cavalcaselle, *A History of Painting in Italy* (1866); A. Venturi, *Storia dell'arte italiana* (1913); W. Bombe, *Perugino* (1914); U. Gnoli, *Pietro Perugino* (1923); F. Canuti, *Il Perugino* (1931); L. Venturi, "A Pietro Perugino" (1932); R. van Marle, *The Development of the Italian Schools of Painting* (1937); F. Santi, *Galleria Nazionale dell'Umbria a Perugia* (1955); *Tutta la pittura del Perugino* (1959); F. Santi, *IV Mostra di opere restaurante* (1963); *L'opera completa del Perugino* (1969); *Pittura in Umbria tra il 1480–1540* (1983); P. Scarpellini, *Perugino,* 1st ed. (1984); F. Santi, *Dipinti* (1985); F. Todini, *La pittura umbra* (1989).

13

MADONNA COL BAMBINO TRA SANTO COSTANZO E SANT'ERCOLANO

(Madonna and Child with Saints Costanzo and Ercolano)

1517
Pietro Perugino
Tempera on panel, 31¾ × 22½ in. (80 × 55 cm)
Galleria Nazionale dell'Umbria, Perugia (no. 262)

PROVENANCE: 1517, commissioned for the kitchen of the Palazzo dei Priori, Perugia;
c. 1800, transferred to the Sala del Consiglio, and then to the Sala del Gonfaloniere,
Palazzo dei Priori, Perugia; c. 1861, transferred to the Accademia di Belle Arti,
now the Galleria Nazionale dell'Umbria.

THE IDEA of a clear separation of church and state is relatively new and would have seemed remarkably foreign to people of the Renaissance. At that time, religious imagery was frequently commissioned and prominently displayed in a variety of civic and secular contexts. This considered, the *Madonna and Child with Saints Costanzo and Ercolano* is an intriguing work: it was originally intended for the kitchen of Perugia's town hall, the Palazzo dei Priori, and hence is often referred to as the *Madonna della Cucina* (Kitchen Madonna). Mary is seated at the center with the Christ Child and considers the audience before her. Christ's attention is drawn to the side, but his right hand is raised in benediction. Directly behind them are the praying figures of the patron saints of Perugia, Costanzo (born in Perugia, martyred A.D. January 29, c. 160) at the left and Ercolano (born in Perugia, martyred A.D. March 1, 547) at the right. Both men were local bishops and their appearance in painting and sculpture is largely limited to Perugia and the surrounding region.

The format of this painting is familiar within Perugino's oeuvre. A notable example is the *Madonna and Child between Saints Rose (?) and Catherine of Alexandria* from the Kunsthistorisches Museum, Vienna (fig. 22).[1] Mary and the Christ Child are featured and two female saints appear immediately behind. Given the popularity of Marian imagery throughout the Renaissance, artists like Perugino would wisely maintain several standard compositions of the Madonna and Child (see Abbott). The representation of the saints or angels would be tailored to reflect the interests or needs of the commission as

Fig. 79. *Madonna and Child*, The Walters Art Gallery, Baltimore

articulated by the patron (see Cole). It was the selection of these saintly or angelic figures which personalized the image and encouraged the notion that, with proper intercession, the divine was accessible. Thus, the *Madonna and Child with Saints Costanzo and Ercolano* was perfectly suited for its placement in the town hall of Perugia.

The Galleria Nazionale panel is dated to the final phase of Perugino's career. The brushwork is typical of this period, sketchy and expressive, and paint has been applied in thin layers. The overall golden hue results from the original varnishes applied and reinforces the halcyon mood of the work.[2] Such qualities are immediately apparent in the monumental altarpiece Perugino executed for the cathedral of Città della Pieve in 1514 (fig. 7).[3] The figures in the *Madonna and Child with Saints Costanzo and Ercolano*, as with others encountered from the master's late period, are decidedly corpulent in comparison to those of his early and mature periods: traces of an athletic, or at least anatomically correct, tone and form, and careful studies of draperies have been supplanted. Emphasis has been placed on general volumes of flesh and material. A largely unknown *Madonna and Child* (dated 1520) from the Walters Art Gallery (fig. 79) is among those paintings executed during the last decade of the artist's life, when such generalizations had become standard. Finally, an image of Saint Catherine of Alexandria (fig. 80) from the Sant'Agostino Polyptych begs comparison with the representation of Mary featured in the *Madonna and Child with Saints Costanzo and Ercolano*.[4] The former is generally attributed to Perugino and assistants, and although the execution of the figure is less refined than the latter, the concept is largely the same.

Fig. 80. Perugino and assistants, *Saint Catherine of Alexandria* (predella detail, Sant'Agostino Polyptych), Galleria Nazionale dell'Umbria, Perugia

NOTES

1. The work has been dated as early as 1483 and as late as 1495. It closely parallels several works by Perugino created during the 1490s, including examples in the Musée du Louvre, Paris, the Staedelsches Kunstinstitut, Frankfurt, and the Palazzo Pitti, Florence.

2. I wish to thank Piero Nottiani for sharing his time and invaluable expertise regarding the restoration and condition of this work.

3. The painting is signed and dated 1514: PETRVS CRISTOFERI VANNUTTI DE CASTRO PLEBIS PINXIT, MDXIIII.

4. For the most recent scholarship on the Sant'Agostino Polyptych, see Vittoria Garibaldi, "The Polyptych of Sant'Agostino" (1996).

LITERATURE

A. Mezzanotte, *Della vita* (1836); J. A. Crowe and G. B. Cavalcaselle, *A History of Painting in Italy* (1866); M. Guardabassi, *Indice-guida* (1872); A. Venturi, *Storia dell'arte italiana* (1913); W. Bombe, *Perugino* (1914); U. Gnoli, *Pietro Perugino* (1923); F. Canuti, *Il Perugino* (1931); Giovanni Cecchini, *La Galleria Nazionale dell'Umbria in Perugia* (Roma: Istituto poligrafico dello Stato, 1932); L. Venturi, "A Pietro Perugino (1932)"; F. Santi, *Galleria Nazionale dell'Umbria a Perugia* (1955); *Tutta la pittura del Perugino* (1959); F. Santi, *IV Mostra di opere restaurante* (1963); *L'opera completa del Perugino* (1969); *Pittura in Umbria tra il 1480–1540* (1983); P. Scarpellini, *Perugino*, 1st ed. (1984); F. Santi, *Dipinti* (1985); F. Todini, *La pittura umbra* (1989).

14

LANDSCAPE *(recto)*

c. 1489
Pietro Perugino
Brush and brown ink with white heightening on prepared paper, 8 × 11 in. (20.4 × 28 cm)

LANDSCAPE *(verso)*

c. 1489
Pietro Perugino
Pen and brown ink on prepared paper, 8 × 11 in. (20.4 × 28 cm)
The Metropolitan Museum of Art, Purchase, Lila Acheson Wallace Gift (1993.327)

PROVENANCE: Herbert List, Munich; Wolfgang Ratjen, Munich; 1992, sold Christie's, London
(as associate of Perugino); Gabrielle Kopelman, New York; 1993, acquired by Ars Libri;
1993, purchase, Lila Acheson Wallace Gift.

THE TREATMENT OF LANDSCAPE is one of the most significant yet quietly considered elements in the art of Pietro Perugino. According to Vasari, audiences of Perugino's day considered the landscapes in his paintings to be extremely beautiful.[1] This double-sided sheet from the Metropolitan Museum of Art is the only known landscape drawing by the master and undoubtedly served as an important resource in the creation of the very type of painted vision his audiences found so appealing. The historical importance of this work is enriched when one understands how rare it is to find pure landscape drawing preserved from the Renaissance. With the exception of Leonardo's *View of the Arno Valley*, dated August 5, 1473 (fig. 81), and this sheet by Perugino, no firmly attributable landscape drawings from the fifteenth century are known.[2]

Both sides of the Metropolitan sheet capture the same terrain—a tranquil, sloping hillside populated by clusters of trees. The verso is a pen and ink study intended to capture the very essence of the environment by a series of quick strokes that define the contours of the hillside and the rotund trees. This sketch was probably executed first, operating as a guide for the more detailed recto study. In the recto study, all forms are given greater definition: terraced ground is fully understood and foliage is discernible. Ink

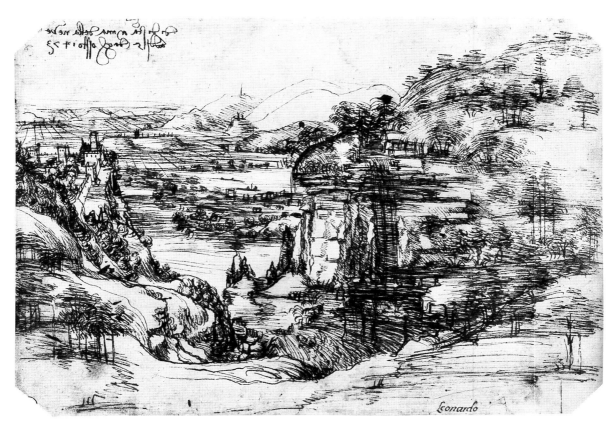

Fig. 81. Leonardo da Vinci, *View of the Arno Valley*, Gabinetto Disegni e
Stampe degli Uffizi, Florence

washes and white highlights attest to the artist's interest in describing natural light and vi-
sualizing the nuances of the atmosphere. Although the specific location that inspired this
drawing has not been identified, the image speaks to the artist's affinity for the countryside of Tuscany and, more poignantly, his native Umbria.

Perugino's drawing was probably executed in preparation for his celebrated *Vision of
Saint Bernard* (fig. 82) altarpiece, which was commissioned in 1489 and completed by 1493
for the Nasi Chapel at the convent of Santa Maria Maddalena in Cestello, known today
as Santa Maria Maddalena dei Pazzi, near Florence. Behind the figures and beyond the
final arch of the portico in this painting is the very landscape envisioned in the Metropolitan's sketches. It has been effectively argued that the spontaneity of the drawing evidenced in the verso, and its evolutionary relationship to the recto, indicate that both works
were created during the formulation of the painting rather than copied.[3] The landscape
in the background of a second, contemporary altarpiece, the *Annunciation* (fig. 83), is strikingly similar to that in the *Vision of Saint Bernard*, attesting to the idea that Renaissance
masters like Perugino effectively utilized a single drawing for multiple end products.[4]

Fig. 82. *Vision of Saint Bernard*, Alte Pinakothek, Munich (see pl. 6)

Fig. 83. *Annunciation*, Church of Santa Maria Nova, Fano

NOTES

1. Giorgio Vasari, *The Lives of the Artists*, trans. Julia Conaway Bondanella and Peter Bondanella (Oxford: Oxford University Press, 1991), p. 258.

2. In his article, George Goldner astutely asserts, ". . . it is reasonable to assume that many other drawings were made—a probability reinforced by the extensive group of landscape studies by Fra Bartolommeo dating from the early part of the next [sixteenth] century" (p. 365).

3. Goldner, p. 366.

4. The *Annunciation* was created for the church of Santa Maria Nova, Fano. A nearly illegible inscription with a date believed to be 1489 is found on this altarpiece.

LITERATURE

B. Berenson, *The Drawings of the Florentine Painters* (1903); Almon Richard Turner, *The Vision of Landscape in Renaissance Italy* (Princeton: Princeton University Press, 1966); Alison Luchs, *Cestello. A Cistercian Church of the Florentine Renaissance* (New York and London: Garland Publishing Co., 1977); S. Ferino Pagden, *Disegni umbri del Rinascimento* (1982); Kenneth Clark, *Leonardo da Vinci*, revised and introduced by Martin Kemp (London: Penguin, 1988); George Goldner, "New Drawings by Perugino and Pontormo," *Burlington Magazine* 136 (1994): 365–67; William M. Griswold, *Metropolitan Museum of Art, Recent Acquisitions: A Selection, 1993–1994* (New York: Metropolitan Museum of Art, 1994).

15

FIVE NUDE INFANTS IN VARIOUS POSES

c. 1500–1505
Attributed to Raphael
Metalpoint, traces of black chalk or charcoal on prepared paper, 21¼ × 16¼ in. (54 × 41.3 cm)
The Metropolitan Museum of Art, Robert Lehman Collection (1975.1.395)

PROVENANCE: n.d., possibly the Conestabile collection, Perugia; n.d., possibly the Thane
collection, London; by 1840, collection of William Esdaile, London; by 1929, collection of
John Heseltine, London; by 1932, collection of Henry Oppenheimer, London; 1936,
collection of Robert Lehman, New York; 1975, Robert Lehman Collection,
The Metropolitan Museum of Art.

THE PROFESSIONAL RELATIONSHIP between Perugino and his most gifted student, Raphael Santi (1483–1520), is the subject of great fascination and debate. Boundaries of attribution are particularly fluid in historical and current discussions involving drawings. This delicately executed work from the Robert Lehman Collection of the Metropolitan Museum of Art is central to such discussions. Since the early nineteenth century, it has been variously assigned to Raphael, Perugino, and the broader, less definitive category of "circle of Perugino and Raphael."[1] Today, *Five Nude Infants in Various Poses* is attributed to Raphael by the Lehman Collection.

It is likely that Raphael entered Perugino's workshop within a year of the death of his father Giovanni, painter to the Urbino court, in 1495. At this point, the young apprentice had access to the preparatory drawings, or cartoons, of his master, whose career was near its zenith. Raphael witnessed Perugino work and eventually served as an assistant in the production of numerous paintings over the course of the next several years. Although no drawings of infants or children survive which can be attributed to Perugino with certainty, the figures in the Lehman sheet clearly recall the very type of fleshy, cherubic infant male featured in numerous religious paintings executed in the years preceding and immediately following 1500, as exemplified by the *Madonna and Child* in the Detroit Institute of Arts (cat. no. 5).

Five Nude Infants in Various Poses is a meticulous study. The outline, or contour, of each figure is particularly strong. Along the jaw line of the child seated on the tree trunk are faintly detectable pouncing marks which would suggest that this drawing may have begun

Fig. 84. Assistant of Perugino, *Study of Fourteen Putti*, Gabinetto Disegni e Stampe degli Uffizi, Florence

Fig. 85. *Family of Saint Anne*, Musée des Beaux Arts, Marseilles

with the transfer of a cartoon. Ironically, this figure is the most Peruginesque in appearance. The contours which define the standing children at the right and the child reclining at the base of the sheet are particularly sinuous in form. Development of the volume of the forms through cross-hatching is consistently sound throughout the drawing. A similar sketch attributed to the circle of Perugino (fig. 84) after Perugino's *Family of Saint Anne* altarpiece (fig. 85), is one of the few known related drawings of this kind. It falls short, however, in each of the elements lauded here in the Lehman drawing.[2]

It has been suggested that *Five Nude Infants in Various Poses* is more than a casual collection of figure studies. With the exception of the reclining child, the other four may be grouped together in a type of *sacra conversazione* (sacred conversation), implying that the seated child is a representation of the young Christ and the others are gathered in homage or toddling adoration.[3] This subject is frequently limited to Christ and the young John the Baptist, who are conducted into the presence of saintly adults, an example of which is depicted in the central panel of Raphael's early Colonna Altarpiece (fig. 86). Having first considered the Lehman drawing, Raphael's conception of Christ and John seems familiar; in fact, the pose and gaze of John are nearly identical to those of the more forward infant in the right pair of figures. This, in combination with the aesthetic merit of the drawing, has promoted the acceptance of the current attribution to the young Raphael.

Fig. 86. Raphael, *Madonna and Child Enthroned, with Saints* (main panel, Colonna Altarpiece), The Metropolitan Museum of Art, Gift of J. Pierpont Morgan, 1916

NOTES

1. A note on the verso labels the drawing "Raffaele." In 1917, Fischel assigned the work to a follower of Perugino. It was listed as Perugino in 1936. In 1978 and 1983, Szabo attributed the work to Perugino, while Ferino Pagden cited the work as a copy after Raphael in her 1982 catalogue. Writing in 1991, Forlani Tempesti attributed the work to the circle of Perugino and Raphael.

2. The *Family of Saint Anne* (also known as the *Family of the Virgin*) was executed between 1500 and 1502. Scholars have questioned the participation of Perugino's workshop in the creation of this work, but it must have been an invaluable resource for younger artists with regard to the variety of poses of the infants.

3. This was first suggested by Szabo.

LITERATURE

B. Berenson, *The Drawings of the Florentine Painters* (1903); O. Fischel, "Die Zeichnungen der Umbrer" (1917); S. Ferino Pagden, *Disegni umbri del Rinascimento* (1982); George Szabo, *Masterpieces of Italian Drawing in the Robert Lehman Collection* (New York: Hudson Hills Press, 1983); Anna Forlani Tempesti, *The Lehman Collection, V. Italian Fifteenth to Seventeenth Century Drawings* (New York: Metropolitan Museum of Art, 1991).

16

PUTTI WITH A WINE PRESS

c. 1500
Follower of Raphael
Oil on panel, 13⅛ in. (33.3 cm) diam.
National Gallery of Art, Washington, D.C., Samuel H. Kress Collection (1952.5.72)

PROVENANCE: until 1933, collection of Prof. Pietro Tosca, Rome; 1933, collection of Count
Alessandro Contini Bonacossi, Florence; 1948, collection of Samuel H. Kress;
1952, donated to the National Gallery of Art.

"TONDO" IS AN ITALIAN TERM for a round painting. The unusual shape captured
the delight of Renaissance patrons and offered artists the opportunity to explore an atypical compositional format. *Putti with a Wine Press* is a small tondo from the National Gallery of Art, Washington, D.C. The subject is mythological in origin and highly imagi-
native. Twelve cherubic nude boys, or putti, are at play in and around a lush grape vine and
a large, wooden wine vat. A single boy, or putto, sits in the vine above the action and seems
to preside over the activities of the others. He could be viewed as a youthful Bacchus, the
Roman god of wine, for he wears the traditional crown of grape leaves, holds a thin scep-
ter in his left hand, and raises a large chalice in his right. Great care has been taken in the
depiction of each of the figures, and the curved shape of the painting has been accentu-
ated by their rounded physique, the bow of the grape vine, and the form of the vat. Both
the author and the function of *Putti with a Wine Press* are a mystery, given the charm and aesthetic merit of the work.

The painting has been attributed to both Perugino and the young Raphael.[1] Mythological subjects were infrequently addressed by Perugino.[2] Of these, his *Combat between Love
and Chastity* (fig. 9) merits consideration in comparison to the National Gallery tondo. The
numerous winged putti in this painting derive from Perugino's depictions of holy children. Although the general forms and rambunctious activity of these putti are loosely related to the children, to suggest a more definitive relationship would be tenuous. Scholars
who have favored an attribution to Raphael feel that *Putti with a Wine Press* reveals his freedom and originality of composition and see a connection to the miniature-like qualities
of early paintings like the *Knight's Dream* and the *Three Graces*.[3] An interesting comparison

Fig. 87. Raphael, *Seven Putti Playing*, The Governing Body, Christ Church, Oxford

Fig. 88. Anonymous Florentine Master, *Children at the Vintage*, Ashmolean Museum, Oxford

may be made with a drawing ascribed to Raphael of seven putti playing (fig. 87). The theme is related, but the work discloses sensitive, even lean contours which are slightly more sophisticated than those of the tondo figures. At best, it can be said that the master of *Putti with a Wine Press* was working beyond the stylistic boundaries of Perugino, yet within the confines established by the young Raphael.

Although most Renaissance art was created with a specific function in mind, the National Gallery of Art tondo eludes such classification. In an age when the art and ideas of classical antiquity were thoroughly considered, images related to Bacchus were not foreign.[4] However, scenes of putti creating and enjoying wine are rare. An interesting engraving by an anonymous Florentine master (fig. 88) is one of the few known related works. The forms are awkwardly rendered and the putti are more industrious, but the theme is the same. It has been suggested that this unique subject would have met with greater approval in Florence than in Perugia, and hence the *Putti with a Wine Press* may have been intended for a domestic interior in the former city.[5]

NOTES

1. Those preferring an attribution to Perugino follow a tradition established by Berenson, while those supporting an attribution to Raphael adhere to the remarks of Gronau.

2. Only Perugino's *Apollo and Marsyas* and *Combat between Love and Chastity* (both in the Louvre) are exclusively mythological. A third painting in the National Gallery of Scotland, now cropped and badly damaged, may also be considered. Perugino's great fresco cycle in the Collegio del Cambio, Perugia, blends Christian, classical, and mythological subjects in the tradition of late fifteenth-century humanism.

3. Suida and Shapley, p. 146.

4. For further reading, see the Renaissance work by Francesco Colonna, *Hypnerotomachia Poliphili.*

5. I wish to thank David Alan Brown of the National Gallery, Washington, D.C., for his suggestions and insights regarding this perplexing painting.

LITERATURE

W. E. Suida and F. R. Shapley, *Paintings and Sculpture from the Kress Collection* (1956); *Tutta la pittura del Perugino* (1959); Francesco Colonna, *Hypnerotomachia Poliphili,* with critical commentary by Giovanni Pozzi and Lucia Ciapponi (Padua: Editrice Antenore, 1964); F. R. Shapley, *Paintings from the Samuel H. Kress Collection* (1968); P. Scarpellini, *Perugino,* 1st ed. (1984); John Walker, *National Gallery of Art, Washington, D.C.* (New York: Abrams, 1984).

17

BAPTISM OF CHRIST *(recto)*

c. 1475
Pietro Perugino
Pen and brown ink; black chalk and brown ink, 7%6 × 7¹³⁄₁₆ in. (19.3 × 19.8 cm)
Verso: *Figure Studies*
National Gallery of Art, Washington, D.C., Pepita Milmore Memorial Fund (1981.64.1)

PROVENANCE: n.d., collection of Dr. Simon Miller, Paris; until 1962, collection of Dr. and
Mrs. Francis Springell (formerly Sprinzels), Prague and London; 1962, sold Sotheby's, London,
to private collection; 1981, National Gallery of Art purchase through David Tunick, from
Galerie Kornfeld and Klipstein, Bern.

RENAISSANCE PAINTERS EXECUTED a great variety of drawings as a means of
realizing both panel paintings and frescoes. Quick figure studies were notations toward
preliminary sketches which, in turn, might give rise to finished drawings to be translated
onto a prepared panel or wall surface. This energetically drawn work from the National
Gallery of Art is a fine example of a preliminary sketch. In the *Baptism of Christ*, Perugino
was able to address the human form in a variety of poses, reference general areas of light
and shadow, investigate the most elemental aspects of the landscape, and collectively secure a basic, balanced composition. Pen strokes may appear whimsical to the modern eye,
but drawings of this detail would have established fundamental guidelines for the production of a painting and been crucial to the qualitative success of a large workshop involving numerous assistants.

The subject of Christ's Baptism by John in the waters of the Jordan River was popular with audiences of the Renaissance and a frequently requested motif.[1] Of the numerous versions Perugino executed, the National Gallery drawing is specifically linked to a
predella panel (fig. 89) for his monumental San Pietro Polyptych. This polyptych was
commissioned in 1495 and completed by 1500 for the abbey church of San Pietro, Perugia.[2]
The panel maintains a great many elements illustrated in the drawing: the position and
gestures of Christ and John are nearly identical, the pairs of kneeling angels in the foreground are similar, and the V-shaped treatment of hillsides leading into a river valley is
sustained. Minor modifications such as the deletion of the kneeling figures in the middle

Fig. 89. Perugino and assistants, *Baptism of Christ*, Musée des Beaux Arts, Rouen

ground and the adjustments to the placement and pose of the standing onlookers ensure the painting's compositional clarity. The San Pietro Polyptych was painted during one of the most active period's of Perugino's career and is generally attributed to the master and his assistants.[3] This considered, drawings like the *Baptism of Christ* were imperative to maintain the standards of the master's workshop.

An arched sheet depicting a study for the Adoration of the Magi by Perugino (fig. 90) in the British Museum, London, reveals the very reinforced outlines of figures and brisk cross-hatching encountered in the National Gallery drawing. Since the early twentieth century, these works have been dated to the second half of the 1470s.[4] If this date is accepted, a gap of more than twenty years separate the *Baptism of Christ* from the predella to which it is linked. It is highly possible that Perugino employed an early drawing to set the composition for the 1495–1500 panel. However, the recent discovery of a double-sided sheet (cat. no. 14) with renderings of a landscape may offer an alternative date. The landscape has been dated to c. 1489, and the verso image bears strong stylistic similarities to the graphic markings which define the *Baptism of Christ*.

On the verso of the National Gallery sheet (fig. 91) is a fairly developed study of a draped figure, possibly a saint, holding a book. The cropping of this study indicates the sheet was originally longer. At the right are two delicate figure sketches which have been identified as a man wielding an ax and a fallen satyr. As general anatomical notations, they could function as points of reference for a more detailed drawing by the artist.[5] The use of both sides of the sheet underscores the highly functional nature of Perugino's drawings.

Fig. 90. *Study for the Adoration of the Magi,* The British Museum, London

Fig. 91. *Figure Studies* (verso of the *Baptism of Christ*), Pepita Milmore Memorial Fund, © Board of Trustees, National Gallery of Art, Washington, D.C.

NOTES

1. For a more complete discussion of Christ's Baptism, see cat. no. 1a–e.

2. The predella series contains three individual, narrative scenes: the *Adoration of the Magi, Baptism of Christ,* and *Resurrection.* The entire polyptych was dismantled in the late eighteenth century, and several individual panels were taken to France. The predella panels are presently preserved in the Musée des Beaux Arts, Rouen.

3. For a more complete discussion, see Scarpellini, pp. 93–94. Perugino assistants Eusebio da San Giorgio and Giovanni di Francesco Ciambella, who are named as witnesses in the contract, are often suggested as the primary assistants on the project.

4. Oskar Fischel suggested the dating in 1917.

5. *Loan Exhibition of Drawings from the Collection of Dr. and Mrs. Francis Springell in London,* p. 21.

LITERATURE

W. Bombe, *Perugino* (1914); O. Fischel, "Die Zeichnungen der Umbrer" (1917); *Loan Exhibition of Drawings from the Collection of Dr. and Mrs. Francis Springell,* exh. cat. (London: Colnaghi & Co., Ltd, 1959); *Important Old Master Drawings of the Italian School,* auction cat., no. 12 (London: Sotheby and Co., 1962); *Graphik und Handzeichnungen Alter Meister,* auction cat. (Bern: Galerie Kornfeld, 1981); S. Ferino Pagden, "Pintoricchio, Perugino or the Young Raphael," *Burlington Magazine* 125 (1983): 87–88; P. Scarpellini, *Perugino,* 1st ed. (1984).

18

ARCHER DRAWING A BOW

n.d.
Follower of Perugino
Black chalk and brown wash drawing, heightened with white and squared for transfer
on laid paper, 10⁵⁄₁₆ × 6⁵⁄₈ in. (26.2 × 16.8 cm)
National Gallery of Art, Washington, D.C., Woodner Family Collection (1991.182.13)

PROVENANCE: until 1987, collection of Rudolph Weigel, Leipzig, as Perugino; 1987, sold
Christie's, London, as workshop of Perugino; by 1990, purchased by Ian Woodner, through
Anna Maria Edlestein, New York; 1990, passed by inheritance to Andrea and Dian Woodner,
daughters of Ian Woodner; 1991, gift to the National Gallery of Art.

PERUGINO'S IMPACT on the history of Umbrian painting cannot be underestimated. The numerous surviving drawings made after his paintings in Perugia and throughout the region testify to the popularity of his figures, landscapes, and compositions among artists throughout the sixteenth century. The *Archer Drawing a Bow* from the National Gallery of Art is one of several related drawings preserved today in Italian, French, and American collections.[1] These drawings are connected to the master's monumental fresco of 1505, the *Martyrdom of Saint Sebastian* (pl. 19) on the altar wall of the confraternity church dedicated to Saint Sebastian in Panicale.[2] The National Gallery drawing carefully follows the form of the archer at the far left of the saint (fig. 92).

Until recently, the paternity of this drawing was assigned to Perugino.[3] The sensitive description of the figure's frontal pose and the three-quarter position of the head with upturned, liquid eyes are hallmarks of the master. This, in combination with the fact that the drawing was squared for transfer, convincingly promoted its attribution to Perugino as a preparatory work for the Saint Sebastian fresco.[4] The author of the National Gallery drawing began to delineate the figure's basic contour with black chalk. Brown ink was then employed to fully realize the form. White lead was effectively used to create highlights. Although of high quality, the rendering of the archer is rather tight as a result of hard outlines—a notion which contrasts with the freedom of shorter, energetic strokes associated with Perugino's draftsmanship.

A nearly exact drawing in the Musée Bonnat, also squared for transfer, is now considered to be the preliminary drawing by Perugino. It possesses the economy of line and

Fig. 92. *Martyrdom of Saint Sebastian* (detail, pl. 19),
Church of San Sebastiano, Panicale

general spontaneity some scholars believe Perugino would have employed while sketching a studio model.[5] The artist of the National Gallery sheet may have had access to Perugino's drawing as well as the fresco, in light of the close relation among the three. A more fanciful interpretation of the archer is found in the Louvre. The style of this drawing, in combination with the heavy contours and bold shadowing, are unique to another hand. Of all other drawings related to the fresco, a sheet in the Gabinetto Disegni e Stampe degli Uffizi (fig. 93) may be the most stylistically compatible with the National Gallery of Art's *Archer Drawing a Bow*.

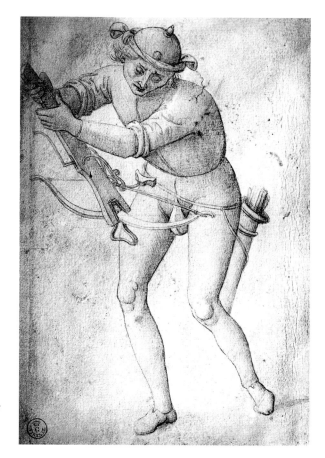

Fig. 93. Attributed to Perugino, *Study of an Archer* (after the Panicale *Martyrdom of Saint Sebastian*), Gabinetto Disegni e Stampe degli Uffizi, Florence

NOTES

1. Related drawings are found in the Galleria degli Uffizi, Musée du Louvre, Musée Bayonne, Musée Condé, and the National Gallery of Art, Washington, D.C.

2. The fresco bears Perugino's name (P[   ] DE CASTRO[   ]) and the date 1505 (A/D/M/DV) on the base upon which Saint Sebastian stands.

3. The attribution to Perugino was initiated with Weigel in 1854 and was maintained through the 1990 exhibition, *Woodner Collection: Master Drawings.*

4. When a measured grid is placed atop a drawing, the drawing is squared. Once squared, drawings can easily be enlarged to meet the desired measurements by transcribing the information from each square to the square in the very same position located on a larger grid of a blank sheet.

5. Van Cleave, p. 124.

LITERATURE

Rudolph Weigel, *Handzeichnungen berühmter Meister aus der Weigel'schen Kunstsammlung in treuen in Kupfergestochenen Nachbildungen* (Leipzig, 1854); B. Berenson, *The Drawings of the Florentine Painters* (1903); O. Fischel, "Die Zeichnungen der Umbrer" (1917); James Byam Shaw, *Drawings by Old Masters at Christ Church, Oxford,* 2 vols. (Oxford: Clarendon Press, 1976); S. Ferino Pagden, *Disegni umbri del Rinascimento* (1982); *Woodner Collection: Master Drawings,* exh. cat. (New York: Metropolitan Museum of Art/Abaris Books, 1990); Claire Van Cleave, "Follower of Perugino, Archer Drawing a Bow," catalogue entry in *The Touch of the Artist: Master Drawings from the Woodner Collection,* exh. cat., ed. Margaret Morgan Graselli (New York: Abrams, 1996); *Dessins italiens du Musée Condé à Chantilly,* vol. 1, *Autour de Pérugin, Filippino Lippi et Michel-Ange,* exh. cat. (Paris: Institut de France, 1995).

19

FIGURE OF AN ARCHER *(recto)*

c. 1500
Style of Perugino
Pen and ink on laid paper, with some tracing marks on the figure of the archer,
10⅝ × 5³⁄₁₆ in. (27 × 13.2 cm)
Verso: *Rider and Standing Draped Man, after the Antique*
National Gallery of Art, Washington, D.C., Pepita Milmore Memorial Fund (1974.20.1.a,b)

PROVENANCE: n.d., collection of Padre Sebastiano Resta, Milan (as Andrea Mantegna); by
1704, collection of Giovanni Matteo Marchetti, Bishop of Arezzo; until 1710, collection of
Cavalier Marchetti, Pistoia; 1710, sold to Lord Somers, London; 1717, Somers collection sold,
London; 1963, sold Sotheby's, London; by 1974, Schaeffer Galleries, New York
(as workshop of Perugino); 1974, National Gallery of Art purchase through
the Pepita Milmore Memorial Fund.

THIS DOUBLE-SIDED SHEET from the National Gallery of Art, Washington, D.C.,
depicts a full-length rendering of an archer drawing a bow, and, on the verso, two figure
studies after antique sources. The attribution to the style of Perugino properly implies the
author's familiarity with the art of the master and a direct or indirect association with his
workshop. The *Figure of an Archer* was undoubtedly made after a painting of the martyrdom
of Saint Sebastian by Perugino; the *Rider and Standing Draped Man, after the Antique* (fig. 95) has
traditionally been discussed as a copy after Roman sculpture. It is an interesting coinci-
dence that the representation of themes and monuments from both Christian and classical traditions on a single sheet poignantly summarizes the primary thematic interests of Renaissance artists and their patrons. Double-sided sheets such as this may have
come from a larger, bound volume containing multiple studies of figures and motifs after
both contemporary sources and monuments from the classical world (see Cole).[1]

The figure of the archer immediately calls to mind the bowmen found in several versions of the martyrdom of Saint Sebastian by Perugino. Although the drawing does not
match a specific painted representation, it is reminiscent of the two archers in the master's
final version of the subject now preserved in the Galleria Nazionale dell'Umbria (fig. 94).[2]
Of particular note is the manner in which the author of the drawing achieves the sense
of depth presented in the painting through the pose of the archer and the slight use of

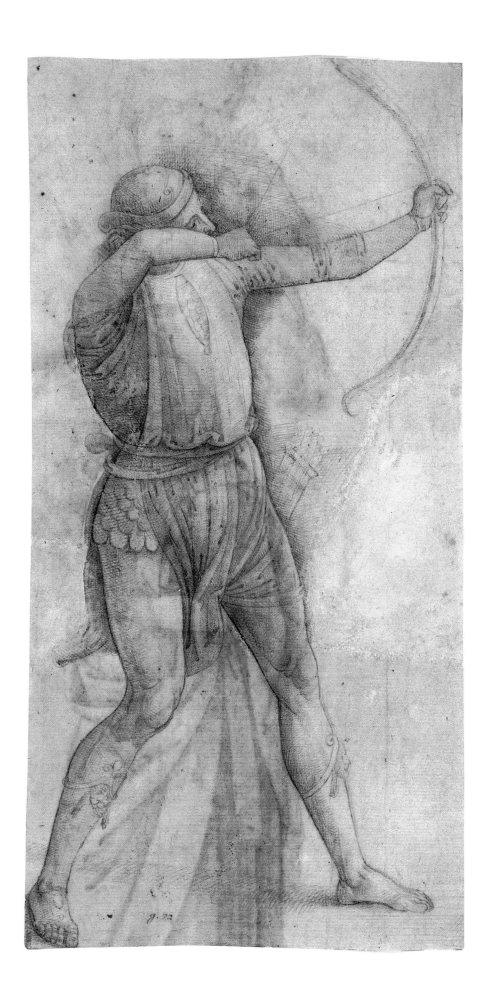

Fig. 94. *Martyrdom of Saint Sebastian*, Galleria Nazionale dell'Umbria, Perugia

foreshortening. On the verso of the sheet (fig. 95), the figures are less animated, even stiff. It has been suggested that the rider is derived from the battle frieze on Trajan's Column or the Arch of Constantine in Rome, and that the standing male corresponds with figures from the Ara Pacis, also in Rome.[3] The attention to the details of classical art perhaps explains why the drawing was formerly attributed to Andrea Mantegna (d. 1506).[4]

The figures on both sides of the drawing are carefully executed. Contours are particularly strong, as are the primary outlines which define their respective costumes. A great deal of attention has been devoted to the study of light and shadow through meticulous cross-hatching, as seen in the torso and head of the archer. The significance of these images as studies is evident, for example, in the folds in the garments worn by the standing figures. The overall lack of spontaneity in draftsmanship signals that these figures were not drawn from life, but copied from existing works of art. In fact, if one accepts the hypothesis that the recto is based on a painting and the verso on sculpture, then the even-handed execution of all forms could have arisen from the artist's having copied other drawings, themselves inspired by, but not taken from, original sources. Such practices were common for Renaissance artists, and consequently, the attribution of drawings to a particular hand can be complicated.

NOTES

1. Konrad Oberhuber articulated this suggestion in an undated document preserved in the drawing's object file at the National Gallery of Art, Washington, D.C.

2. A date of 1518 (A.D.M.D.XVIII) is found on the pedestal beneath the bound saint. The work was originally installed in the Martinelli Chapel in the Church of San Francesco al Prato, Perugia.

3. In his catalogue entry for the National Gallery of Art's 1974 *Recent Acquisitions and Promised Gifts*, Oberhuber discusses the rider in relation to the battle friezes on both the Arch of Constantine and Trajan's Column, and specifically mentions the Aeneas panel from the Ara Pacis as a point of comparison to the standing figure.

4. This attribution to Mantegna was initiated while the drawing was in the collection of Padre Sebastiano Resta. Mantegna's painstaking attention to classical details in his paintings and prints is well-known.

LITERATURE

B. Berenson, *The Drawings of the Florentine Painters* (1903); O. Fischel, "Die Zeichnungen der Umbrer" (1917); *Recent Acquisitions and Promised Gifts, National Gallery of Art* (Washington, D.C.: National Gallery of Art, 1974); Ebria Feinblatt, *Old Master Drawings from American Collections*, exh. cat. (New York: Universe Books, 1976); S. Ferino Pagden, *Disegni umbri del Rinascimento* (1982); *Dessins italiens du Musée Condé à Chantilly*, vol. 1, *Autour de Pérugin, Filippino Lippi et Michel-Ange*, exh. cat. (Paris: Institut de France, 1995).

Fig. 95. *Rider and Standing Draped Man, after the Antique* (verso, cat. no. 19)

20

MAIOLICA PLATE

c. 1500/1535
Deruta Production
Maiolica, 18 in. (45.5 cm) diam.
National Gallery of Art, Washington, D.C., Widener Collection (1942.9.325)
Inscription: AVE/SANTI/SSIMAMA [second "MA" in monogram] /RIA.MATE/RDEI.REG/INA.CELI
[Hail most holy Mary, Mother of God, Queen of Heaven]

PROVENANCE: Maurice Kann, Paris; 1908, Duveen Brothers, Paris; 1910, Peter A. B. Widener,
Elkins Park, Pennsylvania; 1942, National Gallery of Art, through
Joseph E. Widener by inheritance, Elkins Park, Pennsylvania.

MAIOLICA IS A TIN-GLAZED, painted earthenware. During the time of Perugino,
it was a popular and inexpensive ware in Italy. It was produced as early as the thirteenth
century on the peninsula, and several prominent manufacturing centers arose there.
Orvieto emerged first in the region of Umbria with an array of striking designs painted
in sepias and teal greens. The cities of Deruta and Gubbio outside Perugia gained renown
during the Renaissance for their specialization in a spectacular luster technique that endowed their wares with a shimmering iridescent surface.[1] A rich palette of deep opal blues
and greens against deep golden maize is commonly encountered in historical examples.
Such qualities arise from an intense four-step process:

> To achieve the luster of the ware produced in Umbria around the beginning of
> the cinquecento, oxide of silver and oxide of copper were mixed with pigments
> applied to the maiolica after the second firing.
>
> The piece was then fired for a third time in a special kiln into which wood
> smoke was introduced. This removed the oxygen in the pigment and covered
> the specially painted areas with a thin coat of metal which when wiped pro-
> duced wondrous, shimmering hues of golden yellow and ruby red.[2]

In the end, Renaissance maiolica offered audiences affordable works of art which were
both utilitarian and worthy of display.

Fig. 96. *Madonna della Giustizia* (detail, cat. no. 12)

This stunning example from the National Gallery of Art, Washington, D.C., depicts Mary and the Christ Child in the center. The dazzling, patterned rim of the plate serves as a dramatic border to the holy pair. Christ is firmly positioned in his mother's lap; his left hand clutches the hem of her robe and his right hand is raised in benediction. Curiously, neither figure looks directly out toward the viewer. The pose of the figures and the general concept of the youthful Virgin are probably modeled after paintings and perhaps even existing drawings by Perugino and his workshop from the late fifteenth and early sixteenth centuries.

Specifically, one cannot help but draw an immediate comparison to the rendering of the Madonna and Child in the celebrated *Madonna della Giustizia* (fig. 96). The design of the figures from the plate presents a reverse quote of the figures in the painting. Reference lines for the folds in Mary's garment and the attention to her coiffure are decidedly Peruginesque. The National Gallery of Art's maiolica plate was produced at Deruta, in the valley just outside Perugia. During the first quarter of the cinquecento, its author would have had easy access to a multitude of works by Perugino, including the *Madonna della Giustizia*. Religious subjects are frequently encountered in Deruta maiolica. This was probably due in part to the influence of nearby Assisi, a major pilgrimage center, which provided an important market for Deruta products from the fourteenth century onward.[3]

NOTES

1. For a discussion of this luster technique, see M. Bellini and G. Conti's *Le maioliche italiane del Rinascimento* (Milan: A. Vallardi, 1964) as cited in B. Cole's *Italian Maiolica from Midwestern Collections*, p. 9.

2. Ibid., p. 11.

3. Regarding Deruta ware, see U. Nicolini's 1980 catalogue for the Palazzo Ancaiani, Spoleto exhibition, *Antiche maioliche di Deruta* as cited by R. Distelberger et al.

LITERATURE

Inventory of the Objects d'Art at Lynnewood Hall, Elkins Park, Pennsylvania, the Estate of the Late P. A. B. Widener (Philadelphia, 1935); David Finley and John Walker, *Works of Art from the Widener Collections* (Washington, D.C.: National Gallery of Art, 1942); Bruce Cole, *Italian Maiolica from Midwestern Collections*, exh. cat. (Bloomington: Indiana University Art Museum, 1977); Deborah Shinn, *Sixteenth Century Maiolica, Selections from the Arthur M. Sackler and the National Gallery of Art's Widener Collections*, exh. cat. (Washington, D.C.: National Gallery of Art, 1982); Carolyn Wilson, *Renaissance Small Bronze Sculpture and Associated Decorative Arts at the National Gallery of Art* (Washington, D.C.: National Gallery of Art, 1983); Rudolph Distelberger et al., *Western Decorative Arts, Part I: Medieval, Renaissance and Historicizing Styles including Metalwork, Enamels, and Ceramics, Washington, D.C.*, The Collections of the National Gallery of Art, Systematic Catalogue (Washington, D.C.: National Gallery of Art, 1993).

21a MOURNING VIRGIN

c. 1520
Pietro Perugino
Tempera and oil on panel, 8⅜ in. (20.5 cm) diam.
North Carolina Museum of Art, Raleigh, Gift of the Samuel H. Kress Foundation
(GL.60.17.33)

21b MOURNING SAINT JOHN THE EVANGELIST

c. 1520

Pietro Perugino

Tempera and oil on panel, 8⅜ in. (21.3 cm) diam.

North Carolina Museum of Art, Raleigh, Gift of the Samuel H. Kress Foundation

(GL.60.17.34)

PROVENANCE (A AND B): collection of Sir Frederick Cook, Richmond, Surrey; by 1904,
collection of Sir J. Charles Robinson and his son, Charles Newton Robinson, London;
1914, sold R. Lepke's, Berlin; by 1938, collection Contini Bonacossi, Florence;
1938, purchased by Samuel H. Kress; 1960, given to the North Carolina
Museum of Art by the Samuel H. Kress Foundation.

THE FINAL PAINTINGS of Pietro Perugino are perhaps the least well-known and infrequently discussed works of his prolific career. In many ways, these small roundels from the North Carolina Museum of Art summarize many of the stylistic and emotional elements shared among those panels and frescoes executed during the decade preceding the master's death in 1523.[1] The *Mourning Virgin* and *Mourning Saint John the Evangelist* specifically evoke expressive visual parallels to the second phase of images created for the monumental Sant'Agostino Polyptych, and to two frescoes: the lower tier of *Six Saints* in San Severo, Perugia (fig. 34), and the *Pietà* for Santa Maria Maggiore, Spello, which carries an inscription plaque dating it to 1521.[2]

The *Mourning Virgin* and *Mourning Saint John the Evangelist* are created of easily detected, sketchy brushstrokes and a few shallow layers of pigment. Traditional drawing and painting techniques have been united toward an expressive end. The prayerful subjects stand out against dark, solid backgrounds that not only emphasize the application of paint but enrich the color of a modest palette. Mary's mantle and John's tunic are a related gray-green. Interestingly, the yellow of his cape causes the eye to perceive a lighter green, while the burgundy of Mary's tunic contrasts with her paler mantle to suggest a sober gray shroud. Both background and palette establish the sorrow-filled mood which is further conveyed through slightly bowed heads and hands clasped in mourning.

It is likely that the North Carolina panels were once part of an ensemble that formed a large altarpiece. In particular, it would be logical for these figures to have been included in a predella flanking a central figure of the Crucified Christ or Christ at the Sepulcher.[3] An example from the workshop of Raphael, now in the Galleria Nazionale dell'Umbria, Perugia (fig. 97), offers some insight into the proposed original context of Perugino's *Mourning Virgin* and *Mourning Saint John the Evangelist*. Indeed, these panels may once have appeared on either side of a roundel depicting Christ at the Sepulcher in the

Fig. 97. Workshop of Raphael, *Predella with the Pietà, the Magdalen and a Saint*, Galleria Nazionale dell'Umbria, Perugia

Fig. 98. *Dead Christ*, Pinacoteca Civica, Montefortino

Pinacoteca Civica, Montefortino (fig. 98), which is comparable in its dimensions and style to the North Carolina works.[4] In addition, a fourth roundel depicting a male saint, located at the Olana State Historical Site, New York (fig. 37), shares size and compositional format with the North Carolina and Montefortino paintings, and may also have been a part of the same predella series (see Becherer). That the works share the loose brushwork and thin layers of paint that define Perugino's late style further supports this proposal.

NOTES

1. The North Carolina panels have been variously attributed to Perugino, his school, and his circle. In the present catalogue, they are attributed to the master for the stylistic issues discussed in this essay.

2. The Sant'Agostino Polyptych, now conserved in the Galleria Nazionale dell'Umbria, was commissioned in 1502 and was nearly complete at the time of Perugino's death. Two distinct phases of work, pre- and post-1512/13 are apparent. For the most current discussion of the polyptych following its recent restoration, see Garibaldi.

3. According to John 19: 26–28, Christ entrusts the care of his mother to his beloved apostle John at the time of his Crucifixion. From this reading, a tradition developed wherein Christ is depicted between his mother Mary and his beloved apostle John.

4. Scarpellini, p. 127, is the most recent scholar to support the connection of the North Carolina and Montefortino panels.

LITERATURE

J. A. Crowe and G. B. Cavalcaselle, *A History of Painting in Italy* (1866); J. A. Crowe and G. B. Cavalcaselle, *Storia della pittura in Italia* (Florence, 1902); E. Calzini, "La Raccolta Duranti di Montefortino," *Rassegna bibliografica dell'Arte italiana* 7 (1904): 13; B. Berenson, *Central Italian Painters of the Renaissance* (1909); Luigi Serra, *Le Gallerie delle Marche* (Roma: Soc. ed. d'arte illustrata, 1925); *Tutta la pittura del Perugino* (1959); F. R. Shapley, *Paintings from the Samuel H. Kress Collection* (1968); *L'opera completa del Perugino* (1969); B. Fredericksen and F. Zeri, *Census of Pre-Nineteenth-Century Paintings* (1972); Daniela Ferriani, "Un tondo della Bottega del Perugino," in *Urbino e le Marche prima e dopo Raffaello*, ed. Maria Grazia Ciardi Duprè dal Poggetto and Paolo Dal Poggetto (Florence: Salani, 1983); D. A. Brown, *Raphael and America* (1983); V. Garibaldi, "The Polyptych of Sant'Agostino" (1996).

22

STUDY OF A MALE SAINT

n.d.
Giannicola di Paolo
Black chalk, heightened with white; pricked for transfer, 14¹¹/₁₆ × 10⅜ in. (37.3 × 26.4 cm)
Janos Scholz Collection, The Pierpont Morgan Library, New York (1980.67)

PROVENANCE: until 1862, collection of Heinrich William Campe, Leipzig; through 1902,
collection of Karl Edward Hasse, Hanover; 1902, collection of Ernst Ehlers, Göttingen;
n.d., collection of Janos Scholz, New York; 1980, gift of Janos Scholz to the
Pierpont Morgan Library.

GIANNICOLA DI PAOLO (1460–1544), often erroneously referred to as Giannicola Manni, is recognized among Perugino's most prominent students after Raphael. He was born in Perugia and matriculated in the painters' guild in that city in 1500. Numerous works and surviving documents offer ample testimony to his level of popularity. Giannicola is probably best remembered for his frescoes (begun 1513) in the Chapel of Saint John the Baptist, directly adjoining the Sala dell'Udienza, where Perugino's celebrated frescoes in the Collegio del Cambio are housed. As a leading exponent of the Umbrian school throughout the early sixteenth century, Giannicola had ample exposure to the trends of contemporary Florentine, and perhaps even Venetian, painters. His work, however, is best understood within the aesthetic parameters established by his master Perugino.[1]

This fine drawing of a bearded saint from the Pierpont Morgan Library has been variously identified as a study for Saint Peter, Saint Anthony Abbot, or Saint Joseph.[2] Although a rather complete preparatory study, it has not been successfully linked to any painting by Giannicola. This, in combination with the absence of any recognizable attribute or symbol held or located near the figure, enhances the elusiveness of the saint's identity. The drawing can be viewed in comparison to numerous bearded saints with aged but kindly faces who appear throughout the oeuvre of Perugino. Specifically, the disheveled hair, heavy eyes, and lowered head call to mind several versions of Joseph (fig. 99), the earthly father of Christ, a subject with which Giannicola would have undoubtedly been quite familiar. Whether intentionally imitated or unconsciously borrowed, such a comparison underscores the unity of style maintained within the Umbrian school of painting throughout the Renaissance.

The drawing has been masterfully executed in black chalk. Both contours and cross-hatching have been sketched out with assurance. Careful examination of the work reveals it has been pricked for transfer. More than likely, a small pouch of charcoal dust would have been passed across the surface of the drawing. The dust would have transferred an essential "map" of the drawing through the pricked openings to a prepared surface. The loose style of the Pierpont Morgan Library drawing and the very nature of its contours and cross-hatching may be directly related to a sheet preserved in the Uffizi (fig. 100). In this drawing, both the figure of a seated writer and the study of a helmeted head in profile could be considered another quality example by Giannicola di Paolo.

Fig. 99. *Head of Saint Joseph* (detail from *Adoration of the Magi*, pl. 18), Oratory of the Bianchi, Città della Pieve

Fig. 100. Attributed to Perugino, *Drawing of a Seated Figure/Study of a Head*, Gabinetto Disegni e Stampe degli Uffizi, Florence

NOTES

1. For further biographical information, see *Pittura in Umbria tra il 1480 e il 1540.*

2. Ryskamp proposed Saint Anthony Abbot, while Gilbert first suggested a comparison to Saint Joseph.

LITERATURE

Creighton Gilbert, *Drawings of the Italian Renaissance from the Scholz Collection* (New York: Dover, 1958); *Italian Master Drawings, 1350–1800 from the Janos Scholz Collection*, selected and described by Janos Scholz (New York: Dover, 1967); *Nineteenth Report to the Fellows of the Pierpont Morgan Library, 1978–1980*, ed. Charles Ryskamp (New York: Pierpont Morgan Library, 1981); *Pittura in Umbria tra il 1480 e il 1540* (1983).

23

HEAD OF SAINT LAWRENCE

n.d.
After Perugino
Silverpoint, heightened with white on light brown prepared paper,
8⅞ × 6¹³⁄₁₆ in. (22.5 × 17.3 cm)
The Pierpont Morgan Library, New York (I, 10)

PROVENANCE: Charles Fairfax Murray; 1910, purchased by J. Pierpont Morgan.

THIS SENSITIVE RENDERING of a male head is a precise study after the figure of Saint Lawrence in Perugino's celebrated *Decemviri* Altarpiece, completed in 1496 (figs. 64, 101). Lawrence, a deacon and martyr in the early church (d. A.D. 258), appears in the immediate foreground to the right of the enthroned Madonna and Child. Joined by fellow patron saints of Perugia, Ercolano (Herculanus), Costanzo (Constantius), and Louis of Toulouse, his attention is directed downward to the large book in his hands. This explains the lowered glance encountered in the Pierpont Morgan Library drawing. The *Decemviri* Altarpiece was commissioned by Perugia's communal magistrates, known as the *Decemviri*, or Council of Ten, for their chapel in the city's town hall, the Palazzo dei Priori (Palace of the Priors), where it remained until 1797.[1] It is probably in this context that the author of the drawing had the opportunity to study Perugino's figures.

The opportunity to appreciate the artist's skill has not been diminished by the water damage suffered by the sheet. As noted, the form is rendered in silverpoint on prepared paper. This medium is particularly tedious, for it requires the artist to utilize a finely tipped silver rod, or stylus. As the stylus is passed across the surface of the paper, it leaves a slender trace of the metal which instantly oxidizes to a matte gray-brown. As evidenced in the *Head of Saint Lawrence*, white, primarily a lead white, could then be applied to highlight areas such as the forehead, nose, and lips. In short, the silverpoint technique required precise draftsmanship skills, for there was minimal room for error.[2] The highly finished quality of this study results from carefully controlled contours, thin strokes defining shadows, and sparingly applied white highlights. Once combined, these elements offer ample testimony to the skill of the artist. Only the overly taut right edge of the saint's face and

Fig. 101. Saint Lawrence (detail from *Virgin and
Child Enthroned with Saints* [*Decemviri* Altarpiece]),
Musei Vaticani

Fig. 102. *Sketch of a Head*, Gabinetto Disegni e Stampe
degli Uffizi, Florence

Fig. 103. Perugino and assistants, *Saint Nicholas of Tolentino*
(predella detail, Sant'Agostino Polyptych), Galleria
Nazionale dell'Umbria, Perugia

the reworking of the neck beneath the tip of the chin could be considered awkward. However, neither passage possesses enough visual strength to seriously detract from the overall quality of the work.

A drawing attributed to Perugino in the Uffizi (fig. 102) offers a comparison to the Pierpont Morgan Library's *Head of Saint Lawrence*.[3] The Uffizi drawing is a half-length sketch of a young monk displaying the quick strokes traditionally associated with Perugino.[4] The freedom of this style and the more organic quality of this figure differ from the crisply delineated features and general stiffness common to a drawing after an existing work of art, like the Pierpont Morgan Library drawing. A comparison to the panel painting *Saint Nicholas of Tolentino* (fig. 103), from the dismantled Sant'Agostino Polyptych, ascribed to Perugino and assistants, may also be considered. Beyond the similarity of pose (although reversed), a gossamer bond between this painting and the *Head of Saint Lawrence* is formed in the finely crafted facial features and carefully managed contours.

NOTES

1. The work was taken to France by Napoleon's troops in 1797. Upon its return to Italy in 1816, it was sent to Rome. In 1820 it became a part of the Vatican Picture Gallery (now, Pinacoteca, Musei Vaticani), where it remains today. Two full-scale copies of the *Decemviri* Altarpiece are known; one is in the church of Sant'Ercolano, Perugia, and the other is on deposit in the Galleria Nazionale dell'Umbria. The latter was executed by Domenico Garbi in the late eighteenth century following the removal of the original.

2. For a most concise discussion of Renaissance drawing techniques, see M. Clayton's introductory essay in *Seven Florentine Heads: Fifteenth-Century Drawings from the Collection of Her Majesty the Queen.*

3. This drawing was attributed to Perugino by Sylvia Ferino Pagden in her 1982 catalogue, *Disegni umbri del Rinascimento da Perugino a Raffaello.*

4. These general stylistic traits were first articulated by Fischel in 1917.

LITERATURE

B. Berenson, *The Drawings of the Florentine Painters* (1903); O. Fischel, "Die Zeichnungen der Umbrer" (1917); Agnes Mongan, review of *Italian Drawings 1330–1780: An Exhibition at the Smith College Museum of Art*, exhibition, *Art Bulletin* 24 (1942): 93; S. Ferino Pagden, *Disegni umbri del Rinascimento* (1982); M. Clayton, *Seven Florentine Heads: Fifteenth-Century Drawings from the Collection of Her Majesty the Queen* (Toronto: Art Gallery of Ontario, 1993).

24

HOLY FAMILY *(recto)*

LANDSCAPE STUDY *(verso)*

n.d.
School of Perugino
Pen and brown ink, heightened with white on gray prepared paper; gouache;
8⁷⁄₁₆ × 5¹⁵⁄₁₆ in. (21.4 × 15.1 cm)
The Pierpont Morgan Library, New York (1, 11)

PROVENANCE: Bale; Charles Fairfax Murray; 1910, purchased by J. Pierpont Morgan.

IMAGES OF THE HOLY FAMILY (Mary, Joseph, and the infant Christ) often include admiring shepherds or magi in keeping with New Testament tradition. On the recto of this double-sided sheet from the Pierpont Morgan Library, Mary is shown seated and humbly presenting the infant Christ, who is firmly positioned on her lap. Joseph is located slightly behind them. The physical arrangement of the figures, enhanced by the cherubic, forward gaze of Christ, suggests that the scene would be complete only if approaching admirers were present. The very depiction of the Holy Family on the Pierpont Morgan Library sheet is undoubtedly linked to a version of the Adoration of the Magi, originally a predella panel from either Perugino's San Pietro or Sant'Agostino Polyptych.[1] The depiction of the Christ Child revered by three wise men, or magi, was quite popular with audiences of the Renaissance and would often initiate the narrative of a predella series.[2]

Although the artist of the Pierpont Morgan Library sheet may have been familiar with both of the aforementioned altarpieces by Perugino, this representation clearly derives from the predella panel that was once part of the San Pietro Polyptych (fig. 104). The physical description and compositional arrangement of the figures are nearly identical. Even Joseph's grimace and his rather complicated pose are replicated with precision. The work was drawn using pen and brown ink. The heightening with white is unusually powerful. In most Renaissance drawings, white highlights are intended as accents and are applied sparingly, but here they nearly dominate the passages in ink. Examination of the San Pietro *Adoration of the Magi* reveals a strong light emanating from the left which boldly

(recto)

Fig. 104. Perugino and assistants, *Adoration of the Magi*,
Musée des Beaux Arts, Rouen

illuminates the forms. In copying this predella detail, the author of the *Holy Family* must have felt compelled to re-create such a prominent characteristic through the use of white heightening.

The verso of this sheet presents a most unique rendering of a landscape. During the Renaissance, pure landscape drawing was extremely rare and the description of terrain in color washes is rarer still.[3] Considering that Perugino's treatment of landscape was integral to his popularity, it is understandable that an artist creating studies after the master's paintings would carefully consider the available depictions of this subject. Specifically, the *Landscape Study* closely follows the foreground of green hills and valleys, the middle-ground silhouette of a cityscape in dense brown, and the blues of a distant mountain range which appear in each of the San Pietro predella panels. Even the tiny white dots used to convey light playing across the surface of leaves, as seen in the panels, is re-created in the drawing. In many ways, the attention paid to the landscape in this drawing, combined with the use of color, is closely allied with drawing practices north of the Alps and, to a lesser extent, in certain regions of northern Italy and Umbria.[4]

24 (verso)

NOTES

1. Both altarpieces have long been dismantled. The predella panels for the San Pietro Polyptych, completed in 1496, are now in the collection of the Musée des Beaux Arts, Rouen. The predella panels from the Sant'Agostino Polyptych, c. 1512/13–23, are today preserved in the Galleria Nazionale dell'Umbria, Perugia. Both sets of panels are recognized by scholars as the products of Perugino and assistants.

2. The word "magi" comes from *magoi*, which in the Greek translation of the Old Testament (e.g., Daniel 1: 20; 2: 2) is understood as an astrologer and in the New Testament (e.g., Acts 13: 6, 8) is interpreted as a sorcerer: *Illustrated Bible Dictionary*, ed. Herbert Lockyer Sr. (Nashville: Thomas Nelson Publishers, 1982), p. 1104.

3. For a more complete discussion of Renaissance landscape drawings, see cat. no. 14.

4. S. Ferino Pagden, p. 41.

LITERATURE

B. Berenson, *The Drawings of the Florentine Painters* (1903); Almon Richard Turner, *The Vision of Landscape in Renaissance Italy* (Princeton: Princeton University Press, 1966); S. Ferino Pagden, *Disegni umbri del Rinascimento* (1982); Francis Russell, "Perugino and the Early Experience of Raphael," in *Raphael Before Rome*, ed. James Beck, Studies in the History of Art, vol. 17 (Washington, D.C.: National Gallery of Art, 1983), pp. 189–201; George Goldner, "New Drawings by Perugino and Pontormo," *Burlington Magazine* 136 (1994): 365–67; William M. Griswold, *Metropolitan Museum of Art, Recent Acquisitions: A Selection, 1993–1994* (New York: Metropolitan Museum of Art, 1994).

g. 120

25

THE PROPHET JEREMIAH

n.d.
After Perugino
Pen and brown ink, 8⅜ × 5¹¹⁄₁₆ in. (21.3 × 14.4 cm)
Thaw Collection, The Pierpont Morgan Library, New York (1976.42)

PROVENANCE: n.d., collection of Padre Sebastiano Resta, Milan; possibly 1704–10, through
Marchetti collections, Arezzo and Pistoia; 1710–17, collection of John Lord Somers, London;
by 1949, Victor Koch; 1949, Mrs. Flora Koch through Sotheby's, London; collection of
Luigi Grassi; 1967, collection of Mr. and Mrs. Eugene V. Thaw; 1976, gift to the
Pierpont Morgan Library from Mr. and Mrs. Eugene V. Thaw.

THIS DRAWING HAS BEEN ATTRIBUTED to a follower of Perugino. Carefully
executed contours and meticulously rendered cross-hatching imply the work is a study
after an existing work of art, rather than a study from life. The seated figure depicted is
generally considered to be a representation of the Old Testament prophet Jeremiah.[1]
Jeremiah is recognized as one of the four great prophets (along with Isaiah, Ezekiel, and
Daniel), and his imagined likeness appears frequently in art from the Middle Ages
through the Baroque. Jeremiah is traditionally shown aged and bearded. He is commonly
portrayed holding a book or a scroll as the attribute of his prophecies. The artist maintains these conventions in this drawing from the Pierpont Morgan Library, in which the
thick beard and flowing hair frame the face of a distinguished elder, whose right forearm
cradles remnants of a cascading scroll. In truth, it would be virtually impossible to attempt an identification of this figure among innumerable Renaissance drawings of anonymous aged prophets, patriarchs, and statesmen were it not for the direct relationship of
this work to a painting by Perugino.

Jeremiah is the subject of a large circular painting, known as a tondo (fig. 105), which
was once placed to the left of the central panel of Perugino's grand polyptych in San
Pietro, Perugia.[2] From the seated pose to the position of limbs and details of the garment
folds, the Pierpont Morgan Library drawing carefully follows the prophet's depiction in
the tondo. Indeed, the drawing is an exact copy after the painting, with the singular exception of his incomplete left hand. The use of thick cross-hatching in the drawing effectively conveys the concern for shadow and depth found in the painting. In addition, the

Fig. 105. *The Prophet David* (formerly *The Prophet Jeremiah*), Musée des Beaux Arts, Nantes

Fig. 106. *Jupiter* (ceiling detail), Collegio del Cambio, Perugia

figure in the drawing is thinner and more compact—traits that are enhanced by the density of the draftsmanship. It may also be noted that *The Prophet Jeremiah* and the more robust figure from the San Pietro tondo are nearly identical, in reverse, to the enthroned mythological god Jupiter, found among the ceiling frescoes of the Collegio del Cambio, Perugia (fig. 106).[3]

Several well-preserved sheets in the Uffizi are likely to have been drawn by the artist responsible for the Pierpont Morgan Library drawing.[4] The handling of line, treatment of light and dark areas, and even the realization of the face and right hand are analogous. The Uffizi drawing illustrated here (fig. 107) represents the ancient Greek philosopher Socrates and is a study after one of Perugino's figures found on the side wall of the Collegio del Cambio.[5] Like many Umbrian artists of the early sixteenth century, the author of *The Prophet Jeremiah* found it necessary to carefully examine and attempt numerous studies after a variety of paintings that were available for inspection in Perugia. Figures encountered in monumental works like the San Pietro Polyptych and on the walls and ceiling of the Collegio del Cambio served as invaluable resources. Finally, one cannot discount the possibility that Perugino's own drawings may have been accessible for study and replication (see Cole, Mencarelli).

Fig. 107. Assistant of Perugino, *Socrates*, Gabinetto Disegni e Stampe degli Uffizi, Florence

NOTES

1. Jeremiah's prophetic ministry began c. 627 B.C. and continued for more than forty years through the destruction of Jerusalem in 587–586 B.C.

2. The large polyptych was commissioned in 1495 and completed in 1500. Jeremiah and Isaiah are each depicted on tondos that flanked the central panel of *Christ's Ascension.* Scholars have long recognized the participation of other hands in the production of the polyptych. The polyptych was dismantled by French troops in 1797 and most of the panels were sent to Paris. In the early nineteenth century, these panels were distributed among French public collections, and *The Prophet Jeremiah* was received in Nantes in 1809.

3. The ceiling decorations are frequently assigned to Perugino and assistants. For a complete discussion of the fresco cycle in the Collegio del Cambio, consult Scarpellini, pp. 95–99.

4. Three drawings from the Uffizi merit careful consideration in comparison to the Pierpont Morgan Library's *Prophet Jeremiah* and are likely to be by the same artist: a *Study of Socrates* (recto)/*Sketch for the Same Figure* (verso), *The Prophet Elijah*, and *A Study of Pericles* (recto)/*Study of Christ on the Cross* (verso).

5. This drawing has been tentatively attributed to Berto di Giovanni by Sylvia Ferino Pagden in her landmark catalogue of 1982, *Disegni umbri del Rinascimento da Perugino al Raffaello.*

LITERATURE

Rudolph Weigel, *Handzeichnungen berühmter Meister aus der Weigel'schen Kunstsammlung in treuen in Kupfergestochenen Nachbildungen* (Leipzig, 1854); U. Gnoli, "Raffaello, il Cambio di Perugia e I Profeti in Nantes," *Rassegna d'Arte* 13 (1913): 75–83 ; O. Fischel, "Die Zeichnungen der Umbrer" (1917); Felice Stampfle and Cara Denison, *Drawings from the Collection of Mr. and Mrs. Eugene Thaw* (New York: Pierpont Morgan Library, 1975); S. Ferino, "A Master Painter and his Pupils: Pietro Perugino and his Umbrian Workshop," *The Oxford Art Journal* 3 (1979): 9–14; S. Ferino Pagden, *Disegni umbri del Rinascimento* (1982); P. Scarpellini, *Perugino,* 1st ed. (1984).

26

SAINT SEBASTIAN

c. 1500
Follower of Perugino
Oil on panel, transferred to canvas on masonite, 30³⁄₁₆ × 21¹⁄₁₆ in. (76.7 × 53.4 cm)
Gift of the Samuel H. Kress Foundation to the New Jersey State Museum; transferred to
The Art Museum, Princeton University

PROVENANCE: by tradition of former inscription (verso) the Conti degli Oddi, Perugia; by
1847, collection of Edward Solly, London; 1847, sold Christie's, London (as Raphael), to Lord
Northwick, Thirlestane House, Cheltenham, Gloucestershire; 1873, sold through Sir J. Charles
Robinson to Cook collection, Richmond, Surrey (as Giannicola di Paolo); 1875, on view at
Royal Academy, London; n.d., collection of Contini Bonacossi, Florence; 1948, Samuel H. Kress
collection; 1963, given to the New Jersey State Museum, Trenton, by Samuel H. Kress
Foundation; 1994, transferred to The Art Museum, Princeton University.

AS A PROLIFIC PAINTER and the skillful master of an active workshop, Perugino
initiated several standard representations of saintly figures which were frequently reused
by his students and numerous known and unknown followers. Scholars seeking clearer
definition of Renaissance painting in Umbria struggle to identify the authors, dates, and
original contexts of numerous Perugino-related paintings presently found in collections
across the world. This recently rediscovered work from the Art Museum, Princeton University, is a sensitive rendition of Saint Sebastian. The gentle, almost serpentine pose and
upward, otherworldly gaze clearly derive from several images of the popular early Christian saint depicted by Perugino during the final decade of the fifteenth century.[1] The
Princeton painting has been examined by a range of scholars since its acquisition in 1873
for the Cook collection and has been variously assigned to Perugino, Raphael, and
Giannicola di Paolo. Most recently, justified caution has led to the present attribution to
a Follower of Perugino.

Early attributions favor a link to the young Raphael working under the pronounced
influence of his teacher Perugino.[2] This sentiment was fueled by a seventeenth- or
eighteenth-century inscription, "This St. Sebastian was painted by Raphael Sanzio for the
Conti degli Oddi Perugia, I.A.D.S.P.," reportedly found on the back of the original
panel.[3] Scholars willing to accept the studied dependence of *Saint Sebastian* on a prototype

Fig. 108. Perugino and assistant (Eusebio da San Giorgio?), *Madonna and Child with Saints Nicholas of Tolentino, Bernardino of Siena, Jerome, and Sebastian* (Tezi Altarpiece), Galleria Nazionale dell'Umbria, Perugia

Fig. 109. Anonymous (Eusebio da San Giorgio?), *Adoration of the Shepherds*, Duomo, Gubbio

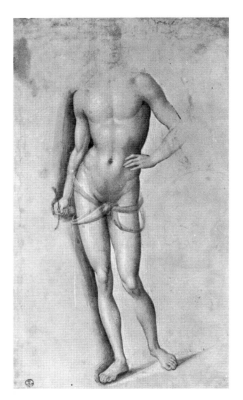

Fig. 110. Follower of Perugino, *Study of a Nude Figure*, Gabinetto Disegni e Stampe degli Uffizi, Florence

established by Perugino, but who are hesitant to embrace the Raphael attribution, have ascribed the work to other pupils of the master, such as Giannicola di Paolo (1460–1544) and Eusebio da San Giorgio (c. 1465–1550?).[4] Although the former proposal has gradually faded as more succinct information on this artist has come to light, the latter attribution merits further consideration.

A painting, *Madonna and Child with Saints Nicholas of Tolentino, Bernardino of Siena, Jerome, and Sebastian* (fig. 108), currently in the Galleria Nazionale dell'Umbria, has been jointly ascribed to Perugino and to Eusebio da San Giorgio.[5] The description of Mary and the infant Christ are in keeping with Perugino's style, but the figures of the four saints are tightly rendered, with contours succinctly defined in the manner of Eusebio. Furthermore, the elongated forms and the description of the flesh of Saint Jerome and Saint Sebastian in the immediate foreground also characterize the Princeton figure. In another altarpiece (fig. 109) attributed to Eusebio in the Duomo of Gubbio, one cannot help but discern the close stylistic relationship between the three musical angels in the sky and the Princeton *Saint Sebastian*. Unfortunately, too little is known of Eusebio's work, so a firm attribution to him is decidedly premature. Another image which merits consideration is the intriguing drawing of a male (fig. 110) in the Uffizi. The sinuous, anatomically pronounced contours are not unlike those encountered in the painting and the intentionally sensual nature of both works is noteworthy. Like the *Saint Sebastian,* the drawing is ascribed to an anonymous follower of Perugino.

NOTES

1. Although eleven representations of Saint Sebastian are known, the Princeton panel is most closely associated with the *Virgin Mary and Child with Saints John the Baptist and Sebastian* panel, Galleria degli Uffizi, Florence, dated to 1493 (fig. 28), and the *Saint Sebastian* panel, Musée du Louvre, Paris (fig. 53).

2. This attribution dates to the mid-nineteenth century when it was listed as a work by Raphael while in the Solly collection; consult the sale catalogue from Christie's, London, May 8, 1847.

3. "Questo S. Bastiano è stato da Raffaelo Sanzio da Urbino Dipinto per I Signori Conti degli Oddi Perugia I.A.D.S.P.," Shapley, p. 101.

4. Tancred Borenius is responsible for the attribution to Giannicola. Berenson tentatively attributed the painting to Eusebio.

5. Scarpellini, p. 102.

LITERATURE

J. A. Crowe and G. B. Cavalcaselle, *A History of Painting in Italy* (1866); B. Berenson, *Central Italian Painters of the Renaissance* (1909); Tancred Borenius, *A Catalogue of the Paintings in the Collection of Sir Frederick Cook* (London: Heinemann, 1913), vol. 1; W. Bombe, *Perugino* (1914); U. Gnoli, *Pietro Perugino* (1923); U. Gnoli, *Pittori e miniatori* (1923); W. Burger, "A tondo by Sinibaldo Ibi," *Burlington Magazine* 55 (1929): 87; W. E. Suida, "The Samuel H. Kress Collection," *Philadelphia Museum Bulletin* 46 (1950): 8; W. E. Suida and F. R. Shapley, *Paintings and Sculpture from the Kress Collection* (1956); *Tutta la pittura del Perugino* (1959); *Catalogue of the Art Collection,* vol. 1: *Italian and French Paintings* (Greenville, S.C.: Bob Jones University, 1962); F. R. Shapley, *Paintings from the Samuel H. Kress Collection* (1968); P. Scarpellini, *Perugino,* 1st ed. (1984); F. Todini, *La pittura umbra* (1989).

27

NATIVITY

c. 1500
School of Perugino
Egg tempera on panel, 16 × 12⅛ in. (40. 6 × 30.8 cm)
Yale University Art Gallery, Bequest of Maitland F. Griggs,
B.A., 1896 (1943.265)

PROVENANCE: 1927, purchased in Paris by Maitland F. Griggs, New York;
1943, bequeathed to the art gallery.

THE *Nativity* from the Yale University Art Gallery is attributed to the school of Perugino. The carefully arranged, symmetrical composition and tranquil mood of this small panel suggest that the anonymous author was quite familiar with several prominent versions of the subject by Perugino and was probably a workshop participant. The visual strength of the painting sustains its current presentation as an independent work of art; however, in its original context, it probably formed part of the predella of an altarpiece. The fact that panel was cut down on all sides, as evidenced by the awkwardly cropped peak of the stable's truss at the top of the image and the slivers of wood shorn from the left and right sides, suggests this function. Of the numerous panels known in public and private collections in Europe and America, this example displays high quality while offering insight into the practices of many artists associated with Perugino's copious workshop.[1]

Perugino addressed the theme of the Nativity, or Adoration of the Shepherds, numerous times. His most renowned version is part of the celebrated fresco cycle of the Collegio del Cambio, Perugia (fig. 27). The general format and placement of the Holy Family, three of the shepherds, the ox, and the ass are repeated in the Yale panel. The figure of Joseph is nearly an exact quote, simply inverted. Most of the human gestures and animal glances have also been carefully translated. Although the significance of the Cambio fresco has long been accepted, another version of the subject by Perugino must be considered as an important resource for the artist who painted the Yale *Nativity*.[2] A large panel which once formed the centerpiece of the apse side of the monumental polyptych in the Church of Sant'Agostino, Perugia, was an equal, or perhaps even greater, source of inspiration (fig. 111).[3] Strong parallels are immediately apparent in the towering

Fig. 111. *Adoration of the Shepherds* (central panel, Sant'Agostino Polyptych), Galleria Nazionale dell'Umbria, Perugia

timber-framed stable and the low-lying hills in the distant haze. Close inspection reveals that the sinuous form of the Virgin in the Yale *Nativity* is the mirrored inversion of the kneeling young mother in the Sant'Agostino panel.

In general, two factors prevent the recognition of the Yale panel as a work by the master: the harsh use of light and dark tones, and the lack of subtleties in the description of human figures. With regard to the former, the author appears uncomfortable with the middle tones which would have softened the appearance of faces and costumes; in reference to the latter, each of the figures reveals a lack of anatomical preparatory study.[4] Although the author of the Yale *Nativity* will probably never be identified by name, a comparison of the work to two of Perugino's most significant commissions in Perugia supports its production in relation to the master's workshop in that city.[5] A fine drawing in the British Museum (fig. 112), pricked for transfer, records the very information presented in the Yale painting and testifies to the widespread dissemination of Perugino's work, which may have aided the Yale master.

Fig. 112. *Adoration of the Shepherds,* The British Museum, London

NOTES

1. For the most complete understanding of documented paintings by the school and anonymous followers of Perugino, see Fredericksen and Zeri, Todini's two-volume work, and the list following Joseph Becherer's essay in this catalogue.

2. The relationship between the Cambio fresco and the Yale panel was most recently published in 1970 as part of the catalogue entry for the work in Charles Seymour Jr.'s *Early Italian Paintings in the Yale University Art Gallery.*

3. The Sant'Agostino Polyptych was commissioned in 1502; however, two distinct phases of work are recognized: from 1502 until 1512, and from 1512/13 until the death of the artist in 1523. The Yale *Nativity* is believed to date to the latter phase.

4. A largely unknown panel also attributed to the School of Perugino, the *Madonna and Child* in the collection of the Dulwich Picture Gallery, London, exhibits similar stylistic traits, as in the face and hands of Mary. This panel is often ascribed to the Master of the Schleissheim Madonna.

5. Perugino maintained workshops in Perugia and Florence throughout his career. A workshop in Rome is also known to have existed.

LITERATURE

R. van Marle, *The Development of the Italian Schools of Painting* (1937); Fernando Bologna, "Un'altra *Resurrezione* giovanile di Raffaello," in *Studies in the History of Art Dedicated to William Suida on His Eightieth Birthday* (London: Phaidon, 1959); Charles Seymour Jr., *Early Italian Paintings in the Yale University Art Gallery* (New Haven and London: Yale University Press, 1970); B. Fredericksen and F. Zeri, *Census of Pre-Nineteenth-Century Italian Paintings* (1972); F. Todini, *La pittura umbra* (1989).

Bibliography for Literature Cited in Catalogue Commentary

Berenson, Bernard. *Central Italian Painters of the Renaissance.* New York and London: G. P. Putnam's Sons, 1909, 1932, 1936, 1968.

————. *The Drawings of the Florentine Painters, Classified, Criticized, and Studied as Documents in the History and Appreciation of Tuscan Art.* New York: Dutton, 1903.

Bombe, Walter. *Perugino, des Meisters Gemälde.* Berlin and Stuttgart: Deutsche Verlags-Anstalt, 1914.

Brown, David Alan. *Raphael and America.* Washington, D.C.: National Gallery of Art, 1983.

Canuti, Fiorenzo. *Il Perugino,* 2 vols. Siena: Editrice d'Arte "La Diana," 1931.

Crispolti, Cesare. *Perugia Augusta Descritta.* Perugia, 1648.

Crowe, Joseph A., and Giovanni B. Cavalcaselle. *A History of Painting in Italy from the Second to the Fourteenth Century.* Ed. Tancred Borenius. 2d ed. Vol. 3. London, 1866. Reprint, New York: C. Scribner's Sons, 1912.

Dipinti, Sculture e Ceramiche della Galleria Nazionale dell'Umbria: Studi e Restauri. Ed. Caterina Bon Valsassina and Vittoria Garibaldi. Florence: Arnaud, 1994.

Ferino Pagden, Sylvia. *Disegni umbri del Rinascimento da Perugino a Raffaello.* Florence: Olschki, 1982.

————. *Die Kirchen von Siena.* Ed. Peter A. Riedl and Max Seidel. Munich: Bruckmann, 1985.

Fischel, Oskar. "Die Zeichnungen der Umber." *Jahrbuch der königlich preussischen Kunstsammlungen* 38 (1917): 1–280.

Fredericksen, Burton, and Federico Zeri. *Census of Pre-Nineteenth-Century Paintings in North American Public Collections.* Cambridge: Harvard University Press, 1972.

Gamba, Carlo. *Pittura umbra del Rinascimento.* Novara: Istituto Geografico De Agostini, 1949.

Garibaldi, Vittoria. "The Polyptych of Sant'Agostino: The Historical and Critical Tradition." *Associazione Comitato Italiano, World Monuments Fund, Annual Report,* 1996.

Gnoli, Umberto. *Pietro Perugino.* Spoleto: C. Argentieri, 1923.

————. *Pittori e miniatori nell'Umbria.* Spoleto: C. Argentieri, 1923.

Guardabassi, Mariano. *Indice-guida dei monumenti pagani e cristiani riguardanti l'Istoria e l'Arte esistenti nella provincia dell'Umbria.* Perugia, 1872.

Lloyd, Christopher. *Italian Paintings before 1600 in The Art Institute of Chicago.* Princeton: Princeton University Press, 1993.

Lupatelli, Angelo. *Catalogo dei quadri che si conservano nella Pinacoteca Vannucci esistente nel piano superiore del Palazzo Municipale di Perugia.* Perugia, 1885.

Mezzanotte, Antonio. *Della vita e delle opere di Pietro Vannucci da Castello della Pieve, cognominato il Perugino—Commentario istorico.* Perugia, 1836.

Morelli, Giovanni F. *Brevi notizie delle pitture e sculture che adornano l'augusta città di Perugia.* Perugia, 1683.

Nelson, Jonathan. "The High Altar-piece of SS. Annunziata in Florence: History, Form, and Function." *Burlington Magazine* 139 (1997): 84–94.

L'Opera completa del Perugino. Ed. Carlo Castellaneta and Ettore Camesasca. Milan: Rizzoli, 1969.

Orsini, Baldassare. *Vita, elogia e memoria dell'egregio pittore Pietro Perugino e degli scolari di esso.* Perugia, 1804.

Pittura in Umbria tra il 1480–1540: premesse e sviluppi nei tempi di Perugino e Raffaello. Milan: Electa, 1983.

Santi, Francesco. *Dipinti, sculture, e oggetti dei secoli XV–XVI.* Rome: Istituto poligrafico dello Stato, 1985.

———. *Galleria Nazionale dell'Umbria a Perugia.* Rome: Istituto poligrafico dello Stato, 1955.

———. *Gonfaloni umbri del Rinascimento.* Perugia: Editrice Volumnia, 1976.

———. *IV Mostra di opere restaurante, Perugia, Galleria Nazionale dell'Umbria.* Perugia: Galleria Nazionale dell'Umbria, 1963.

Scarpellini, Pietro. *Perugino.* 1st ed. Milan: Electa, 1984.

———. *Perugino.* 2d ed. Milan: Electa, 1991.

Shapley, Fern Rusk. *Paintings from the Samuel H. Kress Collection, Italian Schools, XV–XVI Century.* London: Phaidon, 1968.

Siepi, Serafino. *Descrizione topologica-istorica della città di Perugia.* Perugia, 1822.

Suida, William Emil, and Fern Rusk Shapley. *Paintings and Sculpture from the Kress Collection, Washington, D.C., National Gallery of Art.* Washington, D.C.: National Gallery of Art, 1956.

Todini, Filippo. *La pittura umbra. Dal Duecento al primo Cinquecento.* 2 vols. Milan: Longanesi, 1989.

Tutta la pittura del Perugino. Ed. Ettore Camesasca. Milan: Rizzoli, 1959.

van Marle, Raimond. *The Development of the Italian Schools of Painting.* Vol. 16. The Hague: M. Nijhoff, 1937.

Venturi, Adolfo. *Storia dell'arte italiana.* Vol. 7, Part 2. Milan: U. Hoepli, 1913.

Venturi, Lionello. "A Pietro Perugino." *L'Arte* 3 (1932): 422–23.

Zeri, Federico, and Elizabeth E. Gardner. *Metropolitan Museum of Art: Italian Paintings of the Sienese and Central Italian Schools.* New York: Metropolitan Museum of Art, 1980.

MARILYN BRADSHAW

OHIO UNIVERSITY

Pietro Perugino:
An Annotated Chronicle

PIETRO PERUGINO (c. 1450–1523) was an artist famous in his own time and praised
by his contemporaries for his light and color, lyrical line, serene and graceful figures, harmonious balance, perspective, landscape, and draftsmanship. He trained many pupils, but
is best remembered as Raphael's teacher. While born in Umbria and receiving his earliest
training there, his style reached its first mature development in Florence, where in the
1470s he worked in the shop of Andrea del Verrocchio with Sandro Botticelli and
Leonardo da Vinci. Fame came to Perugino in his early thirties when Pope Sixtus IV asked
him to coordinate the largest Roman fresco project of the century, the decoration of the
newly built Sistine Chapel (1481) in Rome. There, he supervised the combined efforts of
Florentine master painters Botticelli, Domenico Ghirlandaio, Cosimo Rosselli, and a
painter from Cortona, Luca Signorelli. Only three of Perugino's six frescoes in the Sistine
Chapel have survived, and among these, it was *The Delivery of the Keys to Saint Peter* that gained
him immediate and considerable renown. He became a favored painter of the Church, the
state, and wealthy nobles, who ordered small- and large-scale religious and secular works
for both public and private settings. Perugino worked for four popes during his lifetime,
making decorations for coronations, chapels, and palaces. Among his many lordly patrons
was Isabella d'Este, Duchess of Mantua, who commissioned a painting for her *studiolo* in
Mantua. The agent of Ludovico Sforza (the Duke of Milan and a military giant) recommended that Perugino be asked to work at the Certosa of Pavia, and Lorenzo de' Medici
(1449–1492) commissioned mythologies from Perugino for his villa at Spedaletto.
Perugino had more patrons than Botticelli and more commissions than his shop could
execute.

However much Perugino's career has been studied, much has remained unexamined
and incompletely understood. "An Annotated Chronicle" brings together pertinent events
and information about Perugino's milieu that will shed new light on the nature of his art

and his contributions to the art of the period. This is a scholarly chronology that includes references to the recorded documents of the period in the form of both the visual (paintings and drawings) and written sources (contracts, letters, payments, and wills). Its commentary gives descriptive and interpretative information that will help illuminate the intent and logic of Perugino's professional decisions. The structure of *An Annotated Chronicle* encourages cross-referencing of data that show the larger patterns of Perugino's career and how it fits with those of his contemporaries.

Perugino's story is uniquely rich and long, spanning nearly three-quarters of a century. As his artistic wisdom grew, he made choices that helped guarantee him immediate economic security as well as durable fame. After his accomplishments at Rome in the Sistine Chapel, he never lacked commissions of significant stature. In 1508, when he was almost sixty years old, his name and style were recognized from Venice to Naples. By 1510 Tuscan and Umbrian artists who had once measured their own art against that of Perugino began to compare their work with that of his student Raphael. This was a pivotal time for Italian art, which began a new course in Rome with Michelangelo's work on the Sistine Ceiling and Raphael's acceptance of the Vatican commission that would change his career. Burgeoning artists continued, however, to study Perugino's work in Perugia, Florence, Siena, and Rome, just as Perugino had studied the work of Masaccio and Giotto.

Our knowledge of Perugino's work remains incomplete, even though Vasari listed about fifty of his paintings and there are some three hundred records about his life and works in existence. However popular Perugino was in his own lifetime, and became again in late eighteenth- and nineteenth-century Europe, Raphael's fame has colored our understanding of his contributions. Our vision of Perugino's art often concentrates on the early style he developed in the decades of the 1480s and 1490s. Questions about attribution continue to engulf Perugino's work and that of the entire Umbrian School. One reason for this confusion is that Perugino's drawings circulated widely among his students, who copied and recopied his figures. Another reason is that Perugino perfected a style that his students could easily emulate and adapt. He designed figures whose distinct postures and gestures signaled specific character types. With few designs, Perugino and his followers could and *did* create multiple paintings. Our appreciation of his unique vision has unfortunately been lessened because some of his ultimate paint surfaces have suffered irreparable damage. These delicate and final touches, especially important in the late works, could not be duplicated by Perugino's students, and were the special marks of this master painter. As the aging artist's experiences multiplied, his vision evolved and his work changed. Perugino developed a late style whose innovations influenced a new generation of artists. His contributions took a new direction, one that could be recognized only by the next generation of painters, the Mannerists.

Pl. 1. Cityscape of Città della Pieve

c. 1450 Pietro di Cristoforo di Pietro Vannucci (Perugino) is born to Lucia di Jacopo Nunzio Betti and Cristoforo di Pietro Vannucci between 1445 and 1450 in Castello della Pieve (now called Città della Pieve), a town about twenty-seven miles from Perugia that had been under Perugia's control since 1198 (pl. 1). Pietro's family enjoyed the rights of citizenship, which means they were more affluent than Vasari described. Pietro got his nickname, *Il Perugino,* "the one from Perugia," from his connection to that city.

1452 Leonardo is born in the town of Vinci near Florence.

c. 1454 Pintoricchio (Bernardino di Betto) is born in Perugia, according to Vasari.

1457 Filippino Lippi is born to the painter and monk Fra Filippo Lippi in the town of Prato, about twenty miles from Florence.

1465–70 Most scholars agree that Perugino's early training began in Perugia. Even Vasari, however, was uncertain about who trained Perugino, identifying his first master as an unaccomplished, nameless artist from Perugia who nevertheless gave young Perugino a respect for skilled artists. Perugino's early work reveals familiarity with the stylistic traits of Umbrian artists in Perugia, including Benedetto Bonfigli (active 1445–1496), Bartolomeo Caporali (active 1440–1503), and Fiorenzo di Lorenzo (active 1460–1522). Afterward, Perugino probably worked in Arezzo with Piero della Francesca (d. 1492), before or after working in Florence with Andrea del Verrocchio (d. 1488). In Verrocchio's shop he became familiar with the art and ideas of Botticelli, Ghirlandaio, the Pollaiuolo brothers, and Leonardo da Vinci (in the shop from 1469 until around 1476). While in Florence, he had the chance to study works by artists of the previous generation. Paintings by Andrea del Castagno (d. 1457) and

Domenico Veneziano (d. 1461) were to influence his early work at Cerqueto (see 1478). The sacred paintings of Angelico (d. 1455) made a lasting impression upon the character type and formal structuring of Perugino's sacred figure groups throughout his career. Angelico and his student Benozzo Gozzoli (d. 1497) had worked in Umbria making images that helped define Umbrian art of the third quarter of the fifteenth century.

1468 In Florence the decoration of a new chapel in San Miniato, built to hold the tomb of Cardinal James Lusitania of Portugal (d. 1459), is completed when Piero and Antonio del Pollaiuolo finish frescoes of angels and an altarpiece panel, *Saints Vincent, James, and Eustace*. For two years Alesso Baldovinetti had worked in the chapel painting frescoes of the Four Evangelists and the Latin Doctors of the Church (1466–67), frescoes of Old Testament prophets and an ornamental frieze with crests of Portugal's royal family (1467), and an Annunciation panel (1467–68).

The entire decoration of the chapel was completed within nine years of the cardinal's death. Many artists worked on the chapel: Antonio Manetti designed the chapel (1460), Giovanni di Matteo del Rossellino carved the architectural stonework for the chapel (1460–61), Luca della Robbia executed a vault of glazed terra-cotta tiles (1462), and Bernardo and Antonio del Rossellino designed and installed the cardinal's marble wall tomb (1461–66). Cardinal James was of royal lineage and his relatives expended great sums of money on this ornate mausoleum. Its lavish decoration must have seemed remarkable compared with the more severe Florentine style prevalent at the time.

In the following years the chapel became a constant source of ideas for artists working in Florence, especially for Perugino. The poised and confident aristocratic figures in the Pollaiuolo brothers' altarpiece, *Saints Vincent, James, and Eustace*, provided the poses and gestures for some figures in Perugino's *Adoration of the Magi* (see 1475; pl. 2) and *Saints Roch, Sebastian, and Peter* (see 1478; fig. 4). Although Perugino appropriated specific gestures, such as the way Eustace's arm wraps around a

strap (for his central magus), his use of the altarpiece as a source for images transcends borrowing. He conflated the characteristic features of the three saints to create distinctive types that he would vary over time. An open, limitless landscape in the Pollaiuolo altarpiece also influenced the deeply receding outdoor settings in Perugino's Sistine Chapel frescoes (see 1480). The sheer wealth of rich patterns and textures coexisting in the Cardinal of Portugal's chapel made a lasting impression on Perugino, one that he remembered as he designed sumptuous frescoes for the Collegio del Cambio. The ceiling frescoes in the Cambio are particularly lively, garnering them immediate attention in a room which could have been dominated by the massive wood paneling, intricately carved and highly decorated with figurative designs (see 1496).

1469 Perugino's name appears as *Petrus Christofori Vannuccioli* in a register of wine purchases in Castello della Pieve.

Antonio del Pollaiuolo works on drawings for embroidered vestments for the San Giovanni Baptistery in Florence. Antonio's designs and workshop practices were to make a lasting impression upon Perugino.

Piero del Pollaiuolo receives a commission to paint images of Cardinal and Theological Virtues for the palace of the *Mercanzia* (a tribunal for commercial law). The *Mercanzia* later commissioned Botticelli to paint the image *Fortitude* for the palace in 1470. Botticelli's and Pollaiuolo's noble women inspired Perugino, whose images of the Virgin Mary as the Mother of God became the quintessential patrician woman: a stately figure having a grand, commanding presence, and a serene demeanor.

Both Antonio and Piero del Pollaiuolo maintain workshops in Florence, with Antonio's being the larger one. Commissions sometimes went from one shop to the other, as the brothers and their assistants were involved in joint projects. Designs by Antonio were frequently reused by him, shared with Piero, and used by the brothers' assistants. Perugino recognized the efficiency of the system they designed to work on multiple commissions simultaneously, using the same drawings for many purposes. Perugino would later establish workshops in Florence and Perugia that ran similarly yet became even larger and were run more efficiently.

Antonio del Pollaiuolo visits Rome.

1470 Perugino depicts the Virgin holding the dead Christ (Pietà) with kneeling Saints Jerome and Mary Magdalene (tempera on canvas), 50⅜ × 65 in. (128 × 165 cm), around 1470 for Franciscan monks at Farneto (since 1863, Galleria Nazionale dell'Umbria, Perugia; cat. no. 9). The *Pietà with Saints Jerome and Mary Magdalene* most likely functioned as a *gonfalone* (processional banner). It reveals Perugino's stylistic closeness to the Umbrian artist Fiorenzo di Lorenzo and to Luca Signorelli, who was possibly trained by Fiorenzo and by Piero della Francesca.

1472 Perugino is inscribed in the *Libro Rosso* (the Red Book: the register of the Florentine *Compagnia di San Luca* [Company of Saint Luke]) as being from Castello della Pieve: *Mag Petrus Christophori de Castro Plebis, vulgariter nuncupatus Perusinus.* The Company of Saint Luke was a religious confraternity whose membership consisted mainly of artists, most of whom were painters.

Filippino Lippi and Leonardo da Vinci are registered in the *Libro Rosso* of the Florentine *Compagnia di San Luca.* Filippino is identified as an apprentice in Botticelli's workshop.

By 1472 Verrocchio had completed a tomb of bronze and marble for the sacristy of San Lorenzo, Florence. It was commissioned by Giuliano and Lorenzo de' Medici for their father Piero and their uncle Giovanni. Verrocchio fashioned a bronze *Putto and Dolphin* fountain for the Medici Villa at Careggi. Perugino's work of the following decades would echo Verrocchio's use of classical motifs in these Medici commissions. As patrons such as Lorenzo de' Medici became more knowledgeable about antique sources, they requested classical mythologies and ornamentation from artists and favored artists having familiarity

with classical imagery. Perugino was soon to be among those valued most by Lorenzo (see 1490).

1473 Perugino and other painters (Pintoricchio, Bartolomeo Caporali, Fiorenzo di Lorenzo, Pietro di Galeotto, and a painter called the Master of 1473) may have painted eight panels that came from a now-dismantled niche which once held the *gonfalone* of Saint Bernardino in the Church of San Francesco al Prato, Perugia. Individual panels display the work of multiple artists. The one panel most often linked with Perugino, *Saint Bernardino Healing the Ulcer of the Daughter of Giovanni Petrazio da Rieti*, 31½ × 22⅜ in. (80 × 56 cm), has the date 1473 inscribed over the arch: A.D. MCCCLXXIII FINIS (now, Galleria Nazionale dell'Umbria, Perugia; fig. 1).

1475 Perugino receives five florins (21 July) for completing work (destroyed) in the Grand Salon of the Palace of the Priors, Perugia's town hall.

Vasari identified an Adoration of the Magi by Perugino for the Servite Order in Perugia as an early painting. He was probably describing the *Adoration of the Magi*, 94⅞ × 70⅞ in. (241 × 180 cm), transferred to Santa Maria Nuova, Perugia, in 1542, when the old Servite church (Santa Maria dei Servi, Colle Landone) was torn down to make room for the Rocca Paolina, a castle built by Pope Paul III. This painting exhibits stylistic traits of Ghirlandaio, Fiorenzo di Lorenzo, and Pintoricchio (since 1863, Galleria Nazionale dell'Umbria, Perugia; pl. 2). The painting likely includes a self-portrait of Perugino in his mid-twenties (the man to the far left, behind the youngest of the magi).

Piero and Antonio del Pollaiuolo complete a panel painting, *Saint Sebastian*, 115 × 80 in. (292 × 203.1 cm), for the Pucci family chapel in the Church of Santissima Annunziata, Florence.

Michelangelo is born at Caprese, about forty miles from Florence.

By 1475 Verrocchio had cast a bronze statue of *David* (Bargello, Florence), commissioned by Lorenzo de' Medici. Lorenzo later sold the statue

Pl. 2. *Adoration of the Magi*, Galleria Nazionale dell'Umbria, Perugia

to the Florentine town hall in 1476. Verrocchio cast two bronze statues for the *Mercanzia: Christ* (1470–76) and *Doubting Thomas* (1479), which were chased and installed at Or San Michele, Florence, by 1483. The early work of Perugino reflects his study of Verrocchio's use of gesture: the nonchalant pose of Verrocchio's young *David* reappears in Perugino's figures of shepherds, magi, soldiers, and Saint Sebastian. Perugino's apostles of *The Delivery of the Keys to Saint Peter* (Sistine Chapel, Vatican; pl. 3) are indebted to Verrocchio's statues of *Christ* and *Doubting Thomas*. As Verrocchio designed preparatory studies and clay models for the figures, Perugino had the chance in Florence to study their poses, drapery, and gestures. Like Verrocchio's *Christ* and *Doubting Thomas*, Perugino's apostles are grand, venerable men. They wear weighty outer cloaks that drape around their lower bodies in thick, broad sweeping folds. Some of them are so closely modeled after Verrocchio's statues that they tilt their heads and hold their expressive hands in nearly the same way.

1476 Domenico and Davide Ghirlandaio complete frescoes for Sixtus IV in the Vatican Library, Rome (now lost). Perugino's professional association with the Ghirlandaio brothers may have paved the way for his subsequent commissions in Rome from Sixtus IV (see 1479).

1478 Perugino paints the fresco of three standing figures, *Saints Roch, Sebastian, and Peter*, for the chapel of Mary Magdalene, Santa Maria Assunta in the parish church of Cerqueto, about twelve miles south of Perugia. The fresco was saved when the town refurbished the church in the eighteenth century, but it was reduced in size to 52⅜ × 35⅜ in. (133 × 90 cm) during the move. While the figure of Sebastian remains intact (fig. 4), the flanking figures of Saints Roch and Peter are now fragments. As Perugino's first signed painting, it is traditionally dated 1478 from a modern inscription beneath the fresco: PETRVS PERVSINVS P/A MCCC.LXXVIII, although it also has been dated as early as 1473. Perugino's knowledge of the work of Verrocchio, Antonio

and Piero del Pollaiuolo, and Piero della Francesca is revealed in the figure of Sebastian.

1479 Perugino completes the apse fresco, *Saints Peter, Francis, Paul, and Anthony of Padua Present a Kneeling Pope Sixtus IV to the Virgin and Child, with Angels*, in a chapel Sixtus built for his own burial in Old Saint Peter's, Rome. Sixtus consecrated the chapel on the Feast of the Immaculate Conception (December 8); upon his death in 1484, the chapel became a mausoleum. The bronze tomb designed for the pope by the Pollaiuolo brothers (see 1483) was placed in the center of the chapel in 1494. With the rebuilding of Saint Peter's in 1606, Sixtus' bronze tomb was moved (now, Treasury of Saint Peter's, Rome) and the entire chapel, including Perugino's apse fresco, was demolished. Only a summary sketch after Perugino's fresco exists, which is noteworthy, considering its significance for Perugino's future: it surely led to his receiving the most important commission of his early career, the supervision of the fresco decoration in the Sistine Chapel (see 1480).

1480 Sometime in 1480, Pope Sixtus IV commissions Perugino to paint frescoes in the newly built Vatican chapel (named the Sistine Chapel after him). Sixtus built the new chapel for a special group of about two hundred men, which included the pope, the College of Cardinals, members of the papal curia, senior churchmen, and notable secular officials. The group, known as the Papal Chapel, annually celebrated some forty masses together and needed a chapel that was large enough to hold the entire membership during religious ceremonies. Until 1477, the largest existing chapel in the Vatican that could hold them was the *cappella magna* (Great Chapel), but Sixtus wanted to put his own stamp on the chapel. In that year, then, he began rebuilding it from its foundations up, and replaced the *cappella magna* with a new structure to house the Papal Chapel.

To achieve his grand plan, Sixtus needed qualified painters to decorate the walls of the new chapel. Sixtus chose Perugino to be the master painter in charge of this formidable fresco

Pl. 3. *The Delivery of the Keys to Saint Peter*, Sistine Chapel, Vatican

project. This was an enormous honor for Perugino, considering the chapel's function. Perugino's earlier work for Sixtus (see 1479) apparently satisfied the pope's expectations and probably attested to Perugino's technical expertise and organizational skills. In Sixtus' new chapel, Perugino worked with five other painters whose names are recorded in papal documents. They painted stories of Christ, Moses, and the Virgin Mary; full-length portraits of the early popes; and curtains bearing Sixtus' family (della Rovere) crest. Upon the completion of the frescoes, Sixtus inaugurated the chapel on the Feast of the Assumption, August 15, 1483.

Work would continue in the chapel over the next fifty years: Michelangelo painted the ceiling (1508–12), Raphael designed tapestries for the lower walls (1515–16), and Michelangelo painted a *Last Judgment* (1536–41) that destroyed Perugino's altar-wall frescoes.

It is likely that Perugino initiated his work in the Sistine Chapel in 1480 with the three frescoes (now destroyed) that covered the altar-wall. By 1483, seventeen frescoes had been executed, covering all four walls of the chapel. Vasari identified Perugino's altar-wall frescoes as *Birth and Finding of Moses*, *Assumption of the Virgin with Pope Sixtus IV* (altarpiece), and *Nativity of Christ*. On October 27, 1481, Perugino signed a contract with three Florentine painters, Cosimo Rosselli, Sandro Botticelli, and Domenico Ghirlandaio, for ten paintings in the chapel. Within three months (January 17, 1482), a document called for the assessment of work already completed in four bays of the chapel. A third contract commissioned work from Bartolomeo della Gatta and Luca Signorelli. Vasari wrote that the Umbrian artist Pintoricchio also helped Perugino on the side walls with the *Baptism of Christ* (fig. 8) and the *Circumcision of Moses' Son.* Bartolomeo della Gatta helped paint *The Delivery of the Keys to Saint Peter* (pl. 3). Both helped Perugino paint some images of early popes on the upper register.

We can imagine that in the early stages of this project, Perugino put together a master plan for painting the enormous chapel that allowed the artists named in the contracts to work together efficiently. They collectively painted yards of wall in a short time. Each individual painter, such as Botticelli, was in charge of particular scenes and hired his own assistants. This procedure effectively created subordinate shops within the larger shop for which Perugino was responsible. By the conclusion of this project, Perugino had improved his visual and technical skills as a fresco painter and gained valuable practical business skills in the process. The success and pattern of his work in the Sistine Chapel helped shape his career and attract patrons for him.

1481 Pintoricchio is documented in the Guild of Painters at Perugia. He makes a payment for a house near his own (in San Fortunato) in Perugia on November 28, making the last payment June 4, 1482. He later bought a second house behind the first, making payments for it in 1484 and in 1485. Records of Pintoricchio's negotiations show him to have been a businessman who bought, leased, and rented properties throughout his career, probably producing a considerable amount of income.

1482 Perugino and Biagio d'Antonio receive a commission (October 5) to decorate one wall of a new council chamber (Sala dei Gigli) in the Florentine town hall (Palazzo Vecchio). Ghirlandaio, Botticelli, and Piero del Pollaiuolo were commissioned to decorate the other walls, but only Ghirlandaio fulfilled his obligations. That these painters won such an esteemed commission in Florence attests to their prestige as a result of their papal commissions. Eventually Perugino's commission was withdrawn and given to Filippino Lippi (December 31), although ultimately neither artist painted the wall. Perugino probably lost the commission for being outside Florence and hence unable to begin work in the council chamber.

Leonardo da Vinci moves to Milan to work as architect and engineer for Ludovico Sforza, ruler of that city. Ludovico later commissioned work from Perugino for the Certosa in Pavia (see 1496, 1497, 1499, 1500). Leonardo's presence in the city

may have encouraged Ludovico to search for other artists working in Florence.

1483 On November 28, Perugino agrees to paint an altarpiece in four months' time for the Chapel of the Priors in the Palace of the Priors, Perugia. One month later (December 31), the *Decemviri* (ten communal magistrates, or priors) discharged him for leaving the city without beginning the painting. He may have delayed this commission because he had work to complete in another city, possibly Rome. The priors, however, continued to request work from him (see 1496, *Decemviri*).

Bartolomeo Bartoli, theologian at Santa Maria Maggiore in Rome and later confessor to Pope Alexander VI, probably commissioned a triptych from Perugino between 1480 and 1485 (pl. 4). The main panel depicts a Crucifixion with Saints John and Mary, 39^{11}/$_{16}$ × 22 in. (101 × 56 cm). Saint Mary Magdalene appears on the left panel and Saint Jerome on the right, with each panel measuring 37^{3}/$_{8}$ × 11^{13}/$_{16}$ in. (95 × 30 cm). Although the original provenance of the triptych is uncertain, by 1695 it was placed in San Domenico, San Gimignano. Prince Galitzin of Moscow bought the painting in 1800, resulting in its being called the Galitzin Triptych; it later became part of the Hermitage Collection in Saint Petersburg (1886). Andrew Mellon bought the painting (1929–31) and bequeathed it to the National Gallery of Art, Washington, D.C., in 1937.

Giuliano della Rovere commissions Antonio del Pollaiuolo to design a bronze tomb for Sixtus IV in Rome. For eleven years (1483–94), Antonio worked on the tomb, which was to go into the mausoleum chapel that Perugino had painted for Sixtus (see 1479). Pollaiuolo's images of Virtues, which are relief sculptures on the tomb, influenced Perugino's frescoes for the *Cambio* (Exchange Guild) in Perugia (see 1500). From 1484 to 1496, Antonio del Pollaiuolo traveled between Florence and Rome, where he worked on the tomb. Antonio's workshop practices in the two cities provided a model for Perugino in defining his own highly productive workshops of the next decades.

Raphael is born in Urbino to Giovanni di Pietro Santi, a painter working for the Duke of Urbino (see 1489).

The Portinari Altarpiece by the Flemish painter Hugo van der Goes arrives in Florence. Tommaso Portinari (a Medici agent working in Bruges) had commissioned the altarpiece for the church of Sant'Egidio, Florence. Hugo's humble, earthy peasants, the bareness of the ground that surrounds the Christ Child, the postures of Mary and the angels, and the tangible seasonal qualities of Hugo's landscapes impressed Perugino and left a visible impact on his paintings.

1484 In Rome on November 20, Perugino, Antoniazzo Romano, and others receive payment for banners, crests, and other decorations ordered for Pope Innocent VIII's coronation (September 12).

Perugino is listed as one of twenty-six members of the large council of Città della Pieve (November 28).

Jacopo Vagnucci, Bishop of Perugia, commissions Luca Signorelli to paint the panel *Mary and Child Enthroned with Saints Honofrius, John the Baptist, Lawrence, and Ercolano*, 87 × 74⅜ in. (221 × 189 cm), for the Chapel of Saint Honofrius in San Domenico, Perugia. Luca's painting reflects a knowledge of Venetian, Florentine, Umbrian, and Flemish art.

Perugino and his Umbrian followers studied Signorelli's images. His figures' expressive gestures and architectonically built forms caught their attention. The swoon of John the Baptist, the earnestness of Lawrence, the devoutness of Honofrius, and the nobility of Ercolano did not escape their notice. They adjusted the harshness of his manner, smoothed over his sharpest crinkles, and toned down his stylistic eccentricities while appropriating some of his pictorial notions. The Umbrians were making a practice of sharing ideas, exchanging sketches, and learning how to harmonize disparate elements. The artist who could do this well was awarded commissions. Perugino quickly became a master as he learned how to incorporate the visual stimuli around him, whether it came from other artists or from classical antiquity firsthand.

Pintoricchio is commissioned to paint frescoes in the Bufalini Chapel in the church of Santa Maria in Ara Coeli in Rome, around 1484 to 1486, soon after working with Perugino in the Sistine Chapel (see 1480). His patron Nicola Bufalini reputedly wanted the frescoes to commemorate the peace that Saint Bernardino (1380–1444) had brought to two families: the Bufalini of Città di Castello and the Baglioni of Perugia.

Pintoricchio's work in this chapel demonstrates his knowledge of classical decoration and his burgeoning penchant for grotesques derived from the study of ancient Roman art. This decorative ornamentation is a fanciful combination of plants, humans, and fabulous animal forms (see 1500). Popes Alexander VI and Innocent VIII later granted commissions to Pintoricchio because of his skill at inventing grotesquerie. Bufalini, a Consistorial Advocate in the papal curia, probably introduced Pintoricchio to the popes. Perugino and Pintoricchio were both in Rome in the 1480s; as their paths continued to cross in the succeeding years, their rivalry grew.

1485 Perugino is living in Città della Pieve on January 18. Five months later he is with Antoniazzo in Rome, where he receives payment for work done in the chapel of the Vatican Palace for Pope Innocent VIII (May 26).

In July, Perugino is in Perugia, where he renews a contract and receives payment for an altarpiece in the Palace of the Priors (see 1483, 1496). On December 26, he becomes a citizen of Perugia, which likely helped him secure commissions there (see 1496). In just a few years Perugino also found the avenues to help him gain commissions in Florence equal to those of Botticelli, Filippino Lippi, and Ghirlandaio (see 1486).

Pintoricchio receives payments for paintings in the Monteluce convent of Perugia. He collected another payment on April 18, 1486.

1486 Perugino joins the Guild of Painters, Perugia.

Working with assistants, possibly with Andrea d'Assisi (l'Ingegno), Perugino executes a fresco, the *Crucifixion* (now a fragment), that, as Vasari observed, faced the monk's choir of Santa Maria degli Angeli in Assisi. When the church was enlarged in 1569, the fresco suffered extensive damage and was later completely repainted (1832).

Between April and August Pintoricchio receives payments for work in the Palace of the Priors, Perugia. The records specifically identify payments for a Madonna over a door to the priors' sleeping quarters.

On February 20, Filippino Lippi completes the large altarpiece *Enthroned Madonna and Child with Saints John the Baptist, Victor, Bernard, and Zenobius* for a council chamber (Sala degli Otto di Pratica) in the Palazzo Vecchio, Florence. Vasari noted that the painting was begun by Leonardo da Vinci and finished by Filippino. Although he confused this altarpiece with another in the Palazzo Vecchio commissioned from Leonardo in 1479, Vasari recognized the importance of Filippino's altarpiece. Records about the altarpiece indicate that Filippino had won Lorenzo de' Medici's approval in

1485. Lorenzo was possibly grooming Filippino for the future. Being the son of the renowned Florentine master Fra Filippo Lippi already enormously improved Filippino's chances for success. In 1488 Lorenzo paid Filippino one hundred gold florins to design a tomb plaque in Spoleto Cathedral for his father Fra Filippo, identifying him as Florentine. The citizens in Spoleto so esteemed Fra Filippo that they claimed him as their own and refused to return the body to Florence.

By 1485, Filippino Lippi and Ghirlandaio had been awarded significant commissions from corporate bodies and wealthy families in Florence. After returning from Rome, Ghirlandaio received prestigious commissions in the Palazzo Vecchio: a mural in the audience chamber in 1482 and an altarpiece in 1483 (not executed). Between 1483 and 1485 he painted Francesco Sassetti's family chapel in the Church of Santa Trinità and signed a contract to paint Giovanni Tornabuoni's family chapel in the Church of Santa Maria Novella in 1486. Filippino signed a contract to paint Filippo Strozzi's family chapel in Santa Maria Novella in 1487 (see 1502). These large-scale projects in Florence brought high visibility to Filippino and Ghirlandaio, and guaranteed them future commissions.

Between 1486 and 1497 Perugino was probably painting cloister frescoes (destroyed) and panels for the Jesuate monks of San Giusto alle Mura, Florence. After the monastery's destruction during the siege of Florence in 1529, when imperial and papal troops attacked the city to restore political power to the ousted Medici family, the Jesuate monks moved to San Giovannino della Calza near the Porta Romana. They took with them the panels that Perugino had painted (see 1493), three of which Vasari identified by subject, including a Crucifixion.

This painting is likely the *Crucifixion*, 79⅞ × 70⅞ in. (203 × 180 cm), with Mary Magdalene by the cross and standing Saints Jerome, Francis, John the Baptist, and the Blessed Giovanni Colombini (since 1904, Galleria degli Uffizi, Florence). The panel was probably executed around 1486. Since the *Crucifixion* displays traits typical

Pl. 5. Designed by Perugino, *Pentecost*, Church of Santo Spirito, Florence

of Signorelli's style, as in the altarpiece of San Domenico, Perugia (see 1484), scholars have postulated that Perugino and Signorelli collaborated in its creation, or that a third Umbrian painter fashioned it. Among the frescoes Vasari mentioned were two Nativity scenes; a Confirmation of the Order; a Virgin, Child, and Saints; and portraits of members of the order. Perugino's largest collective body of work in Florence was in the church and convent of San Giusto alle Mura. Some twenty years after the buildings were destroyed, Vasari remembered the frescoes well enough to give specific descriptive and evaluative observations. He wrote that Verrocchio appeared among the portraits of the *Nativity with Magi*; that the prior of the convent appeared so lifelike that some artists thought it was Perugino's finest work; and that overall, these were the best paintings in fresco Perugino had ever done.

These Jesuate monks became skilled at making stained-glass windows designed by artists such as Perugino, Ghirlandaio, and Filippino Lippi for churches. Between 1490 and 1506 Perugino made drawings for the *Pentecost*, from which the Jesuates made a large stained-glass entrance-wall window for the Church of Santo Spirito in Florence that remains in situ (see 1506; pl. 5).

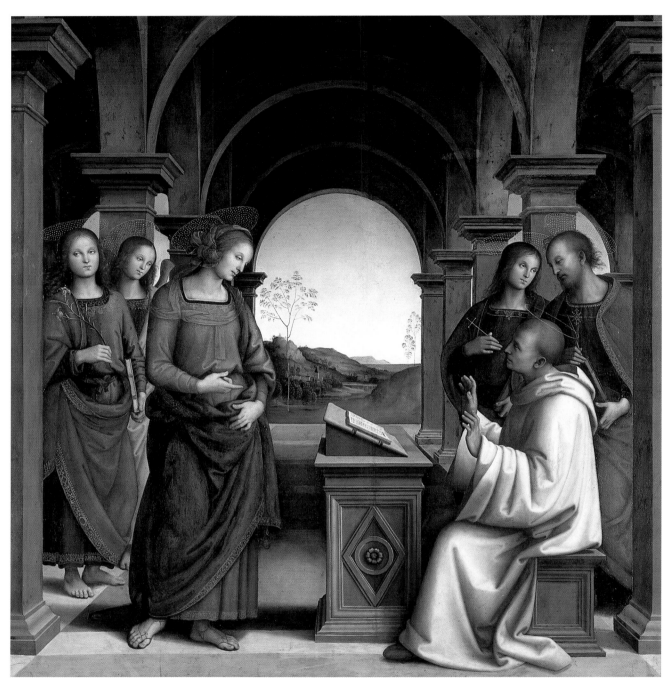

Pl. 6. *Vision of Saint Bernard*, Alte Pinakothek, Munich

Perugino's work for the Jesuate monks won visible prominence for him and shows how Perugino's choice to work for the Jesuates was as much to his benefit as was their decision to employ him.

Pintoricchio receives a commission from Pope Innocent VIII to paint frescoes of city views in the Loggia of the Belvedere in the Vatican, Rome.

Andrea del Sarto is born in Florence, where he became an important master painter. Vasari joined Andrea's workshop in the 1520s.

1487 In July a Florentine judicial body (*Otto di Custodia*) finds Perugino guilty of assaulting someone the previous December (1486). Perugino is fined for his part in the crime, while a fellow defendant, Aulista d'Angelo, is sentenced to flogging and exile from Florence. Perugino's recent commission from the Jesuate monks at San Giusto alle Mura (see 1486) may have helped lighten the judgment against him. Vasari probably confused this court incident with a conflict (probably fictional) he described between Perugino and Michelangelo.

1488 On April 21, the Franciscans of Santa Maria Nova, near San Lazzaro Fano, on the Adriatic seacoast, about twenty miles south of Rimini, commission two altarpieces from Perugino. He may have completed the first altarpiece, *Annunciation*, 83½ × 67¹¹⁄₁₆ in. (212 × 172 cm), soon after receiving the commission (fig. 83). Nevertheless, the lacunae of the inscription make the exact date difficult to read. The painting is signed PETRVS DE CASTR[ ], and was probably dated 1489 (M . CCC[C . LXXX . VI]III) Perugino completed the second altarpiece for the main altar of Santa Maria Nova by 1497, painting it in more than one phase (see 1497).

Giovanni Santi, Raphael's father, is also working in Fano and probably has some contact with Perugino (see 1489).

Michelangelo begins a three-year apprenticeship with Domenico Ghirlandaio in Florence, which probably ended earlier than the stipulated period.

Michelangelo later denied that the apprenticeship had ever taken place.

Filippino Lippi is awarded a commission to paint Cardinal Oliviero Carafa's burial chapel in the Church of Santa Maria sopra Minerva, Rome. Lorenzo de' Medici had recommended the painter to Carafa, and Filippino willingly postponed his Florentine commissions to work in Rome between 1488 and 1493 for his new patron. A distinguished member of the Roman Curia, Cardinal Carafa served his native Neapolitan court as an envoy to Rome. In Naples he had commissioned sculptural family tombs for the Cathedral. In Rome, he decided to prepare an opulent burial chapel for himself, replete with a marble wall tomb, marble balustrade, and frescoes. After his return home, Carafa commissioned Perugino to paint an altarpiece for the Naples Cathedral (see 1508).

1489 Perugino is commissioned by the Nasi brothers to paint the altarpiece *Vision of Saint Bernard*, 68⅛ × 78⅞ in. (173 × 170 cm), for their family chapel in Santa Maria Maddalena (now, Santa Maria Maddalena dei Pazzi) in the Cestello area of Florence. Perugino probably did not finish the painting in time for the consecration of the chapel in 1489; it was completed by 1493. When Carmelite nuns were put in charge of the monastery in 1628, Francesco di Lorenzo took the painting from the family chapel. It may have been transferred to the family's chapel in Santo Spirito, where a seventeenth-century copy of Perugino's painting by Ficherelli still stands on the altar. In 1829 King Ludwig of Bavaria acquired the original painting from the Capponi family (now, Alte Pinakothek, Munich; pl. 6). In the same church, Botticelli completes an Annunciation panel for the family chapel of Benedetto di Ser Francesco Guardi.

While in Fano (July), Perugino receives an emissary from Orvieto asking him to paint the San Brizio Chapel in the Orvieto Duomo. Six months later in Orvieto, Perugino signed a contract (December 30) to paint the San Brizio vaults.

Lorenzo de' Medici describes Antonio del Pollaiuolo as the leading master of Florence in 1489. Sometime between 1478 and 1494 Giovanni Santi, a painter at the Urbino court, praised Perugino, calling him a divine painter. Santi compared Perugino with Leonardo da Vinci in the following verses of the *Cronaca rimata*, a poem chronicling the life of his patron Federico da Montefeltro of Urbino:

> Two young men like in fame and years—
> Leonardo da Vinci and *Pietro Perugino*
> *Of Pieve, a divine painter;*
> Ghirlandaio and the young Filippino Lippi,
> Sandro Botticelli, and from Cortona
> Luca Signorelli of rare talent and spirit.

The Paduan artist Andrea Mantegna (1431–1506) is granted a letter of introduction from Francesco Gonzaga to Pope Innocent VIII in Rome. Gonzaga wrote to Mantegna requesting that he return to help make decorations for his marriage to Isabella d'Este in 1490. Mantegna was painting frescoes in a chapel (destroyed 1781) for Pope Innocent VIII, probably completed in 1491. Records of Mantegna's paintings note the fictive architecture and stucco relief, inscriptions, and similarities with his paintings in the Camera Picta (also known as the Camera degli Sposi) in the Ducal Palace, Mantua. Perugino knew Mantegna's work in Rome, which probably enhanced the development of his own classical vocabulary. Mantegna may have recommended Perugino to Isabella upon his return to Mantua (see 1497).

1490 Perugino is in Rome (May) working in the Vatican, when he is summoned to Orvieto. He remains in Orvieto with his assistant Andrea d'Assisi from September to October and receives prepayment from the *Opera* (Board of Works), Orvieto Cathedral (October 1).

Around 1490 Perugino paints frescoes (now destroyed) for Lorenzo de' Medici at the Villa Spedaletto, Volterra, with Botticelli, Domenico Ghirlandaio, and Filippino Lippi. An agent of Ludovico Sforza later recommended these same four painters to his employer, declaring that Perugino was an exceptional mural painter whose frescoes possessed an *aria angelica* (angelic air) and were *molto dolce* (very sweet). In support of Perugino's talents, he cited the artist's work in the Sistine Chapel and in the Villa Spedaletto. On Sforza's recommendation the monks of the Certosa, Pavia's Carthusian monastery, later hired Perugino (see 1500).

Lorenzo de' Medici invites the Dominican friar Girolamo Savonarola (1452–1498) to Florence to preach the Lenten services in the Cathedral. From a noble family of Ferrara, Savonarola had come to Florence for the first time in 1482 and remained five years. During his second stay in Florence, between 1489 and 1498, he became the most important preacher in the city. He drew immense crowds to the Cathedral and received an esteemed appointment as prior of San Marco in 1491. Pope Alexander VI named him vicar-general of the Dominican Order in Tuscany in 1493 and supported his planned reform for the Order. Savonarola's high-pitched, fevered proclamations against sinfulness and corruption reached broad audiences of people from diverse intellectual, social, and economic backgrounds. His pronouncements incited enthusiastic followers to set bonfires to their vainglorious goods, and he became so awe-inspiring in his prophecies and persuasive in his sermons that Florentines sought both spiritual and political guidance from him in the years following Lorenzo's death.

Savonarola's righteous tongue eventually lashed out against the papacy with dire results: Pope Alexander VI excommunicated him in June 1497 and threatened the Florentines with the same if they allowed him to preach in the Cathedral. Florentine government officials and Roman ecclesiastic authorities put Savonarola and two of his followers on trial and found them guilty of heresy. All three friars were publicly hanged and burned in the town square of Florence on May 23, 1498. It is likely that Savonarola's denouncements and reservations about art affected religious and secular commissions in Florence between 1494 and 1497. Perugino's commissions outside Florence increased during these years (see 1496).

1491 In Florence, Perugino helps judge the competition of façade models for the Cathedral (January 5). Also serving on the panel of judges are Botticelli, Lorenzo di Credi, Domenico Ghirlandaio, and Alesso Baldovinetti.

Perugino is in Orvieto, where money is deposited into his account (April). He never painted the frescoes in the Cathedral's San Brizio Chapel, and Signorelli is eventually hired for the work (see 1499).

In Rome, Perugino may have painted a triptych for Cardinal Giuliano della Rovere in Sant'Apostoli. The central panel consists of a Nativity, inscribed with Perugino's name and the date (1491): PETRVS/DE PERVSIA/PINXIT/M.CCCC.VIIII. PRIMO. The multiple-paneled painting, $55\frac{1}{8} \times 63$ in. (140 × 160 cm), passed from the possession of Cardinal Albani to the Chigi collection (1852) and then to the Torlonia family (since 1866, Villa Albani Torlonia, Rome; fig. 42). Cardinal Giuliano was the nephew of Pope Sixtus IV (Perugino's patron in the Sistine Chapel) and was the future Pope Julius II. As Pope Julius, he commissioned Perugino to work in the Vatican Apartments (see 1508).

1492 Lorenzo de' Medici dies in Florence in the Medici Villa at Careggi (April 8). Perugino may have painted the *Apollo and Marsyas*, $15\frac{3}{8} \times 11\frac{3}{8}$ in. (39 × 29 cm), between 1490 and 1492 for Lorenzo (since 1883, Musée du Louvre, Paris; pl. 7).

While working for Cardinal Giuliano della Rovere in Rome, Perugino receives urgent requests to return to work in Orvieto (June 2).

In June, Pintoricchio is awarded a commission for frescoes in the apse of the Orvieto Cathedral. Between 1492 and 1496 he painted two evangelists and two church fathers (now destroyed). Pintoricchio's work was periodically interrupted because of slow payments and his Roman commissions in the Vatican Apartments (see 1493).

Perugino, Antoniazzo, and Pier Matteo da Amelia make preparations (August) and later receive payments (November 1) for decorations for the coronation of Pope Alexander VI.

1493 In Fiesole, Perugino marries Chiara, daughter of the architect and sculptor Luca Fancelli (September 1). Perugino later deposited Chiara's dowry in Florence (March 26, 1494), from which he drew interest and received money by proxy (October 3, 1494). Chiara's father, Luca, was in the service of Francesco Gonzaga, the Duke of Mantua and husband of Isabella d'Este, who was to be a patron of Perugino (see 1497).

Perugino completes the *Virgin Mary and Child with Saints John the Baptist and Sebastian*, $82\frac{1}{16} \times 64\frac{9}{16}$ in. (178 × 164 cm), for the recently built chapel (1488) of Cornelia di Giovanni Martini Salviati da Venezia in the Church of San Domenico, Fiesole. On a scroll attached to Mary's throne is inscribed PETRVS PERVSINVS/PINXIT AN M.CCCC/LXXXXIII (since 1786, Galleria degli Uffizi, Florence; pl. 8). Vasari noted the high praise Perugino won from Florentine artists for his figure of Sebastian.

Perugino paints a tempera panel, *Virgin and Child with Saints Peter, John the Evangelist, Paul, and John the Baptist*, $73\frac{1}{8} \times 67\frac{11}{16}$ in. (186 × 172 cm), for Giovanni di Cristoforo da Terreno. The inscription on the pedestal reads: PRESBITER . JOHANNES . CHRISTOFORI . DE TERRENO . ERI . FECIT . MCCCC LXXXX . III . Little information about the panel's provenance exists (since 1796, Kunsthistorisches Museum, Vienna).

This painting is similar to Perugino's *Virgin Mary and Child with Saints John the Baptist and Sebastian*, for San Domenico, Fiesole, and to his Sant'Agostino Altarpiece in Cremona (see 1494). The images of Mary and the two foreground saints are nearly identical in drapery and pose to those in the Cremona painting. The Terreno Altarpiece also includes elements to which Perugino returned later in his career, such as the baldachin, the wall behind the figures, and a communal spirit among the saints. Significant paint loss makes it difficult to appreciate the luminosity and tonal variations that unite the figures.

Pintoricchio, commissioned by Pope Alexander VI in 1493, designs frescoes for five rooms in the Vatican Palace: the Rooms of the Mysteries,

Pl. 8. *Virgin Mary and Child with Saints John the Baptist and Sebastian,*
Galleria degli Uffizi, Florence

Pl. 7. *Apollo and Marsyas,* Musée du Louvre, Paris

Pl. 9. *Saint Sebastian*, Musée du Louvre, Paris

Saints, Liberal Arts, Creed, and Sibyls. Pintoricchio was known for his speed and facility, but he had to employ many assistants who could imitate his style in order to complete this immense project in two years.

Around 1493–97 Perugino completed two panel paintings: *Pietà with Saints John the Evangelist, Mary Magdalene, Matthew, and Jerome*, 66⅛ × 69⁵⁄₁₆ in. (168 × 176 cm), and *Agony in the Garden*, 65⅜ × 67⁵⁄₁₆ in. (166 × 171 cm). These are likely the panels that according to Vasari were on the choir screen of San Giusto alle Mura, the Florentine church of the Jesuate monks (see 1486). The monks took both panels with them to the convent of San Giovannino della Calza. From there, after the suppression of the Order of the Jesuates in 1668, the *Agony* was placed in the collection of the Accademia (since 1919, Galleria degli Uffizi, Florence). From San Giovannino the *Pietà* passed into the Medici collection at Villa Imperiale and later to the Palazzo Pitti. Napoleon's troops took the work to France (1799), but returned it to the Palazzo Pitti (1815). In 1831 the *Pietà* became part of the collection of the Accademia in Florence (since 1919, Galleria degli Uffizi, Florence).

In the *Pietà*, Perugino unified the group around Christ by balancing the individual body masses and tensions of the moment: John's dramatic gesture is counterposed against Mary Magdalene's quiet compassion. This *Pietà* may have influenced Michelangelo as he later worked on his own *Pietà*, now in Saint Peter's (see 1499).

Between 1493 and 1497 Perugino probably executed the panel painting *Saint Sebastian*, 66⅞ × 46⅛ in. (176 × 116 cm). At its base is inscribed: SAGITTAE TUAE INFIXE SUNT MICHI. For a time it was in the Barberini collection (seventeenth century), then it passed into the collection of Prince Maffeo Sciarra Colonna, Rome (since 1897, Musée du Louvre, Paris; pl. 9).

Perugino returned to this subject many times in his career. His variations on the figure resulted from his continued study and patrons' requests. Considered an all-powerful protector, Sebastian was invoked against recurring plagues. He was a popular saint, and artists could demonstrate their

Pl. 10. *Portrait of Francesco delle Opere*, Galleria degli Uffizi, Florence

anatomical knowledge by depicting this figure as a beautiful nude. Two paintings of Sebastian are similar to this one: *Saint Sebastian*, 21 × 15⅝ in. (53.3 × 39.5 cm), inscribed PETRVS PERVSINVS PINXIT (The Hermitage Museum, St. Petersburg), and *Saint Sebastian* (panel transferred to canvas), 30³⁄₁₆ × 21¹⁄₁₆ in. (76.7 × 53.4 cm) (The Art Museum, Princeton University, New Jersey; cat. no. 26). One study (metalpoint drawing) connected with the *Saint Sebastian* painting shows the saint in a nearly identical pose, 10¹⁄₁₆ × 5¾ in. (25.6 × 14.6 cm) (The Cleveland Museum of Art, Ohio; cat. no. 4).

1494 Perugino paints the *Virgin and Child Enthroned with Saints John the Evangelist and Augustine* (oil on panel), 66⅞ × 75 in. (170 × 160 cm), for the Church of Sant'Agostino, Cremona, about twenty miles from Milan. He inscribed his name and date (1494) on the Virgin's pedestal: PETRVS . PERVSINVS . PINXIT/MCCCLXXXX. IIII. Taken to France in 1797, the altarpiece was returned to its original site in Cremona in 1817. Scholars debate whether Perugino painted the panel in Florence or on his way to Venice.

This painting bears strong similarities to his earlier painting for San Domenico, Fiesole (see 1493). Both images represent a classic phase in Perugino's career. Mary is grand, noble, sculptural, cosmetically perfect: the quintessential Mother of God. Perugino frequently lowered his horizon lines so that viewers had to look upward to behold the holy figures.

Perugino paints the *Portrait of Francesco delle Opere* (oil on panel), 20½ × 17⁵⁄₁₆ in. (52 × 44 cm). The painting's subject is the brother of gem-engraver Giovanni delle Corniole in Florence. An inscribed scroll rests in the sitter's hand, bearing the words TIMETE DEVM. On the back are inscribed the names of the painter, the subject, and the date (July 1494): *1494 di Luglio/Pietro Perugino pinse franc° de Lopre Peynago.* While in Cardinal Leopold de' Medici's collection, the painting was thought to be by Raphael, but it was reattributed to Perugino in 1815 (since 1833, Galleria degli Uffizi, Florence; pl. 10).

Perugino, Albrecht Dürer, and Michelangelo are all in Venice. Perugino was there to negotiate a commission (August 9) for frescoes in the Hall of the Grand Council in the Doge's Palace. His assigned paintings included portraits of doges (the supreme heads of the Venetian state). His contract also called for a scene with episodes from the life of Pope Alexander III. Perugino's stipulated salary was the impressively high sum of four hundred gold ducats, and included the purchase of expensive materials.

It is likely that Perugino was awarded this prestigious commission on the merits of his celebrated fame and his familiarity with the Umbrian town, Spoleto. The contract called for commemorative portraits of government officials and a continuous narrative scene markedly similar to his work in the Sistine Chapel (see 1480). Since Perugino never fulfilled the commission,

it was later awarded to Titian in 1515. Citing Perugino in his negotiations, Titian sought a comparably high fee, but was apparently unsuccessful in this regard.

In Florence, Perugino buys a house in Borgo Pinti (October 30) for four hundred florins. Perugino knew that maintaining a residence in Florence throughout his career would gain him professional rewards.

Domenico Ghirlandaio dies of the plague in Florence at age forty-three.

Raphael's father (Giovanni Santi) dies. Within the next year Raphael went to Perugia, ostensibly to work with Perugino.

King Charles VIII of France acquires Florentine fortresses from Piero de' Medici, who cedes them without the consent of the town government. The incensed Florentines exile the Medici family (November). Savonarola is hailed as a prophet for having forecast the troubles in Florence. Politics and patronage were changing and, while maintaining considerable popularity within the city, Perugino began to accept more commissions from a variety of patrons outside Florence (see 1490, 1495).

Jacopo Carucci (Pontormo) is born. According to Vasari, Pontormo frequented Mariottto Albertinelli's Florentine shop between 1506 and 1510. Around this time, Albertinelli painted two Annunciation panels for Perugino's Certosa Polyptych (see 1500). During his supposed association with Albertinelli, Pontormo would have become familiar with Perugino and his high altarpiece at Santissima Annunziata (see 1506). Pontormo himself later worked in the Annunziata (1512–16).

Pontormo surely scrutinized Perugino's high altarpiece anew then, as some figures in his cloister fresco *Visitation* reflect a studied familiarity with Perugino's swooning female figures of the *Deposition* and the standing female saints of his side panels. Perugino's standing saints are so tightly bound by the architectural framework, which seems too shallow and narrow for their bulky forms, that they seem mobile, about to

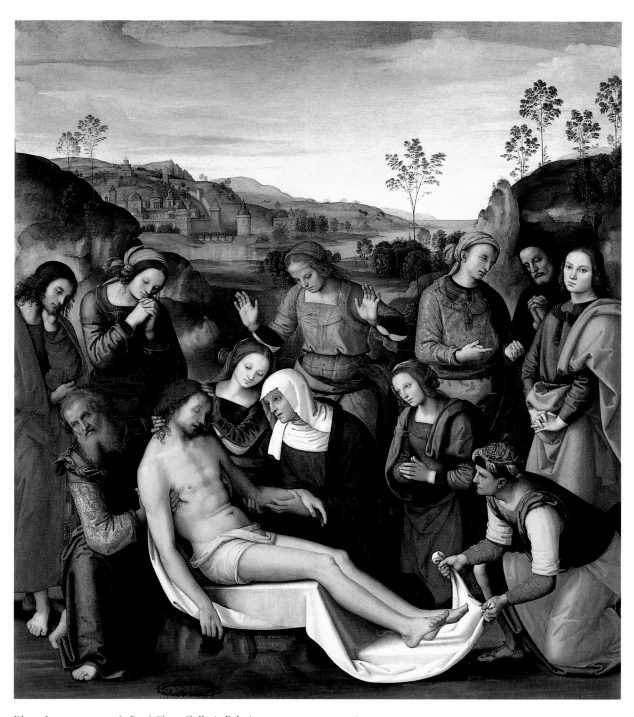

Pl. 11. *Lamentation over the Dead Christ*, Galleria Palatina,
Palazzo Pitti, Florence

expand beyond the confinement of their frames. Pontormo would later experiment with such forms in his own work.

Giovanni Battista di Jacopo di Guaspare (Il Rosso or Rosso Fiorentino) is born in Florence. Il Rosso worked with Andrea del Sarto at Santissima Annunziata (see 1510).

1495 For the nuns of Santa Chiara in Florence, Perugino paints the *Lamentation over the Dead Christ*, 84⁵⁄₁₆ × 76¹³⁄₁₆ in. (214 × 195 cm) (unframed), on which he inscribed his name and date (1495) beneath Christ's body: PETRVS PERVSINVS PINXIT. A. D. MCCCCLXXXXV. (now, Galleria Palatina, Palazzo Pitti, Florence; pl. 11). Vasari commented on its coloring and noted that the painting impressed Francesco del Pugliese so much that he wanted to buy it from the nuns, offering them three times what they had paid.

Perugino receives a sizable commission in Perugia when he signs a contract (March 8) with the Benedictine monks to paint a large polyptych for San Pietro, their abbey church. He was given thirty months to complete the work. Having other commitments that took him outside Perugia, Perugino needed five years to finish this grand altarpiece and possibly the assistance of Eusebio da San Giorgio and Giovanni di Francesco Ciambella, named as witnesses in the contract. He completed the altarpiece by January 13, 1500, when the altar was consecrated.

The chapel's altar, dedicated to Saints Peter and Paul, preserved relics of Saints Catherine and Peter Abbot. The altar had a large central panel, a lunette, and a predella with many panels. Perugino painted *Christ's Ascension* (transferred to canvas, 1845), 110⅛ × 85 in. (280 × 216 cm), for the main altar panel, and *God the Father and Angels*, 44⅞ × 90⅝ in. (114 × 230 cm), for the lunette. Both paintings went to France in 1797 (since 1809, Musée des Beaux-Arts, Lyons). Two tondi were commissioned in 1496: *The Prophet David* (formerly *The Prophet Jeremiah*; fig. 105) and *The Prophet Isaiah*, 50 in. (127 cm) (since 1809, Musée des Beaux-Arts, Nantes). A large number of drawings attributed to Perugino and his followers exist for the many figures in *Christ's Ascension*, a painting that much impressed artists.

Eight of the eleven predella panels are Benedictine saints. Five panels of saints remain in San Pietro in Perugia: *Costanzo*, 13 × 14¹³⁄₁₆ in. (33 × 37.5 cm); *Ercolano*, 12⅝ × 14¹³⁄₁₆ in. (32 × 37.5 cm); *Maurus*, 12⅝ × 11 in. (32 × 28 cm); *Peter in Chains*, 13 × 11 in. (33 × 28.5 cm); and *Scholastica*, 12⅝ × 11⅛ in. (32 × 28 cm). The other three panels of saints are *Placidus*, 12¾ × 11⅜ in. (32.5 × 28.9 cm); *Flavia*, 11⅞ × 10⁹⁄₁₆ in. (30.1 × 26.8 cm); and *Benedict*, 12½ × 9¼ in. (31.8 × 23.6 cm) (since 1820, Musei Vaticani, Rome). Three wider predella scenes illustrate Christ's life: *Adoration of the Magi, Baptism of Christ*, and *Resurrection*, each 12⅛ × 23⅛ in. (31 × 59 cm) (since 1803, Musée des Beaux Arts, Rouen; figs. 104, 89, and 47).

Perugino is in Venice, possibly to paint a canvas (now lost) for the *Scuola di San Giovanni Evangelista* (Confraternity of Saint John the Evangelist), one among five of the *grande* (great) lay corporations in Venice in the 1490s. This confraternity has about five hundred members and considerable funds for the decoration of its chambers. Most commissions went to Venetian artists like Gentile Bellini. His *Procession in the Piazza San Marco*, completed in 1496, shows his knowledge of Perugino's *Delivery of the Keys to Saint Peter* in the Sistine Chapel (see 1480; pl. 3). Gentile's painting echoes and magnifies Perugino's formal, open-space piazza and his calculated files of people. Venetian influences filtered through Perugino's work in the succeeding decade and appear strongest in the light and color of his later paintings.

Pintoricchio is awarded his largest commission in Perugia (February 14). The monks of Santa Maria dei Fossi commission him to paint a multiple-paneled altarpiece for the considerable sum of one hundred and ten florins. It is likely that Pintoricchio's objective for the immense Santa Maria dei Fossi Altarpiece, 201⅝ × 123⅝ in. (512 × 314 cm), was to paint a significant work that would gain him attention and future rewards in his native city. Some scholars consider it his best work in Perugia (see 1502; fig. 65).

Pl. 12. *Virgin and Child Enthroned with Saints* (*Decemviri* Altarpiece),
Musei Vaticani

An alliance known as the Holy League, formed
between the papacy (Pope Alexander VI), Venice, Milan, and the emperor-elect, drives King
Charles VIII and the French out of Italy. Charles
died three years later (1498) in France at age
twenty-eight without an immediate heir. His
cousin the Duke of Orleans became King
Louis XII (see 1499).

1496 Between 1490 and 1496 Duke Ludovico
Sforza of Milan solicited recommendations
about painters from his agent in Florence (see
1490). Sforza needed a painter to decorate his
castle and the Certosa in Pavia. Seeking Perugino's services, Sforza wrote to Archbishop
Arcimboldi of Milan (June 8, 1496), then in
Venice, asking his help. Arcimboldi responded
(June 14) that Perugino had left Venice six
months earlier.

In Perugia, Perugino completes an altarpiece
depicting the Virgin and Child enthroned with
the patron saints of Perugia: Lawrence, Louis of
Toulouse, Ercolano, and Costanzo, 76 × 65 in.
(193 × 165 cm). He inscribed his name on the
throne base beneath Mary's foot: HOC . PETRVS .
DE . CHASTRO . PLEBIS PINXIT. The *Decemviri*
commissioned the altarpiece for their chapel in
Perugia's town hall, the Palace of the Priors. Although Perugino had previously received a commission from the priors in November 1483, they
withdrew it the same year (see 1483).

When they renewed the contract on July 28,
1485, he was paid ten florins. Ten years later
(March 6, 1495), the *Decemviri* gave him one hundred florins and six months to complete the
work, which he did by 1496. About five months
after signing the contract of 1485, Perugino had
become a citizen of Perugia, probably aware of

Pl. 13. *Crucifixion*, Santa Maria Maddalena dei Pazzi, Cestello

the value of this act, for the priors held the commission open to Perugino for ten years this time. Napoleonic troops took the altarpiece from the Palace of the Priors to France (1797). When the work was returned to Italy in 1816, it was sent to Rome (since 1820, Musei Vaticani, Rome; pl. 12).

Perugino fashions another panel painting for the *Decemviri: Dead Christ*, 21⅞ × 22½ in. (55.5 × 57 cm), identified as the upper part of the altarpiece *(cimasa)*. This panel, still in its original frame in 1797, was not removed and remained in Perugia in the *Decemviri* Chapel, Palace of the Priors (since 1863, Galleria Nazionale dell'Umbria, Perugia; cat. no. 8).

Perugino completes (April 20) the *Crucifixion* in the chapter room of Santa Maria Maddalena in Cestello (now, Santa Maria Maddalena dei Pazzi; pl. 13), a Cistercian convent in Florence. Dionigi and Giovanna Pucci had commissioned the fresco in 1492, about the time Perugino was completing his *Vision of Saint Bernard* for the same church (see 1489).

Beneath Christ's cross stand the lamenting figures of Bernard, the Virgin Mary, Mary Magdalene, John the Evangelist, and Benedict. The landscape of the *Crucifixion* derives from the *Vision* but is wide and boundless, spreading like becalmed waves beyond the meditative holy figures. This fresco satisfied both the ritual dictates of a chapter room and the espoused beliefs of Savonarola and his followers that religious images should be free from superfluous objects (see 1490). This painting is stripped to its essentials. The cross seems to lie on the surface of the painting and the body of Christ appears as a real, three-dimensional presence in the room. Worshipers cannot help but fix on Christ's body, as the other figures appear to melt away. Perugino's image offers a perpetual communion between the faithful and a tangible God.

During the completion of work at San Giusto alle Mura, Florence, Perugino begins his masterwork in Perugia: the frescoes of the ground floor Sala dell'Udienza del Collegio del Cambio (audience chamber of the Exchange). The prestigious commission was awarded by the *Cambio* (Guild of the Exchange), whose money exchanges and letters of credit were critical to the town's commercial prosperity. Perugino again has the chance to orchestrate an extensive fresco project, though smaller in scale, fifteen years after his work in the Sistine Chapel. This commission is known as the Collegio del Cambio frescoes (see 1500).

Michelangelo goes to Rome as the guest of Cardinal Riario. Piero del Pollaiuolo dies in Rome and is buried in San Pietro in Vincoli, the church of Cardinal Giuliano della Rovere, a future pope and Sixtus IV's nephew.

1497 Perugino completes the tempera panel altarpiece he had begun nine years earlier (in 1488) for Santa Maria Nova, Fano. He inscribed his name and the date (1497) on the throne: DURANTES. PHANEN AD INTEMERATE/VIRGINIS LAUDE TERCENTU AUREIS ATQ/HUIUS TEMPLI BONO CENTU SUPERADDITIIS/HANC SOLERTI CURA FIERI DEMANDAVIT/MATEO DE MARTINOTIIS FIDEI COMISSARIO PROCURANTE MCCC97/PETRVS PERVSINVS PINXIT.

Sections of panels, however, vary in date. The altarpiece was painted in two distinct phases: parts of the central panel are earliest, while the predella panels belong to the latest. The central panel includes the Virgin Mary and Child enthroned, with Saints John the Baptist, Francis, Louis of Toulouse, Michael, Mary Magdalene, Peter, and Paul, 103⅛ × 84⅝ in. (262 × 215 cm). In the lunette is a Dead Christ, 59⅛ × 98⅜ in. (150 × 250 cm) (fig. 48).

The predella consists of five stories from Mary's life: *Birth of the Virgin, Presentation, Marriage, Annunciation,* and *Assumption,* 11 × 102¹³⁄₁₆ in. (28 × 261 cm). Scholars speculate about Raphael's part in the predella panels and the drawings that were possibly done for them, such as *Studies for Birth of the Virgin* (Gabinetto Disegni e Stampe, Galleria degli Uffizi, Florence).

Perugino painted an altarpiece for Santa Maria delle Grazie in Senigallia between 1497 and 1500. The central panel, *Virgin Mary and Child Enthroned, with Saints John the Baptist, Ludovico, Francis, Peter, Paul, and James,* 110⅜ × 89⅜ in. (280 × 227 cm), is nearly identical to the altarpiece in Fano mentioned above. Scholars have linked these two paintings and speculated about stylistic influence, quality, workshop participation, patronage, and date. Although the patronage of the Senigallia painting is uncertain, the Church of Santa Maria delle Grazie received the attention of Giovanni della Rovere and his wife Giovanna da Montefeltro, from whom Isabella d'Este sought help in locating Perugino (see 1500).

Duke Ludovico Sforza of Milan writes twice to Guido and Ridolfo Baglioni (March 28, November 9) requesting their help in procuring Perugino's services (see 1482, 1496). The Baglioni were Perugia's most politically influential family during Perugino's lifetime. Following the exile of their strongest rival, the Oddi family, in 1488, branches of the family exerted nearly unbroken control over Perugia until 1535. Lorenzo de' Medici had personally supported the Baglioni cause to Pope Innocent VIII in 1490, just after the family had taken charge of Perugia and its government outright. Members of the Baglioni family acquired control over many small towns near Perugia, including Bettona and Spello. Both Perugino and Pintoricchio had patrons in these towns and enjoyed continued popularity in the region, in part as a result of their connection with Perugia and the Baglioni family.

Isabella d'Este, the Duchess of Mantua and a great patron of the arts, writes to Lorenzo de Pavia in Florence (April 3), asking if Perugino were alive so she could engage him to paint a panel for her *studiolo* (study) in the Castello di San Giorgio, Mantua. Lorenzo responds (May 8) that Perugino was willing to work for her. Isabella's agent, Alberto da Bologna, had already informed her in 1496 of Bellini's promise to fashion a painting (never executed) for the study. She intended these two paintings to accompany the two by Mantegna commissioned earlier: *Parnassus* and *Pallas Athena Expelling the Vices from the Garden of Virtue.* Mantegna's paintings were installed in the study around 1498 (now, Musée du Louvre, Paris). It took Isabella copious additional correspondence just to persuade Perugino to sign a

Pl. 14. *Madonna of the Confraternity of the Consolazione*, Galleria
Nazionale dell'Umbria, Perugia

contract in 1503 and then to complete the painting in 1505 (see 1500, 1502, 1503, 1504, 1505).

Pintoricchio is hired to paint the Eroli Chapel in Spoleto Cathedral.

1498 Perugino, Filippino Lippi, Benozzo Gozzoli, and Cosimo Rosselli evaluate Alesso Baldovinetti's frescoes commissioned by the Gianfigliazzi family for the main chapel in Santa Trinità, Florence (January 19).

Perugino completes a *gonfalone* for the Confraternity of Flagellants *(Disciplinati)* of Santa Maria Novella, Perugia. They had commissioned the panel, *Madonna of the Confraternity of the Consolazione,* 72 × 51³⁄₁₆ in. (183 × 130 cm), in April 1496. Perugino received the balance due one year after its completion (April 14). The panel depicts robed confraternity members kneeling in supplication behind a Madonna with Child seated on a bench in the foreground (since 1879, Galleria Nazionale dell'Umbria, Perugia; pl. 14).

An undated portrait, *Saint Mary Magdalene,* with her name inscribed on her bodice, 18½ × 13⅜ in. (47 × 34 cm), was attributed to Perugino in a Medici inventory (1641) at Villa Poggio Imperiale (now, Galleria Palatina, Palazzo Pitti, Florence; pl. 15).

In Florence, Gian Battista, the first of eight children, is born (June 22) to Perugino and Chiara. On September 4, Perugino buys property near his house in Borgo Pinti for one hundred fifty florins (see 1494). Tax records show he rented a shop in the ward of Santa Maria Nuova, Florence.

In Rome, Antonio del Pollaiuolo completes the tomb of Pope Innocent VIII. Antonio dies in Rome and is buried in his brother Piero's tomb in San Pietro in Vincoli. Pintoricchio paints frescoes in the Castel Sant'Angelo for Pope Alexander VI (now destroyed).

1499 On March 2 Perugino receives a commission for the *Resurrection of Christ,* 92½ × 78⅞ in. (233 × 165 cm), to be completed in two months, according to the contract. No records identify when Perugino finished the painting, intended for the chapel of Bernardino di Giovanni da Corneto in San Francesco al Prato, Perugia.

Vasari recorded seeing the *Resurrection of Christ* in the church. Some scholars recognize the portrait of Raphael in one soldier, and others speculate that he worked on the painting as well. After being sent to France (1797), the work remained in Paris until 1815, when it was returned to Rome (since 1816, Musei Vaticani, Rome; pl. 16).

In Perugia, the Confraternity of Saint Joseph awards Perugino a commission to paint an altarpiece of the Virgin's Marriage for the Chapel of the *Santo Anello* (Holy Ring) in San Lorenzo, the Cathedral. In 1486 the confraternity had decided to build the chapel to house their precious relic, the Virgin Mary's wedding ring. Three years later (1489), the confraternity commissioned Pintoricchio to paint an altarpiece depicting the Marriage of the Virgin, but he left Perugia, giving Benedetto Caporali power of attorney to safeguard his rights to this commission. After years of delay and no painting from Pintoricchio, the commission was given to Perugino in 1499 (see 1503).

On April 5 Signorelli signs a contract to paint the vault of the San Brizio Chapel, Orvieto Cathedral, which was finished a year later (April 23, 1500). After waiting years for Perugino, the Cathedral's Board of Works finally chose Signorelli, who was willing to work for less money and was fast and efficient. Signorelli also painted the chapel's walls, completing them by 1502.

From Milan (May 1), Ludovico Sforza writes to Taddeo Vimercati, his agent in Florence, warning that if Perugino and Filippino Lippi did not complete their work at the Certosa of Pavia, he would retract funds already paid to them. Within months, Ludovico could no longer make such threats. The French army under King Louis XII, who had assumed the title Duke of Milan at his coronation, invaded Milan in August and Ludovico fled to Innsbruck. Although Ludovico returned to Milan with an army in 1500, he was taken prisoner and sent to France, where he died in 1508. Filippino never completed his work, while Perugino completed all but the upper panels of his altarpiece (see 1500).

Pl. 15. *Saint Mary Magdalene*, Galleria Palatina, Palazzo Pitti, Florence

Pl. 16. *Resurrection of Christ*, Musei Vaticani

In Florence (September 1), Perugino enters the *Arte dei Medici e Speziali* (Guild of Physicians, Apothecaries, and Spice Dealers), the regulatory guild to which painters belonged and paid fees. After some fifty years of relaxed rules (1444–99), the guild was nearly nonexistent, and in 1499 it renewed efforts to enforce membership. That year even Botticelli entered for the first time (November 15) at age fifty-five.

In Rome, Michelangelo completes the *Pietà*, his masterwork in marble, for the French ambassador to the Holy See, Cardinal Jean Villier (d. August 1499). The *Pietà* was for the Chapel of Santa Petronilla (since 1749, Chapel of the Crucifix, Saint Peter's). Scholars note a probable influence from northern examples of this subject, with which this French patron was familiar. Michelangelo's *Pietà*, though, tempers northern pathos with serenity and repose, two pronounced qualities of Perugino's *Pietà* for San Giusto in Florence, which may have influenced Michelangelo (see 1493).

1500 Perugino completes four panels of a two-tiered polyptych for a chapel in the Certosa, the Carthusian monastery of Pavia about fifteen miles south of Milan (see 1499). He painted three panels for the lower tier: left, *Michael the Archangel*, 45 × 22 in. (114 × 56 cm), inscribed PERVSINV[S]/PINXIT; center, *Virgin and Child with Angels*, 44½ × 25¼ in. (113 × 64 cm); and right, *Tobias and the Archangel Raphael*, 44½ × 22 in. (113 × 56 cm). He painted only one of three panels for the upper tier, the central panel: *God in Glory*, 49¾ × 22¾ in. (126.5 × 58 cm). Other commitments probably kept him from executing the two upper-tier panels meant to flank his image of *God in Glory*.

The Florentine painter Mariotto Albertinelli (1474–1515) completed the altarpiece with two panels depicting an Annunciation, which he executed by 1511: *Archangel Gabriel*, 42¾ × 22 in. (108.5 × 56), and *Virgin Annunciate*, 42¾ × 22 in. (108.5 × 56 cm) (since 1805, Municipality of Geneva; now, Musée d'Art et d'Histoire, Geneva). Only one panel by Perugino, *God in Glory*, remains in the monastery church. Perugino's three lower-tier panels were probably cut down in size before they were taken to Milan in 1784 and, two years later, acquired by the Melzi family (since 1856, National Gallery, London).

Perugino gave extraordinary attention to the side panels with the figures of Michael, Raphael, and Tobias. It is likely that he thought of this painting as his technical and conceptual tour de force that could gain him new commissions from northern Italian patrons. Michael's detailed armor is more refined than that of any other soldier Perugino painted, and every scale of Tobias' fish shines in bright sunlight, giving it a rich tactile surface.

Perugino completes an altarpiece for the abbey church of Vallombrosa, about fifteen miles east of Florence. Vasari recorded a painting by Perugino for the main altar of the abbey without identifying the images. Perugino's painting *Assumption of the Virgin with Saints*, 163⅜ × 96⅞ in. (415 × 246 cm), includes God in Glory above Mary, and below her, four Vallombrosan saints: John Gualberto, Bernard degli Uberti, Benedict, and Michael the Archangel. An inscription at the base of the panel dates it to 1500: PETRVS . PERVSINVS . PINXIT . AD MCCCCC (since 1817, Galleria dell'Accademia, Florence; fig. 26). Perugino was commissioned in 1497, he began work in 1498, and the painting was installed by July 18, 1500.

Two predella panels linked with the altarpiece are now in the Galleria degli Uffizi, Florence: the portraits of *Don Biagio Milanesi*, 11¼ × 10⁷⁄₁₆ in. (28.5 × 26.5 cm), and *Baldassare Vallombrosano*, 10¼ × 10⅝ in. (26 × 27 cm). Inscribed on the first is BLASIO . GEN . SERVO . TVO/ SVCCVRRE, and on the other, D. BALTASAR MONACO/S TUO . SVCCVRRE.

In Perugia, Perugino completes a large polyptych for the abbey church of the Benedictine monks of San Pietro (see 1495). Pintoricchio receives final payment for a small *gonfalone* commissioned by the Confraternity of Sant'Agostino, which he likely completed in one year. Outside Perugia, Perugino buys property near Città della Pieve (April 23).

Perugino completes his work for the Guild of the Exchange *(Cambio)* in Perugia, inscribing the date 1500 beneath his self-portrait (see p. 250) in the audience chamber: ANNO/SALVT/MD/ (see 1496). Vasari recorded that he wrote the following passage under his name: "Even if the craft of painting had been lost, here by the distinguished Pietro of Perugia it was restored; had it been invented nowhere else, Pietro would have done so. In the year of our Lord 1500" (Giorgio Vasari, *The Lives of the Artists*, trans. Julia Conaway Bondanella and Peter Bondanella [Oxford: Oxford University Press, 1991], p. 263). The frescoes took four years to complete and cover the ceiling and lunettes above the extensive wainscoting of figurative intarsia (inlaid wooden panels). Perugino's designs show his familiarity with several life-size depictions of historic figures in Florence: Andrea Castagno's *Famous Men and Women* (Villa Carducci), Verrocchio's *David* (Palazzo Vecchio), and Domenico Ghirlandaio's *Roman Heroes* (Audience Hall, Palazzo Vecchio). In Rome, Antonio del Pollaiuolo's personifications of the Liberal Arts on the *Tomb of Sixtus IV* (Old Saint Peter's) and especially Pintoricchio's grotesques in the Borgia Apartments of the Vatican and the Castel Sant'Angelo provided models.

The humanist scholar Francesco Maturanzio selected the classical subjects and composed the inscriptions. Excerpts from his poetry were inscribed in the painted tablets near the Cardinal Virtues: *Prudence, Justice, Fortitude,* and *Temperance* (see fig. 5). These virtues appear as seated women holding attributes that identify them, two each on the two walls of the audience chamber's south side. Beneath the virtues are images of notable Greek and Roman men extolled in ancient history, each an exemplar of the virtue above him. Fabius Maximus, Socrates, Numa Pompilius, Fulvius Camillus, Pythagoras, and Trajan are on one wall; Lucius Sicinius, Leonidas the Spartan, Horatius Cocles, Scipio, Pericles the Athenian, and Quintius Cincinnatus are on the other wall. Perugino and his workshop painted two images, *Transfiguration* and *Adoration of the Shepherds* (fig. 27), on the walls facing the grand entrance. On the wall next to them are images of standing men and women representing Old Testament Prophets (Isaiah, Moses, Daniel, David, Jeremiah, and Solomon) and Classical Sibyls (Erythrean, Persian, Cumaean, Libyan, Tiburtine, and Delphic). On the entrance wall is the Roman diplomat Cato, symbolizing virtuous Wisdom. Benedetto da Maiano's seated image of Justice (1493), flanked by two images of the griffin (Perugia's emblem), appears on the sixth lunette in the room, directly above the benches where the bankers sat. Images of the planets decorate the eight quadrants of the ceiling: Apollo covers two quadrants in the center, and is surrounded by Jupiter (fig. 106), Saturn, and Mars on the three quadrants farthest from the entrance. Mercury, Venus, and Diana as the Moon are on the three quadrants nearest the entrance.

The ceiling with its geometric patterns and grotesques, is the most distinctive feature of the room. These ceiling divisions derive from Nero's Golden House in Rome (rediscovered c. 1480), a perpetual font of information which attracted Perugino and had a profound impact on artists in Rome. Pintoricchio studied the ruins (he scratched his name on a wall during one visit) and became a master of grotesquerie. Perugino's ceiling designs surely derive as much from Pintoricchio's work (see 1484) as from the Golden House. The Cambio frescoes, the most complex and luxurious paintings of Perugino's career, inspired the young Raphael's decoration of the Vatican Apartments (Stanza della Segnatura) eight years later in Rome.

From Mantua, Isabella d'Este, still interested in employing Perugino, writes to Giovanna da Montefeltro in Senigallia (September 22) for help in contacting the artist. Between 1501 and 1503 Isabella exchanged with her friends and agents more than fifty letters concerning Perugino and the painting she wanted from him for her study (see 1497).

In October Pintoricchio visits the encampment of Cesare Borgia (son of Pope Alexander VI) in Deruta, seeking help in obtaining subsidies from the government of Perugia. Cesare, who reputedly esteemed this Perugian artist for the works he did for the Borgia family, sent letters on his behalf.

Agostino Chigi, writing to his father Mariano in Siena (November 7), advises him that Perugino is the best painter in Italy.

1501 Sant'Andrea della Giustizia (a confraternity devoted to helping those condemned to death) submits a petition to the Ten Priors of Perugia to remake a much-used *gonfalone*. Their old processional banner probably offered thanks to the Madonna for deliverance from the plague. It is likely that Perugino's new banner, *Madonna della Giustizia* (wood transferred to canvas), 85⅞ × 55⅛ in. (218 × 140 cm), replaced it. Records show the confraternity bought a crown for the Madonna in 1509. When the Confraternity of Sant'Andrea united with that of San Bernardino (1534), they transferred the banner to the Oratory of San Bernardino (since 1879, Galleria Nazionale dell'Umbria, Perugia; cat. no. 12).

Perugino rents two rooms as workshop space in the Palazzo Nuovo dell'Ospedale della Misericordia in Perugia (January 1). He is also elected a prior of Perugia for a two-month term in 1501.

Leonardo da Vinci works on a cartoon, the *Madonna, Child, and Saint Anne* (lost), for the high altar of the Church of Santissima Annunziata, Florence. When Leonardo abandoned the project, Filippino Lippi was awarded the commission, and Perugino finished it after Filippino's death (see 1506).

Pintoricchio signs and dates frescoes in the Baglioni Chapel, Santa Maria Maggiore, Spello, for Troilo Baglioni, prior of the church and member of a branch of the Perugian Baglioni family (see 1497). Pintoricchio painted a self-portrait in the *Annunciation*, imitating Perugino's self-portrait in the Cambio in Perugia (1500). Both are framed, bust-length portraits that look like ex-voto images (see 1512) and are given a prominence usually reserved for images of patrons. Perugino would paint two frescoes in the same church twenty years later (see 1521).

Shortly after returning to Florence, Michelangelo receives the contract for the *David*. It took three years to finish the colossal marble statue, which his contemporaries nicknamed "The Giant" (see 1504).

Raphael completes an altarpiece for Sant'Agostino in Città di Castello depicting the *Coronation of Saint Nicholas of Tolentino* (now in fragments). In 1500 the prominent Baronci family jointly awarded this commission to Raphael and to Evangelista da Pian di Meleto, a former assistant in the shop of Raphael's father. It is likely that the Baronci chose Raphael because he had mastered some of Perugino's techniques and had inherited some professional connections from his father (in this case, a collaboration with Evangelista). Raphael's mastery of Perugino's style immeasurably helped the seventeen-year-old attract patronage in Umbria, where Perugino's reputation was highly respected (see 1503).

1502 Mariano Chigi (Agostino Chigi's father) commissions Perugino to paint an altarpiece with predella scenes (dispersed) for the family chapel in Sant'Agostino, Siena. Although Perugino was obliged to complete the work in one year, it took four years (see 1506) to finish the *Crucifixion with Saints Augustine, Monica, Virgin Mary, Catherine, Mary Magdalene, John the Evangelist, John the Baptist, and Jerome*, 157½ × 113¹³⁄₁₆ in. (400 × 289 cm), which still remains in the chapel. Vasari cited the *Crucifixion with Saints* as being in Sant'Agostino, but did not mention a predella.

Had Perugino painted predella panels, they would likely have represented scenes from Christ's life. Scholars, therefore, have linked five specific panels to the Chigi Altarpiece. The five panels were together from the mid-nineteenth century until their sale in 1892. Four panels (transferred from panel to canvas) are now in the same collection (since 1933, The Art Institute of Chicago): *Adoration of the Christ Child*, 10⁵⁄₁₆ × 18¼ in. (26.2 × 46.4 cm); *Baptism of Christ*, 10¾ × 18¼ in. (27.3 × 46.3 cm); *Christ and the Woman of Samaria*, 10¾ × 18¼ in. (27.3 × 46.3 cm); and *Noli me Tangere*, 10¾ × 18¼ in. (27.3 × 46.3 cm) (cat. no.

1a–c, e). The fifth panel is in the Metropolitan Museum of Art, New York (since 1911): *Resurrection*, 10½ × 18 in. (26.7 × 45.7 cm) (cat. no. 1d).

Scholars have also linked the five panels with the high altarpiece of Santissima Annunziata, Florence (see 1506). Two paintings from Perugino's San Pietro Polyptych were probably the models for the *Baptism of Christ* and *Resurrection* panels (see 1495).

Pintoricchio is commissioned by the nephew of Pope Pius II, Cardinal Francesco Todeschini-Piccolomini, to paint the Piccolomini Library in Siena Cathedral (June 29). Francesco is elected Pope Pius III in September 1503, but dies within one month. Pintoricchio had completed the library frescoes by 1509, when his final account was settled. Both Perugino and Pintoricchio were working in Siena concurrently, although Perugino's other commissions often took him away from the city.

Baccio d'Agnolo works on the inlaid wooden choir of the Church of Sant'Agostino in Perugia, following Perugino's design. For the same church, Perugino receives a commission to paint an immense polyptych, the purported compensation for which was a sum of money, a house, and a farm. He began in 1503 and completed some twenty panels during the next two decades, working at intervals and with the help of his assistants: between 1503 and 1507; in 1512; in 1513; and between 1514 and 1520. In 1523 Eusebio da San Giorgio completed panels for the altarpiece. Perugino's paintings were placed into a double-sided altarpiece frame fashioned by Mattia di Tommaso da Reggio in 1495 and altered in 1512, when the side panels were added (see 1512, 1520).

In Florence, Filippino Lippi completes his work in the Strozzi Chapel in the Church of Santa Maria Novella, signing and dating the *Raising of Drusiana* (see 1486). When their paths overlapped in Rome and Florence (1486–1502), Perugino took notice of Filippino's lyrical figures, adapting Filippino's designs and incorporating his types into his own paintings (see the *Family of Saint Anne* below). In Perugino's hands, Filippino's gyrating figures, such as the Strozzi *Virgin and Child* stained-glass window and the women and children (*Drusiana* fresco), became subdued and timeless.

Perugino completes the altarpiece *Family of Saint Anne*, 108 11/16 × 96½ in. (296 × 259 cm), for Santa Maria dei Fossi in Perugia (since 1802, Musée des Beaux-Arts, Marseilles; fig. 85). The inscription on Mary's throne, PETRVS DE CHASTRO PLEBIS . PINXIT (modern), identifies Perugino from Città della Pieve and once included the date 1502 (still legible in the seventeenth century). This altarpiece has been linked to the patronage of Angelo Conti, who set aside funds in 1492 for the execution of a chapel and an altarpiece honoring Saint Anne by a master painter, to be completed within two years of his death. Conti later changed his will and in 1500, awarded the altarpiece contract solely to Perugino based on a design he had received from the painter. Santa Maria dei Fossi was the same convent church where Pintoricchio had executed his finest and largest altarpiece in Perugia some years earlier (see 1495).

Although Perugino's painting is more modest in its scale and surface ornamentation than Pintoricchio's, it is distinctive for its uncommon subject: the contract called for the depiction of Anne; her three daughters (the Virgin Mary, Mary Cleophae, and Mary Salome) and their sons (unnamed); the Virgin Mary's husband (Joseph); and her father (Joachim). Few Italian paintings of this theme were available to Perugino for comparison. Though pictures of Christ's earthly family (called the Holy Family) had become increasingly popular devotional images by 1500, the figures most frequently depicted with Christ were his parents, his cousin John the Baptist, and his grandmother Anne. Patrons did not usually request a family reunion of Saint Anne's progeny from three marriages with the specific figures that Conti's contract stipulated. The depiction of Anne's genealogy (called the Holy Kinship) was more common in northern Europe. There, such images had become biblical family portraits embellished by regional folklore. So Perugino's prototypes for the *Family of Saint Anne* came from different themes within his own work, namely the Fano and Senigallia Altarpieces (see 1497), and from other works that exalted holy figures, namely, the paintings of Masaccio and Bellini.

In Venice, Perugino had seen Bellini's Frari Altarpiece (1488, Santa Maria dei Frari), with its vaulted ceiling and elevated stepped throne, and he recalled the coffered vault of Masaccio's *Trinity* fresco in Florence (c. 1425, Santa Maria Novella). Perugino pictured Mary's mother, Anne, rising above Mary (portrayed as the mother of God), just as Masaccio had done with his exalted figure of God towering over Christ. Perugino's architecture, like Masaccio's, is somber and austere. His geometric-patterned, stark, cold stone vault and supporting piers call attention to the dominant matriarchal pyramid onto which Perugino imposed round, fleshy infant bodies.

These babies control the spirit of Perugino's painted room, as buzzing energy issues from each of them and invites joyful celebration. Their inspiration came from Filippino Lippi. Perugino scrutinized his images of youthful women and healthy, lively children in the Strozzi Chapel frescoes in Florence (see above) and in the *Allegory of Music* (now, Kaiser Friedrich Museum, Berlin). Both artists succeeded at depicting young children interacting naturally, as do the two boys seated on Perugino's throne step. These artists (and their Umbrian and Florentine followers) probably learned how to depict babies by studying real infants. The subject was especially challenging, and the artists of Perugino's circle made frequent sketches that developed their skills at combining active figures: e.g., a metalpoint and charcoal drawing of *Five Nude Infants in Various Poses*, 21¼ × 16¼ in. (54 × 41.3 cm) (now, Robert Lehman Collection, The Metropolitan Museum of Art, New York; cat. no. 15).

Unfortunately, the poor condition of Perugino's *Family of Saint Anne* restricts our unqualified appreciation of Perugino's finesse with this subject, but both Raphael (1505, Ansidei Madonna for San Fiorenzo, Perugia) and Fra Bartolommeo (1510–12, Saint Anne Altarpiece [unfinished] for

the Great Council Hall, Palazzo Vecchio, Florence) learned from it (see 1505, 1510).

Isabella d'Este writes to Francesco Malatesta, her agent in Florence (September 15), prodding him to find Perugino. She still wanted to hire Perugino because she considered him among the most excellent painters in Italy. Francesco responds (September 23) that Perugino would be in Siena for the next ten days and cautions her against hiring him, saying he was infamous for his delays. Francesco also wrote that he had independently negotiated with two other famous and reputable painters, Filippino Lippi and Botticelli. Isabella continued to favor Perugino. By October 24, Perugino had accepted the commission when Francesco wrote to Isabella asking her to send specific instructions. From Mantua (November 22), she forwards information about the subject, size, and price of the painting and sends twenty-five ducats to Francesco (December 23) to be paid into Perugino's account (see 1503–5).

Leonardo da Vinci becomes the military engineer for Cesare Borgia, who is in central Italy leading the armies of his father, Pope Alexander VI. Cesare drives the Baglioni from Perugia in 1502. Rival families of the Baglioni return to Perugia from exile in 1503, where they remain briefly (February to September) until the Baglioni reclaim the city (see 1503).

1503 Perugino completes the *Marriage of the Virgin*, 92⅛ × 72¹³⁄₁₆ in. (234 × 185 cm), for the Chapel of the Holy Ring in the Cathedral of Perugia. The Confraternity of Saint Joseph had awarded Perugino the commission (see 1499), and it is likely that he completed it before 1504 (1797, removed to France; since 1804, Musée des Beaux Arts, Caen; pl. 17). Scholars have speculated that Lo Spagno executed the painting on Perugino's design. The design for the painting and for specific figures influenced both Pintoricchio (*Meeting of Frederick III and Eleonora of Aragon*, Piccolomini Library, Siena Cathedral, 1502–9) and Raphael (*Marriage of the Virgin*, Città di Castello, 1504). Pintoricchio painted his work after 1502, but exactly when is not certain.

Pl. 17. *Marriage of the Virgin*, Musée des Beaux Arts, Caen

In Florence (January 19), Francesco Malatesta, acting for Isabella d'Este, has Perugino sign an agreement to paint the *Combat between Love and Chastity* (see 1505). Isabella's instructions about the poetic theme to be represented were precise: Pallas Athena and Diana (signifying chastity) were to fight against Venus and Cupid (signifying lasciviousness). Although she gave Perugino some freedom (e.g., the number of figures he could include), she was punctilious about how he construct the struggles between Pallas, Diana, Venus, and Cupid. She also required that he paint the images of chaste nymphs fighting "fiercely" and "victoriously" against fauns, satyrs, and several thousand cupids. Francesco presented Perugino with only twenty ducats instead of the twenty-five Isabella had instructed him to give to the painter. Isabella later reprimanded Francesco (January 26) for not tendering Perugino the total amount.

In Florence, a second son, Francesco, is born to Perugino and Chiara (February 1). Perugino's name appears in the register of the Florentine Company of Saint Luke. It was listed there again in 1504 and 1505.

From Mantua (June 10), Isabella d'Este writes to Angelo del Tovaglia in Florence lamenting that Perugino had not begun her painting, promised for June. Angelo responds (October 23) that Perugino had apologized for the delay, due to illness, and would start work immediately.

Leonardo da Vinci is inscribed in the register of the Florentine Company of Saint Luke and, in the same year, Piero Soderini, the Republican governor of Florence, commissions him to paint a fresco for the Great Council Hall (now, Sala dei Cinquecento) in the Palazzo Vecchio. The room had political importance: it was built in 1495 under Savonarola's guidance to hold the citizens' council (see 1490). Soderini commissioned murals of Florentine military history from both Leonardo and Michelangelo (see 1504) to inspire temerity in the citizens, then struggling to retake the city of Pisa.

Leonardo began (but never completed) his painting of the Florentine military victory of 1440, the *Battle of Anghiari*. He executed a cartoon (a full-scale working drawing) for it in the studio space provided for him in the papal quarters at Santa Maria Novella. The cartoon remained on display in the hall of the papal quarters for some time after he left Florence in 1506. Perugino and other artists studied the cartoon there, adapting parts of the design for their own compositions (see 1505). Around 1503 Leonardo began painting the *Mona Lisa* in Florence.

Raphael signs the altarpiece *Crucifixion with Angels and Saints Mary the Virgin, John the Evangelist, Jerome, and Mary Magdalenee*, 110½ × 65 in. (280.7 × 165 cm), made for the Gavari Chapel in San Domenico, Città di Castello (since 1924, National Gallery, London). Raphael inscribed his name in metallic letters, identifying himself as a painter from Urbino: RAPHAEL/VRBIN/AS/P. As Vasari noted, had Raphael not signed the painting, this work would have been attributed to Perugino. Raphael made his signature prominent by strategically placing it at the base of the cross, beneath Jerome's poignant gesture.

Although both the color and design are indebted to Perugino's earlier work, the young Raphael lacked Perugino's subtlety of figure placement. But his method of selecting character types and gestures appropriate for specific content and mood reveals his Umbrian training and Perugino's guidance. The image of the Virgin Mary derives from Perugino's *Crucifixion* of Santa Maria Maddalena dei Pazzi (see 1496), and Raphael's John the Evangelist mimics the male figure standing to the far right in Perugino's *Lamentation over the Dead Christ* (see 1495).

Upon Pope Alexander VI's death (August), a struggle erupts as military nobles scramble to recover lost estates taken by Cesare Borgia seeking to enlarge the Papal States. The Baglioni recovered Perugia on September 9 with Florentine help (see 1506).

Perugino receives payment in Perugia (November 22) for painting the arms of Pope Julius II on the city gate and in the Palace of the Priors.

Perugino writes to Isabella d'Este from Florence (December 10), asking about the measurements for the foreground figures in his painting and how his figures would compare with those of the other paintings in her study. From Mantua (January 12, 1504), Isabella then sends him the sizes of the foreground figures in Mantegna's paintings (see 1497). She encourages him to finish quickly, as she continued to do in her correspondence until the completion of the painting in 1505.

1504 Perugino completes the *Adoration of the Magi* in fresco, 255⅞ × 275⅝ in. (650 × 700 cm), for the Confraternity of Santa Maria dei Bianchi in Città della Pieve, the town of his birth (pl. 18). The date 1504 (A D M.D.IIII) is inscribed below the Holy Family. Vasari mentioned the fresco, without naming it, in both editions of the *Lives*. In the first edition he wrote that it was unimportant; in the second, that it remained unfinished. Some scholars see Raphael's participation as well as his portrait in this fresco. As partial payment for the work, Perugino was to receive a house, valued at twenty-five florins, in Città della Pieve (March 29, 1507). Several drawings have been connected with the painting, including a silverpoint drawing, *Two Standing Youths*, 8½ × 6¹⁵⁄₁₆ in. (21.7 × 17.6 cm), which may be studies for the young king (Robert Lehman Collection, The Metropolitan Museum of Art, New York).

Perugino serves on a committee with Botticelli, Giuliano da Sangallo, Cosimo Rosselli, and Leonardo in Florence (January 25) to determine

Pl. 18. *Adoration of the Magi,* Oratory of Santa Maria dei Bianchi, Città della Pieve

a suitable Florentine site for Michelangelo's marble *David* (see 1501).

From Mantua, Isabella d'Este writes to Perugino in Florence (February 19), requesting that he adjust the overall size of his painting because she was altering the design of her study and had reduced the area allotted to the paintings. Some four inches from the top of each of Mantegna's two paintings were tucked under their frames to fit the new scheme.

Filippino Lippi dies in Florence (April 18). On the day of his burial, all the shops along the Via dei Servi closed in mourning. Perugino and other artists had their workshops in this area and the *Compagnia di San Luca* met nearby in the Church of Santissima Annunziata (see 1508).

On August 4 Michelangelo is awarded a commission to paint the *Battle of Cascina* in the Grand Council Hall of the Palazzo Vecchio, Florence (see 1503). A large portion of the cartoon was probably finished by April 1505. Incomplete, it was transferred (possibly in 1506) to the Great Council Hall. It is likely that Michelangelo's cartoon influenced the battle scene that Perugino was painting for Isabella d'Este in 1505 (see 1505).

Raphael signs and dates the *Marriage of the Virgin,* 66⅞ × 46⅛ in. (170 × 117 cm), for the Albizzini

family altar of the Saint Joseph Chapel in San Francesco, Città di Castello (since 1806, Pinacoteca di Brera, Milan). Raphael had developed patrons in this city and this was the third of his large altarpieces for prominent families there (see 1501, 1503). Although Perugino did not work in Città di Castello, Raphael gave the citizens his best imitations of Perugino in all three altarpieces. For this painting he studied Perugino's *Delivery of the Keys to Saint Peter* (pl. 3) and quoted directly from the *Marriage of the Virgin* (pl. 17). Raphael's position shifted after this painting: from Perugino's imitator, Raphael became his rival. Having absorbed certain technical skills, working methods, and business practices from Perugino, he now had the means to realize his ambitions.

Giovanna da Montefeltro, the wife of Giovanni della Rovere, writes to Soderini, head of the Florentine Republic (October 1) that "Raphael, a painter of Urbino of considerable talent, would like to move to Florence."

Agostino Stroza, Abbot of Fiesole, informs Isabella d'Este in Mantua (November 27) that Perugino had made small progress beyond a drawing for her painting. Isabella's agent in Florence, Luigi Ciocca, then criticized Perugino's

Pl. 19. *Martyrdom of Saint Sebastian,* Church of San Sebastiano, Panicale

work (December 29), saying it strayed from Isabella's instructions. Isabella's anticipation grew with each delay and in the early months of 1505 she exchanged many letters with Ciocca, Stroza, and Angelo del Tovaglia, asking them to monitor Perugino's progress.

1505 Perugino signs his name and the date (1505): P[ ] DE CASTRO[ ] A./.D./.M./.D.V. in the fresco the *Martyrdom of Saint Sebastian* in the Church of San Sebastiano, Panicale, about five miles from Città della Pieve (pl. 19). Scholars have associated several drawings with this fresco, among which are two studies now in the National Gallery of Art, Washington, D.C.: *Archer Drawing a Bow,* black chalk, 10⁵⁄₁₆ × 6⅝ in. (26.2 × 16.8 cm) and *Figure of an Archer* (recto), pen and ink, 10⅝ × 5³⁄₁₆ in. (27 × 13.2 cm) (cat. nos. 18, 19).

Francesco Malatesta tells Isabella d'Este in Mantua (June 9) that Perugino has completed the *Combat between Love and Chastity,* 62⅞ × 75⅛ in. (160 × 191 cm). Perugino took many years to

paint this picture, and it is distinctive in his oeuvre. Rarely did he paint violent actions or battle scenes. The friezelike arrangement of the figures in his *Combat* was probably inspired by antique art, namely the continuous narrative reliefs of Roman sarcophagi. It is even more likely that his rhythmic, figure-locked groupings were influenced by the explosive, intertwined figures of Michelangelo's and Leonardo's battle cartoons for the large project underway in the Palazzo Vecchio (see 1503, 1504). Isabella paid to have the *Combat* transported to Mantua and installed in her study. She wrote to Perugino that the painting greatly pleased her (June 30), and he thanked her (August 10). Four paintings in her study (two by Mantegna and one each by Perugino and Lorenzo Costa) later passed into the collection of Cardinal Richelieu. It is likely that while in Richelieu's collection, a strip of canvas about four inches in height was added to Perugino's painting (since 1801, Musée du Louvre, Paris; pl. 20).

Raphael completes the altarpiece *Madonna and Child Enthroned with Saints John the Baptist and Nicholas of Bari,* commissioned by Bernardino Ansidei for his family chapel in San Fiorenzo dei Serviti in Perugia (since 1885, National Gallery, London). Raphael inscribed the date MDV (1505) on the hem of Mary's gown. Altarpieces by Signorelli and Perugino in Perugia provided Raphael with models for figures and architecture: Signorelli's Ercolanus (1484, San Domenico Altarpiece) for Raphael's Nicholas and Perugino's youngest magus (1475, *Adoration of the Magi,* Santa Maria dei Servi; pl. 2) for his figure of John. The architectural setting for Raphael's altarpiece is derived from Perugino's *Family of Saint Anne* (see 1502).

Raphael is working in Florence, and Leonardo begins painting the *Battle of Anghiari* in the Palazzo Vecchio (see 1503).

1506 Perugino finishes the *Deposition of Christ from the Cross,* 131⅛ × 85¹³⁄₁₆ in. (333 × 218 cm), begun by Filippino Lippi in 1503 but incomplete at his death in 1504. The *Deposition* (Galleria dell'Accademia, Florence; pl. 21) was part of a double-sided altarpiece designed by Baccio d'Agnolo in

Pl. 20. *Combat between Love and Chastity*, Musée du Louvre, Paris

1500 for the Florentine Servite church, Santissima Annunziata.

Perugino also painted the large panel for the opposite side, *Assumption of the Virgin*, 131⅛ × 85¹³⁄₁₆ in. (333 × 218 cm), which remained in the church until the Servite priests dismantled the altarpiece and sold eight of its paintings around 1650.

Six panels depict saints: *Helen*, 65⅞ × 25½ in. (167.5 × 64.8 cm) and *Filippo Benizzi* (?), 62³⁄₁₆ × 25⅜ in. (158 × 64.5 cm) (both now in the Lindenau Museum, Altenburg, Germany); *John the Baptist*, 63 × 26⅜ in. (160 × 67 cm), and *Lucy*, 65¹¹⁄₁₆ × 26⅜ in. (167 × 67 cm) (both now in The Metropolitan Museum of Art, New York; figs. 41a, b); *Nicholas of Tolentino*, 31⅛ × 24⅜ in. (79 × 62 cm) (Galleria Nazionale, Rome); and *Catherine of Alexandria* (?) (private collection, South Africa).

Perugino probably painted a predella for the altarpiece. Scholars have linked the panels, the *Adoration of the Christ Child, Baptism of Christ, Christ and the Woman of Samaria, Resurrection,* and *Noli me Tangere,* with the Santissima Annunziata Altarpiece (cat. no. 1a–e; see 1502). Perugino's work at the Annunziata had untold significance for him and for other artists (see 1508, 1510).

Perugino completed his *Pentecost* design between 1500 and 1506 from which the Jesuate monks

made a stained-glass window for the façade of Santo Spirito in Florence (see 1486; pl. 5). Perugino's format brings together ideas that flow through his many Ascensions and Assumptions. But this image is like a bolt of lightning: it encapsulates the energy and fever of an extraordinary, excited moment when the ethereal holy spirit descends upon mortals. These physically enervated yet spiritually vitalized figures anticipated those of his later work. Perugino's use of a high wall, which appeared earlier in the Terreno Altarpiece (see 1493), now tightly contains the figures.

Il Rosso probably modeled his *Assumption* fresco in the cloister of Santissima Annunziata after Perugino's *Assumption of the Virgin* in the same church and his *Pentecost.* Like Perugino, Il Rosso also depicted a dropped ceiling, low viewpoint, and heaven seen from below by saints. While Il Rosso never overtly imitated Perugino, he did absorb Perugino's compositional structure and the geometric purity of his emotionally forceful works.

Perugino is paid (June 13, August 10) for the altarpiece he had completed for Mariano Chigi's family chapel in Sant'Agostino, Siena (see 1502). In Siena he also works on the altarpiece *Birth of*

Pl. 21. Filippino Lippi and Perugino, *Deposition of Christ from the Cross* (from the Annunziata Altarpiece), Galleria dell'Accademia, Florence

the *Virgin Mary* (completed in 1508) for the chapel of Girolamo and Bernardino di Giovanni Vieri in San Francesco (destroyed by fire, 1655). When asked to evaluate the painting (September 5, 1510), four painters (Gerolamo di Benvenuto, Pacchiarotti, Genga, and del Pacchia) judge it to be well executed and rule that he should be paid according to the contract.

Around 1506 Raphael paints portraits of a Florentine couple married since 1503: *Angelo Doni* and *Maddalena Strozzi Doni*, each 24¹³⁄₁₆ × 17¹¹⁄₁₆ in. (63 × 45 cm) (since 1826, Galleria Palatina, Palazzo Pitti, Florence). The portrait of Angelo resembles Perugino's *Portrait of Francesco delle Opere* (see 1494; pl. 10) in the sitter's directness and in the landscape's breadth and color.

After laying the cornerstone of the new Saint Peter's in April, Pope Julius II leaves Rome to reclaim papal land, commanding some five hundred soldiers armed for battle. They march first to Perugia, where Julius reputedly enters the city with only a small group of his curia and takes it without bloodshed from the tyrant Giampaolo Baglioni. The pope continues northward with his troops and also reclaims Bologna.

1507 By 1507 Perugino finishes the *Baptism of Christ*, 175³⁄₁₆ × 89¾ in. (445 × 228 cm), for the Chiesa della Nunziatella, Foligno, about eighteen miles from Perugia. An image of God in Glory is depicted above the Baptism. On the entablature dividing the two images is an inscription that identifies the patron as Giovanni Battista Morganti. In the nineteenth century, the inscription purportedly still bore the artist's name and partial date as well: OPERA PETRI ANNO DOMINI MD[ ]. Several drawings attributed to him were possibly sketches for some figures of the fresco: *Kneeling Figure and Two Heads*, 8⅝ × 5⅜ in. (21.9 × 13.7 cm) (now, Sterling and Francine Clark Art Institute, Williamstown, Massachusetts; cat. no. 3).

In Perugia, executors of Giovanni di Matteo Schiavone's will (d. 1507) commission Perugino to paint a Virgin of Loreto with two saints, Jerome as Cardinal and Francis of Assisi (June 7), for Schiavone's chapel in Santa Maria dei Servi.

Perugino is given four months (i.e., until September 1507) to finish the painting and to have a frame made for it. The painting mentioned in the contract is probably *Virgin and Child with Saints Jerome and Francis*, 73 × 60 in. (185.5 × 152.5 cm), which was taken to Santa Maria Nuova when Santa Maria dei Servi was demolished in 1542 to make room for the Rocca Paolina, the castle of Pope Paul III (since 1879, National Gallery, London; fig. 72). Scholars speculate that Perugino did not finish the painting by 1507; that the painting is not by his hand alone, as specified in the contract; and that the contract stipulated a predella, without identifying the subjects.

Scholars have proposed that three panels by Perugino from Santa Maria dei Servi formed a predella for the Virgin of Loreto Altarpiece: the *Annunciation*, 6⅝ × 14¾ in. (16.8 × 37.2 cm); *Adoration of the Christ Child*, 6⅜ × 14⅝ in. (16.2 × 37 cm); and *Baptism of Christ*, 6¾ × 14⅜ in. (17.1 × 36.6 cm) (since 1863, Galleria Nazionale dell'Umbria, Perugia; cat. no. 10a–c). These same panels have also been connected with the *Transfiguration* from Santa Maria dei Servi (see 1517; fig. 71).

During 1507, Raphael signs and dates the *Entombment*, 72⅜ × 69⁵⁄₁₆ in. (184 × 176 cm), for the Church of San Francesco al Prato in Perugia (1608, Cardinal Scipione Borghese, Rome; 1809, Camillo Borghese, Paris; since 1815, Galleria Borghese, Rome). Atalanta Baglioni ordered the painting to commemorate her son Griffone, assassinated in 1500 in a family struggle to control Perugia. Raphael executed some twenty drawings for the commission, and the early studies imply close study of Perugino's *Lamentation over the Dead Christ* in Florence (see 1495; pl. 11).

1508 Perugino supervises the design and painting of a ceiling in the Vatican Apartments for Pope Julius II, carried out mostly by his pupils. The ceiling quadrants include *Christ Flanked by Justice and Grace*, *God the Father with Angels*, *Christ Tempted*, and *Christ and the Apostles with God the Father*. The room, later named the Room of the Fire (Stanza dell'Incendio), was where the *Segnatura* (the tribunal of the papal curia) met to decide disputes and hear papal decisions to appeals. Raphael and his pupils later painted the walls of this room for Pope Leo X (1514–17).

Around 1508 Perugino paints an *Assumption of Mary,* 196⅞ × 129⅞ in. (500 × 330 cm), for the main altar of Naples Cathedral (moved within the Cathedral after 1774). In this painting Saint Gennaro presents the patron, Cardinal Oliviero Carafa of Naples, to Mary. This same patron had commissioned frescoes from Filippino Lippi for a burial chapel in Rome (see 1488). After returning to Naples, he built a second burial chapel in Naples Cathedral between 1497 and 1508.

Negotiations with Perugino probably started about this time. Perugino was a likely choice for Carafa, whose ties with Perugia dated to his early schooling there and who probably became familiar with Perugino's work in Rome. Perugino had become the master painter of Assumptions, completing two paintings for Pope Sixtus IV in Rome (see 1480), and others for Santa Maria Nova, Fano (see 1497), for the Vallombrosans (see 1500), and for Santissima Annunziata, Florence (see 1506). Vasari recorded that Perugino painted an Assumption with the apostles standing around Mary's tomb for the Bishop's Palace in Naples. Vasari probably meant this painting, although no tomb is depicted, nor was the work ever in the palace.

Perugino's son Michelangelo is born in Florence.

Andrea del Sarto joins the *Arte dei Medici e Speziali* in Florence. Andrea worked with the painter Franciabigio in a shop near the Palazzo Vecchio, but they later moved to a building near Santissima Annunziata. This quarter was one of the most active parts of the city, especially popular because of the religious and social festivals that attracted pilgrims to the church and piazza. By 1508 the Annunziata was like a picture gallery of today and artists made pilgrimages there to study the works of nearly every valued painter working in Florence: Baldovinetti, Castagno, the Pollaiuolo brothers, Cosimo Rosselli, Leonardo (see 1501), Filippino Lippi, and Perugino (see 1506).

For many years the *Compagnia di San Luca* met in the Annunziata. Vasari and others met again at the Annunziata in 1560, when the *Compagnia* was defunct for purposes of reviving the old practices (such as burial and prayers) extended to members of the painters' confraternity. What Vasari started in 1560 became an academy for painters, the first in Europe. Shortly afterward, in 1573, the academy in Perugia was founded with the Florentine *Accademia del Disegno* as its model. An analogous academy in Rome was not established until 1593.

Sponsorship of these academies became critical to their creation: in Florence, support for the academy came from the Medici Grand Duke; in Perugia, from both the papal governor and the bishop of Perugia. Perugino and the artists of his circle knew the value of having wealthy patrons and the importance of having their work seen by others. Of the many commissions that advanced Perugino's career, his work at the Annunziata was his most prominent accomplishment in Florence. He later chose this same church for his burial (see 1515).

Michelangelo begins work on the Sistine ceiling for Julius II and finishes it within five years (see 1513). Some early studies reveal his first designs were of a geometrically patterned ceiling, closer to Perugino's Cambio ceiling and Pintoricchio's Piccolomini Library ceiling than to his final design.

1509 Around 1509 Perugino's daughter Paola is born in Florence. Paola later joined the monastery of Saint Catherine in Perugia.

Perugino probably completes an altarpiece, the *Ascension,* 130⅞ × 104¹¹⁄₁₆ in. (332.5 × 266 cm), for the Duomo of San Sepolcro, about seventy miles southeast of Florence, by the time his patron Abbot Simone de' Graziani, dies in 1509. Vasari recorded the name of the patron and the altarpiece's great size. Scholars have theorized about the participation of Gerino da Pistoia, a member of Perugino's Florentine workshop; about its closeness and chronological relationship to *Christ's Ascension* in San Pietro, Perugia; and about how some existing drawings of standing apostles may be related to one or the other panel (see 1495).

According to Vasari, the Florentine sculptor Jacopo Sansovino (1486–1570) made wax models for Perugino in Rome (see 1517). Vasari noted that both Sansovino and Perugino lived in Domenico della Rovere's palace while the latter was working in the Vatican for Pope Julius II, another member of the della Rovere family (see 1508). While in Rome (1505–11), Sansovino may have been working for Julius in the choir of Santa Maria del Popolo.

Pope Julius II awards Raphael a commission to paint a room (Stanza della Segnatura) in the Vatican Apartments. This commission changes his career and he soon becomes the most popular and respected artist in Rome.

Pintoricchio completes work for Pope Julius II in the choir of Santa Maria del Popolo, Rome. Julius was continuing the patronage of his uncle Sixtus, who had previously commissioned Pintoricchio to paint in this church. Perugino too retained della Rovere patronage, working for both Sixtus and Julius in the Vatican complex (see 1479, 1480, 1508).

1510   Perugino probably completed the altarpiece *Saint John the Baptist between Saints Francis of Assisi, Jerome, Sebastian, and Anthony of Padua*, 79½ × 68½ in. (202 × 173 cm), between 1505 and 1510 for San Francesco al Prato in Perugia. The four saints are positioned around the Baptist, who stands on a mound of earth. Vasari recorded that Perugino painted an oil panel of the Baptist for the Franciscan convent and listed it with Perugino's *Resurrection of Christ* (see 1499). In 1797 the painting was sent to Paris (since 1863, Galleria Nazionale dell'Umbria, Perugia; pl. 22).

Sandro Botticelli dies in Florence and is buried in the cemetery of the Church of All Saints (Ognissanti) on May 17.

Andrea del Sarto is working in the small cloister of Santissima Annunziata, Florence, built from 1444 to 1455 by Antonio Manetti following Michelozzo's design. Shortly after the cloister was completed, the Servites began ordering frescoes for the walls of its sixteen bays. Only two frescoes from before 1500 are still extant: Alesso Baldovinetti's *Nativity* (1460) and Cosimo Rosselli's *Vocation of Filippo Benizzi* (1476).

Activity in the cloister greatly increases during the first decade of the sixteenth century as Andrea del Sarto depicts six episodes from Filippo Benizzi's life between 1508 and 1510. He continued to work in the cloister painting stories from the lives of Christ and Mary. Three painters worked together with him between 1511 and 1516. A fourth painter, Francesco (di Lazzaro) Indaco, was commissioned as well to paint two scenes, a *Magi before Herod* and a *Vision of the Virgin's Nativity* in 1513 (never executed). The painters worked concurrently on five different paintings: a *Journey of the Magi* (1511–12) and a *Birth of the Virgin* (1513–14) by Andrea del Sarto; a *Marriage of the Virgin* (1513) by Franciabigio; a *Visitation* (1515–16) by Pontormo; and an *Assumption* (1513–14) by Il Rosso.

This cloister area became a large production studio resembling the project in the Sistine Chapel supervised by Perugino in the 1480s. The activities were as similar as were the results. Del Sarto's style drastically changed in the years he painted there and Perugino's high altarpiece may have provided one of the catalysts in this process (see 1506, 1508).

Fra Bartolommeo (1472–1517) is commissioned (November 16) to paint an altarpiece for the Great Council Hall of the Palazzo Vecchio in Florence. Filippino received the first commission for this altarpiece in 1496 but died in 1504 without executing the painting. Meanwhile, Leonardo and Michelangelo had been commissioned to paint battle scenes in the same hall (see 1503 and 1504), but by 1510 both had left Florence.

Fra Bartolommeo's contract called for the depiction of an enthroned Madonna, Child, and Saint Anne surrounded by Florentine saints. Anne was a popular Florentine saint, whose presence, along with that of the other saints, lent political weight to the town hall. Fra Bartolommeo worked for two years on this important painting, but it never progressed beyond the underpainting

Pl. 22. *Saint John the Baptist between Saints Francis of Assisi, Jerome, Sebastian, and Anthony of Padua*, Galleria Nazionale dell'Umbria, Perugia

stage. Fra Bartolommeo was a Dominican friar living at the convent of San Marco near Santissima Annunziata, where he studied the works of Perugino and Leonardo.

Pintoricchio completes the *Assumption of the Virgin* for Paolo Tolosa's chapel in Monte Oliveto, Naples (now, Museo Nazionale di Capodimonte, Naples). Vasari ascribed this panel to Pintoricchio, but Eusebio da San Giorgio, an assistant, probably executed most of it. The painting closely imitates Perugino's lost *Assumption* fresco in the Sistine Chapel (see 1480), as recorded in a drawn copy of the painting (Albertina, Vienna).

1511 Giorgio Vasari is born in Arezzo (July 30).

After his Roman sojourn, Jacopo Sansovino returns to Florence, where between 1511 and 1518 he shared a studio near Piazza Santissima with del Sarto, for whom he fashioned sculptural models (see 1509).

1512 Perugino signs and dates the canvas banner *Saint Anthony of Padua and a Patron*, 56¼ × 26¾ in. (143 × 68 cm), for Sant'Antonio, Bettona (now Pinacoteca Comunale, Bettona; fig. 62). It bears an inscription identifying the patron, painter, and date: BOLO . DE MARAGLIA . DE PEROGA . QVANDO FO PREGIONE DE FRANCIOSE / CHE FO ADDI . XI DE FEBRAIO . MDXII . PETRVS PINXIT . DE CASTRO . PLEBIS. The patron, Bartolomeo di Maraglia of Perugia, a lieutenant in the army of Giampaolo Baglioni (see 1502, 1503, 1506), was captured in the battle of Marignano by the French and probably commissioned the banner as an ex-voto (an offering in fulfillment of a vow) shortly after his liberation. It was apparently carried in processions, which accounts in part for its abrasion and wear.

Perugino renews his contract (June 16) for the polyptych in Sant'Agostino, Perugia (see 1502). The altarpiece was to increase in size and become grander in its overall appearance. On November 24, the friars of Sant'Agostino contracted Giambattista Bastone to make additions to the altarpiece frame according to Perugino's design. The enormous double-sided structure was freestanding and stood between the nave and choir. In the

sixteenth century the two central panels were replaced by a tabernacle. The altarpiece frame was completely dismantled in the seventeenth century during the renovation of the church. Individual panels were relocated in the church and some have since disappeared. Twenty-six panels have been attributed to Perugino and assistants and four panels to Eusebio da San Giorgio.

On the side that faced the nave were three tiers, including the predella, with the following panels: in the center of the upper tier was *God the Father*, 53⅞ × 53½ in. (137 × 136 cm) (now, Galleria Nazionale dell'Umbria, Perugia); two tondi flanked *God the Father* with Old Testament sages, *The Prophet Daniel*, diam. 24 in. (61 cm) and *The Prophet David*, diam. 24 in. (61 cm) (both, Galleria Nazionale dell'Umbria, Perugia); in the center of the middle tier, the *Baptism of Christ*, 104⅜ × 58¼ in. (265 × 148 cm) (now, Galleria Nazionale dell'Umbria, Perugia; pl. 23); two panels flanked the *Baptism* on the upper middle tier, *Young Saint with a Sword*, diam. 40⅛ in. (102 cm) (now, Musée du Louvre, Paris), and *Saint Bartholomew*, 35¼ × 29½ in. (89.5 × 74.8 cm) (now, Birmingham Museum of Art, Alabama); two panels flanked the *Baptism* on the upper middle tier, with two saints in each, *Saint John the Evangelist and Saint Augustine*, 68⅛ × 35⅞ in. (173 × 91 cm) (since 1801, Musée des Augustins, Toulouse) and *Saint Ercolano and Saint James the Less*, 68⅛ × 35⅞ in. (173 × 91 cm) (now, Musée Municipal des Beaux-Arts, Lyons).

Six panels were in the predella (all now in the Galleria Nazionale dell'Umbria, Perugia): the *Baptist Preaching*, 15½ × 33⅛ in. (39.5 × 84 cm), the *Marriage at Cana*, 15½ × 33¼ in. (39.5 × 84.5 cm), and four panels of saints: *Monica, Nicholas of Tolentino* (fig. 103), *Lucy,* and *Jerome,* each panel measuring 15⅜ × 10¹³/₁₆ in. (39 × 27.5 cm).

On the side that faced the choir were three tiers, including the predella, with the following panels: in the center of the upper tier, the *Pietà*, 56¾ × 59⅞ in. (144 × 152 cm) (now San Pietro, Perugia); in the center of the middle tier, the *Adoration of the Shepherds*, 104⅜ × 57½ in. (265 × 146 cm) (now, Galleria Nazionale dell'Umbria, Perugia; fig. 111); two panels flanked the *Adoration*

Pl. 23. *Baptism of Christ* (central panel, Sant'Agostino Polyptych),
Galleria Nazionale dell'Umbria, Perugia

on the upper left, *Gabriel*, diam. 40⅛ in. (102 cm) (now, Galleria Nazionale dell'Umbria, Perugia), and on the upper right, the *Virgin Annunciate*, 40⅛ in. (102 cm) (?) (formerly, Musées Municipaux, Strasbourg; destroyed by fire, 1871); two panels flanked the *Adoration* on the lower middle tier, with two saints in each, *Saint Irene and Saint Sebastian*, 74½ × 37⅜ in. (189 × 95 cm) (since 1811, Musée des Beaux-Arts, Grenoble), and *Saint Jerome and Saint Mary Magdalene*, 64⅛ × 37¾ in. (163 × 96 cm) (now, Galleria Nazionale dell'Umbria, Perugia; fig. 75).

Six panels were in the predella (all now in the Galleria Nazionale dell'Umbria, Perugia): the *Adoration of the Magi*, 15½ × 33½ in. (39.5 × 85 cm), the *Presentation in the Temple*, 15½ × 32⅞ in. (39.5 × 83.5 cm), and four panels of saints: *Lawrence, Louis of Toulouse, Costanzo*, and *Catherine of Alexandria* (fig. 80), each panel measuring 15⅜ × 10¹³⁄₁₆ in. (39 × 27.5 cm).

Vasari saw the altarpiece before it was dismantled and commented on the rich freestanding decorative frame. He briefly mentioned the saint panels, identified the central panels (*Baptism* and *Adoration*) by name, and then complimented Perugino on the care he took in executing the small figures of the predella panels. Vasari probably recognized in these predella panels the fluid way Perugino organized his figures, the subtlety of his color choices, and the fineness of his descriptive surface detail, which unfortunately has been cleaned away in places.

Perugino's blended pastel colors seem more fragile, capable of absorbing and reflecting light. Veils of colors help us perceive figures breathing and nature flexing. One striking difference in the late work is his brush technique. It more lightly touches the surface, delicately picking out the particular details that will spark quiet action, inject emotional strength into single figures, and provide flowing energy to groups. The works of the last decade of Perugino's career reflect the certainty of the master and his new direction (see 1514, 1521).

Perugino again works for the priors in Perugia, this time designing a silver boat as table decoration. The Perugian goldsmith Giovanni Battista di Mariotto Anastagi was hired on December 30 to execute Perugino's design.

1513 Perugino and his assistants paint the *Assumption of Mary*, 89 × 58¹¹⁄₁₆ in. (226 × 149 cm), for Santa Maria at Corciano, near Perugia. This painting bears strong similarities to his earlier *Assumption of Mary* in Naples Cathedral (see 1508) and his San Pietro Polyptych, Perugia (see 1495). Some gestures and positions of the apostles are common to all three panels. The predella consists of the *Annunciation* and *Nativity*, each 12³⁄₁₆ × 30¹¹⁄₁₆ in. (31 × 78 cm). Each scene has an openness and airy quality that characterizes the work of Perugino's late period. The composition of the *Nativity* shows its certain debt to an earlier Nativity predella panel (*Adoration of the Christ Child*, now, The Art Institute of Chicago, cat. no. 1a; see 1502).

Leonardo da Vinci moves to Rome in the service of Giuliano de' Medici, brother of Pope Leo X. He was given a studio in the Belvedere and living quarters in the Vatican. Raphael is completing frescoes in the Vatican and Michelangelo is working on the tomb of Julius. Pintoricchio dies in Siena.

1514 Four years after receiving a commission to paint the high altarpiece of the Cathedral of his hometown, Città della Pieve, Perugino completes the *Virgin and Child with Four Saints*, 94½ × 86⅝ in. (240 × 220 cm) (fig. 7). An inscription on the low retaining wall behind the figures gives his family name, Vannucci, and his birthplace, Città della Pieve: PETRVS CHRISTOFERI VANNUTTI DE CASTRO PLEBIS PINXIT MD.XIIII. In this altarpiece, Mary is shown seated on clouds and holding the Christ Child above the heads of four standing saints (Gervase, Peter, Paul, and Protasius). Two of the saints hold banners bearing the town's crest.

In this work, scholars have posited the hand of Perugino's local assistants, particularly Giacomo di Guglielmo, an artist from Città della Pieve, in part because the style of this painting is so different from that of Perugino's earlier works. But Perugino's style *did* change during the last decade of his life. No longer do we see the muscular and sculptural forms of the earlier figures; instead, the most distinguishing feature about these late figures is their human frailty. They are less perfect, less groomed, less cosmetically appealing. The changes he made seem purposeful, as though he were searching for new types. Vasari criticized Perugino's work for not changing, and scholars have taken for granted that his art stagnated. But in more than fifty years of painting, Perugino's work continually manifested change. The changes were due to the technical expertise Perugino acquired, his own practical nature, and a sensitivity to life that allowed him wide vision rather than to issues of patronage, old age, or many workshop assistants and followers.

1515 Perugino paints the *Adoration of the Child* in fresco, 78¾ × 118⅛ in. (200 × 300 cm), for a niche in San Francesco, Montefalco, about twenty-two miles south of Perugia.

Perugino acquires a sepulcher for himself and his family in Santissima Annunziata, Florence (July 30). His wife, Chiara, paid the balance for the sepulcher while Perugino was absent from Florence (September 21).

1517 Perugino's painting the *Transfiguration*, 114⅛ × 72¹³⁄₁₆ in. (290 × 185 cm), was transferred to the new Servite church of Santa Maria Nuova, Perugia, when Santa Maria dei Servi was destroyed in 1542. Its design owes much to his earlier *Transfiguration* fresco in the Collegio del Cambio (1496–1500). The altarpiece is probably the one Perugino completed for Adreana Signorelli on December 17, 1517 (since 1863, Galleria Nazionale dell'Umbria, Perugia; fig. 71). This may be the *Transfiguration* Vasari recorded as an early work of Perugino at Santa Maria dei Servi. Some scholars posit that three panels (see 1507) formed a predella for this altarpiece: the *Annunciation, Adoration of the Christ Child,* and *Baptism of Christ* (now, Galleria Nazionale dell'Umbria, Perugia; cat. no. 10a–c).

Perugino is nominated (June 16) head of the Painters' Guild in Perugia from July to December.

Perugino completes frescoes for the Confraternity of Santa Maria della Stella in Santa Maria dei Servi, Città della Pieve. He depicted a Deposition on one wall and an Eternal Father on the adjoining wall above sorrowful figures that flank a niche once filled with a terra-cotta Pietà. An inscription bearing the date and the names of both the painter and the patron runs along the bottom of both frescoes: [QU]ESTA.HOPERA FERO DEPENGERE . LA CONPAGNIIA . DELLA S[TELLA] . COSSI . DICTA IN LI ANNI D.N I.M.D. XVII.PETR[US de castro plebis pinxit].

Both walls have suffered substantive paint loss, and opinions vary about the merits of these frescoes. The *Deposition* has been both praised for being expressive of Perugino's graceful, mature work and dismissed for being derivative. Some see in it the work of his assistant Giacomo di Guglielmo. Scholars have speculated that the chapel originally had two more walls with frescoes of an Annunciation and Entombment, destroyed during a seventeenth-century transformation of the church.

Perugino's *Deposition* is distinctive for its triple ladders, its broad array of mourners, its two attentive figures supporting the Virgin who has fainted, and the two men carrying Christ from the cross (a large section of which is missing). These figures are nearly identical to those in the *Deposition* sculpted in gilt wax and wood by Jacopo Sansovino around 1510 (now, Victoria and Albert Museum, London). Vasari recorded that Jacopo executed wax models for Perugino in Rome, including a Deposition that was later collected by the Florentine Giovanni Gaddi (see 1509).

While scholars have posited that Perugino ordered the Deposition model for a painting (presumed lost) done around 1510, the Città della Pieve *Deposition* closely follows this Sansovino model, although Perugino's painting is far more subdued. His bereaved, contemplative figures have the broad shoulders and delicate, shot-silk garments of his late works. Human resolve resonates through these accordion-like bodies that stand tightly together, their upper torsos gently fanning outward and emitting hushed sobs in unison. One lively figure stationed between the crosses draws our attention to the Virgin. This is the only active figure beneath the crosses who looks toward the Virgin, and *not* toward Christ. It is likely that Il Rosso thought of Perugino's *Deposition* some years later while completing his own *Deposition* panel in Volterra (1521), for he positioned figures beneath the crosses in a similar manner.

1518 Perugino designs a door for the Grand Salon in the Palace of the Priors, Perugia (November 26). Around this time, he paints the panel *Madonna and Child with Saints Costanzo and Ercolano,* 31¾ × 22½ in. (80.5 × 57 cm), for the palace. The panel, which shows the intimacy he brought to the palpable figures of his late period, was once in the palace kitchen (since 1861, Galleria Nazionale dell'Umbria, Perugia; cat. no. 13).

1519 Perugino makes two trips to Florence. During the first trip, he collects the interest from Chiara's dowry (October 5) and during the second, he reconfirms his power of attorney to Jacopo d'Antonio (December 20).

Leonardo da Vinci dies in Amboise, France (May 2).

1520 Perugino collects interest from Chiara's dowry in Florence (February 11).

Raphael dies in Rome and is buried in the Pantheon.

1521 Perugino paints the fresco *Pietà with Angels and Saints John the Evangelist and Mary Magdalene* (detached) in the presbytery of Santa Maria Maggiore, Spello. He inscribed his name and date (1521) on two plaques that hang from the throne: PETRVS .DE/CHASTRO . PLEB/PINSIT . AD/M. D. XXI; and the patron's name on the base of the throne: MICHALAGELVS . ANDINE. He painted a second fresco in the presbytery, *Virgin Mary and Child Enthroned between Saints Biagio and Catherine of Alexandria* (detached). The base of Mary's throne is inscribed in like fashion with the patron's name and date (April 25, 1521): EX . SPEIS . IOANNE . BERNARDELLI/AD MD XXI . DIE XXV . APRILIS.

Pl. 24. Perugino and Raphael, *Trinity with Six Benedictine Saints Above and Six Other Saints Below,* Church of San Severo, Perugia

Perugino paints the *Adoration of the Magi* fresco in Santa Maria delle Lacrime, Trevi. He inscribed his name at the base of Mary's throne: PETRUS . DE CASTRO PLEBIS . PINXIT. In the arch above the Adoration he depicted an Annunciation: Gabriel appears in one roundel and Mary in the other. He depicted Saints Paul and Peter on the sides, in painted niches with their names inscribed beneath them.

For the Camaldolese monastery church of San Severo in Perugia, Perugino completes work on the lower part of a fresco begun by Raphael years earlier (around 1505–7). On the upper part of the chapel wall, Raphael painted six seated Benedictine saints flanking a Trinity (pl. 24). In 1521 Perugino adds six standing Benedictine saints beneath Raphael's work. Each of Perugino's saints holds a book and is identifed below: Scholastica, Jerome, John the Evangelist, Pope

Gregory the Great, Boniface, and Martha. An inscribed plaque on the lower right gives Perugino's name and the date: PETRVS DE CAST[R]O PLEBIS PERVSINUS/TEMPO[RE] DOMINI SILVESTRI STEPHANI/VOLATERRANI A DESTRIS ET SINISTRIS/DIVAE CHRISTIPHERAE SANCTOS/SANCTASQUE/PINXIT. AD. MDXX[I]. Vasari cited the painting, noting that Perugino was an old man when he painted the fresco in San Severo and that Raphael had begun the work while he was Perugino's student.

In Perugino's late works we see the age of the man. His maturity and humanity show. The surface of this fresco has unfortunately suffered much from abrasion, paint loss, and many years of repainting. Nevertheless Perugino's figures may be perceived as more vulnerable, more human, and more emotionally and spiritually alive than those of Raphael in the fresco above. Indi-

vidual figures are seemingly closer to our space and touchable. They lack grand manners and are imperfect human specimens, approachable and real. Proportions shift in the last decade of Perugino's career: the heads are smaller and the bodies rounder and softer. These bodies seem more fluid and their poses more spiritually expressive.

The underpainting in Perugino's last works shows fine, sure lines that define basic contours over which he applied thin layers of paint. He drew more with his brush in the last paintings, and the more sketchy definition and the final brushstrokes that deftly pull the image into focus made his style especially difficult for his students to replicate. It also makes it difficult for contemporary eyes to evaluate the contribution of the late years, especially when modern repainting has replaced his final brushstrokes.

Times were changing in Italy. Rather than looking backward, Perugino looked forward, full of wisdom and experience. He continued to experiment and reflect ideas current in the circle of Andrea del Sarto. His last works made an impression on the next generation of painters: Pontormo, Il Rosso, Beccafumi, and Domenico Alfani. Perugino's broad, angular, and massive yet delicate and weightless forms draped in shot-silk and pastel complementary colors inspired these artists. The new generation of Florentine artists continued to explore ideas present in Perugino's style, the same elements later identified as characteristic of Mannerism.

1522 Perugino paints a fresco of an enthroned Madonna and Child for the Oratory of the Annunciation, Fontignano (pl. 25). Inscribed on the base of Mary's throne are the name of the patron and the date (1522): ANGNIOLVS TONI ANGELI/FECIT FIERI MDXXII. In this work, one of his last paintings, Perugino did not depict Mary as a noble patrician woman, as he had done in the 1490s. Mary appears less exalted and remote, more fragile, humble, and likely to move from her bench. This Madonna and Child seems ready to offer comfort to a patron in times of uncertainty. His image captures the essence of what this type

Pl. 25. *Madonna and Child*, Oratory of the Annunciation, Fontignano

Pl. 26. Castle ruin, Fontignano, site of Perugino's death

Pl. 27. Perugino's commemorative tomb, Oratory of the Annunciation, Fontignano

meant to people living in the early sixteenth century. It gives hope in the face of old age, misery, and plague, and most of all, it offers encouragement in the face of death and accountability—issues perhaps nagging his own thoughts in 1522.

1523 Around February, Perugino dies of the plague in Fontignano. His body is interred in the countryside (pl. 26).

1524 To settle their debt to Perugino (December 30), the friars of Sant'Agostino (Perugia) agree to pay his heirs and move his corpse from Fontignano to their church for an honorable burial. About eight months later, they apparently gave Perugino's sons the agreed-upon sum, though no further mention was made of moving the corpse (pl. 27). Perugino's wife, Chiara, was buried in Santissima Annunziata, Florence (1541).

For information on the written documents, please consult the following texts:

Walter Bombe, *Geschichte der Peruginer Malerei bis zu Perugino und Pinturicchio auf Grund des Nachlasses Adamo Rossis und eigener archivalischer Forschungen* (Berlin: Cassirer, 1912).

Fiorenzo Canuti, *Il Perugino*, 2 vols. (Siena: Editrice d'Arte "La Diana," 1931).

Sylvia Ferino Pagden, *Disegni umbri del Rinascimento da Perugino a Raffaello* (Florence: Olschki, 1982).

Umberto Gnoli, *I documenti su Pietro Perugino* (Perugia: Unione Tipografica Cooperativa, 1923).

Pittura in Umbria tra il 1480 e il 1540: premesse e sviluppi nei tempi di Perugino e Raffaello (Milan: Electa, 1983).

Pietro Scarpellini, *Perugino*, 2d ed. (Milan: Electa, 1991).

Filippo Todini, *La pittura umbra. Dal Duecento al primo Cinquecento*, 2 vols. (Milan: Longanesi, 1989).

Giorgio Vasari, *Le vite de' più eccellenti pittori, scultori, ed architettori*, ed. Gaetano Milanesi, 9 vols. (Florence, 1878–85).

Jeryldene Wood, "The Early Painting of Perugino" (Ph.D. diss., University of Virginia, 1985).

Works by Perugino Cited in This Catalogue

COMPILED BY JODY SHIFFMAN

Index of People and Places

COMPILED BY JODY SHIFFMAN

Gabriel, Archangel, 14, 176, 282, 299, 301
Gaddi, Agnolo, 26
Gaddi, Giovanni 300
Gaddi, Taddeo, 25, 28
Galitzin, Alexander, Prince, 110, 260
Galitzin, Theodore, Prince, 110
Garbi, Domenico, 231 n. 1
Genga, Girolamo, 293
Gennaro, Saint, 294
Gentile da Fabriano, 155
Gerino da Pistoia, 26, 68, 105, 119, 294
Gerolamo di Benvenuto, 293
Gervase, Saint, 299
Ghiberti, Lorenzo, 25
Ghirlandaio, Davide, 25, 258
Ghirlandaio, Domenico, 4, 6, 9, 24, 25, 30, 102, 251,
        254, 256, 258, 259, 260, 262, 263, 265, 266, 267,
        272, 283
Giacomo di Guglielmo, 299, 300
Gianfigliazzi family, 279
Giannicola di Paolo, 44, 117–18, 225, 226, 227 n. 1, 240,
        243, 243 n. 4
Giannicola Manni, 116, 225
Giorgione, 123 n. 29
Giotto, 22, 25, 26, 28, 33, 83, 99 n. 50, 102, 252
Giovanni delle Corniole, 272
Giuliano da Sangallo, 288
Gonzaga, Francesco, Duke of Mantua, 266, 267
Gozzoli, Benozzo, 255, 279
Granacci, Francesco, 117
Graziani, Simone de', Abbot, 294
Gregory the Great, Pope, 181, 301–2
Guardi, Benedetto di Ser Francesco, 265
Gubbio, 103, 150, 216
    Duomo, 242, 243

Hals, Frans, 110
Helen, Saint, 291
Herod, 295
Honofrius, Saint, 261, 262
Horatius Cocles, 283

Ibi, Sinibaldo, 102, 103, 116, 117
Indaco, Francesco (di Lazzaro), 295
Innocent VIII, Pope, 261, 262, 265, 266, 277, 279
Innsbruck, 279
Irene, Saint, 15, 151 n. 2, 299
Isaiah, 237, 239 n. 2, 274, 283

Jacob, 132
Jacopo d'Antonio, 301
James, Saint, 255, 277
James the Less, Saint, 14, 297
James of the Marches, 70, 163–65
Jarves, James, 102, 103, 122 nn. 6, 7, 9
Jeremiah, 237–38, 239 nn. 1, 2, 4, 283
Jerome, Saint, 10, 15, 78, 87, 108, 109, 114, 116, 117, 119,
        120, 160, 161, 170, 172, 178, 181–83, 183 n. 1, 2,
        242, 243, 256, 260, 261, 263, 271, 284, 293, 295,
        296, 297, 299, 301
Jerusalem, 239 n. 1
Joachim, 285
John the Baptist, Saint, 62, 72, 75, 76, 111, 112, 114, 121,
        130–31, 132, 137 n. 2, 149, 157 n. 3, 176, 198, 205,
        225, 243 n. 1, 261, 262, 263, 267, 269, 277, 284,
        285, 290, 291, 295, 296
John the Evangelist, Saint, 10, 59, 72, 94, 105, 107, 108,
        109, 114, 119, 139, 169, 169 n. 3, 221, 222, 223 n. 3,
        260, 261, 267, 271, 276, 284, 288, 297, 301
John Gualberto, Saint, 30, 282
Joseph, 119, 129, 172, 176, 187, 225, 226, 227 n. 2, 232,
        244, 285
Joseph of Arimathaea, Saint, 72, 139, 142, 143 n. 2
Judas, 59
Julius II, Pope. See Della Rovere, Giuliano
Jupiter, 238, 283

Kress, Samuel H., 110, 113, 114, 115, 116, 117, 118, 119, 120

Landucci, Luca, 56, 57, 64 n. 4
Lawrence, Saint, 166, 228, 230, 231, 261, 262, 275, 299
Leo X, Pope. See Medici, Giovanni de'
Leonardo da Vinci, 4, 34, 44, 69, 96, 102, 123 n. 29, 172,
        192, 194, 251, 254, 256, 260, 262, 266, 284, 286,
        287, 288, 290, 294, 295, 297, 299, 301
Leonidas, 283
Lippi, Filippino, 13, 15 n. 3, 92, 99 n. 51, 111, 254, 256,
        260, 262–63, 265, 266, 279, 284, 285, 286, 289,
        290, 292, 294
Lippi, Fra Filippo, 53, 56, 68, 254, 263
Lorenzetti, Pietro, 55
Lorenzo de Pavia, 277
Lorenzo di Credi, 4, 17 n. 21, 267
Lo Spagno (Giovanni di Pietro), 117, 118, 286
Louis of Toulouse, Saint, 54, 166, 228, 275, 277, 299
Louis XII, King of France, 275, 279
Lucius Sicinius, 283
Lucy, Saint, 111, 112, 114, 291, 297

CAPTIONS FOR DETAIL ILLUSTRATIONS

Front cover: *Madonna and Child*, cat. no. 5

Back cover: *Madonna della Giustizia*, cat. no. 12

Frontispiece: detail, *Pietà with Saints Jerome and Mary Magdalene*, cat. no. 9

Page vi: detail, *Christ and the Woman of Samaria*, cat. no. 1c

Page xxii: detail, *Virgin and Child Enthroned with Saints*, pl. 12

Page 2: detail, *Adoration of the Magi*, pl. 2

Page 18: detail, *Combat between Love and Chastity*, pl. 20

Page 36: detail, *Madonna della Giustizia*, cat. no. 12

Page 52: detail, *Madonna and Child*, cat. no. 5

Page 66: detail, *Virgin Mary and Child with Saints John the Baptist and Sebastian*, pl. 8

Page 82: detail, Perugino and Raphael, *Trinity with Six Benedictine Saints Above and Six Other Saints Below*, pl. 24

Page 100: detail, *The Crucifixion with the Virgin, Saint John, Saint Jerome, and Saint Mary Magdalene*, pl. 4

Page 124: detail, *San Girolamo*, cat. no. 11

Page 134: detail, *Noli Me Tangere (Touch Me Not)*, cat. no. 1e

Page 140: detail, *Sepulcrum Christi (Christ at the Sepulcher)*, cat. no. 2

Page 250: *Self-portrait*, detail from the frescoes of the Sala dell'Udienza, Collegio del Cambio, Perugia

Page 253: detail, *The Delivery of the Keys to Saint Peter*, pl. 3